CREATIVITY AND COLLABORATIVE LEARNING

A PRACTICAL GUIDE TO EMPOWERING STUDENTS AND TEACHERS

edited by

Jacqueline S. Thousand, Ph.D.
Department of Education and
The University Affiliated Program of Vermont
University of Vermont
Burlington

Richard A. Villa, Ed.D.
Bayridge Educational Consortium
Colchester, Vermont

and

Ann I. Nevin, Ph.D.
Education Unit
Arizona State University–West
Phoenix

·P·A·U·L·H·
BROOKES
PUBLISHING C°

Baltimore • London • Toronto • Sydney

Paul H. Brookes Publishing Co.
P.O. Box 10624
Baltimore, Maryland 21285-0624

Typeset by Brushwood Graphics, Inc., Baltimore, Maryland.
Manufactured in the United States of America by
BookCrafters, Falls Church, Virginia.

Permission to reprint the following quotations is gratefully acknowledged:

Page 219:   Quotation from Silverstein, S. (1981). The little boy and the old man. In
A light in the attic (p. 95). New York: Harper & Row. Copyright © 1981 by Evil Eye Music,
Inc. Reprinted by permission of the HarperCollins Publishers.
Pages 272–273:   Quotation from WINNIE-THE-POOH by A.A. Milne. Copyright 1926 by
E.P. Dutton, renewed 1954 by A.A. Milne. Used by permission of Dutton Children's Books, a
division of Penguin Books USA Inc.
Page 296:   Article from Durovich, C. (1990, February 9). Becky belongs. *Spartan Warrior*,
p. 2. Reprinted by permission.
Pages 331–332:   Quotation from Giangreco, M.F. (1993). Using creative problem solving
methods to include students with severe disabilities in general education classroom activities. *Journal of Educational and Psychological Consultation, 4,* 113–135. Reprinted by
permission of Lawrence Erlbaum Associates.

Most of the case studies that appear in this book are based on synthesized composites of the
authors' experiences in using cooperative group learning techniques. However, a few of the
case studies are based on actual cases; fictitious names have been used in these instances.

Library of Congress Cataloging-in-Publication Data

Creativity and collaborative learning : a practical guide to empowering students and teach-
   ers / edited by Jacqueline S. Thousand, Richard A. Villa, and Ann I. Nevin.
      p.   cm.
   Includes bibliographical references and index.
   ISBN 1-55766-158-8
   1. Group work in education—United States.   2. Peer-group tutoring of students—United
States.   I. Thousand, Jacqueline S., 1950–   .   II. Villa, Richard A., 1952–   .
III. Nevin, Ann.
LB1032.C73   1994
371.3'95—dc20   93-43006
                                                                              CIP
British Library Cataloguing-in-Publication data are available from the British Library.

To The Future

To our children

Rebecca
Chang
David
Jonathan
Ruth
Rosemarie

and

grandchildren

Rith
Junior
Nyda
Jme Suanna
Shawn
Jodie

With love and hope
that your education
has and will be
creative, collaborative,
and empowering

1994

CREATIVITY AND
COLLABORATIVE
LEARNING

CONTENTS

About the Editors

Jacqueline S. Thousand, Ph.D., Research Associate Professor, Department of Education and The University Affiliated Program of Vermont, 449C Waterman Building, University of Vermont, Burlington, Vermont 05405-0160

Since 1986, Jacqueline S. Thousand has coordinated a graduate training program that prepares *Integration Facilitators,* advanced educational leadership personnel who work with administrators, teachers, and families to redesign the delivery of special education services. This enables learners with extensive educational and psychological challenges to experience quality educational and social opportunities within their local general education and community environments. Dr. Thousand's most recent research is in the areas of collaborative consultation and teaming, school-based systems change strategies, cooperative group learning and partner learning, transition planning, attitudinal change strategies, and international educational exchange.

Richard A. Villa, Ph.D., President, Bayridge Educational Consortium, 6 Bayridge Estates, Colchester, Vermont 05446-1435

Richard A. Villa's primary field of expertise is the development of administrative support systems for educating all students within general education settings. Dr. Villa has taught a number of subjects at both the middle and secondary school levels, including biology, chemistry, physics, government, and special education; his administrative experiences include serving as a special education administrator, pupil personnel services director, and director of instructional services. Dr. Villa is currently President of the Bayridge Educational Consortium and an adjunct professor at the University of Vermont, Trinity College, and St. Michael's College; he teaches courses and supervises practica in the development of effective administrative and instructional skills for accommodating all students within general education classrooms.

Ann I. Nevin, Ph.D., Professor, Education Unit, Arizona State University–West, Phoenix, Arizona 85069-7100

Ann I. Nevin has a Ph.D. in Educational Psychology from the University of Minnesota and is currently a professor in the Education Unit at Arizona State University—West. Dr. Nevin has been involved with experimental education programs for the past 25 years and has field tested the cooperative and collaborative learning processes described in this book. She has taught both graduate and undergraduate students since 1969 at several major universities in several states (e.g., California, Hawaii, Indiana, Minnesota, Vermont).

Dr. Nevin is an internationally recognized expert in collaborative consultation and the integration of learners with disabilities into the general education classroom. She helped establish the Vermont Consulting Teacher Program, an innovative system to help classroom teachers and special educators plan, implement, and evaluate instruction for students with disabilities in general education classes. Her publications reflect her commitment to discovering what teachers can do to effectively accelerate the learning of their students.

About the Authors

Barbara J. Ayres, Ph.D., Assistant Professor, School of Education and Human Services, Department of Special Education and Reading, Eastern Montana College, 1500 North 30th Street, Billings, Montana 59101-0298

Barbara J. Ayres teaches both undergraduate and graduate courses in special education and consults in the areas of inclusive education, cooperative learning, and positive approaches. Her research interests include working collaboratively with teachers to create a close match between their goals and practices through the creation of cooperative classrooms, developing and using portfolios in teacher education programs, and promoting the use of cooperative learning in higher education.

Chigee J. Cloninger, Ph.D., Research Associate Professor, Center for Developmental Disabilities, College of Education, 499C Waterman Building, University of Vermont, Burlington, Vermont 05405-0160

Chigee J. Cloninger is Coordinator of the State of Vermont I-Team, a statewide training and technical assistance team providing intensive special education supports to children with disabilities. She also is Director of the Vermont State Project for Children and Youth with Deaf-Blindness. A frequent national presenter on issues pertaining to inclusive education, Dr. Cloninger is especially interested in the use of creative problem-solving approaches to facilitate educational leadership and inclusive education. Along with several other publications, Dr. Cloninger is coauthor of *Choosing Options and Accommodations for Children: A Guide to Planning Inclusive Education* (Giangreco, Cloninger, & Iverson, Paul H. Brookes Publishing Co., 1993).

Neil Davidson, Ph.D., Curriculum and Instruction Department, Benjamin Building, University of Maryland, College Park, Maryland 20742

Neil Davidson is a frequent presenter at national and international conferences and a consultant on cooperative learning for many school districts, colleges, and universities. He is the author of numerous articles on the use of cooperative learning. His most recent books include *Cooperative Learning in Mathematics: A Handbook for Teachers* (Addison-Wesley, 1990) and *Enhancing Thinking Through Cooperative Learning* (with Toni Worsham, Teachers College Press, 1992). He is current President of the International Association for the Study of Cooperation in Education. He is Professor in the Curriculum and Instruction Department at the University of Maryland, where he directs a doctoral program in staff development.

Ruth E. Dennis, OTR, M.Ed., Lecturer, Center for Developmental Disabilities, College of Education, 499C Waterman Building, University of Vermont, Burlington, Vermont 05405-0160

Ruth E. Dennis is the Occupational Therapy and Essential Early Education Consultant for the State of Vermont I-Team, a statewide training and technical assistance team providing intensive special education supports to children with disabilities. A doctoral candidate at the University of Vermont, her professional interests focus on home, school, and community partnerships as well as quality of life issues for people with disabilities. She is coauthor of several articles about various aspects of educating students with significant disabilities.

Janet Duncan, Doctoral Candidate, Special Education Programs, Syracuse University, 805 South Crouse Avenue, Syracuse, New York 13244-2280

Janet Duncan is currently teaching at State University of New York–Cortland and is a doctoral candidate in special education at Syracuse University. Her research interests include facilitated communication, cooperative learning, and inclusion of students with significant disabilities in regular education classes.

Susan W. Edelman, PT, M.Ed., Lecturer, Center for Developmental Disabilities, College of Education, 499C Waterman Building, University of Vermont, Burlington, Vermont 05405-0160

Susan W. Edelman is Coordinator of the Vermont State Project for Children and Youth with Deaf-Blindness and Physical Therapy Consultant for the State of Vermont I-Team, a statewide training and technical assistance team providing intensive special education supports to children with disabilities. A doctoral candidate at the University of Vermont, her current professional interests focus on the roles of related service providers to support students with disabilities in general education classrooms. She is coauthor of several articles about various aspects of educating students with significant disabilities.

Mary A. Falvey, Ph.D., Professor of Special Education, California State University, Los Angeles, 5151 State University Drive, Los Angeles, California 90032

Mary A. Falvey is Professor in the Division of Special Education at California State University, Los Angeles. She was a teacher and administrator in the public schools, responsible for teaching and administering programs for students with and without significant disabilities. She received her doctor of philosophy degree in 1980 from the University of Wisconsin–Madison. She has authored numerous chapters, several articles, and the two editions of *Community-Based Curriculum: Instructional Strategies for Students with Severe Handicaps* (Paul H. Brookes Publishing Co., 1986, 1989). She has served on the International Board of The Association for Persons with Severe Handicaps (TASH) and is currently on the California TASH Board of Directors.

Marsha Forest, Ed.D., Director of Education, Centre for Integrated Education and Community, 24 Thome Crescent, Toronto, Ontario M6H 255 Canada

Marsha Forest is the founder and Director of Education of the Centre for Integrated Education and Community (CIEC) and Inclusion Press. Dr. Forest has more than 25 years' experience as a teacher and advocate for children and families. She has worked in special education and holds her doctorate in teacher education, leadership, and administration. She is a widely known and popular keynote speaker, workshop leader, and video producer. She is an editor of many books on inclusive education. Dr. Forest is Adjunct Professor at McGill University and Director of the McGill Summer Institute on Integrated Education and Community.

Michael F. Giangreco, Ph.D., Research Assistant Professor, Center for Developmental Disabilities, College of Education, 499C Waterman Building, University of Vermont, Burlington, Vermont 05405-0160

Prior to joining the faculty at the University of Vermont in 1988, Michael F. Giangreco spent several years working directly with people with disabilities as a counselor in community residential services, a special education teacher, and a special education coordinator. His research and training efforts have focused primarily on teamwork and coordination of related services, curriculum planning and adaptation, and other strategies to facilitate inclusive education. Dr.

Giangreco is a coauthor of several publications including *Choosing Options and Accomodations for Children: A Guide to Planning Inclusive Education* (Giangreco, Cloninger, & Iverson, Paul H. Brookes Publishing Co., 1993).

Gregory F. Harper, Ph.D., Professor of Education, Department of Education, State University of New York–College at Fredonia, Fredonia, New York 14063

Gregory F. Harper is a specialist in the psychological foundations of education. A former school psychologist, he remains committed to identifying and evaluating effective instructional strategies that are easily implemented in classroom settings. In addition to research on peer-mediated and cooperative learning, he is involved in research aimed at improving undergraduate teacher preparation. He is the author of more than 50 articles, chapters, and monographs.

Tracy Harris, M.S., Integration Specialist, The Baird Center for Children and Families, 1110 Pine Street, Burlington, Vermont 05401

Tracy Harris has advocated for inclusionary practices to support children and youth in her roles as public school educator, team leader, foster parent, collaborative consultant, educational surrogate, and public speaker. She currently facilitates an interagency approach for integrating students who experience emotional and behavioral challenges into their local public schools.

David W. Johnson, Ed.D., Department of Educational Psychology, College of Education, University of Minnesota, Minneapolis, Minnesota 55455

David W. Johnson is Professor of Educational Psychology at the University of Minnesota. He has published more than 300 research articles and book chapters and has authored more than 30 books. His research interests focus on cooperation and competition, conflict resolution, team effectiveness, organizational change, experiential learning, relationships among diverse team members, and the implications of that research for training and instruction. Dr. Johnson has received awards for outstanding research from the American Personnel and Guidance Association, the Society for the Psychological Study of Social Issues (Gordon Allport Award), the Association for Specialists in Group Work (Division of American Association for Counseling and Development), the American Society for Engineering Education, and the National Council for Social Studies. He has received the Award for Outstanding Contribution to American Education from the Minnesota Association for Supervision and Curriculum Development. He is a Fellow of the American Psychological Association. He is a past editor of the *American Educational Research Journal* (1981–1983), and is listed in *Marquis Who's Who in the World*.

Roger T. Johnson, Ed.D., Department of Curriculum and Instruction, College of Education, University of Minnesota, Minneapolis, Minnesota 55455

Roger T. Johnson is Professor of Curriculum and Instruction with an emphasis in science education at the University of Minnesota. He holds a master of arts degree from Ball State University and a doctor of education degree from the University of California in Berkeley. Dr. Johnson's public school teaching experience includes kindergarten through 8th grade instruction in self-contained classrooms, open schools, nongraded situations, cottage schools, and departmentalized (science) schools. At the college level, Dr. Johnson has taught teacher preparation courses for undergraduate through Ph.D. programs. He is the author of numerous articles and book chapters, and coauthor with David W. Johnson of *Learning Together and Alone* (3rd edition, Prentice Hall, 1990) and *Circles of Learning: Cooperation in the Classroom* (Association of Supervision and Curriculum Development, 1984; revised edition, Interaction Book Company, 1986, 1990).

Brian Kelly, M.Ed., Student Services Consultant/Psychometrist, School District 12, Woodstock, New Brunswick EOJ 2BO Canada

Brian Kelly's work has focused on inclusive education for students with challenging behaviors, students at risk of leaving school, crisis intervention, and alternative assessment techniques. As a volunteer, he has been a board member and chairperson for the community's early intervention agency and residential living board, serving individuals with special needs.

Norman Kunc, M.Sc., Axis Consultation and Training, 4623 Elizabeth Street, Port Alberni, British Columbia V9Y 6L8 Canada

Norman Kunc is a family therapist and an educational consultant. Born with cerebral palsy, he attended a segregated school for children with physical disabilities. At age 13, he was integrated into a regular school. From there, he went on to complete an honors degree in Humanities at York University. Upon graduation, he received the Murray G. Ross Award for academic excellence and outstanding contribution to the university. He then completed a master of science degree in family therapy at the University of Guelph. He is the author of *Ready, Willing and Disabled* (Frontier College, Toronto, 1984), and has a book chapter and several journal articles to his credit.

Laurie LaPlant, M.Ed., Consulting/Collaborating Teacher, Swanton Central School, Swanton, Vermont 05488

Laurie LaPlant presently teaches at the middle school level in the Swanton, Vermont, Schools, a fully inclusive public school. In her past 10 years of working to facilitate with children and families opportunities to receive quality education and social opportunities in their home schools, she has concentrated her efforts in developing systems change activities, collaborative teaming relationships, cooperative learning, and partner learning programs. She has shared her learnings from the educators, families, and children with whom she has worked in various courses and workshops throughout the United States.

Herbert L. Leff, Ph.D., Associate Professor of Psychology, University of Vermont, Burlington, Vermont 05405

Herbert L. Leff's work over the past 2 decades has focused on metacognitive techniques for the enhancement of experience and creativity. Most recently, his research and publications have centered on "turning learning inside out"—developing procedures that enable students to apply academic learning meaningfully and creatively in their lives outside school.

Larry Maheady, Ph.D., Professor of Education, Department of Education, State University of New York–College at Fredonia, Fredonia, New York 14063

Larry Maheady is a certified school psychologist and special education teacher. He is on the editorial board of four leading special education and psychology journals and has published more than 50 articles in refereed journals. He is also the coauthor of a text entitled *Educating Students with Behavior Disorders* (Prentice Hall, 1992). Dr. Maheady is interested primarily in the development, implementation, and evaluation of classroom-based interventions designed to improve the academic or interpersonal performance of children who are at risk for failure in school. In addition, he is presently involved in the restructuring of preservice teacher preparation programs and the development of school–university partnerships.

Barbara Mallette, Ph.D., Associate Professor of Education, Department of Education, State University of New York–College at Fredonia, Fredonia, New York 14063

Barbara Mallette teaches coursework that addresses the needs of exceptional learners, child development, preschoolers with special needs, and classroom management. Dr. Mallette's research interests involve peer-mediated instructional strategies, training preservice educators, and dealing with families of youngsters with special needs. Dr. Mallette is involved with education majors through the Teacher Education Club. She is also Director of the Office of Internships and International Education.

Mary McNeil, Ed.D., International Educational Consultant, Director of Special Education and Evaluation, Merced Union High School District, 3105 North G Street, Merced, California 95348

Mary McNeil is Director of Special Education and Evaluation for the Merced Union High School District, Merced, California. She has taught at the graduate and undergraduate levels while on the faculty of the University of Vermont, served as coeditor of *Teacher Education and Special Education,* the journal of the Council for Exceptional Children, Teacher Education Division; and was President of the Partners of the Americas Vermont–Honduras Partnership. Dr. McNeil published widely in the area of special education, and is an international consultant in Europe and Latin America. Her specialty areas include partner learning, collaborative consultation, and systems change.

Frank B. Murray, Ph.D., Dean, College of Education, and H. Rodney Sharp Professor in the Departments of Educational Studies and Psychology at the University of Delaware, Newark, Delaware 19716

Frank B. Murray has been Dean of the College of Education at the University of Delaware since 1980. He earned his bachelor's degree from St. John's College and a master of arts in teaching degree and doctorate from The Johns Hopkins University. He serves on the editorial boards of several journals in educational and developmental psychology and is a Fellow of the American Psychological Association and the American Psychological Society. Currently, he chairs the National Board of the Holmes Group and is President of the Project 30 Alliance, a consortium of faculty in education and liberal arts. He is editing a handbook on the knowledge base for teacher educators for the American Association of Colleges for Teacher Education and serves on the Teacher Programs Council of the Educational Testing Service, which is developing a new national teacher examination, *Praxis.*

Jack Pearpoint, B.A., Executive Director, Centre for Integrated Education and Community, 24 Thome Crescent, Toronto, Ontario M6H 2S5 Canada

Jack Pearpoint is the founder and Executive Director of the Centre for Integrated Education and Community (CIEC) and President of Inclusion Press. He has more than 25 years' experience running innovative adult education and literacy organizations. He spent 5 years in Nigeria and Ghana with Canadian University Services Overseas, then was President of Frontier College, Canada's oldest adult education institution, for more than 15 years. He has designed and developed with his colleagues and friends the PATH process. Presently, he is an adjunct professor at McGill University, and spends his time advocating, writing, and lecturing about a vision of a world in which "Kids Belong Together."

Richard L. Rosenberg, Ph.D., Vocational Coordinator and Coordinator of Training, Whittier Union High School District, 9401 South Painter Avenue, Whittier, California 90605

Richard L. Rosenberg is Vocational Coordinator and Coordinator of Training at Whittier Union High School District and the Career Assessment and Placement Centers Adult Services component. He has been responsible for establishing Supported Living Options for a number of individuals utilizing the future planning process of MAPs, PATH, and Circles of Support. He received his doctor of philosophy degree in 1980 from the University of Wisconsin–Madison. He has provided technical assistance to a number of schools, adult services agencies, and individual families in Los Angeles as well as across the United States. He has served as a board member of California's chapter of The Association for Persons with Severe Handicaps for a number of years as well as President of CHOICESS, a nonprofit adult support organization in Los Angeles.

Mara Sapon-Shevin, Ed.D., Professor, Teaching and Leadership Programs, Syracuse University, 150 Huntington Hall, Syracuse, New York 13244-2340

Mara Sapon-Shevin prepares teachers for inclusive, heterogeneous classrooms through Syracuse's new Inclusive Elementary and Special Education Teacher Education Program. She is a board member of the International Association for the Study of Cooperation in Education and gives workshops on cooperative learning and cooperative games for the classroom. The author of many articles and book chapters on cooperative learning, full inclusion, diversity education, and the politics of gifted education, she is the author of the forthcoming book *Playing Favorites: Gifted Education and the Disruption of Community* (SUNY Press).

Fred Schrumpf, M.S.W., M.Ed., Trainer-Consultant, 1429 South Walnut Street, Spokane, Washington 99203

Fred Schrumpf holds master's degrees in both social work and education from the University of Illinois at Urbana-Champaign. He has practiced school social work for the past 20 years, and has taught at the University of Illinois, Idaho State University, and Eastern Washington University. He is currently a trainer-consultant delivering workshops on conflict resolution, peer mediation, and life skills. He is the coauthor of *Peer Mediation: Conflict Resolution in the Schools* (Research Press, 1991), *Life Lessons for Young Adolescents* (Research Press, 1993), and *The Peaceable School* (Research Press, 1994).

Karl A. Smith, Ph.D., Professor, Department of Civil and Mineral Engineering, University of Minnesota, 500 Pillsbury Drive SE, Minneapolis, Minnesota 55455

Karl Smith has worked with David and Roger Johnson for more than 10 years, has conducted many cooperative learning workshops. He has published numerous articles on the active learning strategies of cooperative learning and structured controversy, knowledge representation and expert systems, and instructional uses of personal computers. He teaches courses on building models to solve problems for civil engineering systems and for project management and leadership. He is coauthor of *How to Model It: Problem Solving for the Computer Age* (McGraw-Hill, 1990), *Active Learning: Cooperation in the College Classroom* (Active Interaction Book Co., 1991), and *Cooperative Learning: Increasing College Faculty Instructional Productivity* (ASHE-ERIC Report on Higher Education, 1991).

Susan B. Stainback, Ed.D., and **William C. Stainback, Ed.D.,** Professors, College of Education, University of Northern Iowa, Cedar Falls, Iowa 50614

Susan and William Stainback are professors of education at the University of Northern Iowa. They received their doctorates from the University of Virginia in the early 1970s. Their professional experiences involve elementary-, secondary-, and university-level teaching. The Stainbacks have coauthored or coedited more than 150 publications, including books, monographs, chapters in books, and articles in professional journals. Their current professional interests include how to address the educational needs of all students in regular schools and classrooms.

Jonathan Udis, M.Ed., Consultant in Effective Instruction, Discipline, and Leadership, P.O. Box 3368, R.D. #3, Middlesex, Vermont 05602

Over the years, Jonathan Udis has taught students at the elementary and secondary levels; served as a building principal; and provided training, support, and consultation to various agencies promoting educational and social change. His primary areas of expertise and interest include adult teaming, conflict resolution for adults and students, discipline and full inclusion of students with behavioral and emotional challenges, especially as they relate to interagency cooperation and conflict. For the past 4 years, he has taught courses for St. Michael's College (Colchester, Vermont) on teaming, cooperative group learning, and consultation.

Alice Udvari-Solner, Ph.D., University of Wisconsin, Departments of Curriculum and Instruction and Rehabilitation Psychology and Special Education, 225 North Mills Street, University of Wisconsin–Madison, Madison, Wisconsin 53706

Alice Udvari-Solner is Assistant Professor at the University of Wisconsin–Madison where she holds a joint appointment in the Department of Curriculum and Instruction and the Department of Rehabilitation Psychology and Special Education. She teaches graduate and undergraduate courses to general and special education students that examine strategies for including learners with disabilities in general education classes. Dr. Udvari-Solner is currently the principal investigator of a federal research grant to examine how the design and use of effective curricular adaptations influence the participation of students with disabilities in general education. In addition to her interests in curricular adaptations, her research and publications focus on collaborative teamwork, fostering natural supports in the workplace, community-based instruction, longitudinal vocational training, transition from school to work, supported employment, and communication systems for individuals with dual sensory impairments.

Emma Van der Klift, Axis Consultation and Training, 4623 Elizabeth Street, Port Alberni, British Columbia V9Y 6L8 Canada

Emma Van der Klift is a consultant who provides training and consultation in the areas of inclusive education, employment equity, conflict management, and labor relations. During the past 18 years, she has worked to support people with disabilities in a variety of capacities, including supported employment, the development of residential options for people leaving institutions, and as a program director. Formerly the Labour Relations Director for a large nonprofit organization on Vancouver Island, she is currently completing a diploma in Conflict Resolution and Mediation at the Justice Institute in Vancouver, British Columbia.

Nadine Zane, M.Ed., Collaborating Teacher, JFK Elementary School, 70 Normand Street, Winooski, Vermont 05404

Nadine Zane has taught students in both regular and special education programs at levels ranging from elementary students to graduate students. She has participated in many presentations and training sessions related to inclusive schooling, collaboration, adaptations, accommodations, behavior management, and peer support systems. She is currently a special educator serving elementary students in an inclusive school.

PREFACE

We, the three coeditors, have focused our professional and much of our personal lives on working with educators, parents, and students to restructure schools so that all children may be educated together. History is at a point when inclusive education is no longer an idealistic vision but an inescapable reality and obligation.

In our collective years of work, we discovered that students supporting other students is a critical element for successful academic and social inclusion of children with disabilities. Furthermore, we learned to broaden our discussions to include *all* children, rather than focusing only on a subset of the school population (e.g., "special" education, "general" education).

Our career paths intertwined as we each pursued unique work opportunities that demanded collaboration, consultation, and cooperation with people who had differing ideas about educating students with various educational challenges. Through these interactions, we learned many of the principles and processes that we showcase in this book. We learned from experience that practices such as cooperative learning, partner and peer-mediated learning, and creative thinking increase the likelihood of success for all students.

Our vision in writing this book was to go beyond the rhetoric of explaining *why* students with disabilities must be educated in regular education and community settings. Instead, we wanted to show how peer support in instruction, advocacy, and decision making can be structured to facilitate the success of learners with and without disabilities in general education. Furthermore, we wanted to offer adults and children techniques for enhancing their creative thinking and problem-solving capacities.

From the start, we knew that none of us could write or edit this book alone. Yet, together and with the help of the creative partnerships of the contributing authors, we believe we have created a text that provides detailed ways for teachers to facilitate learning for an increasingly diverse student population. Our book features case studies, sample lesson plans, and other specific "how to" strategies for meaningfully involving a diverse student body in learning. We emphasize practical ways for classroom teachers, students, special educators and other support personnel, curriculum coordinators, administrators, and university professors to invent schools and classrooms in which students with differing abilities can be creatively and actively involved in their own and others' academic and social learning.

Included in this book are research reviews presented in everyday language, sample lesson plan formats, suggestions for peer coaching, and forms and materials that teachers may duplicate. Our partnerships involved classroom teachers, graduate students, and other school personnel whose experiences are represented in the cooperative group lesson plans at the end of Section I. We include a variety of grade levels (e.g., preschool, primary, upper elementary, middle, high school, college), curriculum areas (e.g., science, mathematics, language arts, career/vocation, oral expression, art), and specific adaptations to meet the unique needs of students with varying abilities (e.g., significant disabilities, gifted and talented, emotional challenges, and special education needs). In addition, there are two lesson plans that introduce cooperative learning methods to middle school teachers and other adult learners. To facilitate use, the book has been printed with a special "layflat" paperback binding. Our hope is that this book will become the most useful and most used book in any educator's library. Our dream is that educators will use this book to celebrate diversity in the classroom, to capitalize on their students' individual differences, and to welcome each and every child as an important member of a caring classroom community.

INTRODUCTION

William C. Stainback and Susan B. Stainback

Schools such as Hansen Elementary in Cedar Falls, Iowa; the Winooski School District in Winooski, Vermont; Saint Francis in Waterloo County, Ontario; Brook Forest in Oak Brook, Illinois; and Ed Smith Elementary School in Syracuse, New York, have attracted the attention of parents, educators, and concerned community members. They are examples of a new breed of schools that are effective, caring, and inclusive. Educators, parents, and students in all these schools have consistently stated in interviews, in conference presentations, and in various publications that a major key to their success is the involvement of students, along with teachers, specialists, and parents working in collaboration with each other. Students in these schools are involved in circles of friends; as advocates for fellow students; in cooperative learning situations; as peer tutors and partners; and on educational planning teams as equal members with teachers, administrators, and parents.

Although there are a small but growing number of schools throughout the United States of America similar to the ones mentioned above, these schools are still the exception rather than the rule. That is, there remains an enormous amount of work to achieve effective, fully inclusive, and caring schools on a widespread basis.

In the early 1990s, a Massachusetts scholar clearly summarized a major obstacle. He stated:

> Our society's current infatuation with the word "competitiveness" which has leached into discussions about education encourages a confusion between two very different ideas; excellence and the desperate quest to triumph over other people. (Kohn, 1991, p. 497)

He went on to say:

> At a tender age, children learn not to be tender. A dozen years of schooling often do nothing to promote generosity or a commitment to the welfare of others. To the contrary, students are graduated who think that being smart means looking out for number one. (p. 498)

Growing numbers of practitioners, researchers, and scholars (e.g., Coleman & Hoffer, 1987; Flynn, 1989; Kohn, 1991; Sapon-Shevin, 1992; Solomon, Schaps, Watson, & Battistich, 1992; Stainback & Stainback, 1992; Thousand & Villa, 1992) have argued in recent years that far too many of today's schools have lost or are losing a sense of community; that is, students and teachers learning to care about, work cooperatively with, and support each other. In addition, there is growing empirical evidence that in schools where students and teachers do not establish friendships, commitments, and bonds with each other (i.e., where there is an absence of community), there are increased problems with underachievement, student dropouts, drug abuse, exclusion of students with disabilities from the mainstream, and gang activity (Coleman & Hoffer, 1987; Maeroff, 1990). As a result, Coleman and Hoffer have hypothesized that some of the present-day problems in education, including the exclusion of some students from the mainstream, are due, at least in part, to a lack of community in many schools in an increasingly urban, complex, and depersonalized society.

This is one major reason why *Creativity and Collaborative Learning: A Practical Guide to Empowering Students and Teachers* is timely and important. It provides numerous practical suggestions regarding how students can grow up together, work cooperatively, and care about and support each other. It also explains why doing these things is critical to enhancing students' social, educational, and life achievements.

This book is composed of 17 chapters, lesson plans, an epilogue, and a glossary, divided into three sections. Section I, Cooperative Group Learning, includes a chapter designed to describe why cooperative learning may be the essential means by which the minds of students and teachers construct knowledge and create meaning. There are also chapters on which models of cooperative learning may be best; cooperative learning in the context of integration; issues in structuring cooperative group lessons; how classroom teachers, special educators, support personnel, and students can serve as equal members of cooperative education teams; the role of cooperative group learning in modifying behavior; and a discussion of the role of cooperative group learning in higher education instruction.

Following Section I are sample creative cooperative group lesson plans. These examples are intended to stimulate the reader's creativity in designing cooperative group lessons.

Section II, Partner Learning, Peer Tutoring, and Peer Mediation, consists of five chapters that focus on practical ways students can help each other in academic and social endeavors and situations. In the first chapter of this section, the authors provide a user-friendly review of the research on peer-mediated instruction and partner learning systems. Specific steps for organizing and managing peer partner learning is the topic of Chapter 10. Chapter 11 presents case studies that illustrate the variations of how partner learning may be carried out within a classroom or across a school or school district. Chapter 12 provides an overview of conflict resolution strategies and the role of peers in modifying conflict. The final chapter in this section details the long-term effects of various peer support systems (e.g., peer tutors, peer buddies, students on IEP and transition planning teams) in facilitating the academic success and social inclusion of a young woman with Down syndrome during her high school years.

The four chapters in Section III, Cooperatively Creating New Responses and New Behaviors, illustrate the power of collaborative and creative processes. The first chapter of Section III offers conceptual tools for enhancing the creativity and quality of the solutions generated by collaborative teams. In Chapter 15, case studies are presented that illustrate how students have employed creative problem-solving strategies to assist teachers in identifying instructional accommodations for classmates, to manage their own and classmates' behavior, and to plan for students' transitions. Included in Chapter 16 are examples of the MAPs and PATHS future planning processes, Circles of Friends, and peers acting as advocates on student educational planning teams. The final chapter in this section details multiple strategies for empowering students who are experiencing emotional challenges by creating caring communities and teaching responsibility.

The book concludes with an epilogue that emphasizes the need for power and belonging for both the adults and students who work in our school systems. The need for reciprocity in relationships is highlighted. The glossary defines key ideas for easy referral.

As you read the chapters of this book, it becomes evident that there is a great deal of emphasis on students and teachers helping and supporting each other. There are a number of basic principles of support networking that have emerged during the past several decades that may be helpful to keep in mind.

1. Support networking is based on the premise that everyone has capabilities, strengths, gifts, and talents, including students classified as having disabilities, that they can use to provide support and assistance to their fellow community members.

2. In support networking, all people are involved in helping and supporting one another in both formal and informal support arrangements. Relationships are reciprocal, rather than some people always serving as helpers and others always being helped.

3. Natural supportive relationships in which individuals support one another as peers, friends, or colleagues are as important as providing professional support. A focus on natural supports helps connect people together in classrooms and schools and, therefore, fosters supportive communities.

4. Individuals are unique and differ in what they require; their needs often change over time. Thus, any supports inherent in support networking should not be based on a predefined, ironclad list of support options that cannot be modified.

5. Support networking works best in integrated, heterogeneous classrooms and schools. The diversity inherent among the members increases the likelihood that all class and school members, including students, teachers, parents, specialists, administrators, and other school personnel will have the assets and resources necessary to support the needs of and become interdependent with each other.

6. Supports should be consumer driven. That is, the focus should be on what the consumer (the person receiving support) wants and needs as stated by him or her. (Or, if the person is very young or unable to communicate effectively to the provider, his or her advocate should state what the consumer wants and needs.)

7. Any support provided should focus on empowering a person to assist himself or herself and others. This includes empowering a person to seek assistance when required and provide assistance to others.

8. School personnel in administrative or decision-making situations need not only to provide opportunities for informal support development among all members of the school community, but also, when possible, to empower and encourage people to provide support to each other.

9. Support networking should be a natural and ongoing part of the school and classroom community. It should not be episodic or reserved only for times of difficulty or crisis.

10. Support networking should be run by insiders (i.e., those individuals directly involved in the school and classroom community). This may include students, teachers, secretaries, administrators, parents, specialists, other school personnel, and community volunteers.

11. Support networking is for everyone. Plans that focus on and operate for a single

student or teacher generally are inefficient in promoting and maintaining the development and operation of an inclusive, supportive community.

12. Support networking starts with an examination of the social interactions and supportive characteristics that naturally operate in regular classrooms and school environments and builds upon these.

13. An inherent danger in providing some types of support is that, if done incorrectly, it can make the person unnecessarily dependent upon the support. For example, if someone helps a particular student find his or her way to the school cafeteria without at the same time helping the student learn the route and the skills necessary to do it alone, then that student may never learn to travel to the cafeteria independently. Thus, it is critical in supportive classroom communities that everyone understand that the goal is to provide support to others whenever it is needed, but in the process of doing so always work to empower people to assist and support themselves and others.

This book is one that all educators, parents, and students interested in effective schools, empowerment of students and teachers, community building, and heterogeneous education should keep close at hand.

REFERENCES

Coleman, J., & Hoffer, T. (1987). *Public and private high schools: The impact of communities.* New York: Basic Books.

Flynn, G. (1989, November). *Toward community.* Paper presented at the 16th Annual TASH Conference, San Francisco.

Kohn, A. (1991). Caring kids: The role of the schools. *Phi Delta Kappan, 72*(7), 496–506.

Maeroff, G. (1990). Getting to know a good middle school. *Phi Delta Kappan, 71,* 505–511.

Sapon-Shevin, M. (1992). Celebrating diversity, creating community: Curriculum that honors and builds on differences. In S. Stainback & W. Stainback (Eds.), *Curriculum considerations in inclusive classrooms: Facilitating learning for all students* (pp. 19–36). Baltimore: Paul H. Brookes Publishing Co.

Solomon, D., Schaps, E., Watson, M., & Battistich,

V. (1992). Creating caring school and classroom communities for all students. In R.A. Villa, J.S. Thousand, W. Stainback, & S. Stainback (Eds.), *Restructuring for caring and effective education: An administrative guide to creating heterogeneous schools* (pp. 41–60). Baltimore: Paul H. Brookes Publishing Co.

Stainback, S., & Stainback, W. (Eds.). (1992). *Curriculum considerations in inclusive classrooms: Facilitating learning for all students.* Baltimore: Paul H. Brookes Publishing Co.

Thousand, J.S., & Villa, R.A. (1992). Collaborative teams: A powerful tool in school restructuring. In R.A. Villa, J.S. Thousand, W. Stainback, & S. Stainback (Eds.), *Restructuring for caring and effective education: An administrative guide to creating heterogeneous schools* (pp. 73–108). Baltimore: Paul H. Brookes Publishing Co.

COOPERATIVE GROUP LEARNING

WHY UNDERSTANDING THE THEORETICAL BASIS OF COOPERATIVE LEARNING ENHANCES TEACHING SUCCESS

Frank B. Murray

There are many people who think that a well-meaning, college-educated person can teach after a little on-the-job practice and coaching. The problem with this idea is that it works only when the teacher and the students are similar. It can be expected to fail when the teacher and the students come from markedly different backgrounds. In cases where the teacher is not comfortable with the students, it is known that novice teachers will rely, about 80% of the time (Hawley & Rosenholtz, 1984), on two traditional and limiting teaching techniques—telling and assigning seat work exercises.

It is also known that "untrained" teachers, however well-intentioned, will make a number of pedagogical errors. These errors may be viewed one day as educational malpractice. They are errors that can be avoided if the prospective teacher can understand why they are problematic and is willing to practice some of the alternative teaching techniques described throughout this book.

Without disciplined study and practice, it can be expected, for example, that amateurs, especially those with the best and most decent intentions, will blunder when they teach pupils who are very different from themselves. They will, for example, treat pupils for whom they have low expectations in the following ways: They will seat them farther away from their desk, they will treat them as a group rather than as individuals, and they will look at them and call on them less often. When they do call on them, they will ask them questions that require lower level cognitive responses and give them less time to respond and fewer hints than they give pupils for whom they have higher expectations. They will give them less praise, even when they are correct, and more blame when they are wrong than they give pupils for whom they have higher expectations (see Brophy & Good, 1986; Hawley & Rosenholtz, 1984). Furthermore, they will do all of this out of a mistaken sense of kindness because they do not wish to humiliate a pupil they believe does not know the answer by calling upon him or her, by prolonging the question interval with hints even when an easy question has been asked, and so forth. It takes concentrated practice and understanding to eliminate these and other documented mistakes that novice teachers inevitably make, particularly with those pupils who are in the most need of professional care.

Teaching these students is not easy, even when the prospective teacher is exposed to modern views of educational practice. Smith (1990) has shown that even under ideal teacher-coaching conditions—one to one—highly motivated and experienced teachers were still unsure and shaky after 10 months of practice in their efforts to implement a new teaching technique, even though they had practiced the technique in a variety of environments, had analyzed their teaching performance through video and stimulated recall, had personal feedback of their efforts, and so forth.

ROLE OF UNDERSTANDING

There is no question that ordinary common sense, although helpful to the novice teacher (see, for example, Gardner & Rogoff, 1982, on mothers' teaching), is not a sufficient guide for many of the problems teachers face. Upon what else does the novice teacher draw when asked to consider whether some educational innovation should be introduced into the school? How should teachers and administrators in the 1970s have decided, for example, whether to require, as they did, one quarter of the nation's pupils to learn to read in a special alphabet (*ita*, the initial teaching alphabet) that "regularized" English orthography by having a separate letter or symbol for each of the 45 sounds that make up spoken English? How would they have evaluated the history of spelling reform efforts that claimed to simplify reading; what would they make of the fact that *ita* was but a version of "phonataby," another alphabet used in the 1860s that was discarded after it failed to live up to its promise? Could they have predicted that the shift from *ita* to the regular alphabet would harm the pupil's spelling and writing even though it would actually help reading somewhat (Gillooly, 1966)? How could they have evaluated the claims for the benefits of *ita* more wisely than they did? What else did they need to consider?

Along the same lines, how would the novice avoid advocating widely believed, but wrong-headed policies, such as the failure to accelerate gifted pupils (Kulik & Kulik, 1984), or giving their pupils bad advice, such as not changing answers to multiple-choice questions because the first guess is supposed to be best (Reile & Briggs, 1952)? How would the novice come to know that, for more than 80 years, researchers and policy makers have studied whether the benefits of holding unsuccessful pupils back to repeat a grade outweigh the harm failure causes? They need to know that only about 7% of the 650 studies conducted since 1930 on this topic meet acceptable research standards and that these sound studies, conducted in grades one to six across the country, compared 4,208 pupils who were not promoted to the next grade with 6,294 pupils of comparable accomplishment who were "socially" promoted (i.e., pupils who were promoted even though they were not ready for the next level) (Holmes &

Matthews, 1984). These socially promoted pupils outscored those who were held back by about 17 percentile ranks in academic achievement and about 11 percentile ranks in social adjustments. As the decision to promote or hold back pupils cannot be avoided by the teacher, those who decide to keep academically weak children in an elementary grade for an additional year, as common sense might have it, do so despite considerable evidence that the children would have done better in school had they been promoted with their classmates.

A SOURCE OF EDUCATIONAL UNDERSTANDING

Educational theory and research is really knowledge teachers might have used, or could have used, to explain and justify their decisions and performance in teaching. Teachers' literacy in the fields of educational history, philosophy, sociology, psychology, and research is critical to the improvement of teaching practices because it challenges common sense and the widespread naive theories of education.

To establish that a teacher could have, might have, or even should have based his or her teaching performance on some knowledge of educational theory or some body of research is not evidence that he or she did, or would ever, base his or her performance on that knowledge. While we all could have formed our speech in conformity to our tutored understanding of English grammar and syntax, we know that most of us, particularly young children, speak the language unencumbered by any conscious knowledge of the very linguistic rules that explain correct speech. It would be wise, therefore, to base the instruction of educational theory upon the knowledge teachers would *actually use* in their performance, unless, of course, the goal of instruction is literacy for its own sake, whether or not it actually influences what the teacher does when he or she teaches.

There are many reasons why it is beneficial to have teachers who are literate in the discipline (or disciplines) of education, of course, but the primary goal in teacher education is to have students acquire that mixture of knowledge, skill, and disposition that truly affects what the teacher does.

Unfortunately, very little is known about how teachers actually think about their teaching and how that knowledge develops, other than, similar to children's teaching (Koester & Bueche, 1980), it tends to be direct (i.e., show and tell) and teachers tend to see the goal of instruction as the transmission of information to the pupil. The goal of teacher education is to have the teacher develop a mature *structure* of reasoning about teaching and schooling. In the end, it is this structure that is important, not the specific content or information, but rather the system of the teacher's reasoning about his or her teaching.

Given that so much rests upon teachers' ways of thinking and expectations about schooling, there is a need to be sure that teachers can evaluate evidence, can spot a fad or an unsound proposal for innovation, have an educated view of how a pupil's mind develops, have a reasoned and informed position on the major public policy issues that affect schooling, and so forth. Upon what reserve does the teacher draw when he or she faces a novel problem? Surely, teachers ought to have acquired more than a pop-psychological view of how the mind works or a pop-sociological view of how, for example, families, schools, and cultures thrive. Amateurs make bad guesses and predictions and they have no defenses against destructive educational fads because their common sense and folk wisdom only work in the easy cases.

WAYS OF THINKING ABOUT COOPERATIVE LEARNING

The term *cooperative learning* refers to a family of instructional practices in which the teacher gives various directions to groups of pupils about how to work together. It is a teaching practice, as the remainder of this book shows, that is rarely employed by novices as it has very little in common with the novice methods of "telling" and individual seat work assignments; yet, it is a powerful, if somewhat counterintuitive, teaching technique.

In a cooperative learning exercise, the class typically is divided into groups of three to six children usually of the same age, but differing in ability, ethnicity, and gender. The directions the teacher gives are designed, one way or another, to have the children work together as a team on some academic task. The children learn to cooperate to follow the teacher's instructions; however, cooperation itself, while a worthy curriculum objective, is not the principal objective in cooperative learning instruction. The claim of cooperative learning practitioners, usually supported in field research, is that ordinary school learning is enhanced considerably when children, following one of the cooperative learning procedures, learn in groups rather than on their own or in competition with other pupils (see Davidson, chap. 2, and Johnson & Johnson, chap. 3, this volume, for further details).

Schooling invariably takes place in groups, largely for reasons of economy and efficiency. Overall academic achievement is usually, but not always, superior when the groups are small—optimally about seven students—and when the members of each group are of different or mixed academic levels of achievement. A disproportionate share of the academic benefits in mixed classrooms of 30 or so pupils tend to go to those of lower academic accomplishment when the instructional approach is traditional and success is measured conventionally by a teacher's grades or standardized tests.

Although traditional classroom instruction has always entailed a degree of cooperation and competition among pupils, cooperative learning practices *require* pupils to cooperate as a team as a *necessary* condition of acquiring academic information. This usually means that the instructional outcome results from the pupils' shared efforts, and that the instructional goal is shared and each pupil's success depends upon and is linked with every other pupil's success and never their failure. Cooperative learning practices typically have pupils share materials, divide up the labor required to complete the assignment, assist the other members of the group, and receive rewards based upon the group's performance.

SUCCESS AND UNDERSTANDING

The link between successful teaching practice and the teacher's understanding of the reasons for the success of the practice is subtle (Floden & Klinzing, 1990). On the one hand, sound practices can be derived from sound theories; on the other hand, surprisingly, they also can be validly derived from unsound theories. Thus, the fact that practice works does not guarantee that the theory from which it was derived is sound. Technically, unsound practices cannot be derived from sound theories, but theories in education or the behavioral sciences are rarely stated with the precision that one would need to make a proper deduction from them in any case. Nevertheless, the way in which the teacher thinks about the practice is important in determining which aspects of the pupil's accomplishment will be stressed and cultivated.

The instructions teachers give when they ask their pupils to work cooperatively are based on four theoretical perspectives: 1) social learning theory, 2) Piagetian theory, 3) Vygotskian theory, and 4) the newer cognitive science theories. Each of these perspectives is focused on one of the following characteristics of cooperative learning: *teamwork* (social learning theory), *conflict resolution* (Piagetian theory), *community collaboration* (Vygotskian theory), and *tutoring* (cognitive science theory).

Social Learning Theory: Teamwork

Practices derived from the social learning tradition are the most widely used in schools. They are based upon the common principle that pupils will work hard on those tasks for which they secure a reward of some sort and will fail to work on tasks that yield no reward or yield punishment. In cooperative learning instruction, the teacher employs the approval of other pupils and the expectations of the group, and relies on the ability of the pupil to imitate the academic behavior of others. These are the tools of the cooperative learning teacher in the social learning tradition.

When individuals work together toward a common goal, their mutual dependency often motivates them to work harder to help the group, and thereby themselves, to succeed. In addition, they often must help specific members of the group do well and they often come to like and value the members of the group.

The several cooperative learning practices in the social learning tradition are designed to provide incentives for the members of the group to participate in a group effort because, for example, children will not spontaneously help their colleagues or work toward a common goal. Thus, it is critical that the teacher reward a pupil *only* when all members of the group succeed in learning the assignment or, in the case where a teacher assigns the pupils different parts of a complicated task, only on the basis of the group's overall achievement and not according to the merit of any individual pupil's contribution to the group's effort.

Also, the teacher must ensure that the contributions of the weaker members of the group are genuinely important so that the group's success cannot be attributable merely to the work of one or two pupils. If the teacher merely instructs the pupils to work together and to help each other, the academic gains are generally no greater than had the pupils worked alone on the task.

The most thoroughly researched cooperative learning practices are these: Learning Together; Student Teams-Achievement Divisions (STAD) or STAD Group Investigation; Team Assisted Individualization (TAI); Teams-Games-Tournaments (TGT); and Jigsaw (see Slavin, 1986; Stallings & Stipek, 1986).

In a typical cooperative learning exercise the teacher might divide academic material into parts and have each member of the team read and study one of the parts. Then the members of the different teams who have studied the same parts might meet to discuss and clarify their sections, after which they would return to their original group to teach and quiz their teammates about their section; or they might enter into an academic game contest with their counterparts on the other teams to determine who performed the best. Often, each student takes an individual examination, with no help from the others, on the entire subject matter and a score for the group is computed from the individual scores by a scheme that allows each member to contribute to the team's score in a significant way (e.g., the team score might be based upon the amount of improvement in each member's grasp of the subject matter). The team with the highest group score is often rewarded with a certificate or some other attractive form of recognition. In some schemes, the grade the student receives is the team score and in others the grade follows the conventional practice and is based solely upon the pupil's own work.

Johnson, Maruyama, Johnson, Nelson, and Skon (1981) found 108 studies in which cooperation promoted higher academic achievement than independent work, 6 studies in which the reverse was true, and 42 in which no difference was found. Slavin (1986), in a review of selected research studies that had equivalent control groups and took place in real schools over a period of at least 2 weeks, found that the cooperative group achieved at higher levels than the control group in 22 of the 33 studies, with no difference being found in 10 studies.

Some cooperative schemes have been carefully researched; TGT, for example, has been evaluated in sample sizes ranging from 53 to 1,742 at both elementary and secondary levels and in several subject matter domains (Stallings & Stipek, 1986). In these studies, TGT was administered by classroom teachers with random assignment of teachers and pupils to the cooperative and control groups and with both groups having the same curriculum materials and objectives. On four of the seven standardized achievement tests and eight of the nine classroom tests, the TGT group outscored the control group as well as showed positive effects for race relations, friendship, attitudes toward school, and self-esteem.

Piagetian Theory: Conflict Resolution

Teachers, working within the Piagetian tradition, use cooperative learning lessons to accelerate a pupil's intellectual development by forcing him or her to systematically confront another child who holds an opposing point of view about the answer to some school task. Basically, the teacher places two pupils who disagree about the answer to a problem in a group, called a *dyad*, and tells them to work together until they can agree or come to a common answer, at which time the lesson will conclude. Once the pupils agree, usually in about 5 minutes, the teacher who tests the children alone usually finds that the pupils who initially did poorly on the problem can now, on their own, solve the problem in a way that is indistinguishable from the way a correct problem solver solved it in the first place (see Murray, 1986, for a review of this literature).

In some instances, teachers also may instruct the pupils in the dyad to simply imitate a correct problem solver, and on other occasions the teacher may instruct one child, in the presence of the other, to pretend to reason in a mature way. In other words, the teacher places the pupil in some social situation where he or she is forced to take a viewpoint that conflicts with his or her own point of view.

The practice of using dyads works best if the teacher ensures that one pupil understands the task. Some cognitive growth occurs, however, when neither child knows the correct answer to the problem and each initially offers an incorrect answer that contradicts the other's answer.

Overall, these social interaction or cooperative learning effects, documented consistently in some 30 studies, are limited to mental tasks that have srong relationships with age. They occur across a variety of such tasks with groups of various sizes (2–5), grades (K–5), and ethnic and social diversity. These developmental tasks, nevertheless, are important parts of the school curriculum because they are about information that is necessarily true (e.g., if A is older than B and B is older than C, then A is also older than C). Such social interaction versions of cooperative learning, apart from being effective ways to promote cognitive growth, are also more effective for developmental tasks in the school curriculum than traditional instructional practices that are based upon direct teaching or conditioning.

The techniques are rooted in the Genevan notion of *egocentrism,* or the tendency of young children to center on one aspect of a situation, usually their own perspective. The techniques are designed to address this pivotal factor in a child's reasoning by encouraging a child to attend to other dimensions and perspectives and to integrate these and his or her prior views into a new, more inclusive view of the problem.

Throughout the 1960s and early 1970s, it was widely held that one implication of Piagetian theory was that the young child (below the age of 7 years) was structurally incapable of taking a cognitive point of view different from his or her own (Cox, 1980). Researchers all over the world confirmed the young child's stubborn egocentrism in scores of laboratory studies, and extensions of the fact of egocentrism were found in curriculum and instructional designs that accepted the immutability of the young child's limited competence.

When teachers and mothers researched these issues, however, based upon their own unique familiarity with children and as part of their own graduate research training in the 1970s, they quickly devised experiments that showed that young children were able to take the point of view of others in many situations. These experiments led to substantial modifications in the prevailing interpretations of the child's cognitive competence that in turn supported the invention of pedagogical techniques, such as cooperative learning, that now presuppose the young pupil's competence to take the point of view of another pupil.

Vygotskian Theory: Community Collaboration

Even though few American educators are aware of it, the most compelling theoretical rationale for cooperative learning comes from the Russian psychologist, L.S. Vygotsky. He claimed that our distinctively human mental functions and accomplishments have their origins in our social relationships. Mental functioning in this view is the internalized and transformed version of the accomplishments of a group. The theory gives great weight to a group's common perspectives and solutions to problems as they are arrived at through debate, argument, negotiation, discussion, compromise, and dialectic.

This collaboration by a community of learners is seen as indispensable for cognitive growth. Its role is more than a mere facilitator of events; it is the means by which such growth occurs and a provision for it must be made in schooling. (See Connelly & Clandinin, 1990, for a related point about the inherent collaborative requirements in narrative inquiry as a pedagogical device in which the object of instruction is the pupil's story or narrative that confers meaning on the objectives of the curriculum.)

Researchers and teachers often find that the dyad can solve a problem when individuals working on their own cannot solve it. There is a distance that Vygotsky called a *zone of proximal development* between what the pupil can do on his or her own and what the pupil could achieve if he or she worked under the guidance of teachers or in collaboration with more capable peers. Thus, teachers who wish to maximize what the child can accomplish will minimize the time the child works alone on school tasks.

Research in this tradition (Forman & Cazden, 1985) so far has not resulted in novel practices in the schools, but it has provided a demonstration of the growth in individual children's problem solving when the problems are approached collaboratively and when the teacher sees the other children in the class as an indispensable part of the lesson and not as a barrier to each pupil's accomplishments. The other pupils are an instructional resource in this approach.

Cognitive Science Theory: Tutoring

The characteristics of ideal learning environments from the cognitive science perspective (Collins, Brown, & Newman, 1986) closely follow many features that are embedded in the common cooperative learning formats, all of which make provisions for modeling, coaching, and scaffolding, for example. However, some novel cooperative learning procedures, such as *reciprocal teaching,* have been developed by cognitive scientists for classroom instruction.

Reciprocal teaching, developed by Palincsar and Brown (1984), is a method of teaching reading in which the teacher and students take turns as the teacher. This works as follows: Both the teacher and students read a passage to themselves and the teacher demonstrates the process of formulating a question based upon the passage, summarizing the passage, clarifying it, and making predictions based on the information contained in it. When a pupil takes a turn as the teacher, the teacher carefully coaches the pupil in these skills of comprehension and offers prompts and criticism until none is needed by the pupil, at which time the teacher's role becomes more passive.

Both laboratory and classroom studies have demonstrated that reciprocal teaching is effective in significantly raising and maintaining the reading comprehension scores of poor readers (Collins et al., 1986; Symons, Snyder, Cariglia-Bull, & Pressley, 1989). Basically, the method is thought to be successful because the pupil gradually, but solidly, develops a new conceptual model for the skill and couples it with specific strategies that are used by expert readers. The cooperative learning features of these expert-novice teaching procedures lead the pupil to integrate the multiple roles that the successful problem solver inevitably masters. Thus, student writers are assisted when they read and critique other pupils' work and when they have their own work read by others. By taking turns writing and reading, they acquire a more comprehensive view of the writing task and a new conceptual model for it—a model closer to that possessed by the expert writer.

Tutoring, when it is viewed from the perspective of the benefits that accrue to the tutor, is also a form of cooperative learning. It is difficult, however, to know to what to attribute the benefits for the tutor—the tutoring act itself, the preparation for tutoring, the kind of study the tutor engages in, or some interactive combination of these factors (Hufnagel, 1984).

CONCLUSION

The research literature supports the claim that teachers can increase their pupils' performances on academic tasks when they assign their pupils to work on tasks in groups of two to six with rules that the pupils teach each other, coach each other, and succeed as a group. These gains occur only if teachers show their pupils how to do and think about these things and if they reward the pupils, individually and as a group, for doing them.

At least four theories explain how the cooperative learning innovations produce their impressive results—social learning theory, Piagetian theory, Vygotskian theory, and cognitive science theory. These theories guide the teacher in ways of dealing with novel problems presented in the lesson.

Over and above accomplishment on school tasks, cooperative learning—between pupils and pupils and between pupils and teachers—may be the essential means, as both Vygotsky and Piaget claimed, by which the mind constructs knowledge and invents meaning. Techniques that fail to make a provision for this kind of cooperation run the risk that pupils, while they may learn their lessons and may imitate their teachers, will not understand their lessons. The meaning derived from the instructional experience, in other words, will fall short of what would have been possible. The teacher who grasps the reasons behind a successful, even if counterintuitive, teaching strategy, such as cooperative learning, will be guided to the core of education, namely the development of the child's mind and the child's ability to use it well.

REFERENCES

Brophy, J., & Good, T. (1986). Teacher behavior and student achievement. In M. Wittrock (Ed.), *Handbook of research on teaching* (3rd ed.) (pp. 328–375). New York: Macmillan.

Collins, A., Brown, J., & Newman, S. (1986). Cognitive apprenticeship: Teaching the craft of reading, writing, and mathematics. In L. Resnick (Ed.), *Cognition and instruction: Issues and agendas* (pp. 1–41). Hillsdale, NJ: Lawrence Erlbaum Associates.

Connelly, F., & Clandinin, D. (1990). Stories of experience and narrative inquiry. *Educational Researcher, 19*(4), 2–14.

Cox, M.V. (Ed.). (1980). *Are young children egocentric?* New York: St. Martin's Press.

Floden, R., & Klinzing, H. (1990). What can research on teacher thinking contribute to teacher preparation? A second opinion. *Educational Researcher, 19*(5), 15–20.

Forman, E., & Cazden, C. (1985). Exploring Vygotskian perspectives in education: The cognitive value of peer interaction. In J.V. Wertsch (Ed.), *Culture, communication and cognition: Vygotskian perspectives* (pp. 323–347). New York: Academic Press.

Gardner, W., & Rogoff, B. (1982). The role of instruction in memory development: Some methodological choices. *Quarterly Newsletter of the Laboratory of Comparative Human Cognition, 4,* 6–12.

Gillooly, W. (1966). The promise of *ita* is a delusion. *Phi Delta Kappan,* 545–550.

Hawley, W., & Rosenholtz, S. (1984). Good schools: What research says about improving student achievement. *Peabody Journal of Education, 61*(4).

Holmes, C., & Matthews, K. (1984). The effects of nonpromotion on elementary and junior high school pupils: A meta-analysis. *Review of Educational Research, 54,* 225–236.

Hufnagel, P. (1984). *Effects of tutoring on tutors.* Unpublished doctoral dissertation, University of Delaware.

Johnson, D., Maruyama, G., Johnson, R., Nelson, D., & Skon, L. (1981). Effects of cooperative, competitive, and individualistic goal structures on achievement: A meta-analysis. *Psychological Bulletin, 89,* 47–62.

Koester, L.S., & Bueche, N.A. (1980). Preschoolers as teachers: Where children are seen but not heard. *Child Study Journal, 10,* 107–118.

Kulik, J., & Kulik, C. (1984). Effects of accelerated instruction on students. *Review of Educational Research, 54,* 409–425.

Murray, F. (1986). Micro-mainstreaming. In J. Meisel (Ed.), *The consequences of mainstreaming handicapped children* (pp. 43–54). Hillsdale, NJ: Lawrence Erlbaum Associates.

Palincsar, A., & Brown, A. (1984). Reciprocal teaching of comprehension-fostering and monitoring activities. *Cognition and Instruction, 1,* 117–175.

Reile, P., & Briggs, L. (1952). Should students change their initial answers on objective-type tests: More evidence regarding an old problem. *Journal of Educational Research, 43,* 373–375.

Slavin, R. (1986). Small group methods. In M. Dunkin (Ed.), *The international encyclopedia of teaching and teacher education* (pp. 237–243). Elmsford, NY: Pergamon Press.

Smith, D. (1990). *The role of teacher knowledge in teaching conceptual change science lessons.* Unpublished doctoral dissertation, University of Delaware.

Stallings, J., & Stipek, D. (1986). Research on early childhood and elementary school teaching programs. In M. Wittrock (Ed.), *Handbook of research on teaching* (3rd ed.) (pp. 727–753). New York: Macmillan.

Symons, S., Snyder, B., Cariglia-Bull, T., & Pressley, M. (1989). Why be so optimistic about cognitive strategy instruction? In C. McCormick, G. Miller, & M. Pressley (Eds.), *Cognitive strategy research: From basic research to educational applications* (pp. 1–32). New York: Springer-Verlag.

COOPERATIVE AND COLLABORATIVE LEARNING

AN INTEGRATIVE PERSPECTIVE

Neil Davidson

This chapter explores some of the diversity in the field of cooperative and collaborative learning. In contrast to some other innovations, there is no single guru on cooperative learning who is accepted on all points. The field has a number of diverse viewpoints, which can result in arguments over which approach is better or more "right." However, diversity can be viewed as a source of strength in terms of flexibility and mutually enriching perspectives, with all approaches having more similarities than differences. This chapter outlines six major approaches to cooperative and collaborative learning and examines commonalities and variations among the approaches. The approaches are Student Team Learning (Slavin, 1983a, 1983b, 1990); Learning Together (Johnson & Johnson, 1987, 1989a, 1989b); Group Investigation (Sharan & Hertz-Lazarowitz, 1980, 1982; Sharan & Sharan, 1992); the Structural Approach (Kagan, 1992); Complex Instruction (Cohen, 1986); and the Collaborative Approach (Barnes, Britton, & Torbe, 1986; Britton, 1970; Reid, Forrestal, & Cook, 1989).

As shown in Table 1, five attributes are common to all the cooperative/collaborative approaches; nine attributes vary. In this chapter, each cooperative/collaborative learning approach is explained and analyzed in terms of common and varying attributes.

Drafts of this chapter were sent for review to at least one of the major authors for each of the approaches. The final version reflects their comments and suggestions.

Since July, 1990, Neil Davidson has served as President of the International Association for the Study of Cooperation in Education (IASCE). This paper is based on a portion of his keynote address for the IASCE Convention in Baltimore, Maryland, in July, 1990.

Table 1.   Common and varying attributes among cooperative and collaborative learning approaches

Attributes common to all approaches

1. Common task or learning activity suitable for group work
2. Small-group learning
3. Cooperative behavior
4. Interdependence (often referred to as positive interdependence)
5. Individual accountability and responsibility

Attributes that vary among approaches

6. Grouping procedure (e.g., heterogeneous, random, student selected, common interest)
7. Structuring positive interdependence (e.g., goals, tasks, resources, roles, division of labor, rewards)
8. Explicit teaching of interpersonal, relationship, cooperative, or collaborative skills
9. Reflection (or processing) on social skills, academic skills, or group dynamics
10. Climate setting through class-building, team-building, trust-building, or cooperative norms
11. Group structure
12. Attention to student status by the teacher (identifying competencies of low-status students and focusing peers' attention on them)
13. Group leadership
14. Teacher's role

STUDENT TEAM LEARNING

The Student Team Learning (STL) approaches were developed by Robert Slavin (1983a, 1983b, 1986, 1990) and his associates at The Johns Hopkins University. Student Teams Achievement Divisions (STAD), Teams-Games-Tournaments (TGT), and Jigsaw II are examples of STL methods. Some STL techniques, notably Team Assisted Individualization (TAI) in math and Cooperative Integrated Reading and Composition (CIRC) have specific curriculum materials to go with them. In STAD, worksheets and quizzes are provided to help teachers, but these are not intended to be complete or prescriptive.

A central feature of STL is the combination of individual accountability and either group rewards or group goals. This combination is cited by Slavin (1983b, 1990) as a central finding in the research for increasing student achievement.

Space allows for an analysis of only one STL method, namely STAD. A different analysis would be required for TAI or CIRC. In STAD, students are grouped heterogeneously based upon past achievement, race, ethnicity, and gender. This is also true of the other STL methods. Groups are called "teams" in order to transfer some of the motivational dynamics of team sports into the classroom arena. Typically, the teacher follows a cycle of teacher presentation/direct instruction, team study and practice, individual quizzes, and team recognition. Individual students receive grades based upon their own quiz scores. Teams also receive points based upon individual members' improvement over past performance (i.e., individuals earn improvement points that are used solely for team recognition). Recognition often takes place through class newsletters, bulletin boards, and posters; team names are prominently featured.

In terms of the five common and nine varying attributes of cooperative/collaborative approaches, STAD is structured as follows.

Common attributes:

1. The task for group work is for all members to practice and master facts and skills, as well as solve problems in math and identify main ideas in literature.

2. Student interaction occurs in small teams of four or, occasionally, five members. Students often practice in pairs within their teams.
3. Cooperative behaviors include students discussing the problems or questions together, comparing their answers, explaining, and correcting any misconceptions or mistakes. Peer norms support academic effort and achievement.
4. Positive interdependence occurs when teammates encourage each other to do their best; individual learning is important for team success. The only way for the team to succeed is to concentrate on the learning of every team member.
5. Individual accountability occurs when all team members take individual quizzes and receive individual grades. Individual improvement points contribute to team recognition, not grades.

Varying attributes:

6. Team formation is heterogeneous, based on past academic performance (i.e., a high performer, two medium performers, and a low performer), gender, and race/ethnicity.
7. Positive interdependence is structured in a variety of ways. Goals are for all team members to master the material or improve their own past performances and for the team to receive recognition or a reward. Tasks require discussion and mutual help for all team members to succeed. Resources are limited; there are two worksheets for a team of four. Roles typically are not assigned, but team members sometimes take turns quizzing each other. Team rewards are based on the team's average improvement points. Rewards include certificates or other team recognition via a newsletter or bulletin board, special privileges, or small prizes.
8. Explicit teaching of social skills does not occur unless there is a specific need for it.
9. Reflection (or processing) on team functioning is not highly emphasized.
10. Climate setting occurs via team-building through the use of and emphasis upon team names.
11. Group structure is not specified, except that practice often occurs in pairs within teams.
12. Attention to student status treatments is not emphasized.
13. Group leadership is not specified; no single leader is selected for a team.
14. The teacher's role varies in different phases of the instructional cycle. The teacher presents information; circulates among and praises the teams; computes base scores, improvement points, and team improvement scores; and presents certificates or rewards to high-performing teams.

LEARNING TOGETHER

David and Roger Johnson (1987, 1989a, 1989b) at the University of Minnesota have designed a conceptual approach to cooperative learning, sometimes known as Learning Together as in the title of their book, *Learning Together and Alone* (1975/1991). The Johnsons emphasize the distinction among cooperative, competitive, and individualistic learning situations. In the cooperative learning situation, students perceive that their goal achievements are positively related—"We sink or swim together." In competition, students work against each other. In individualistic learning situations, students work individually to accomplish goals unrelated to those of their peers.

The Johnsons emphasize certain basic elements of cooperative learning, including positive interdependence, face-to face interaction, direct teaching of interpersonal and small-group skills, processing of those skills, and individual accountability. They use a group discussion procedure, often with assigned roles (e.g., facilitator, encourager, praiser). Interdependence is structured in various ways. The Learning Together method of cooperative learning is used for both higher cognitive processes as well as mastery of basic facts and skills and has been extensively researched over many years (Johnson & Johnson, 1989a).

The Johnsons' conceptual approach to cooperative learning does not involve direct application curriculum packages or specific strategies applied in detailed or structured ways. Following is the Learning Together approach analyzed in terms of the common and varying attributes of cooperative learning models.

Common attributes:

1. Common tasks or learning activities suitable for group work can occur at all cognitive levels; however, more conceptual learning requires more discussion, explanation, and elaboration.
2. Small-group learning occurs in groups of two, three, or four members, with groups of three preferred.
3. Cooperative behaviors are emphasized. Students work together, discuss, listen, question, explain, elaborate, share ideas and materials, encourage, and so forth.
4. Positive interdependence is interpreted as the perception that one is linked with others so that one cannot succeed unless the other team members also succeed. Groups are structured so students seek outcomes that are beneficial to their group mates.
5. Individual accountability or responsibility is attained by checking responses on individual worksheets, randomly selecting one group member to explain, or giving individual quizzes or tests. Group members are to hold one another accountable for their learning.

Varying attributes:

6. Grouping typically is done heterogeneously by mixing gender, race/ethnicity, social class, and achievement levels (i.e., high, medium, low). However, a teacher may sometimes form homogeneous groups of students who need to work on a specific skill, procedure, or set of facts.
7. Positive interdependence is structured in multiple ways. Goal achievements by students are positively correlated; that is, students perceive that they can reach their learning goals if and only if group mates also reach their goals. The mutual learning goals are to learn the assigned material and to make sure that all group members do the same. Tasks require students not only to agree upon answers, but to be able to explain their group's reasoning or strategies. Resource materials can be limited to one copy per group or jigsawed with each member having different materials. Division of labor sometimes occurs for suitable tasks. Roles are assigned and rotated frequently. Each member is assigned a role that is essential to the group's functioning (e.g., reader, checker, relater/elaborator, accuracy coach, summarizer, encourager, confidence builder). Rewards may be given in the form of bonus points if all members of a group achieve a preset criteria of excellence.

8. Interpersonal and small-group skills of leadership, decision making, trust building, communication, and conflict management are purposefully and explicitly taught. Skills often are practiced while performing assigned roles.

9. Reflection (processing) on social skills, academic skills, and group dynamics occurs regularly after group work is completed. Students discuss how well group members are learning and maintaining effective working relationships. They also identify helpful or unhelpful behaviors of members and behaviors to continue or to change.

10. Climate-setting occurs within teams and across the whole class through a variety of trust-building activities (see Johnson & Johnson, 1991).

11. Group structure is not prescribed in detail; teachers apply the basic elements in planning their own lessons.

12. Attention to status treatments for individual students' sometimes occurs, but is not emphasized.

13. Shared leadership occurs through assigning and rotating roles essential to a group's work.

14. The teacher's role is complex and varies in different phases of the lesson. The teacher specifies academic and social objectives, makes a number of decisions prior to instruction, explains the academic task and cooperative goal structure, monitors and intervenes during group work, and evaluates learning and facilitates processing. All these teacher actions are described in detail in the varied works by the Johnsons. (See also Sapon-Shevin, Ayres, & Duncan, chap. 4, and Nevin, Thousand, & Villa, chap. 9, this volume.)

The Johnsons employ a combination of ad-hoc informal cooperative learning groups that last up to one class period, formal cooperative learning groups that last up to several weeks, and base groups with stable membership for long-term mutual support. Note that the analysis above applies to the basic conceptual model of cooperative learning. For more advanced information, see the Johnsons' works on leading the cooperative school (1989b), creative conflict (1987), and cooperation in the college classroom (Johnson, Johnson, & Smith, 1991).

GROUP INVESTIGATION

The Group Investigation model, based upon the ideas of Thelen (1967, 1981), has been applied and investigated extensively in Israel in the works of Sharan and Sharan (1992) and Sharan and Hertz-Lazarowitz (1980, 1982). In the Group Investigation model, a complex topic is divided into multiple subtopics to be studied by different research groups. The model has six components or stages:

1. The class determines subtopics and organizes into research groups.

2. Groups plan their investigations—what they will study, how they will go about it, and how they will divide the work among the group members.

3. Groups carry out their investigations. Members of each group gather, organize, and analyze information on their subtopic.

4. Groups plan their presentations. Members share and discuss their data with their group and plan the group report together.

5. Groups make their presentations. Reports are delivered to the entire class in a variety of forms and with the participation of all group members.

6. Teachers and students evaluate the group investigation individually, in groups, and as a class. There are varied means for assessing contributions of individual members as well as the group presentation as a whole.

The six stages of the model, including the teacher's role and the students' role at each stage, have been described in detail by Sharan and Sharan (1992). Additional stages may be added if needed with a particular project. Critical components of the model are investigation, interaction, interpretation, and intrinsic motivation. Positive effects of the group investigation model have been found on student achievement, intrinsic motivation, and social interaction. Below the Group Investigation model is analyzed in terms of the common and varying attributes of cooperative learning.

Common attributes:

1. The common task or learning activity is to investigate a complex topic divided into subtopics for groups to research. The task should allow all group members to readily participate and have an opportunity to talk, and should require members to make choices and group decisions.
2. Small-group learning takes place in research groups with no more than four or five members.
3. Cooperative behavior includes jointly planning the investigation using detailed suggestions given for cooperative planning. Students work together and sometimes individually; assign roles and divide the tasks among themselves; exchange materials, ideas, and information; plan their presentation together; and give feedback to their classmates.
4. Positive interdependence begins with the identification of a broad problem of common concern to the class, which then leads to jointly planning, coordinating, and conducting the investigation. Interdependence takes different forms at different phases of the complex undertaking.
5. Individual accountability or responsibility occurs when students divide up and take responsibility for a part of the task; carry out their investigations; present their findings with all members taking part; receive feedback and perhaps written evaluations of their work; and take individual tests.

Varying attributes:

6. Grouping procedures include random assignment, common interest in a topic, and student or teacher selection. Factors to consider in grouping include individual student characteristics, task characteristics, and duration of the group investigation.
7. Structuring positive interdependence is promoted when: a) common goals are set by the class through cooperative planning and tasks are jointly determined by each research group, b) resources for the investigation are exchanged and divided among and within groups, c) roles are determined and assigned by each research group, and d) division of labor occurs as the class and each group divide the research topics and tasks associated with each subtopic. Rewards are not used to promote interdependence; instead, intrinsic motivation is strongly emphasized.
8. Explicit teaching of cooperative skills often occurs prior to the investigation. In addition to establishing a climate for interactive talk, the teacher may conduct

skill-building exercises to develop students' skills in discussion and reaching consensus. Cooperative skills are taught during the investigation only if a need arises.

9. Reflection by the group members may occur in the final stage of the investigation by students identifying and analyzing what happened, generalizing their learning outcomes to different situations, and setting goals for the improvement of group behavior. Students may be asked to reflect on their own academic and social learnings, as well as on the presentations of others.

10. The climate is set for interactive talk through cooperative norms, such as mutual help and sharing ideas and information, teacher modeling of listening with respect, teacher encouragement of student talk, and establishing cooperative planning.

11. Group structure is not made explicit by the teacher, but is determined by the student groups at different stages of the investigation.

12. Attention to student status may occur, but is not a prominent part of this method.

13. Shared leadership occurs when students plan together and select their tasks and roles in the investigation. There are no assigned leaders and no pre-assigned roles.

14. The teacher's role changes at different stages in the investigation. The teacher leads exploratory discussions to determine subtopics; helps groups formulate their plans; helps maintain cooperative norms; helps students find information and use study skills; coordinates planning, presentations, and feedback; and evaluates learning of information, higher-level thinking, and cooperative behavior.

STRUCTURAL APPROACH

The Structural Approach (Kagan, 1992) represents and derives its name from an array of simple group structures (e.g., Think-Pair-Share, Roundtable, Numbered Heads Together, Three-Step Interview, Jigsaw, and Pairs Check) that teachers can readily add to their repertoire and use immediately. The goal is for teachers to become skilled with the individual simple structures and then begin to combine and sequence them in a meaningful and artistic way to form more complex lessons. Kagan recommends trying one new structure at a time, working it solidly into the repertoire of both the teacher and students. In the Structural Approach, there are structures for practice and mastery, structures that foster thinking, structures for information sharing, and so forth. The job of the teacher is to choose and use the structure(s) most appropriate for the task at hand.

The Structural Approach incorporates some procedures from other models of cooperative and collaborative learning. For example, STAD is considered a lesson design for developing mastery and Jigsaw II is a "division of labor" design. One design, Co-op Co-op, is the Sharans' (1992) Group Investigation model, expanded from 6 to 11 steps.

Kagan often refers to the five basic elements of the Johnsons' Learning Together model, especially the elements of positive interdependence and individual accountability. However, he recommends teaching the structures first and then examining them in terms of basic elements. Kagan also discusses an additional principle, "simultaneous interaction." A goal of group learning is to maximize the number of students who can speak at any given time in order to maximize "simultaneous interaction" (e.g., pairs allow for more simultaneous interaction than groups of four).

There is some research support for the Structural Approach in that it incorporates procedures from other models that have an established research base. However, there is a need to research specific structures as well as their effectiveness in a multistructural lesson. The Structural Approach may be described in terms of the attributes of cooperative and collaborative learning as follows.

Common attributes:

1. Common tasks or learning activities for group work can be designed at all cognitive levels, ranging from mastery of basic facts and skills to the development of higher level thinking skills. Different structures are matched to different types of tasks.
2. Small-group learning occurs in teams of four, which sometimes divide into pairs.
3. Cooperative behaviors include listening, paying attention, giving ideas, praising, encouraging, and a host of other behaviors that are taught through a variety of methods.
4. Interdependence is a key concept in the Structural Approach. Kagan distinguishes among weak, intermediate, and strong forms of positive interdependence. The strength of the interdependence depends on the degree to which success of each team member is linked to the success of other team members.
5. Individual accountability or responsibility is structured for: a) student achievement (e.g., the team recognition score is based upon *individual* scores), b) participation (e.g., using "talking chips"), and c) listening (e.g., using a three-step peer interview process). Grades are based upon individual performance, not upon any form of team scoring.

Varying attributes:

6. Grouping may be heterogeneous, random, common interest, or homogeneous by language. Each grouping procedure is used for a different purpose and has distinct advantages and disadvantages.
7. Structuring of positive interdependence varies depending on the academic and social goals of the lesson and the specific structure employed. In some lessons, group members have the same goal, such as producing an essay, model, or mural. Tasks may be structured so that no individual is able to do them alone. Resources are shared among group members. Roles are chosen so they are complementary and necessary (e.g., materials monitor, coach, encourager, reflector, quiet captain, praiser, checker). Division of labor (e.g., Jigsaw II) occurs in some lesson designs. Rewards are used differently in various reward structures. Team scores and rewards are used to promote cooperative relations *within* a team; team scores contributing to a total class score fosters cooperation *among* teams.
8. Explicit teaching of social skills occurs through a "structured natural approach." Teachers set up a "social skills center" where important information about each social skill may be found. They select and introduce a skill-of-the-week, develop roles that use the skill, and identify the verbal and nonverbal behaviors needed to fulfill the role. Next, they choose a cooperative structure that requires or fosters that skill (e.g., listening is required for the "interview"

and "round-robin" structures). Finally, they model and reinforce the skill and guide students to reflect on their use of the skill.

9. Teachers encourage reflection on academic and group performance through varied means such as reflection questions, linking with the social skills center, using a particular cooperative structure for reflection, student self-monitoring, observers, and formal reflection forms.

10. Class and team climate-building efforts attempt to help students get acquainted, develop class and team identity, provide mutual support, value differences, and experience synergy through interactions. Numerous techniques are used to accomplish these purposes.

11. Group structure is highly explicit in the Structural Approach. Numerous specific, simple structures are offered for organizing the interaction of individuals in a classroom or small group.

12. Attention to students' status may occur, but is not a principal feature of this approach.

13. Leadership is shared through the use of varied structures and rotating roles that develop social skills.

14. The teacher's role is complex. It involves selecting academic and social goals, choosing the appropriate cooperative structure(s) to accomplish the goals, observing and consulting during group work, and so forth. The teacher also employs a cooperative classroom management system that includes the use of a quiet signal, the setting of class norms or rules, positive attention for following norms, and public recognition systems.

COMPLEX INSTRUCTION

Complex Instruction, a model developed by Elizabeth Cohen and associates (1986), is complex both in terms of the tasks given the students and the way in which student groups are organized. Complex Instruction originally was designed for investigations in math and science, using the Finding Out/Descubrimiento curriculum of DeAvila, Duncan, and Navarette (1986). Now, the method is being applied in other subject areas as well.

In Complex Instruction, the class is divided into groups of four or five. Each group has a different learning station and roles are assigned to group members. Different groups often investigate related phenomenon (e.g., issues related to the melting point of ice) and then report their results to the entire class. Complex Instruction is similar to Group Investigation approaches, except that it is organized and orchestrated by the teacher and members of groups work together rather than separating into individual investigations. Multiple-ability tasks are designed to incorporate all levels of performance—not only cognitive, but psychomotor, visual, organizing skills, and so forth. Tasks are designed so that all members of the group are needed; each individual brings unique talents or knowledge to the task. The Complex Instruction model also employs a cooperative management system involving delegation of authority to students, cooperative norms, assigned roles, and group decision making.

A unique and prominent feature of Cohen's approach is the attention to individual students' status within the classroom. The multiple-abilities orientation sets the stage for the *assignment of competence*. This occurs by the teacher first identifying low-status students and looking for their areas of competence. The teacher then specifically identifies that competence when it is displayed and calls it to the attention of teammates and other classmates. Students who are publicly recognized as competent in one area may perceive themselves more positively and become motivated to develop competence in other areas.

The Complex Instruction model may be characterized in terms of the 14 common and varying attributes of cooperative learning as follows.

Common attributes:

1. Common tasks and learning activities are multiple-ability tasks that require skills in manipulating materials, observing, reasoning, organizing, recording, and communicating. Tasks are designed to be intrinsically motivating and highly challenging.
2. Learning takes place in groups of five or, sometimes, four members.
3. Cooperative behavior is established through a system of cooperative norms (e.g., asking for help when necessary, providing assistance, taking turns, giving everyone an opportunity to contribute).
4. Interdependence is stimulated, in part, by the delegation of authority; that is, students must act as resources for one another to be able to complete a task successfully. Children cannot move on to the next learning center unless *all* group members have completed the task and their individual worksheets. Although Cohen does not emphasize the concept of positive interdependence, it is provided in many ways.
5. Individual accountability and responsibility are promoted when students perform their assigned roles and complete their individual worksheets. Students are responsible for their own learning and task engagement.

Varying attributes:

6. Grouping is random in the context of a heterogeneous classroom (e.g., academic, social, and linguistic heterogeneity). Groupings also are heterogeneous with respect to gender, ethnic background, and linguistic proficiency.
7. Positive interdependence is promoted incidentally and directly with the Complex Instruction method. Students have a common goal—to explore and learn about a challenging, intrinsically interesting phenomenon. Conceptual learning, including the development of thinking skills and problem-solving strategies, is the main objective; however, this requires interpersonal interactions— opportunities to talk and work together on the task. Tasks are designed so that multiple abilities are required for their completion; thus, children must work together to successfully complete these tasks. Resources, such as manipulative materials and activity cards (available in English and Spanish), are limited and must be shared at each learning center. Depending on the task, various roles are assigned and rotated (e.g., facilitator, checker, reporter, safety officer, clean-up supervisor, equipment manager, harmonizer). Division of labor occurs between groups; different groups work with different materials and perform different tasks. Rewards are *not* used in Complex Instruction, as tasks are designed to be intrinsically motivating.
8. Cooperative behaviors are taught using procedures from social learning theory; that is, new behaviors are labeled and discussed, recognized when they occur, practiced, and reinforced. Cooperative behaviors are learned through structured games and exercises and practiced during group work.

9. Reflection on the quality of group work is accomplished in several ways. For teachers, there is an observation guide and a participation scoring instrument for use by an "outside observer." During the wrap-up phase of the lesson, the teacher gives specific feedback to groups and individuals, comments on groups' collaborative processes, discusses with the class how group functioning could be improved in the future, and emphasizes connections among activities.

10. The climate is set for cooperation by training students to use specific cooperative behaviors, setting norms for equal participation and cooperation, and discussing the importance of being responsive to the needs of members within a group.

11. Group structure is affected by the system of assigned roles and task directions, but otherwise is not specified.

12. Student status issues are attended to through the multiple-abilities orientation and by highlighting the competence of students with low-status characteristics. The teacher publicly and specifically identifies and acknowledges quality performances of a child of (potential) low status.

13. Shared leadership develops as students perform their assigned roles.

14. The teacher's role may be described as "letting go and teaming up." The teacher's cooperative management system involves setting cooperative norms; assigning groups and roles; describing specific cooperative behaviors; and giving clear, specific orientation and instructions for the task. During group work the teacher plays a supportive role, but does not directly supervise groups. The teacher asks questions to stimulate and extend children's thinking, provides specific feedback to groups and individuals during group work or the wrap-up, and addresses "status" issues as needed.

COLLABORATIVE APPROACH

The Collaborative Approach is most often associated with theories about language and learning developed by James Britton (1970) and Douglas Barnes (1976). Used initially in language arts and literature, the Collaborative Approach is practiced extensively in the United Kingdom, Australia, Canada, and the United States. Its intention is to focus on the creation of personal meaning and internally persuasive understandings through dialogue and discussion. The methodology of Collaborative Learning is described by Barnes et al. (1986); Barnes and Todd (1977); Brubacher, Payne, and Rickett (1990); and Reid et al. (1989).

In the Collaborative Learning model described by Reid et al. (1989), instruction is organized into five phases labeled engagement, exploration, transformation, presentation, and reflection. In the *engagement* stage, the teacher provides a perspective to the whole class, producing the basis for the ensuing group activities. In the *exploration* stage, students engage in initial exploration of ideas or information; this is done in small groups called "home groups." In the *transformation* stage, students in home groups engage in an activity to "reshape" the information—organize, clarify, elaborate, or practice the information. In the *presentation* phase, students present their findings to an interested and critical peer audience, a "sharing group." Sharing groups are larger than home groups and are formed by combining together or reconstituting home groups. In the final *reflection* phase, students "look back" at what they have learned and the process they experienced. Reflection may be done by individuals, pairs, small groups, or the whole class.

This particular collaborative approach is like a "Jigsaw" procedure with a more leisurely pace and less structure. There is no attempt to directly teach social skills, even though social skills may be discussed during processing. Students are given plenty of time to do their work. In addition, they are given discretion in how they organize themselves, as long as they get the task done. The intent is to foster meaning and understanding of the world and one's place in it and for people to come to know and articulate their own values and beliefs.

Historically, there has been some tension between "collaborative" and "cooperative" learning approaches, with some (but not all) cooperative learning approaches tending to be more structured and focused upon specific behaviors and rewards. Those of the collaborative learning tradition tend not to "micro manage," not to break tasks into small component parts, and not to provide rewards. While interdependence and individual accountability are clearly present in collaborative models, they are emphasized less than in cooperative approaches.

In analyzing Collaborative Learning in terms of the 14 common and varying attributes of small-group approaches, it should be noted that the analysis presented below for items 2, 5, 6, 9, 10, and 14 is based mainly on the one model of collaborative learning described by Reid et al. (1989). These items are marked with an asterisk below.

Common attributes:

1. The common task or learning activity is clarified so group members know the purpose of the group discussion and its desired outcomes are clear to them.
2. Small-group learning takes place in "home groups" with four members and in larger "sharing groups."*
3. Cooperative behavior involves a lot of discussion in which everyone takes part in clarifying the task, listening, disagreeing, and honestly stating ideas.
4. Interdependence is present in collaborative learning more as an underlying assumption than a technique. The assumption is that learning that takes place in daily life is predominantly social, with language as a primary means of communication. Thus, social and collaborative interaction are fundamental in human learning and the classroom is a place where language should flow readily and freely among the learners.
5. Individual accountability and responsibility occur as students take notes and keep their own records. Students also must make their findings public and receive feedback in their sharing groups. During the presentation stage, students are accountable for clear and precise communication about their findings (Reid et al., 1989).*

Varying attributes:

6. Grouping is done by "friendship selection" in home groups. The teacher helps compose the sharing groups.*
7. Interdependence is loosely structured. It is assumed that an innate need to make sense and meaning of the world and curiosity about the learning situation will motivate groups to jointly work toward a goal. An explicit goal for the home group is to prepare a public presentation of its findings. Tasks require dialogue in exploration, discussion, elaboration, and critique and typically are structured so students must be interdependent in order for the task to be completed. Tasks also culminate with a presentation of the group's findings. Re-

sources are shared within groups, but different materials may be used for different home groups. Roles are not explicitly assigned. Division of labor may occur when different groups perform different tasks or activities. Rewards are not used; instead, emphasis is placed on engaging intrinsic motivation to inquire and make sense of our world.

8. Explicit teaching of social skills does not occur in a structured way.

9. Reflection on group dynamics and learning takes place during a final reflection stage, both individually and collaboratively. Reflective use of a group checklist helps students understand group process.*

10. Climate setting includes providing introductory lessons to help students understand how groups work. These experiential lessons deal with students as learners, working in small groups, and characteristics of effective and ineffective groups.*

11. Group structure is not made explicit.

12. Attention to student status issues may occur, but is not emphasized.

13. Shared leadership occurs through the different leadership functions (e.g., recording, reporting) assumed by different group members at different times. A group of four does not need a designated leader to "chair" discussions.

14. The teacher's role includes carefully structuring the learning experiences, assisting students with their learning, listening carefully to small-group discussions, and making personal contact with students. The teacher's role in planning each phase of the lesson, monitoring small groups, and facilitating whole-class discussion is described in detail by Reid et al. (1989).*

OTHER MODELS AND RESOURCES

There are many more approaches to cooperative and collaborative learning than the ones described in this chapter. For example, McCabe and Rhoades (1990; Rhoades & McCabe, 1992) have developed a "simple cooperation" model that features: 1) direct instruction of social skills in a somewhat sequential manner based on a social skills continuum, 2) use of group rewards and bonus points instead of group grades, 3) three authentic assessment techniques, 4) processes for effective meeting management, 5) distributed leadership, 6) a direct link between cooperative learning and varied thinking behaviors and thinking processes, and 7) an outcomes-based learning model.

The reference list and bibliography at the end of this chapter includes selected additional references for cooperative and collaborative learning. A more comprehensive listing of resources may be found in *1993 Resource Guide* (Graves, 1993), which is a special issue of the *Cooperative Learning Magazine* published by the International Association for the Study of Cooperation in Education (IASCE).

CONCLUSION

Six major approaches to cooperative and collaborative learning are described and compared in this chapter. Five attributes considered "critical attributes" of cooperative and collaborative learning are identified as common to all six approaches. These attributes are: 1) a common task or learning activity suitable for group work, 2) small-group learning, 3) cooperative behavior, 4) interdependence, and 5) individual accountability and responsibility.

Table 2. Analysis of attributes that vary among approaches

	STAD	Learning Together	Group Investigation	Structural Approach	Complex Instruction	Collaborative Approach
6. Grouping procedure	Heterogeneous	Usually heterogeneous	Varied	Varied	Random heterogeneous	Friendship
7. Structuring positive interdependence						
Goals	Everyone masters material; improves over own past performance	Mutual learning goals; make sure everyone learns	Set by cooperative planning	Sometimes to produce a group product	Conceptual learning goals	Arise from need to make sense and meaning of the world
Tasks	Require mutual help	Require ability to explain reasoning or strategies	Set by cooperative planning	Designed so they cannot be done alone	Require multiple abilities	Include use of language and presentation of findings
Resources	Limited	Limited or jigsawed	Shared; divided among groups	Shared	Limited; shared	Shared
Roles	No	Yes	Set by group	In some structures	Yes	Not explicitly assigned
Division of labor	No	Sometimes	Within and between groups	In some designs	Between groups	Sometimes between groups
Rewards	Yes, team recognition	Sometimes, bonus points	No	Team recognition scores	No	No
8. Explicit teaching of social skills	Only as needed	Major emphasis	As needed, sometimes prior to Group Investigation	Structured natural approach	Using Social Learning theory	No

Attribute						
9. Reflection on social and academic skills or group process	Not emphasized	Yes	May occur in final stage	Yes	Yes	Yes
10. Climate setting	Team-building via team names	Trust-building activities	Cooperative norms	Class-building; team-building	Cooperative norms and training for cooperation	Sometimes through introductory lessons
11. Group structure	Not specified; sometimes paired practice	Not prescribed; affected by roles	Determined by students	High degree of explicit structure	Not specified; affected by roles	Not specified
12. Attention to student status	Not emphasized	Not emphasized	Not emphasized	Not emphasized	Highly emphasized	Not emphasized
13. Group leadership	Not designated	Shared via roles	Not designated; develops in joint planning	Shared via structures and roles	Shared via roles	Shared via assuming different functions
14. Teacher's role	Complex and varied	Complex and varied	Complex and varied	Complex and varied	Complex and varied	Complex and varied

The numbering of the attributes (6–14) in the table above corresponds to the numerical order of the varying attributes that follow an analysis of each of the six collaborative approaches presented in this chapter.

Beyond these five critical attributes, nine attributes are identified that are employed to varying degrees in the different models of cooperative/collaborative learning. Table 2 on pages 26–27 provides a summary analysis of the approaches presented in this chapter, using the nine attributes that vary among approaches.

In the author's opinion, it is useful for teachers to emphasize the five attributes common to all cooperative and collaborative approaches. Teachers can then make careful selections among approaches and additional attributes that fit their own personal philosophies, instructional goals, and classroom settings. The five common attributes establish a coherent unity underlying all of the diverse approaches to cooperative and collaborative learning. The diversity of approaches within this underlying unity provides flexibility based upon a strong conceptual foundation.

REFERENCES AND BIBLIOGRAPHY

Albert, L. (1989). *A teacher's guide to cooperative discipline: How to manage your classroom and promote self-esteem*. Circle Pines, MN: American Guidance Service.

Aronson, E., Blaney, N., Stephan, C., Sikes J., & Snapp, M. (1978). *The jigsaw classroom*. Beverly Hills: Sage Publications.

Barnes, D. (1976). *From communication to curriculum*. Portsmouth, NH: Boynton/Cook.

Barnes, D., Britton, J., & Torbe, M. (1986). *Language, the learner and the school* (2nd ed.). Portsmouth, NH: Boynton/Cook.

Barnes, D., & Todd, F. (1977). *Communicating and learning in small groups*. London: Routledge, Kegan Paul.

Bellanca, J., & Fogarty, R. (1990). *Blueprints for thinking in the cooperative classroom*. Palatine, IL: Skylight Publishing.

Bennett, B., Rolheiser-Bennett, C., & Stevahn, L. (1991). *Cooperative learning: Where heart meets mind*. Toronto: Educational Connections.

Britton, J. (1970). *Language and learning*. Portsmouth, NH: Boynton/Cook.

Brubacher, M., Payne, R., & Rickett, K. (1990). *Perspectives on small group learning: Theory and practice*. Oakvale, Ontario, Canada: Rubicon Publishing Inc.

Bruffee, K. (1993). *Collaborative learning: Higher education, interdependence, and the authority of knowledge*. Baltimore: Johns Hopkins University Press.

Clarke, J., Wideman, R., & Eadie, S. (1990). *Together we learn*. Englewood Cliffs, NJ: Prentice Hall.

Coelho, E., Winer, L., & Winn-Bell Olsen, J. (1989). *All sides of the issue. Activities for cooperative jigsaw groups*. Englewood Cliffs, NJ: Prentice Hall.

Cohen, E. (1986). *Designing groupwork: Strategies for the heterogeneous classroom*. New York: Teachers College Press.

Cooper, J., Prescott, S., Cook, L., Smith, L., & Cuseo, J. (1989). *Cooperative learning and college instruction: Effective use of student learning teams*. Carson, CA: Center for Quality Education.

Dalton, J. (1985). *Adventures in thinking*. Melbourne, Australia: Thomas Nelson Australia.

Davidson, N. (Ed.). (1990). *Cooperative learning in mathematics: A handbook for teachers*. Reading, MA: Addison-Wesley.

Davidson, N., & Worsham, T. (Eds.). (1992). *Enhancing thinking through cooperative learning*. New York: Teachers College Press.

DeAvila, E., Duncan, S., & Navarette, C. (1986). *Finding out/Descubrimiento*. Northvale, NJ: Santilla Publishing Company.

Dishon, D., & O'Leary, P. (1984). *A guidebook for cooperative learning: A technique for creating more effective schools*. Holmes Beach, FL: Learning Publications, Inc.

Ellis, S., & Whalen, S. (1990). *Cooperative learning: Getting started*. New York: Scholastic Professional Books.

Fogarty, R., & Bellanca, J. (1989). *Patterns for thinking, patterns for transfer: A cooperative team approach for critical and creative thinking in the classroom*. Palatine, IL: IRI Group.

Gibbs, J. (1987). *Tribes: A process for social development and cooperative learning*. Santa Rosa, CA: Center Source Publications.

Glasser, W. (1986). *Control theory in the classroom*. New York: HarperCollins.

Graves, T. (1993). 1993 resource guide. *Cooperative Learning Magazine, 12*(4).

Graves, N., & Graves, T. (1990). *What is cooperative learning? Tips for teachers and trainers*. Santa Cruz, CA: Cooperative College of California.

Hassard, J. (1990). *Science experiences*. Reading, MA: Addison-Wesley.

Hertz-Lazarowitz, R., & Davidson, J. (1990) *Six mirrors of the classroom: A pathway to cooperative learning*. Westlake Village, CA: Joan B. Davidson.

Hertz-Lazarowitz, R., & Miller, N. (Eds.). (1992) *Interaction in cooperative groups: The theoretical anatomy of group learning*. New York: Cambridge University Press.

Johnson, D.W., & Johnson, R. (1975/1991). *Learning together and alone: Cooperative, competitive, and individualistic learning*. Englewood Cliffs, NJ: Prentice Hall.

Johnson, D.W., & Johnson, F. (1991). *Joining to-*

gether: Group theory and group skills. Englewood Cliffs, NJ: Prentice Hall.

Johnson, D.W., & Johnson, R. (1987). Creative conflict. Edina, MN: Interaction Book Company.

Johnson, D.W., & Johnson, R. (1989a). Cooperation and competition: Theory and research. Edina, MN: Interaction Book Company.

Johnson, D.W., & Johnson, R. (1989b). Leading the cooperative school. Edina, MN: Interaction Book Company.

Johnson, D.W., Johnson, R., & Holubec, E. (1986). Circles of learning: Cooperation in the classroom (rev. ed.). Edina, MN: Interaction Book Company.

Johnson, D.W., Johnson, R., & Smith, K. (1991). Active learning: Cooperation in the college classroom. Edina, MN: Interaction Book Company.

Kagan, S. (1992). Cooperative learning: Resources for teachers. San Juan Capistrano, CA: Resources for Teachers.

Kohn, A. (1986). No contest: The case against competition. Boston: Houghton Mifflin.

Kohn, A. (1990). The brighter side of human nature: Altruism and empathy in everyday life. New York: Basic Books.

Lyman, L., & Foyle, H. (1990). Cooperative grouping for interactive learning: Students, teachers and administrators. Washington, DC: National Education Association.

Male, M., Johnson, D., Johnson, R., & Anderson, M. (1986). Cooperative learning and computers: An activity guide for teachers. Santa Cruz, CA: Educational Apple-cations.

McCabe, M., & Rhoades, J. (1990). The nurturing classroom. Sacramento, CA: ITA Publications.

Moorman, C., & Dishon, D. (1983). Our classroom: We can learn together. Bay City, MI: Personal Power Press.

Newmann, F., & Thompson, J. (1987). Effects of cooperative learning on achievement in secondary schools: A summary of research. Madison, WI: National Center on Effective Secondary Schools.

Reid, J., Forrestal, P., & Cook, J. (1989). Small group learning in the classroom. Scarborough, Australia: Chalkface Press. Portsmouth, NH: Heinemann.

Rhoades, J., & McCabe, M. (1992). Outcome-based learning: A teacher's guide to restructuring the classroom. Sacramento, CA: ITA Publications.

Roy, P. (1990). Cooperative learning groups: Students learning together. Richfield, MN: Patricia Roy Company.

Schmuck, R., & Schmuck, P. (1988). Group processes in the classroom. Dubuque, IA: William C. Brown Company.

Schniedewind, N., & Davidson, E. (1983). Open minds to equality: A sourcebook of learning activities to promote race, sex, class and age equity. Englewood Cliffs, NJ: Prentice Hall.

Schniedewind, N., & Davidson, E. (1987). Cooperative learning—cooperative lives: A sourcebook of learning activities for building a peaceful world. Dubuque, IA: William C. Brown Company.

Sharan, S. (1980). Cooperative learning in small groups: Recent methods and effects on achievement, attitudes, and ethnic relations. Review of Educational Research, 50, 241–271.

Sharan, S. (1990). Cooperative learning: Theory and research. New York: Praeger.

Sharan, S. (Ed.). (1993). Handbook of cooperative learning methods. Westport, CT: Greenwood.

Sharan, S., Hare, P., Webb, C.D., & Hertz-Lazarowitz, R. (Eds.). (1980). Cooperation in education. Provo, UT: Brigham Young University Press.

Sharan, S., & Hertz-Lazarowitz, R. (1980). A group investigation method of cooperative learning in the classroom. In S. Sharan, P. Hare, C. Webb, & R. Hertz-Lazarowitz (Eds.), Cooperation in education (pp. 14–46). Provo, UT: Brigham Young University Press.

Sharan, S., & Hertz-Lazarowitz, R. (1982). Effects of an instructional change program on teachers' behavior, attitudes and perceptions. Journal of Applied Behavioral Science, 18, 185–201.

Sharan, S., Kussell, P., Hertz-Lazarowitz, R., Bejarano, Y., Raviv, S., & Sharan, Y. (1984). Cooperative learning in the classroom: Research in desegregated schools. Hillsdale, NJ: Lawrence Erlbaum Associates.

Sharan, Y., & Sharan, S. (1992). Expanding cooperative learning through group investigation. New York: Teachers College Press.

Shaw, V. (with Kagan, S.). (1992). Community building in the classroom. San Juan Capistrano, CA: Kagan's Cooperative Learning Co.

Slavin, R. (1983a). Cooperative learning. New York: Longman.

Slavin, R. (1983b). When does cooperative learning increase student achievement? Psychological Bulletin, 94, 429–445.

Slavin, R. (1989, December/1990, January). Research on cooperative learning: Consensus and controversy. Educational Leadership, 47(4), 52–55.

Slavin, R. (1990). Cooperative learning: Theory, research and practice. Englewood Cliffs, NJ: Prentice Hall.

Slavin, R.E. (1986). Using student team learning. (3rd ed.). Baltimore: Johns Hopkins University, Center for Research on Elementary and Middle Schools.

Slavin, R., Sharan, S., Kagan, S., Hertz-Lazarowitz, R., Webb, C., & Schmuck, R. (Eds.). (1985). Learning to cooperate, cooperating to learn. New York: Plenum.

Smith, B.L., & MacGregor, J. (1992). What is collaborative learning? In A. Goodsell, M. Maher, V. Tinto, B.L. Smith, & J. MacGregor. (Eds.), Collaborative learning: A sourcebook for higher education (pp. 9–22). University Park, PA: National Center on Postsecondary Teaching, Learning, and Assessment.

Solomon, R.D., Davidson, N., & Solomon, E.C.L. (1993). The handbook for the fourth r: Relationship activities for cooperative and collegial learning (Volume III). Columbia, MD: National Institute for Relationship Training, Inc.

Solomon, R., & Solomon, E.C. (1987a). The handbook for the fourth r: Relationship skills. Columbia, MD: National Institute for Relationship Training, Inc.

Solomon, R., & Solomon, E.C. (1987b). The handbook for the fourth r II: Relationship skills for group discussion and process. Columbia, MD: National Institute for Relationship Training.

Solomon, D., Watson, M., Battistich, V., Schaps, E., & Delucchi, K. (1992). Creating a caring community: Educational practices that promote children's prosocial development. In F. Oser, A. Dick, & J. Patry, (Eds.), Effective and responsible teaching: The new synthesis (pp. 383–396). San Francisco: Jossey-Bass.

Solomon, D., Watson, M., Schaps, E., Battistich, V., & Solomon, J. (1990). Cooperative learning as part of a comprehensive classroom program designed to promote prosocial development. In S. Sharan (Ed.), Cooperative learning: Theory and research (pp. 231–260). New York: Praeger.

Stahl, R. (1993). Cooperative learning in social studies: A handbook for teachers. Reading, MA: Addison-Wesley.

Thelen, H. (1967). Group interactional factors in learning. In E. Bower & W. Hollister (Eds.), Behavioral science frontiers in education (pp. 257–287). New York: John Wiley & Sons.

Thelen, H. (1981). The classroom society. London: Croom Helm.

Webb, N.M. (1991). Task-related verbal interaction and mathematics learning in small groups. Journal for Research in Mathematics Education, 22(5), 366–389.

Wiederhold, C. (1990). Cooperative learning and critical thinking: The question matrix. San Juan Capistrano, CA: Resources for Teachers.

AN OVERVIEW OF COOPERATIVE LEARNING

*Roger T. Johnson
and David W. Johnson*

*Without the cooperation of its members society
cannot survive, and the society of man has survived because the cooperativeness of its members made survival possible. . . . It was not an
advantageous individual here and there who
did so, but the group. In human societies the
individuals who are most likely to survive are
those who are best enabled to do so by their
group.*

(Ashley Montagu, 1965)

How students perceive each other and interact with one
another is a neglected aspect of instruction. Much training
time is devoted to helping teachers arrange appropriate
interactions between students and materials (i.e., text-
books, curriculum programs) and some time is spent on
how teachers should interact with students, but how students should interact with one another is relatively ignored. It should not be. How teachers structure student–
student interaction patterns has a lot to say about how
well students learn, how they feel about school and the
teacher, how they feel about each other, and how much
self-esteem they have.

There are three basic ways students can interact with
each other as they learn. They can compete to see who is
"best," they can work individualistically toward a goal
without paying attention to other students, or they can
work cooperatively with a vested interest in each other's
learning as well as their own. Of the three interaction patterns, competition is presently the most dominant. Research indicates that a vast majority of students in the
United States view school as a competitive enterprise

where one tries to do better than other students. This competitive expectation is already widespread when students enter school and grows stronger as they progress through school (Johnson & R. Johnson, 1991). Cooperation among students who celebrate each other's successes, encourage each other to do homework, and learn to work together regardless of ethnic backgrounds or whether they are male or female, bright or struggling, disabled or not, is still rare.

BASIC DEFINITIONS

Even though these three interaction patterns are not equally effective in helping students learn concepts and skills, it is important that students learn to interact effectively in each of these ways. Students will face situations in which all three interaction patterns are operating and they will need to be able to be effective in each. They also should be able to select the appropriate interaction pattern suited to the situation. An interpersonal, competitive situation is characterized by negative goal interdependence where, when one person wins, the others lose; for example, spelling bees or races against other students to get the correct answers to a math problem on the blackboard. In individualistic learning situations, students are independent of one another and are working toward a set criteria where their success depends on their own performance in relation to an established criteria. The success or failure of other students does not affect their score. For example, in spelling, with all students working on their own, any student who correctly spells 90% or more words passes. In a cooperative learning situation, interaction is characterized by positive goal interdependence with individual accountability. Positive goal interdependence requires acceptance by a group that they "sink or swim together." A cooperative spelling class is one where students are working together in small groups to help each other learn the words in order to take the spelling test individually on another day. Each student's score on the test is increased by bonus points if the group is successful (i.e., the group totals meet specified criteria). In a cooperative learning situation, a student needs to be concerned with how he or she spells and how well the other students in his or her group spell. This cooperative umbrella can also be extended over the entire class if bonus points are awarded to each student when the class can spell more words than a reasonable, but demanding, criteria set by the teacher.

There is a difference between simply having students work in a group and structuring groups of students to work cooperatively. A group of students sitting at the same table doing their own work, but free to talk with each other as they work, is not structured to be a cooperative group, as there is no positive interdependence. Perhaps it could be called individualistic learning with talking. For this to be a cooperative learning situation, there needs to be an accepted common goal on which the group is rewarded for its efforts. If a group of students has been assigned to do a report, but only one student does all the work and the others go along for a free ride, it is not a cooperative group. A cooperative group has a sense of individual accountability that means that all students need to know the material or spell well for the whole group to be successful. Putting students into groups does not necessarily gain a cooperative relationship; it has to be structured and managed by the teacher or professor.

ELEMENTS OF COOPERATIVE LEARNING

It is only under certain conditions that cooperative efforts may be expected to be more productive than competitive and individualistic efforts. Those conditions are:

1. Clearly perceived positive interdependence
2. Considerable promotive (face-to-face) interaction
3. Clearly perceived individual accountability and personal responsibility to achieve the group's goals
4. Frequent use of the relevant interpersonal and small-group skills
5. Frequent and regular group processing of current functioning to improve the group's future effectiveness

All healthy cooperative relationships have these five basic elements present. This is true of peer tutoring, partner learning, peer mediation, adult work groups, families, and other cooperative relationships. This conceptual "yardstick" should define any cooperative relationship.

Positive Interdependence

The first requirement for an effectively structured cooperative lesson is that students believe that they "sink or swim together." Within cooperative learning situations, students have two responsibilities: 1) learn the assigned material, and 2) ensure that all members of the group learn the assigned material. The technical term for that dual responsibility is *positive interdependence*. Positive interdependence exists when students perceive that they are linked with group mates in such a way that they cannot succeed unless their group mates do (and vice versa) and/or that they must coordinate their efforts with the efforts of their group mates to complete a task. Positive interdependence promotes a situation in which students: 1) see that their work benefits group mates and their group mates' work benefits them, and 2) work together in small groups to maximize the learning of all members by sharing their resources to provide mutual support and encouragement and to celebrate their joint success. When positive interdependence is clearly understood, it establishes that:

1. Each group member's efforts are required and indispensable for group success (i.e., there can be no "free-riders").
2. Each group member has a unique contribution to make to the joint effort because of his or her resources and/or role and task responsibilities.

There are a number of ways of structuring positive interdependence within a learning group.

Positive Goal Interdependence   Students perceive that they can achieve their learning goals if and only if all the members of their group also attain their goals. The group is united around a common goal—a concrete reason for being. To ensure that students believe they "sink or swim together" and care about how much each other learns, the teacher has to structure a clear group or mutual goal, such as "learn the assigned material and make sure that all members of the group learn the assigned material." The group goal always has to be a part of the lesson.

Positive Reward—Celebrate Interdependence   Each group member receives the same reward when the group achieves its goals. To supplement goal interdependence, teachers may wish to add joint rewards (e.g., if all members of the group score 90% correct or better on the test, each receives 5 bonus points). Sometimes teachers give students: 1) a group grade for the overall production of their group, 2) an individual grade resulting from tests, and 3) bonus points if all members of the group achieve the criterion on tests. Regular celebrations of group efforts and success enhance the quality of cooperation.

Positive Resource Interdependence   Each group member has only a portion of the resources, information, or materials necessary for the task to be completed; the members' resources have to be combined for the group to achieve its goals. Teachers may wish to highlight the cooperative relationships by giving students limited resources that must be shared (one copy of the problem or task per group) or giving each student part of the required resources that the group must then fit together (the Jigsaw procedure).

Positive Role Interdependence   Each member is assigned complementary and interconnected roles that specify responsibilities that the group needs in order to complete the joint task. Teachers create role interdependence among students when they assign them complementary roles such as reader, recorder, checker of understanding, encourager of participation, and elaborator of knowledge. Such roles are vital to high-quality learning. The role of checker, for example, focuses on periodically asking each group mate to explain what is being learned. Rosenshine and Stevens (1986) reviewed a large body of well-controlled research on teaching effectiveness at the pre-collegiate level and found "checking for comprehension" to be one specific teaching behavior that was significantly associated with higher levels of student learning and achievement. Although the teacher cannot continually check the understanding of every student, the teacher can engineer such checking by having students work in cooperative groups and assigning one member the role of checker.

There are other types of positive interdependence. Positive task interdependence exists when a division of labor is created so that the actions of one group member have to be completed if the next member is to complete his or her responsibility. Positive identity interdependence exists when a mutual identity is established through a name or motto. Outside threat interdependence exists when groups are placed in competition with each other. Fantasy interdependence exists when a task is given that requires group members to imagine that they are in a hypothetical situation.

We have conducted a series of studies investigating the nature of positive interdependence and the relative power of the different types of positive interdependence (Hwong, Caswell, Johnson, & Johnson, 1993; Johnson, Johnson, Ortiz, & Stanne, 1991; Johnson, Johnson, Stanne, & Garibaldi, 1990; Lew, Mesch, Johnson, & Johnson, 1986a, 1986b; Mesch, Johnson, & Johnson, 1988; Mesch, Lew, Johnson, & Johnson, 1986). Our research indicates that positive interdependence provides the context within which promotive interaction takes place. Group membership and interpersonal interaction among students do not produce higher achievement unless positive interdependence is clearly structured. The combination of goal and reward interdependence increases achievement over goal interdependence alone and resource interdependence does not increase achievement unless goal interdependence is present also.

Face-to-Face Promotive Interaction

> *In an industrial organization, it's the group effort that counts. There's really no room for stars in an industrial organization. You need talented people, but they can't do it alone. They have to have help.*
>
> (John F. Donnelly, President, Donnelly Mirrors)

Positive interdependence results in promotive interaction. Promotive interaction may be defined as individuals encouraging and facilitating each other's efforts to achieve, complete tasks, and produce in order to reach the group's goals. Although positive interdependence in and of itself may have some effect on outcomes, it is the face-to-face promotive interaction among individuals fostered by the positive interdependence, that most powerfully influences efforts to achieve, caring and committed relationships, and psychological adjustment and social competence. Promotive interaction is characterized by individuals providing each other with efficient and effective help and assistance; exchanging needed resources, such as information and materials, and processing information more efficiently and effectively; providing each other with feedback in order to improve their subsequent performance; challenging each other's conclusions and reasoning in order to promote higher quality decision making and greater insight into the problems being considered; advocating the exertion of effort to achieve mutual goals; influencing each other's efforts to achieve the group's goals; acting in trusting and trustworthy ways; being motivated to strive for mutual benefit; and maintaining a moderate level of arousal characterized by low anxiety and stress.

Individual Accountability/Personal Responsibility

What children can do together today, they can do alone tomorrow.

(Lev Vygotsky, 1962)

Among the early settlers of Massachusetts there was a saying, "If you do not work, you do not eat." Everyone had to do their fair share of the work. The third essential element of cooperative learning is individual accountability, which exists when the performance of individual students is assessed, the results are given back to the individual and the group, and the student is held responsible by group mates for contributing his or her fair share to the group's success. It is important that the group knows who needs more assistance, support, and encouragement in completing the assignment. It is also important that group members know they cannot "hitchhike" on the work of others. When it is difficult to identify members' contributions, when members' contributions are redundant, and when members are not responsible for the final group outcome, they may be seeking a free ride (Harkins & Petty, 1982; Ingham, Levinger, Graves, & Peckham, 1974; Kerr & Bruun, 1981; Latane, Williams, & Harkins, 1979; Moede, 1927; Petty, Harkins, Williams, & Latane, 1977; Williams, 1981; Williams, Harkins, & Latane, 1981). This is called social loafing.

The purpose of cooperative learning groups is to make each member a stronger individual in his or her own right. Individual accountability is the key to ensuring that all group members are, in fact, strengthened by learning cooperatively. After participating in a cooperative lesson, group members should be better prepared to complete similar tasks by themselves.

To ensure that each student is individually accountable to do his or her fair share of the group's work, teachers need to assess how much effort each member is contributing to the group's work, provide feedback to groups and individual students, help groups avoid redundant efforts by members, and ensure that every member is responsible for the final outcome. Common ways to structure individual accountability include:

1. Keeping the size of the group small. The smaller the size of the group, the greater the individual accountability may be.
2. Giving an individual test to each student.
3. Randomly examining students orally by calling on one student to present his or her group's work to the teacher (in the presence of the group) or to the entire class.

4. Observing each group and recording the frequency with which each member contributes to the group's work.
5. Assigning one student in each group the role of checker. The checker asks other group members to explain the reasoning and rationale underlying group answers.
6. Having students teach what they learned to someone else. When all students do this, it is called *simultaneous explaining*.

There is a pattern to classroom learning. First, students learn knowledge, skills, strategies, or procedures in a cooperative group. Second, students apply the knowledge or perform the skill, strategy, or procedure alone to demonstrate their personal mastery of the material. Students learn it together and then perform it alone.

Interpersonal and Small-Group Skills

I will pay more for the ability to deal with people than any other ability under the sun.

(John D. Rockefeller)

The fourth essential element of cooperative learning is the appropriate use of interpersonal and small-group skills. In order to coordinate efforts to achieve mutual goals, students must: 1) get to know and trust each other, 2) communicate accurately and unambiguously, 3) accept and support each other, and 4) resolve conflict constructively (Johnson, 1990, 1991; Johnson & F. Johnson, 1991). Placing socially unskilled students in a group and telling them to cooperate does not guarantee that they have the ability to do so effectively. We are not born instinctively knowing how to interact effectively with others. Interpersonal and small-group skills do not magically appear when they are needed. Students must be taught the social skills required for high quality collaboration and be motivated to use them if cooperative groups are to be productive. The whole field of group dynamics is based on the premise that social skills are the key to group productivity (Johnson & F. Johnson, 1991).

The more socially skillful students are and the more attention teachers pay to teaching and rewarding the use of social skills, the higher the achievement that can be expected within cooperative learning groups. In their studies on the long-term implementation of cooperative learning, Lew and Mesch (Lew et al., 1986a, 1986b; Mesch et al., 1988; Mesch et al., 1986) investigated the impact of a reward contingency for using social skills as well as positive interdependence and a contingency for academic achievement on performance within cooperative learning groups. In the cooperative skills conditions, students were trained weekly in four social skills and each member of a cooperative group was given two bonus points toward the quiz grade if all group members were observed by the teacher to demonstrate three out of four cooperative skills. The results indicated that the combination of positive interdependence, an academic contingency for high performance by all group members, and a social skills contingency promoted the highest achievement.

Group Processing

Take care of each other. Share your energies with the group. No one must feel alone, cut off, for that is when you do not make it.

(Willi Unsoeld, Renowned Mountain Climber)

The fifth essential component of cooperative learning is group processing. Effective group work is influenced by whether or not groups reflect on (i.e., process) how well they are functioning. A process is an identifiable sequence of events taking place over time, and process goals refer to the sequence of events instrumental in achieving outcome goals (Johnson & F. Johnson, 1991). Group processing may be defined as reflecting on a group session to: 1) describe what member actions were helpful and unhelpful, and 2) make decisions about what actions to continue or change. The purpose of group processing is to clarify and improve the effectiveness of the members in contributing to the collaborative efforts to achieve the group's goals.

While the teacher systematically observes the cooperative learning groups, he or she attains a "window" into what students do and do not understand as they explain to each other how to complete the assignment. Listening in on the students' explanations provides valuable information about how well the students understand the instructions, the major concepts and strategies being learned, and the basic elements of cooperative learning.

There are two levels of processing—small group and whole class. In order to ensure that small-group processing takes place, teachers allocate some time at the end of each class session for each cooperative group to process how effectively members worked together. Groups need to describe what member actions were helpful and not helpful in completing the group's work and make decisions about what behaviors to continue or change. Such processing: 1) enables learning groups to focus on maintaining good working relationships among members, 2) facilitates the learning of cooperative skills, 3) ensures that members receive feedback on their participation, 4) ensures that students think on the metacognitive as well as the cognitive level, and 5) provides the means to celebrate the success of the group and reinforce the positive behaviors of group members. Some of the keys to successful small-group processing are allowing sufficient time for it to take place, providing a structure for processing (e.g., "List three things your group is doing well today and one thing you could improve."), emphasizing positive feedback, making the processing specific rather than general, maintaining student involvement in processing, reminding students to use their cooperative skills while they process, and communicating clear expectations as to the purpose of processing.

In addition to small-group processing, the teacher should periodically engage in whole-class processing. When cooperative learning groups are used, the teacher observes the groups, analyzes the problems they have working together, and gives feedback to each group on how well they are working together. The teacher systematically moves from group to group and observes them at work. A formal observation sheet may be used to gather specific data on each group. At the end of the class period the teacher can then conduct a whole-class processing session by sharing with the class the results of his or her observations. If each group has a peer observer, the results of their observations may be added together to get overall class data.

An important aspect of both small-group and whole-class processing is group and class celebrations. It is feeling successful, appreciated, and respected that builds commitment to learning, enthusiasm about working in cooperative groups, and a sense of self-efficacy in terms of subject-matter mastery and working cooperatively with classmates.

RESEARCH RATIONALE

Working together to get the job done can have profound effects on students and staff members. A great deal of research has been conducted on the relationship among cooperative, competitive, and individualistic efforts and instructional outcomes (Johnson & R. Johnson, 1974, 1978, 1983, 1989a; Johnson, Johnson, & Maruyama, 1983; Johnson, Maruyama, Johnson, Nelson, & Skon, 1981; Pepitone, 1980; Sharan, 1980; Slavin, 1983). These research studies began in the late 1890s when Triplett (1898) in the United States and Mayer (1903) in Germany conducted a series on the factors associated with competitive performance. The amount of research that has been conducted since then is staggering. During the past 90 years, more than 600 studies have been conducted by a wide variety of researchers in different decades with different age subjects, in different subject areas, and in different environments. We know far more about the efficacy of cooperative learning than we know about lecturing, age grouping, beginning reading instruction at age 6, departmentalization, or almost any other facet of education.

Building on the theorizing of Kurt Lewin (1935) and Morton Deutsch (1949), the premise may be made that the type of interdependence structured among students determines how they interact with each other, which in turn largely determines instructional outcomes. The quality of peer relationships, furthermore, has widespread and powerful impact on individuals' cognitive and social development.

Cooperative Efforts and Achievement/Productivity

The highest and best form of efficiency is the spontaneous cooperation of a free people.

(Woodrow Wilson)

How successful competitive, individualistic, and cooperative efforts are in promoting productivity and achievement is the first question pragmatists ask about social interdependence. More than 375 studies have been conducted during the past 90 years to give an answer (Johnson & R. Johnson, 1989a). When all of the studies were included in the analysis, the average cooperator performed at about two thirds a standard deviation above average student learning within a competitive (effect size = 0.66) or individualistic situation (effect size = 0.63). When only the high-quality studies were included in the analysis, the effect sizes are 0.86 and 0.59 respectively. Cooperative learning, furthermore, resulted in more higher level reasoning, more frequent generation of new ideas and solutions (i.e., process gain), and greater transfer of what is learned within one situation to another (i.e., group-to-individual transfer) than did competitive or individualistic learning.

The fact that working together to achieve a common goal produces higher achievement and greater productivity than does working alone is so well confirmed by so much research that it stands as one of the strongest principles of social and organizational psychology. Cooperative learning is indicated whenever learning goals are highly important, mastery and retention are important, a task is complex or conceptual, problem solving is desired, divergent thinking or creativity is desired, quality of performance is expected, and higher-level reasoning strategies and critical thinking are needed.

Participants in the research have varied widely as to economic class, age, sex, and cultural background. A variety of tasks and measures of the dependent variables have been studied. Studies have been conducted by many different researchers with markedly different orientations working in different environments and in different decades. This means that the overall body of research on social interdependence has considerable generalizability, as shown in Table 1.

Table 1. Social interdependence: Weighted findings

	Mean	Standard deviation	n^a
Achievement			
Cooperative vs. competitive	0.66	0.94	128
Cooperative vs. individualistic	0.63	0.81	182
Competitive vs. individualistic	0.30	0.76	39
Interpersonal attraction			
Cooperative vs. competitive	0.65	0.47	88
Cooperative vs. individualistic	0.62	0.59	59
Competitive vs. individualistic	0.08	0.70	15
Social support			
Cooperative vs. competitive	0.59	0.39	75
Cooperative vs. individualistic	0.71	0.45	70
Competitive vs. individualistic	−0.12	0.37	18
Self-esteem			
Cooperative vs. competitive	0.60	0.57	55
Cooperative vs. individualistic	0.44	0.40	37
Competitive vs. individualistic	−0.19	0.40	18

[a]n = number of studies in sample

Interpersonal Relationships and Acceptance of Differences

One of the most important and long-standing goals of American education is to promote constructive relationships and positive attitudes among heterogeneous students. Almost every school district has acceptance of differences as one of their stated
goals for students. Legislation exists that proclaims it is unlawful to segregate any
student for educational purposes unless it is absolutely necessary. Ethnic minor-
ities, students with disabilities, non–English-speaking students, and even females
interested in science and math are examples of areas of students who need to be integrated with a wide variety of peers. Acceptance of differences is a central issue for all
students.

Cooperative learning experiences, compared with competitive, individualistic,
and "traditional" instruction, promote considerably more liking among students (effect sizes = 0.65 and 0.62 respectively) (Johnson & R. Johnson, 1989a; Johnson et al.,
1983). This is true regardless of differences in ability level, sex, disability, ethnic
membership, social class differences, or task orientation. Students who collaborate
on their studies develop considerable commitment and caring for each other no
matter what their initial impressions of and attitudes toward each other were when
they started. They also like the teacher more and perceive the teacher as being more
supportive and accepting academically and personally.

It is when students with disabilities are liked, accepted, and chosen as friends
that inclusion becomes a positive influence on the lives of students with and without
disabilities. Thus, any definition of inclusion that does not recognize the importance
of relationships among students with and without disabilities is incomplete. It is
peers without disabilities who provide students with disabilities entry into the typical life experiences of their age groups, such as going to dances, taking buses, going to
movies, shopping, knowing what is "cool" and what is not, and dating. Constructive
peer relationships are not only an absolute necessity for maximal achievement and

healthy social and cognitive development, they may be the primary relationship within which development and socialization take place. Students with disabilities especially need access to peers who are highly motivated and behave appropriately. Placing students with disabilities in the corner of a classroom and providing individualistic learning experiences is not effective inclusion.

Inclusion is not something teachers do for a few students. It is something teachers do for every student in their class. The instructional procedures needed for the constructive inclusion of students with disabilities also benefit the shy student sitting over by the window, the over-aggressive student who seeks acceptance through negative behaviors, the bright but stereotyped student sitting in the front row, and the average student in the center of the classroom who needs very little help and is often neglected. *All* students need to be accepted and benefit from a classroom where it is acceptable to be different. We have also found in our research that when students without disabilities collaborate with their peers with disabilities on instructional tasks, the result is increased empathy, altruism, and an ability to view situations from a variety of perspectives. Even the most well-adjusted and hard-working students benefit from the instructional techniques associated with inclusion when it is structured effectively.

Accuracy of Perspective Taking

Social perspective taking is the ability to understand how a situation appears to another person and how that person is reacting cognitively and emotionally to the situation. The opposite of perspective taking is egocentrism, the embeddedness in one's own viewpoint to the extent that one is unaware of other points of view and of the limitations of one's perspectives. Cooperative learning experiences tend to promote greater cognitive and affective perspective taking than do competitive or individualistic learning experiences (Johnson & R. Johnson, 1989a).

Creativity

Cooperative learning promotes creative thinking by increasing the number of ideas, quality of ideas, feelings of stimulation and enjoyment, and originality of expression in creative problem solving (Bahn, 1964; Bolen & Torrance, 1976; Dunnette, Campbell, & Jaastad, 1963; Falk & Johnson, 1977; Peters & Torrance, 1972; Torrance, 1970, 1971, 1973; Triandis, Bass, Ewen, & Mikesell, 1963). It is not surprising that students are "triggered" by the ideas of others and that different perspectives cause group members to consider a larger number of alternatives. The cooperative relationship also provides a context to consider and appreciate other group members' ideas instead of ignoring (individualistic) or trying to come up with a better one (competition).

Self-Esteem

The data in Table 1 indicate that cooperation produced higher levels of self-esteem than did competitive and individualistic efforts (effect sizes of 0.58 and 0.44 respectively) with regard to self-esteem. Individuals with low self-esteem tend to (Johnson & R. Johnson, 1989a):

1. Have low productivity due to setting low goals for themselves, lacking confidence in their ability, and assuming that they will fail no matter how hard they try.
2. Are critical of others as well as themselves by looking for flaws in others and trying to "tear them down."

3. Withdraw socially due to feeling awkward, self-conscious, and vulnerable to rejection.
4. Are conforming, agreeable, highly persuadable, and highly influenced by criticism.
5. Develop psychological problems such as anxiety, nervousness, insomnia, depression, and psychosomatic symptoms.

Within competitive situations, self-esteem tends to be based on the contingent view of one's competence that, "If I win, then I have worth as a person, but if I lose, then I have no worth." Winners attribute their success to superior ability and attribute the failure of others to lack of ability, both of which contribute to self-aggrandizement. Losers, who are the vast majority, defensively tend to be self-disparaging, apprehensive about evaluation, and tend to withdraw psychologically and physically. Within individualistic situations, students are isolated from one another, receive little direct comparison with or feedback from peers, and perceive evaluations as inaccurate and unrealistic. A defensive avoidance, evaluation apprehension, and distrust of peers results. Within cooperative situations, individuals tend to interact, promote each other's success, form multidimensional and realistic impressions of each other's competencies, and give accurate feedback. Such interaction tends to promote a basic acceptance of oneself as a competent person.

Understanding Interdependence

Cooperative learning simultaneously models interdependence and provides students with the experiences they need to understand the nature of cooperation (Johnson & Johnson, 1989a). The future of the world depends on the constructive and competent management of world interdependence as well as interdependence in family, work, community, and societal environments. Students who have had 12–20 years of cooperative learning and who have had opportunities to work cooperatively with students who vary in ability, ethnicity, gender, and so forth will be better able to build positively interdependent relationships than will students who have had 12–20 years of competitive and individualistic learning.

RELATIONSHIPS AMONG OUTCOMES

There are bidirectional relationships, as shown in Figure 1, among achievement, quality of interpersonal relationships, and psychological health (Johnson & Johnson, 1989b). Each influences the others. Caring and committed friendships come from a sense of mutual accomplishment, mutual pride in joint work, and the bonding that results from joint efforts.

The more students care about each other, the harder they will work to achieve mutual learning goals. Long-term and persistent efforts to achieve do not come from the head; they come from the heart (Johnson & Johnson, 1989b). Individuals seek out opportunities to work with those they care about. As caring increases, so do feelings of personal responsibility to do one's share of the work, a willingness to take on difficult tasks, motivation and persistence in working toward goal achievement, and a willingness to endure pain and frustration on behalf of the group. All these contribute to group productivity.

In addition, the joint success experienced in working together to get the job done enhances social competencies, self-esteem, and general psychological health. The more psychologically healthy individuals are, the better able they are to work with

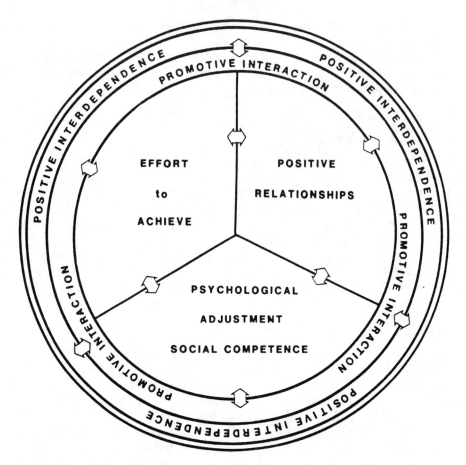

Figure 1.   Outcomes of cooperation.

others to achieve mutual goals. Joint efforts require coordination, effective communication, leadership, and conflict management. States of depression, anxiety, guilt,
shame, and anger decrease the energy available to contribute to a cooperative effort.

Finally, the more positive interpersonal relationships are, the greater the psychological health of the individuals involved. Through the internalization of positive
relationships, direct social support, shared intimacy, and expressions of caring, psychological health and the ability to cope with stress are built. Destructive relationships and the absence of caring and committed relationships tend to increase psychological pathology. Moreover, depression, anxiety, guilt, shame, and anger decrease
an individual's ability to build and maintain caring and committed relationships.
The more psychologically healthy individuals are, the more they can build and maintain meaningful and caring relationships.

With the amount of research evidence available, it is surprising that classroom
practice is so oriented toward individualistic and competitive learning and schools
are so dominated by a competitive/individualistic structure. It is time for the discrep-
ancy to be reduced between what research indicates is effective in teaching and what
teachers actually do.

BACK TO THE BASICS

Our research and the research of many others dating back to the late 1800s has established that having students work together cooperatively is a powerful way for them to learn and has positive effects on the classroom and school climate. This has been verified by teachers in classrooms from preschool through graduate school. However, the importance of emphasizing cooperative learning in classrooms goes beyond just achievement, positive relationships, and psychological health.

The ability of all students to learn to work cooperatively with others is the keystone to building and maintaining stable marriages, families, careers, and friendships. Being able to perform technical skills, such as reading, speaking, listening, writing, computing, and problem solving, are valuable but of little use if the person cannot apply those skills in cooperative interaction with other people in career, family, and community environments. The most logical way to emphasize the use of students' knowledge and skills within a cooperative framework, such as they will meet as members of society, is to spend much of the time learning those skills in cooperative relationships with each other. We need to get back to the basics, reconcile school practices with current research, and encourage that a healthy portion of instruction is cooperative.

REFERENCES

Bahn, C. (1964). *The interaction of creativity and social facilitation in creative problem solving.* Doctoral dissertation, Columbia University, Ann Arbor, MI. (University Microfilms No. 65-7499)

Bolen, L., & Torrance, E. (1976, April). *An experimental study of the influence of locus of control, dyadic interaction, and sex on creative thinking.* Paper presented at the American Educational Research Association, San Francisco.

Deutsch, M. (1949). A theory of cooperation and competition. *Human Relations, 2,* 129–152.

Dunnette, M., Campbell, J., & Jaastad, K. (1963). The effect of group participation on brainstorming effectiveness of two industrial samples. *Journal of Applied Psychology, 47,* 30–37.

Falk, D., & Johnson, D.W. (1977). The effects of perspective-taking and ego-centrism on problem solving in heterogeneous and homogeneous groups. *Journal of Social Psychology, 102,* 63–72.

Harkins, S., & Petty, R. (1982). The effects of task difficulty and task uniqueness on social loafing. *Journal of Personality and Social Psychology, 43,* 1214–1229.

Hwong, N., Caswell, A., Johnson, D.W., & Johnson, R. (1993). Effects of cooperative and individualistic learning on prospective elementary teachers' music achievement and attitudes. *Journal of Social Psychology, 133*(1), 53–64.

Ingham, A., Levinger, G., Graves, J., & Peckham, V. (1974). The Ringelmann effect: Studies of group size and group performance. *Journal of Personality and Social Psychology, 10,* 371–384.

Johnson, D.W. (1990). *Reaching out: Interpersonal effectiveness and self-actualization* (4th ed.). Englewood Cliffs, NJ: Prentice Hall.

Johnson, D.W. (1991). *Human relations and your career* (3rd ed.). Englewood Cliffs, NJ: Prentice Hall.

Johnson, D.W., & Johnson, F. (1991). *Joining together: Group theory and group skills* (4th ed.). Englewood Cliffs, NJ: Prentice Hall.

Johnson, D.W., & Johnson, R. (1974). Instructional goal structure: Cooperative, competitive, or individualistic. *Review of Educational Research, 44,* 213–240.

Johnson, D.W., & Johnson, R. (1978). Cooperative, competitive, and individualistic learning. *Journal of Research and Development in Education, 12,* 3–15.

Johnson, D.W., & Johnson, R. (1983). The socialization and achievement crisis: Are cooperative learning experiences the solution? In L. Bickman (Ed.), *Applied social psychology annual 4* (pp. 119–164). Beverly Hills: Sage Publications.

Johnson D.W., & Johnson, R. (1989a). *Cooperation and competition: Theory and research.* Edina, MN: Interaction Book Company.

Johnson, D.W., & Johnson, R. (1989b). *Leading the cooperative school.* Edina, MN: Interaction Book Company.

Johnson, D.W., & Johnson R. (1991). *Learning together and alone: Cooperation, competition, and individualization* (3rd ed.). Englewood Cliffs, NJ: Prentice Hall.

Johnson, D.W., Johnson, R., & Maruyama, G. (1983). Interdependence and interpersonal attraction among heterogeneous and homogeneous individuals: A theoretical formulation and a meta-analysis of the research. *Review of Educational Research, 53,* 5–54.

Johnson, D.W., Johnson, R., Ortiz, A., & Stanne, M. (1991). Impact of positive goal and resource interdependence on achievement, interaction, and attitudes. *Journal of General Psychology, 118*(4), 341–347.

Johnson, D.W., Johnson, R., Stanne, M., & Garibaldi, A. (1990). Impact of group processing on achievement in cooperative groups. *Journal of Social Psychology, 130,* 507–516.

Johnson, D.W., Maruyama, G., Johnson, R., Nelson, D., & Skon, L. (1981). Effects of cooperative, competitive, and individualistic goal structures on achievement: A meta-analysis. *Psychological Bulletin, 89,* 47–62.

Kerr, N., & Bruun, S. (1981). Ringelmann revisited: Alternative explanations for the social loafing effect. *Personality and Social Psychology Bulletin, 7,* 224–231.

Latane, B., Williams, K., & Harkins, S. (1979). Many hands make light work: The causes and consequences of social loafing. *Journal of Personality and Social Psychology, 37,* 822–832.

Lew, M., Mesch, D., Johnson, D.W., & Johnson, R. (1986a). Components of cooperative learning: Effects of collaborative skills and academic group contingencies on achievement and mainstreaming. *Contemporary Educational Psychology, 11,* 229–239.

Lew, M., Mesch, D., Johnson, D.W., & Johnson, R. (1986b). Positive interdependence, academic and collaborative-skills group contingencies and isolated students. *American Educational Research Journal, 23,* 476–488.

Lewin, K. (1935). *A dynamic theory of personality.* New York: McGraw-Hill.

Mayer, A. (1903). Uber einzel und gesamtleistung des schul kindes. [About individual and overall achievement of school children]. *Archiv for die Gesamte Psychologie, 1,* 276–416.

Mesch, D., Johnson, D.W., & Johnson, R. (1988). Impact of positive interdependence and academic group contingencies on achievement. *Journal of Social Psychology, 28,* 345–352.

Mesch, D., Lew, M., Johnson, D.W., & Johnson R. (1986). Isolated teenagers, cooperative learning and the training of social skills. *Journal of Psychology, 120,* 323–334.

Moede, W. (1927). Die richtlinien der leistungspsychologie [Guidelines for the psychology of performance]. *Industrielle Psychotechnik, 4,* 193–207.

Montagu, A. (1965). *The human revolution.* New York: World Pub Co.

Pepitone, E. (1980). *Children in cooperation and competition.* Lexington, MA: Lexington Books.

Peters, R., & Torrance, E. (1972). Dyadic interaction of preschool children and performance on a construction task. *Psychological Reports, 30,* 747–750.

Petty, R., Harkins, S., Williams, K., & Latane, B. (1977). The effects of group size on cognitive effort and evaluation. *Personality and Social Psychology Bulletin, 3,* 575–578.

Rosenshine, B., & Stevens, R. (1986). Teaching functions. In M. Wittrock (Ed.), *Handbook of research on teaching* (3rd ed.) (pp. 376–391). New York: Macmillan.

Sharan, S. (1980). Cooperative learning in teams: Recent methods and effects on achievement, attitudes, and ethnic relations. *Review of Educational Research, 50,* 241–272.

Slavin, R. (1983). *Cooperative learning.* New York: Longman.

Torrance, E. (1970). Influence of dyadic interaction on creative functioning. *Psychological Reports, 26,* 391–394.

Torrance, E. (1971). Stimulation, enjoyment and originality in dyadic creativity. *Journal of Educational Psychology, 62,* 45–48.

Torrance, E. (1973, February). *Dyadic interaction in creative thinking and problem solving.* Paper presented at the American Educational Research Association annual meeting, New Orleans.

Triandis, H., Bass, A., Ewen, R., & Mikesell, E. (1963). Teaching creativity as a function of the creativity of the members. *Journal of Applied Psychology, 47,* 104–110.

Triplett, N. (1898). The dynamogenic factors in peacemaking and competition. *American Journal of Psychology, 9,* 507–533.

Vygotsky, L. (1962). *Thought and language.* Cambridge, MA: MIT Press.

Williams, K. (1981). *The effects of group cohesiveness on social loafing.* Paper presented at the annual meeting of the Midwestern Psychological Association, Detroit.

Williams, K., Harkins, S., & Latane, B. (1981). Identifiability as a deterrent to social loafing: Two cheering experiments. *Journal of Personality and Social Psychology, 40,* 303–311.

COOPERATIVE LEARNING AND INCLUSION

Mara Sapon-Shevin,
Barbara J. Ayres, and Janet Duncan

As schools move closer to the goal of providing education for all children within inclusive classrooms and schools, increasing amounts of attention and energy are being devoted to developing pedagogical approaches that are appropriate in heterogeneous classrooms. It has become clear that physical inclusion of students with disabilities in the classroom is not sufficient to ensure they will develop meaningful relationships with others. Teachers must structure the educational and social environment so that students develop the skills and attitudes required to interact across perceived differences and disabilities. Teachers who are working in inclusive classrooms are eager to develop modes of instruction that do not isolate and stigmatize learners with different needs: "Everyone write your book reports, and Michael, come over here and draw a picture" is an approach that not only separates children unnecessarily, but also denies all children the opportunity to learn and interact with others in ways that will enhance their academic and social growth. The realization that complete individualization is not a practical or even desirable solution to meeting the diverse needs of children within a single classroom has led many inclusion advocates to promote cooperative learning as the pedagogy of choice.

One of the principles of cooperative learning is the principle of heterogeneous grouping. Cooperative learn-

In keeping with the content and philosophy of this book, this chapter was written cooperatively by the three authors, who combined their knowledge and energy to produce something better than any one could have accomplished alone.

A special thank you is extended to the teachers who participated in the summer course in language arts held at Acadia University, Wolfville, Nova Scotia, during July and August 1992.

ing advocates support the idea that diversity is something to be worked with, not negotiated around, and that the richness of the educational experience is improved for all students when they are active participants in a mutually supportive environment.

Cooperative learning has been used extensively within "regular education" classrooms and "special education" classrooms, but because "inclusive classrooms" are a relatively recent phenomenon, there has not been extensive documentation of the use of cooperative learning strategies within classrooms that serve a range of students within the same environment. Many of those who teach about and promote cooperative learning are also products of and still work within an educational system that segregates and tracks students by ability and prepares teachers for this dual system; therefore, they may still identify themselves as "regular education teachers" or "special education teachers."

Putting the principles of cooperative learning together with the principles of inclusion involves extending the concept of heterogeneous grouping beyond more common notions of children who read at different levels or are at different math skill levels to thinking about and planning for students whose disabilities are more extensive (Sapon-Shevin, 1990, 1991). This chapter addresses the principles of planning for, implementing, and evaluating cooperative learning within inclusive classrooms that serve all students within a common framework. Sharing students' labels does little to help us plan for them educationally; educational programming is maximized by looking at students' abilities and gifts and by describing their educational needs in descriptive rather than evaluative ways. However, because many children are currently labeled (e.g., "severely handicapped," "cognitively delayed," "physically handicapped") and we do believe that children with labels should be and can be included in cooperative learning activities, we identify children's specific educational and physical limitations and needs so that it is clear to the reader that we are, in fact, talking about all children.

This chapter begins with the presentation of three beliefs about cooperative learning. We then explore some principles of cooperative learning that must be implemented in order to maximize academic and social goals for all students. Finally, we discuss the application of cooperative learning beliefs and principles.

BELIEFS ABOUT COOPERATIVE LEARNING

In writing this chapter we were guided by three beliefs about the importance of cooperative learning and inclusion: 1) it benefits all students, 2) it is an integral part of current school reform efforts, and 3) it promotes collaboration between educators who have traditionally worked in isolation from others.

Cooperative Learning Is Good for All Students

Cooperative learning makes sense in inclusive classrooms because it builds upon heterogeneity and formalizes and encourages peer support and connection. However, cooperative learning is not of value only to children with disabilities. Cooperative learning is of value for all students including those who have been identified as "at risk," "bilingual," "gifted," and "normal." *All* students need to learn and work in environments where their individual strengths are recognized and individual needs are addressed. *All* students need to learn within a supportive community in order to feel safe enough to take risks.

Some educators have challenged the use of cooperative learning in classrooms with students who are identified as "gifted," claiming that gifted students become permanent tutors and are resentful of having to work with students of differing abilities (Matthews, 1992). Such arguments must be examined critically; we must ask ourselves what we want students to learn in school. Beyond academic subjects, don't we want all students to be comfortable with and accepting of individual differences (their own and others)? Don't we want all students to have sophisticated social skills that will enable them to work with people they perceive as "different" or even "difficult"? Furthermore, don't we want to model inclusion and community and demonstrate in the microcosm of the classroom what a society in which all people are valued would look like?

One student we know who was initially resistant to group work commented, "What I like best about this class is that everyone cooperates and shares" (Ayres, O'Brien, & Rogers, 1992, p. 26). Surely this is an important lesson for all students to learn, not just students with disabilities. Another student said, "Sometimes I can't understand Jingyu—it's kind of hard to understand him but he can read pretty good. He, um, like on math problems, people say, 'Why don't you help Jingyu?', but sometimes he helps us. He is good at his math" (Ayres & Carnicelli, in preparation). Thoughtfully implemented cooperative learning disrupts typical hierarchies of who is "smart" and who is not, and allows all students to work together, each student experiencing the role of teacher and of learner.

If teachers or students are uncomfortable with cooperative learning, it is often because they have adopted a technique without a firm understanding of the underlying principles and without sufficient support to implement creative, multilevel cooperative learning activities. Teachers must be encouraged to be thoughtful about all aspects of cooperative learning (Sapon-Shevin & Schniedewind, 1989/1990) and to garner enough support for themselves so that they are not isolated and overwhelmed by the truly complex task of meeting the needs of many different children within the same environment.

Cooperative Learning Is Part of Comprehensive School Reform

Teachers are confronted on a regular basis with educational innovations that must be incorporated into their teaching: whole language, critical thinking, authentic assessment, and so forth. Some teachers (and administrators) hope they can ignore these "fads" in education, and, by waiting for them to pass and be replaced by "the next thing," save themselves the time and energy needed to learn about and implement new practices. Yet, not only is cooperative learning supported by a compelling research base, it is also fully compatible with other "best practices" currently being promoted.

Whole language, which involves having students read literature and write stories, has been implemented very successfully in cooperative groups, and many of the practices promoted by whole language experts are inherently cooperative (e.g., editing conferences, book sharing, collaborative writing). One teacher, for example, had each student in the class write an "I like" book; some of the students wrote long narratives—"I like walking in the rain in my new boots"—whereas others cut out pictures of things they liked and pasted them in the book. Every child was able to complete a book, engaging in the literacy activity. Every child was able to partner with another and share his or her book by "reading" it to an attentive listener. In contrast to grouping children into homogeneous reading groups by skill, this activity was structured in heterogeneous cooperative groups so that all children could succeed at their own level.

Important skills such as critical thinking, creative problem solving, and the synthesis of knowledge can easily be accomplished through cooperative group activities in inclusive classrooms. In addition, authentic assessment (anecdotal reporting, portfolio assessment, and observational recording) is fully compatible with cooperative learning and inclusion.

Teachers need not envision cooperative learning as "one more thing" they need to do, but rather as an organizing value and principle for all the instruction in their classroom. Building a cooperative, inclusive classroom community can be the framework within which other teaching strategies and practices are woven.

Cooperative Learning Means Teachers Cooperating

In order for cooperative learning to be successful in inclusive classrooms, teachers who have traditionally worked in isolation will need to find new ways of collaborating and sharing their expertise. This kind of collaboration can be challenging because it involves sharing responsibilities and communicating with others, but it can also be exciting and rewarding. One teacher commented that planning cooperative learning lessons was stimulating: "For us, it really gets the creative juices flowing." Another teacher said, "It's fun, there are no two ways about it, it's fun. How can it not be fun? Plus [the students] get to know each other's abilities and they can get excited about each other's growth, even though it's not the same as theirs" (Ayres et al., 1992, pp. 25, 26).

Not only can students get to know each other's abilities within a cooperative process, but teachers can as well. A general education teacher and a special education teacher planning together often find that they have unique skills and ideas to contribute to the process. The general education teacher may have a broader perspective on the curriculum and on curriculum integration, whereas the special education teacher may have special skills in modifying instruction and developing adaptations that benefit many children. General education teachers who are used to working with larger groups of children often can contribute important classroom management and organizational strategies to balance some of the individualized approaches proposed by the special education teacher.

It is often acknowledged that when students are learning to work in groups they need support and encouragement to get them over the rough spots. "I don't want to work with Pam," or "Danny's taking over the whole project" are indications that time and attention must be devoted to developing appropriate social skills for negotiating conflict and moving toward consensus. Similarly, teachers learning to work together may encounter struggles over turf, expertise, ownership, and responsibility—these also need to be negotiated. Teachers must find ways to support one another as they learn to be cooperative, inclusive educators at the same time they support their students in this goal. Learning how to use the expertise of the speech therapist or physical therapist, for example, or how to balance a child's individualized education program (IEP) objectives with broader classroom objectives requires time for teachers to meet, talk, listen, plan, and develop a trusting working relationship. Implementing cooperative learning in inclusive classrooms can benefit not only the students, but also provide an important opportunity for educators to develop their own teaching skills. Supportive administrators have found creative ways of providing teachers with adequate planning and preparation time so that inclusion becomes an opportunity for better teaching rather than an imposed burden.

PRINCIPLES OF INCLUSIVE COOPERATIVE LEARNING

Once teachers have decided that they will begin to implement formal cooperative group lessons in their classrooms, there are many decisions that must be made. Teachers must decide how they will incorporate cooperative learning lessons within their classroom structure, how they will decide the content to be taught using cooperative learning, how they will form groups, how they will ensure active participation for all students, and how they will evaluate students' learning. On the following pages we explore some principles of inclusive cooperative learning that must be taken into consideration for successful implementation.

Cooperative Learning Means
Establishing a Cooperative Classroom Ethic

For cooperative learning to be maximally effective, it must take place within an overall context of cooperation and peer support. Attempts to implement cooperative learning activities when the classroom norms are those of isolation, competition, or interpersonal indifference are apt to result in contradictory messages to students and have limited positive impact on the goal of creating a safe, inclusive community.

Creating a safe, caring community for all students within which cooperative learning is simply the formalized expression of classroom values and orientations involves attention to overall community and connections, open communication about differences and classroom practices, and helping.

Overall Community and Connections Cooperative learning should not be something that is done on Tuesdays and Thursdays from 9 to 10, nor should it be something we do only when we have children with disabilities included. For example, in one school, a sign on a wall announced "Cooperative Learning, May 14th." When a visitor inquired about the sign, she was told, "That's the day the trainable mentally retarded students go into the third grade classroom to work."

A feeling of cooperation, community, and connection should be part of everything that happens in the classroom. For example, hanging up for display only those papers graded with "A"s communicates to students that not everyone's work is valued. Teachers might instead want to hang up a "proud paper" from every student or let students decide what they would like to display. Having students line up for music and gym in a girls' line and a boys' line communicates that gender divisions are important ones (and pity the boy who accidentally gets in the girls' line). There are an infinite number of other ways to line students up that encourage them to interact with a variety of their classmates across boundaries of race, gender, and ability. Behavior management strategies that single students out for praise or punishment (names on the board, statements such as "I like the way Nicole is sitting") must be challenged with reference to how such practices affect the way students look at one another and their differences. Classroom holiday celebrations, posters on the wall, and the racial and ethnic representation of the books in the classroom library all affect the school community and the extent to which students feel that they are (or are not) a valued part of the classroom. Teachers must be encouraged to think about all aspects of their classroom practice in reference to questions such as the following:

Will this practice contribute to or detract from a sense of classroom community? Will what I say or do in this situation encourage students to see each other positively or negatively?

Open Communication About Differences and Classroom Practices Creating a classroom community in which all students feel comfortable and supported in their learning requires that teachers deal directly with issues that affect the classroom. When a child in the classroom is displaying some challenging behavior, for example, other students are generally aware of this. Not talking about the situation and exploring various solutions with students may leave them frightened or disenfranchised, wondering why something so obvious is not being discussed and what their role in the classroom should be. Teachers certainly need to be thoughtful about how and when they talk to students about Mark's biting or the fact that LeAnn is being teased on the playground because she smells. However, ignoring such issues in the hope that they will "work themselves out" often results not only in escalation of the problem but a classroom atmosphere in which students do not feel empowered to talk about what is happening or to explore their role in generating and implementing solutions.

In Johnson City, New York (Salisbury, Palombaro, & Hollowood, 1993), students and teachers employ a collaborative problem-solving process in which they identify issues, generate possible solutions, screen solutions for feasibility, choose a solution to implement, and then evaluate it. Teachers have used this system to address barriers to inclusion at multiple levels: physical (How can Marie be involved in the puppet show her group has written when she cannot stand up and hold her puppet at the same time?), social (What might Taylor be trying to communicate when he pulls hair?), and instructional (What are some ways we can help Luis, who has a hearing impairment, learn to count?). Including children in identifying problems and generating and implementing solutions sends the clear message that we can talk about what is happening in our classroom, and, as a group, we can figure out ways to do things so that everyone is included.

Similarly, teachers who implement more formal cooperative learning strategies should also talk to students about why they are doing so, what they hope to accomplish, and what some of the barriers might be. Students who are involved in the process of cooperative learning, as opposed to those who are simply doing what the teacher told them to, are far more likely to take ownership of cooperative activities and generalize them to other areas of classroom and home life.

Helping Establishing norms about when, how, and why we help others is critical to the full implementation of cooperative learning. Because many teachers and students have received cultural messages that say that "needing help is bad or shameful" and "offering help to others will embarrass them," it is important to establish new classroom norms. Two of the most critical values are: 1) Everyone is good at something and can help others, and 2) Everyone is entitled to and can benefit from help and support from others. Teachers may want to help students structure a "Classroom Classifieds" in which students identify their own strengths and skills and name these as "Help Offered" (can help with multiplication, good at jumping rope, can teach sign language, know a lot about frogs). Concurrently, they can identify their needs and learning goals and identify these as "Help Wanted" (want to learn to make friendship bracelets, need help with spelling, want to learn how to play ball games at recess). It is important that such activities be structured so that every child is both a teacher and a learner, as a way of challenging rigid notions that there are some people who give help and some people who need help. It is important to create a classroom space for people to proudly claim what they are good at and safely ask for the help and support they need without fear or embarrassment, humiliation, or isolation. When fourth grade teacher Cathleen Corrigan implemented this activity in her inclusive fourth grade class, she found that many of the students had difficulty identifying something they were good at. She observed that when students announced that "they weren't good at anything," other students jumped in to remind them about their strengths ("You're really good at the computer," "You're a good artist.").

Cooperative Learning Facilitates Teaching Meaningful Content

Unfortunately, neither deciding to have an inclusive classroom nor implementing cooperative learning guarantees that the curriculum will be creative or meaningful. Teachers who feel constrained by or limited to a fixed curriculum or set of materials often try to "bend" the child to fit the curriculum, and we have seen cooperative learning used to encourage children to complete unimaginative worksheets and dittos.

Including a child with a significant disability in an activity and structuring that activity cooperatively gives us an opportunity (and sometimes forces us) to examine the curriculum critically and unleash our creative pedagogical and curricular inventiveness. Not only is memorizing the states and their capitals an inappropriate curriculum objective for Manuel, but neither is it the best way to teach map skills and geography to other students. Combining a commitment to inclusion with an orientation toward cooperative learning can be a catalyst for thinking carefully about the following questions: What is really important for students to learn? How can I make learning meaningful and functional for all students?

One of the often unexpected but welcome benefits of including children with specific behavioral and educational challenges in the classroom is that teachers are encouraged to rethink previous beliefs and practices related to the curriculum and pedagogy. The teacher who decides to use manipulatives for math (instead of worksheets) because one child quite clearly requires that approach often finds that many other students also benefit from this hands-on, participatory approach. Teachers who move away from text-based question-and-answer approaches to teaching in order to accommodate students who require more active involvement in the curriculum are generally pleased to find that such an orientation is of benefit to *all* students.

Cooperative learning in inclusive classrooms will be more effective when it is multilevel, multimodal, and integrated across subject areas. Multilevel teaching involves students working on similar objectives or with the same material, but at different levels. All students may be using the telephone book, for example, but some students might be learning to dial 911 in case of an emergency while others learn to compute and compare long distance charges and optimum calling times. Or, all students may be working on map skills, but at different levels. Perhaps Maria is learning about lines of latitude and longitude while Robin is learning the directions "up" and "down," "left" and "right."

Multimodality teaching involves moving away from pencil and paper tasks to other forms of active involvement. Writing and performing a puppet show, for example, might involve writing, reading, building a set, singing, cutting, talking, dancing, and so forth. An activity like a puppet show or a unit on space can also be used to integrate curriculum across subject matter. When one class studied the moon, for example, they incorporated science (facts about the moon and astronomy), creative writing (poems and stories about the moon), social studies (cross-cultural beliefs and traditions around the moon), math (computing distance, density, air pressure), and much more. Broadening the curriculum in these ways provides many opportunities both to include students who work at significantly different levels and to design cooperative learning activities in which students can help and support one another in their learning while still maintaining a common theme and a sense of community.

Cooperative Learning Depends on Supportive Heterogeneous Groups

In classrooms where teachers are working to communicate norms of cooperation, students can work together in a number of different ways. In many cooperative classrooms, students sit in heterogeneous base groups so that teachers can structure both informal and formal opportunities for cooperation between students throughout the day. For example, students can start their day with an informal group activity at their desk clusters; complete class jobs with a partner from their group; and engage in formal, structured cooperative learning activities with group members. In most classrooms, teachers leave cooperative learning groups together for 1 month or 6 weeks so that students have an opportunity to get to know and work together with group members, but then also have an opportunity to learn to work with other classmates throughout the year. The goal is for students to have worked in cooperative groups with all their classmates by the end of the year.

One important aspect of creating cooperative learning groups is maximizing the heterogeneity of the students within the small groups. Students should be placed in groups that are mixed by academic skills, social skills, personality, race, and sex. It is often helpful for teachers to work with others who are familiar with their students when groups are being formed. With all of the different aspects of student diversity that need to be taken into consideration, forming groups can seem like an onerous task that will be too difficult for any one person.

Many teachers structure cooperative groups very deliberately. In classrooms where students are functioning at different levels in regard to academic and social abilities, it is important that the teacher structures the groups to ensure heterogeneity, particularly in the beginning of the year or when new students enter.

Two first grade teachers who team teach in a classroom that includes the full range of learners work together to plan cooperative learning groups. They begin the process by identifying one aspect of student diversity and placing one student with this quality in each group. For example, they start with academic diversity and place one student in each group who is able to read. Next they look at the students who are nonreaders and place them into groups. As they place this second student they always consider how this student and the first student match up in regard to supporting one another socially. For the third student in each group they also consider social aspects—they look for a student who can complement the other two students and help pull the group together. One day their discussion when forming groups went as follows:

> This is a nice combination but Katie and Andrew are both quiet. I was thinking about Rachel and Katie because of Rachel's style—she may be more assertive with Katie to help stimulate her involvement. (Ayres et al., 1992, p. 6)

> What about Doug and Brent? I'm thinking of this because of Doug's abilities. In many ways Brent is similar but it may build some self-esteem for Brent in that setting. He can really do things but he doesn't think he can do as much as he can. (p. 6)

Maybe Madeline should be with Brad because she is so strong in everything—and in that group it is going to take a little more work from two people instead of three. Plus, she is comfortable with Brad and I think she will come up with strategies to involve him—she is real bright and she is good at modifying things. This group is going to have to be able to change and not have to be doing exactly what every other group is doing, and not get upset about it. (p. 6)

The comments made by these teachers illustrate the level of complexity of thought that goes into structuring supportive heterogeneous groups. Through careful planning, students have a greater opportunity to receive the social support that is important for establishing a sense of belonging and group membership in the classroom.

In forming groups, some teachers focus on student choice, asking students who they would *like* to work with. Although it makes sense for teachers to provide students with multiple opportunities to choose within the school day, student choice may not be the best way to form groups. When students choose their own groups and work only with others they already know, the groups often tend to be same gender, race, and ability. These more homogeneous groups work against the broader goals of cooperative learning in which teachers are striving to help the students learn to value the diversity that exists in the classroom and in society.

There are ways, however, that teachers can incorporate some aspects of student choice into group formation. For example, Deborah Quick, a fourth grade teacher, forms new groups periodically throughout the year and asks each student to respond (privately) to a number of questions including: "Who are two people you think you could work well with?", "Who are two people you don't know well and would like to know?" By asking students these questions, she is allowing them to participate in group formation, but also emphasizing that although it is important to work with students they already know, it is also important to learn to accept, value, and work with others they do not know well yet. Once students have learned to work with many others, allowing more choice in group formation may be appropriate.

Cooperative Learning Requires Structures that Ensure the Active Participation of All Students

Equally important to establishing supportive heterogeneous groups is ensuring the active participation of all students within inclusive cooperative learning lessons. All too often students are placed into groups and given a task to complete without the provision of structures that will promote the active, equitable participation of all members. Key components of participation include the division of labor and materials, flexible interpretation of roles, and individualized student responsibilities.

Division of Labor and Materials   The participation of all group members is more likely when teachers carefully structure the cooperative group task. Through the division of labor and materials, the students are given a clear message that each student has an important contribution to make toward the completion of the group's task. In the beginning, or when new groups have formed, it is important that teachers structure this interdependence among the group members. Planning for equitable participation becomes especially important in inclusive classrooms where the participation of some students may be dependent on the structure that is provided. For example, with a student who is reserved and responds more slowly than her classmates due to a physical disability, if labor and materials are not divided it is possible that group members will do the task for her. As was mentioned previously in this chapter, it is also important for teachers to talk with students about the goals of working together and the importance of everyone contributing. In one classroom, the teacher talked to individual groups and asked the students how they were going to make sure that all group members were given a turn.

Flexible Interpretation of Roles To promote active, equitable participation within groups, roles must be interpreted flexibly. Instead of creating static roles for students, flexible roles allow for the individualization that will ensure that all group members are able to assume each role at some point in time. For example, in one classroom, the roles remained the same across time (e.g., writer, reader/questioner, checker), but the responsibilities of the roles changed depending on the task and the students who would be given the role on that particular day (Ayres et al., 1992). Through these flexible roles, a student who is unable to write the letters of the alphabet could be the writer when the task is designed so that the writers are gluing something instead of writing words. Another aspect of individualizing roles occurs when teachers think of creative ways for students to fulfill the role responsibilities. Teachers might ask themselves, "What are the different ways that students could encourage group members for this lesson?" or "How could Rachel, who doesn't speak, encourage others?" When teachers work to broaden their thinking about the equitable participation of students, they can come up with many different ways for students to be active contributors (e.g., encourage others by giving a "high five," passing a card with a positive statement or a smiley face written on it to a group member).

Individualized Student Responsibilities Adaptations can be made within groups to promote the active, equitable participation of all members. Sometimes adaptations are necessary to promote the participation of an individual student. For example, in Mary Rita Carnicelli's classroom, heterogeneous cooperative learning groups worked together on math story problems. One student, Kris, whose goals for math included writing numbers from 1 to 50 and using a calculator to compute problems, was given the role of writer/checker within her group. The other students in the group determined what mathematical function to use for the problem, helped Kris write down the problem on the worksheet by dictating the numbers, solved the problem, and dictated to Kris the numbers to write down for the answer. Kris was then responsible for checking the group's response on her calculator. In another classroom, Brad was a first grade student whose educational objectives included grasping and holding objects and indicating his preference by choosing between two objects. During a lesson on community helpers, Brad's group was given the role of a doctor to study so that he would be able to use a play doctor's kit to learn about medical instruments. The addition of the hands-on materials provided an opportunity to address his educational objectives of grasping objects and indicating preference (Ayres et al., 1992).

When students are placed in supportive heterogeneous groups and issues of active, equitable participation are addressed by teachers, all students can benefit from the use of cooperative learning in the classroom. Through these considerations and individualized adaptations, all students are seen as important group members in the eyes of their peers. Although these components initially require more thought and time on the part of teachers, they will reap the rewards as students begin to support and expect the maximum involvement of all group members.

Cooperative Learning Provides Opportunities for Ongoing Evaluation

One important and often complex aspect of instruction with cooperative learning is evaluation. How can educators be certain that students are attaining their educational goals within cooperative groups? How should students be evaluated and how should that evaluation be communicated? How can an evaluation system help modify and refine cooperative learning instructional programs? These questions can guide educators as they work to design appropriate evaluation methods for cooperative learning activities. Effective evaluation of cooperative learning in inclusive classrooms must focus on both the content and the process of the group experience.

The issue of grading in inclusive cooperative classrooms is difficult. Educators who are concerned about the self-esteem of all learners reject the use of practices that promote competition between students. Group grades or group rankings work against encouraging cooperation among students and may make group members less willing to support a classmate with a disability. Evaluation should not be structured so that one student's difficulty becomes a group's liability or the cause (real or perceived) of group failure. It is imperative to avoid situations in which students can accurately report that "Tyrone brought our grade down." Teachers must be careful that the structure of group evaluation accounts for differing abilities.

In inclusive cooperative classrooms, teacher-made tests of subject matter or standardized tests with norm-referenced criteria may not be sufficient or appropriate for assessing achievement. The students who have IEPs may be working at different levels than their peers, a modification we wish to encourage, rather than discourage, through excessive standardization. Separating students into fixed ability groups that are evaluated through a variety of criterion-referenced tests is not the solution either, particularly as such a process tends to isolate and stigmatize individuals ("You're only on the red book.").

Teachers must find ways to assess students who are engaging in significantly different activities within a common structure and begin to describe and evaluate what students have learned and how they are working with their peers. Cooperative learning provides an opportunity for students to complete an activity with an emphasis on group dynamics and interpersonal skills as well as the academic goals of the lesson. Cooperative learning also allows for ongoing evaluation on the part of students and teachers, both during and after group activities.

If we intend to evaluate students on their group process and product, it is crucial that cooperative learning lessons are designed to be just that—cooperative. This can be accomplished through the creation of activities that incorporate many of the principles presented in this chapter, including teaching meaningful content, creating supportive heterogeneous groups, and using structures that ensure the active participation of all students. Many different types of activities are appropriate for the evaluation of students who are working in cooperative groups. Dippong (1992) advocates for evaluation through activities such as group reports, problem solving, seminars and debates, and simulations and role-plays.

In inclusive cooperative classrooms, teachers may want to assess individual as well as group effort and, perhaps, grade students on individual goals and/or on the basis of improvement. Individual goals can be both academically oriented and social-skill related. For example, one of Martin's objectives might be to say encouraging things to his classmates during the group lesson; Kara's objectives might relate to her writing skills or organizational leadership.

During cooperative learning activities both teachers and students can assume responsibility for evaluating the skills and contributions of group members. While students are engaging in group activities, educators often collect and share information on how groups are functioning in regard to the academic and social aspects of the lesson. This information is shared with groups both during and after the lesson. Direct observation is a valuable tool for teachers who are concerned about a student's performance in a specific area. For example, do all group members have a chance to talk, including the child who uses an alternative communication device? If not, equitable participation can be addressed with this group at the time they most need the feedback—when they are working together to complete a task. In addition, as part of cooperative learning lessons, students are often asked to discuss how they worked together to accomplish the task. This information is shared within small groups and then with the entire class. An important part of cooperative learning includes the instruction of students in how to observe, evaluate, and provide feedback to group members in positive ways. Peer evaluation affords students a chance to appreciate and critique the efforts of their peers with the group project in mind. Self-evaluation can also be a part of cooperative learning activities in which students set their own goals and share them with group members.

There are several strategies that can be used to provide a more comprehensive examination of progress within cooperative learning activities (see Cullen & Pratt, 1992). The following methods are more qualitative in nature and provide rich information about students that could not be ascertained as readily through traditional testing. For example, some teachers use a cumulative record file review system that outlines teachers' comments in subject areas, patterns of strengths as well as areas that need improvement, and affective observations. This information includes observations of students in cooperative learning groups and comments about their growth in academic and social skills. Other teachers collect both individual and group work in portfolios that can be reviewed by teachers, parents, and students on a periodic basis. The student–teacher interview is another option. Through interviews the teacher can glean much information about students' interests, motivation, knowledge, and perspectives on their contribution to the group. All of these approaches are compatible with cooperative learning and the use of authentic assessment, which is gaining attention as an important approach to determining whether students have acquired skills to select and use important concepts in authentic open-ended situations (Hibbard, 1992).

Cooperative learning activities provide a unique opportunity to evaluate important collaborative outcomes, such as interactive communication, active listening, taking the perspective of others, acceptance and accommodation of individual differences, and the evaluation of a final product developed through group effort.

APPLYING COOPERATIVE LEARNING BELIEFS AND PRINCIPLES

Knowing where to begin the process of developing cooperative learning lessons for heterogenous groups may seem daunting. There is not one "right way" to do it; one simply must jump in—with the help of some colleagues (see Villa & Thousand, chap. 6, this volume, for collaborative learning strategies for designing and implementing cooperative group lessons).

Some teachers begin by designing lessons for their whole class and then later create individualized adaptations for specific students. Others prefer to begin with one student's interests and needs and then expand the teaching concept for the whole group. Regardless of the process, the goal is to meet learning goals for individual students within a heterogeneous, cooperative learning lesson (Duncan et al., 1991).

Recently, educators attending a university course in language arts curricula development designed several cooperative learning units for their classes so that students with specific disabilities could be equal members of groups and meet their IEP goals. To guide their planning, the teachers reflected on the five elements of cooperative learning by Johnson, Johnson, Holubec, and Roy (1984): 1) face-to-face interactions, 2) positive interdependence, 3) individual accountability, 4) interpersonal and small-group skills, and 5) group processing. These elements formed the cornerstones of the lessons.

The first step teachers took was to select a grade level and a topic of interest. Working in small groups of three and four, the teachers generated ideas for the topic that could be developed into a unit of study. The five most frequently named concepts were chosen as the focal point for the unit. Once the basic lessons were sketched out, attention was turned to making adaptations for students with disabilities. Each student was described in terms of his or her learning style, interests, talents, and areas in need of support. Teaching strategies for the student were written in terms that teachers found useful; IEP goals were articulated in familiar, everyday phrases. The teachers then answered the following questions: What would be the best student composition of the groups? How would the student be best supported in a group? How would the student offer his or her talents to the group? Finally, effective evaluation strategies for the class were determined. (See Udvari-Solner, chap. 5, this volume, for specific strategies for adapting curriculum in the context of cooperative groups to accommodate students with educational and other challenges.)

One lesson developed for second grade students focuses on "dinosaurs." All aspects of the curriculum (i.e., mathematics, reading, science, social studies) are included in the unit. Students brainstorm research questions about different dinosaurs and transfer their information to a poster with illustrations. For a student with difficulty printing and recording information, coloring the illustrations with jumbo crayons is an appropriate adaptation.

Another lesson concerns "aspects of flight and flying things" for fifth grade students. Propulsion is the topic to be explored, with balloons as the primary tool in the experiment. A series of instructions are given and a lab report is the final product. For a student with difficulty reading and staying on task, instructions are provided to his or her group in a pictorial format accompanied by words. To record the results of the experiment, the student dictates his or her responses to a partner.

These two examples, as well as those detailed in the Creative Cooperative Group Lesson Plans following Section I, this volume, illustrate how students with disabilities may be meaningfully and effectively included in cooperative learning lessons. Through the consideration of the beliefs and principles articulated in this chapter, teachers can structure cooperative learning lessons that ensure active participation in learning for all students.

CONCLUSION

In this chapter, we suggest that cooperative learning is good for all students and that it is part of comprehensive school reform efforts. To achieve this reform, teachers must work together to build networks within their school community. Teachers must also establish a cooperative classroom ethic that emphasizes overall community building, open communication about differences and classroom practices, and reciprocal helping relationships. Meaningful content in cooperative lessons is critical for the success of all students. For students to succeed within their groups, careful consideration regarding group heterogeneity must be given in conjunction with roles that ensure active, equal participation by all students. Creative assessment practices must be developed to document achievement of meaningful outcomes for students. All of these considerations require planning and structure in order for the teaching to be successful.

Some of the early literature on mainstreaming assumed that children with special education needs could be considered eligible for participation in the general education classroom when they were able to *compete* successfully with other children. This orientation implies that the burden of change is on the child and that the general education classroom is a fixed, immutable environment in which some practices, such as competition, are unamenable to change or modification. A more exciting and far-reaching way of thinking about inclusion and cooperation is based on the belief that all children belong in the general education classroom. By creating a community that is cooperative and inclusive, children's acceptance and success in the general education environment will be greatly enhanced. All students and all teachers have much to gain by structuring the classroom and school environment so that it provides generous support for learning, connecting, and caring.

REFERENCES

Ayres, B., & Carnicelli, M.R. (in preparation). *Third grade students' perspectives on cooperative learning.*

Ayres, B., O'Brien, L., & Rogers, T. (1992). *Working together, sharing, and helping each other: Cooperative learning in a first grade classroom that includes students with disabilities.* Syracuse, NY: Inclusive Education Project, Syracuse University.

Cullen, B., & Pratt, T. (1992). Measuring and reporting student progress. In S. Stainback & W. Stainback (Eds.), *Curriculum considerations in inclusive classrooms: Facilitating learning for all students* (pp. 175–196). Baltimore: Paul H. Brookes Publishing Co.

Dippong, J. (1992). Two large questions in assessing and evaluating CL: Teacher challenges and appropriate student tasks. *Cooperative Learning, 13*(1), 6–8.

Duncan, J., Hedeen, D., Henneberry, M.B., Kraus, J., Weber, C., Jackson, L., Trubisky, M., & Seymour, A. (1991). *Cooperative learning lessons which promote full inclusion of students with disabilities.* Syracuse, NY: Teacher Leadership Inservice Project, Syracuse University.

Hibbard, K.M. (1992). Bringing authentic performance assessment to life with cooperative learning. *Cooperative Learning, 13*(1), 30–32.

Johnson, D.W., Johnson, R.T., Holubec, E.J., & Roy, P. (1984). *Circles of learning.* Alexandria, VA: Association for Supervision and Curriculum Development.

Matthews, M. (1992). Gifted students talk about cooperative learning. *Educational Leadership, 50*(2), 48–50.

Salisbury, C., Palombaro, M.M., & Hollowood, T.M. (1993). On the nature and change of an inclusive elementary school. *Journal of The Association for Persons with Severe Handicaps, 18*(2), 75–84.

Sapon-Shevin, M. (1990). Student support through cooperative learning. In W. Stainback & S. Stainback (Eds.), *Support networks for inclusive schooling: Interdependent integrated education* (pp. 65–79). Baltimore: Paul H. Brookes Publishing Co.

Sapon-Shevin, M. (1991). Cooperative learning in inclusive classrooms: Learning to become a community. *Cooperative Learning, 12*(1), 8–11.

Sapon-Shevin, M., & Schniedewind, N. (1989/1990). Selling cooperative learning without selling it short. *Educational Leadership, 47*(4), 63–65.

A Decision-Making Model for Curricular Adaptations in Cooperative Groups

Alice Udvari-Solner

This chapter begins with a brief examination of traditional instructional arrangements and the problems they pose for facilitating the inclusion of students with disabilities. As an alternative to these traditional approaches, the cooperative learning model, Learning Together, conceptualized by Johnson and Johnson (1975), is justified. Following this rationale, the teacher's role in formulating successful lessons is articulated. Within the context of cooperative learning, additional curricular and instructional adaptations to accommodate students with disabilities are explored. The remainder of the chapter outlines a decision-making model for collaborative problem solving between general and special educators to plan for the participation of students with unique learning needs.

LEARNING TOGETHER: A MODEL OF COOPERATIVE LEARNING TO ACCOMMODATE STUDENTS WITH DIVERSE LEARNING NEEDS

The general education population has become significantly more diverse as growing numbers of students with mild, moderate, and severe disabilities receive instruction in regular classes in their neighborhood schools. School districts that have adopted the practice of inclusive or heterogeneous schooling operate from a philosophical base that all children can learn together and that the multiplicity of learning styles found in diverse groups of children is valued (Biklen, 1985; Forest, 1987; Stainback & Stainback, 1992). In accordance with this philosophy comes a renewed emphasis on facilitating constructive interactions among students in order to build respect for others with different interests, back-grounds, and abilities. Consequently, general and special educators are faced with the challenge of designing learning experiences that ensure meaningful and active participation for all class members while at the same time fostering social and emotional growth.

When planning instruction, the first decision a teacher must make is *what* to teach. Immediately following, and inherently linked to this decision, is the question of *how* to teach the selected content. Deciding how to teach a subject, activity, or task is not a trivial or random event; instead, it must be consciously engineered to account for the various learning styles of students who comprise the class. The instructional arrangement a teacher selects directly influences how subject matter is taught. For any given subject or lesson, there are a number of instructional arrangements from which to choose. The most common alternatives for student groupings include: 1) large-group or whole-class instruction; 2) teacher-directed small-group instruction; 3) small-group learning; 4) partner learning, peer tutors, or cross-age tutors; 5) one-to-one teacher/student instruction; 6) independent or individual seat work; and 7) cooperative learning groups. Each of these instructional arrangements is defined in Table 1.

Whole-class instruction and independent seat work, which are still predominant practices in many classrooms, can be particularly problematic for students with disabilities. When whole-class instruction is used, all students receive information in the same manner and at the same rate, and they are expected to keep pace with the teacher. A high degree of attention and effective listening are usually expected in these environments. For many students with disabilities who have difficulty processing, understanding, and integrating information, it is difficult, if not impossible, to assimilate and make sense of all the information. By the nature of their size, large-group arrangements offer fewer opportunities for students to respond and stay actively involved. An underlying competitive goal structure exists within large-group question-and-answer sessions because students are in contention with one another to supply the correct answer first (Kagan, 1990). A student who supplies the correct answer essentially eliminates the opportunity for other students to participate. The most gregarious, outgoing, and assertive students are those who benefit most from this arrangement. Furthermore, students who are unable to sit attentively for an extended period (which often includes students with disabilities) have difficulty remaining focused in larger groups.

When engaged in independent seat work, students are expected to perform in a quiet, self-reliant manner while working at their desks. Long periods of independent seat work can pose similar difficulties for students with disabilities as those identified in large-group environments. Additionally, students with disabilities often require prompts, cues, and assistance to interpret classroom material used during independent seat work. Whereas many students have acquired skills to work independently, others need supervision and instruction to perform independently or even semi-independently.

Teacher-directed groups and small-group learning offer more opportunities for teacher–student and student–student contact than either large-group instruction or independent seat work. However, these arrangements do not necessarily facilitate constructive interactions between peers or build social skill repertoires.

Fortunately, there is a growing realization among educators that practices relying heavily upon teacher-directed, whole-class learning or requiring a high degree of

Table 1. Alternatives for instructional arrangements

Large-group or whole-class instruction The entire class learns the same content from the teacher. The teacher is the primary source of information. Students are usually expected to assimilate the information and work at approximately the same rate.

Teacher-directed small-group instruction The teacher instructs a small group of students, usually between five and eight. The instruction pertains to a particular topic, subject, or content area.

Small-group learning Students are allowed to work together to complete a project or they are allowed to socialize and share ideas while completing individual work. This arrangement differs from cooperative learning groups because students are not necessarily assigned roles or asked to work together to complete a common task.

Partner learning, peer tutors, or cross-age tutors The student is coached on a particular topic or assignment by a classmate or older student. Students may take turns as tutor or tutee for different subjects.

One-to-one teacher/student instruction The student receives direct instruction, supervision, or guidance from an adult. Instruction may be provided by the classroom teacher, specialist, related services personnel, classroom volunteer, and so forth.

Independent or individual seat work The student is expected to work alone on assigned homework or material that has been presented in class or previously explained.

Cooperative learning groups Students work together in groups ranging in size from two to six individuals. The students work cooperatively to achieve a common goal. Interdependence and social skills are fostered by assigning roles and responsibilities to each group member. The completion of the task is dependent upon the participation of all group members.

independent performance do not capture or capitalize on the unique learning characteristics of the majority of students in heterogeneous classrooms (Goldman & Gardner, 1989; Johnson & Johnson, 1989; Oakes & Lipton, 1990; Stainback, Stainback, & Moravec, 1992). The decision to depart from traditional instructional arrangements and employ cooperative learning or partner learning may be the single most effective step to facilitate the inclusion of a student with disabilities. As substantiated in previous chapters, cooperative learning promotes peer interaction, establishes options for participation through a division of responsibility, and provides frequent opportunities for student initiation and the application of skills.

Since the early 1970s, a variety of cooperative learning models have emerged, each with their own value and application. A few of the most well-known techniques are Jigsaw (Aronson, Blaney, Stephan, Sikes, & Snapp, 1978); Student Teams—Achievement Divisions (Slavin, 1978); Group Investigation (Sharan & Sharan, 1976); Teams-Games-Tournament (DeVries & Slavin, 1978); and Team Assisted Individualization (Slavin, Leavey, & Madden, 1986). (For a concise summary of various cooperative learning models, see Johnson & Johnson, 1991; Kagan, 1990; and Slavin, 1990. Also see Johnson & Johnson, chap. 3, this volume.) These models also have been referred to as *cooperative structures* because they offer a series of steps for organizing instruction (Kagan, 1990). Although each of these techniques has merit, the cooperative learning model designed by Johnson and Johnson (1975), known as Learning Together, is particularly well suited for use in heterogeneous classrooms. Johnson and Johnson (1991) characterize their model as a *conceptual approach* to group learning, whereas the other models cited are considered *direct approaches*. Direct approaches are associated with very specific strategies that have different functions or domains of usefulness (Kagan, 1990). The Johnsons' approach emphasizes that teachers must learn the essential elements of positive interdependence, face-to-face interaction, individual accountability, social skills, and group processing, and then apply the concepts to their unique instructional circumstances. This approach is content-free; that is, it is not linked to any particular academic task or objective and can be used across grade levels (Sapon-Shevin, 1990). Consequently, the use of this model becomes metacognitive, allowing teachers to manipulate any lesson.

Another clear advantage of the Learning Together model is its concentration on the development and use of social skills. Social interactions are not viewed as mere by-products of group work; instead, social contact is used as a tool for fostering learning (Sharan & Sharan, 1976). By virtue of its strong theoretical framework, Learning Together offers a model to design lessons across content areas, across grade levels, and across students with very divergent social and academic skills.

THE TEACHER'S ROLE IN DESIGNING LESSONS

When cooperative groups are utilized, the teacher's role shifts from that of information giver to facilitator and manager of learning. The teacher is pivotal in ensuring the success of groups and must engage in a number of critical instructional decisions. Seven steps enable the teacher to establish the principles of positive interdependence, individual accountability, face-to-face interaction, social skills, and group processing. These steps are: 1) identify academic and social objectives; 2) determine group size, membership, and duration of group affiliation; 3) arrange the learning environment; 4) establish positive interdependence; 5) explain the criteria for academic and social success; 6) monitor student performance; and 7) provide closure to the lesson and evaluate the product and progress of group work. Each of these steps is discussed on the following pages.

Identify Academic and Social Objectives

Before the lesson begins, the teacher must specify two types of objectives: academic and social. Academic objectives relate to the curricular content of what is to be learned. Most teachers are familiar with designing academic objectives; however, when planning for cooperative groups keep in mind that the academic goals can be group-oriented or relate to individual performance. For example, in a seventh grade social studies class, students working in cooperative groups were expected to design a survey and poll a random sample of classmates regarding their opinions about the presidential candidates. The academic objectives related to *group* performance were:

1. Each group will submit a list of five survey questions related to the presidential campaign.
2. Each group will submit one graph of their survey findings, which is labeled and charted correctly (title, numeration, labeling of X and Y axis).

An academic objective related to *individual* performance for the same activity was:

3. After completion of the project, each group member will be able to summarize the survey findings in a written paragraph.

All three objectives address academic performance. These examples illustrate that objectives can be formulated to encourage both group and individual accountability.

The second type of objective that must be designated is social or collaborative in nature. The teacher may select one or several social skills to emphasize during a lesson. Based upon its composition, each classroom has its own social climate and level of social competence. Key skills may surface within a classroom that require ongoing practice across activities, such as active listening or encouraging. Sometimes social skills are selected that relate directly to the completion of the activity. For example, an activity in which students must contribute ideas to make up a futuristic society requires the use of consensus seeking skills. The teacher has the freedom to select the highest priority skills for a class or particular activity. It is important to note that students will need repeated exposure to and practice in any social skill before it is internalized and used spontaneously. A list of potential social skills for consideration is found in Table 2.

Determine Group Size, Membership, and Duration of Group Affiliation

The size of cooperative learning groups usually ranges from two to six members. An upper limit of six members is imposed to preserve the element of face-to-face interaction and maintain meaningful participation of all participants. Bennett, Rolheiser-Bennett, and Stevahn (1991) offer the following guidelines to determine group size:

1. Partner work tends to promote involvement because interaction opportunities are more frequent within a dyad. Students new to cooperative methods may do better in groups of two or three.
2. Tasks that demand diversity in thinking or a range of skills and expertise can be best accomplished with larger groups of three to four members.
3. Larger groups require members to be more adept at fostering working relationships.
4. The nature of the task or availability of materials may dictate the group size. For example, a task that neatly divides into four distinct steps may be well suited to a group of four students.
5. The shorter the time period, the smaller the groups need to be to maximize participation.

As a general rule, the membership of groups should be heterogeneous across ability level, ethnicity, gender, and socioeconomic level. More perspective-taking, elaborative thinking, and exchange of information have been noted as beneficial outcomes of heterogeneous groups when compared to their homogeneous counterparts (Johnson & Johnson, 1991; Slavin, 1990). Groups may be formed on a temporary or long-term basis. *Base groups* may be formed for a semester, entire year, or maintained for several years. This long-term affiliation is designed to provide peer support both socially and academically, as well as to hold members accountable for performance. *Formal groups* are focused on the completion of specific learning tasks and

Table 2. Potential social skills for consideration

Contributing ideas	Exhibiting self-control (managing anger, keeping hands to self)
Asking questions	
Expressing feelings	Sharing materials
Encouraging members to participate	Perspective-taking
Providing constructive feedback	Active listening
Disagreeing without criticizing	Summarizing
Elaborating on a comment or answer	Paraphrasing
Checking for understanding	Staying on task
Using humor to enhance group cohesiveness	Staying with the group
Expressing support and acceptance toward ideas	Turn-taking
Expressing warmth and empathy toward group members	Resolving conflicts
	Asking for help

may form for a number of days or stay together across several weeks. *Informal groups* differ from the previous two arrangements because they are short-term (i.e., one discussion or class period) and less structured. Within partnerships or groups of three, students help each other focus on class material, organize information into manageable increments, and debrief one another after receiving information.

Arrange the Learning Environment

To facilitate interaction, students should be arranged in circles or clusters. Space constraints may be artificially imposed to avoid students "staking out" a location away from their groups. A helpful rule of thumb is to keep sufficient space between teams to reduce distractions and allow easy access by the instructor. Because the intent is to keep students "eye to eye" or "knee to knee," it may be necessary to make arrangements for a group to move to the floor if a team member who uses a wheelchair must be transferred for positioning or comfort reasons.

Establish Positive Interdependence

Positive interdependence is achieved when students feel linked by a common bond or purpose. Structuring a team goal and establishing division of responsibility are central to establish team cohesiveness. The fundamental categories of interdependence are goal, resource, role, and incentive.

Goal Interdependence Goal interdependence occurs when a common purpose has been established. This usually involves the completion of one product to which each group member has contributed. A common social objective may also be the focus of interdependence. Success might be gauged by each member engaging in the desired behavior.

Resource Interdependence Resource interdependence can be engineered by arranging one set of shared materials or distributing information among group members so that single elements must be interfaced for the completion of the product.

Role Interdependence Role interdependence requires that each group member assume a specified responsibility that is interconnected to the functioning of other group members. Roles may be created and assigned to capitalize on students' strengths or compensate for a weakness. Roles can be task oriented or social. A few examples of useful roles include reader, writer, summarizer, coach, observer, encourager, jargon-buster, materials manager, quality controller, and illustrator. Often the nature of the task will dictate the type and number of appropriate roles.

Incentive Interdependence Incentive interdependence results when the same reward, grade, or advantage is given to group members for the successful performance of all teammates.

Other forms of interdependence may be pertinent also. When students are placed in competition with some external element (i.e., other groups, time, the group's previous score), outside interdependence is achieved. Group cohesiveness can be enhanced by employing identity interdependence through the use of a group name, motto, song, or secret code.

The use of the four fundamental categories of interdependence creates a firm structure within which students can operate. When planned correctly, students can see their part in the accomplishment of the "whole" and they become motivated by the responsibility to others.

Explain the Criteria for Academic and Social Success

To ensure class members understand their charge as a group, the instructor must take a leadership role in presenting the performance expectations. Performance expectations are the criteria by which students will be evaluated in both the academic and social domains. For example, criteria for success might be to complete a task, meet key quality standards, answer a minimum number of questions correctly, or exhibit a specific social skill. At this time the teacher should make a distinction between group goals and the requirements for individual accountability. The teacher may provide examples and models of the desired skills. An explanation of their importance to the students' current and future endeavors can be helpful to establish the usefulness and validity of selected skills.

Monitor Student Performance

The teacher's role intensifies once students are working in their groups. Even though groups may be engaged in a task, it does not mean students are employing group skills with ease. Consequently, teachers must move about the room to monitor performance and determine whether intervention is necessary. Unobtrusive observations can determine whether students understand the academic task and utilize cooperative skills. Teachers can use an observation sheet designed so that data on the frequency and quality of appropriate behaviors can be gathered. This data collection signals the teacher when intervention is necessary for task assistance or instruction in collaborative skills. When a group is not working well together, the teacher should first look for ways of turning the problem solving back to group members.

The teacher usually has a primary role in monitoring group performance; however, student monitoring can be powerful in promoting group reflection. Students can be assigned as observers within groups or across several groups. When students are learning to be observers, it is advisable to limit the number of skills observed; limit the observation time; rotate the role of observer among students; and, above all, provide instruction so that students can accurately identify the skills of concern (Bennett et al., 1991).

Provide Closure to the Lesson and
Evaluate the Product and Progress of Group Work

At the conclusion of the lesson, the teacher facilitates a review of the desired outcomes. This is a time to summarize important points and answer any remaining questions posed by students. Time is allotted for students and the teacher to evaluate achievement of the academic and social objectives. Direct feedback is provided about the quantity and quality of work as it compares to the criteria for success. This is not the sole responsibility of the teacher; thus, student opinions can be solicited regarding each group's accomplishments. Before the lesson ends, students engage in group processing—a self-assessment of how well the group functioned. The quality of collaboration can be appraised by asking students to generate examples of actions they performed, as a group and individually, that helped them work together. The teacher can also compare his or her observations to the group's perception. This discussion should lead to the identification of new personal and group goals for subsequent activities.

The seven steps in the teacher's role are fundamental in planning for any cooperative learning situation and serve as the foundation for organizing heterogenous groups of students. When students with disabilities are integral members of a class, additional accommodations are often necessary to ensure meaningful participation and desired learning outcomes. A decision-making model to design appropriate curricular and instructional adaptations is described in the following section.

MAKING CURRICULAR ADAPTATIONS IN THE CONTEXT OF COOPERATIVE GROUPS

In a general sense, a curricular adaptation may be defined as any adjustment or modification in the environment, instruction, or materials used for learning that enhances a person's performance or allows at least partial participation in an activity (Baumgart et al., 1982; Udvari-Solner, 1992). The purpose of an adaptation is to assist the individual to compensate for intellectual, physical, sensory, or behavioral challenges (Nisbet et al., 1983). Furthermore, an adaptation allows the individual to use his or her current skill repertoire while promoting the acquisition of new skills. Embedded in this definition is the concept of *partial participation*. Partial participation is considered to be *at least some degree of active involvement in a task or activity* (Baumgart et al., 1982; Ferguson & Baumgart, 1991). The principle of partial participation acknowledges that many students, particularly those with severe disabilities, might never learn the skills to perform an activity with complete independence. Partial participation is central to the involvement of students with all types of disabilities in general education classrooms because it reinforces the idea that a student should not be excluded from an activity due to the fact only a portion of the required skills can be performed.

Modifications that relate specifically to instruction or curricular content in general education environments are referred to as *curricular adaptations*. Curricular adaptations fit the general definition offered; however, they also serve the important function of preventing a mismatch between the student's skills and the general education lesson content (Giangreco & Putnam, 1991). Curricular adaptations can make the difference between a student merely being present in the classroom and being actively involved in daily school life. When collaboratively engineered, curricular adaptations can minimize the differences between students with varied abilities. Successful modifications individualize the lesson content and help create a match between the student's learning style and the instructor's teaching style. Therefore, most adaptations employed in the general education classroom address either the way instruction is arranged and delivered or the way the student takes part in an activity. In many ways, these two factors are interrelated because the way instruction is delivered directly affects how the student is expected to respond and participate.

The first and foremost modification teachers can make to accommodate students with disabilities is to arrange cooperative learning groups. Teachers must examine their existing instructional arrangements and determine when large-group or teacher-directed tasks can be appropriately transformed into cooperative structures. As an alternative to independent seat work, the use of partner learning or peer tutors should be seriously considered.

Within the context of cooperative learning, additional adaptations for students with disabilities may be needed in the areas of: 1) lesson format (Ferguson & Baumgart, 1991; Ford & Black, 1989; Ford & Davern, 1989; Peterson, LeRoy, Field, & Wood, 1992); 2) teaching style or delivery of instruction (Ferguson & Jeanchild, 1992; Hoover, 1987; Wood & Meiderhoff, 1988; Wood & Rosbe, 1985); 3) curricular goals and evaluation criteria (Carpenter, 1985; Ferguson & Baumgart, 1991; Giangreco & Putnam, 1991; Salend, 1990; Stainback et al., 1992; Wood & Aldridge, 1985); 4) environmental and social conditions (Piuma & Udvari-Solner, 1993; Udvari-Solner, 1992); 5) learning materials (Bigge, 1988; Cassella & Bigge, 1988; Udvari-Solner, 1992); and 6) level of support (Rainforth, York, & Macdonald, 1992).

The process to select and utilize appropriate adaptations can be operationalized as an eight component decision-making model. This eight component model, summarized in Table 3, is framed by a series of questions to facilitate communication between general and special educators *before* instructional decisions have been made for the entire class. The adaptation strategies move from the least intrusive to more intrusive means of modification. By addressing eight key questions, teachers are guided to consider changes in the structure of instruction, demands and evaluation criteria of the task, learning environment, the way the task is done, and the student's support structure. The first question addresses changes in instructional arrangements that related to the previous discussion of the structure and benefits of coopera-

Table 3. Eight component decision-making models for designing curricular adaptations to cooperative learning lessons

Change the Structure of the Instruction

1. Can the student's participation be increased by arranging the lesson in:
   Cooperative groups?
   Partner learning?
   Peer tutors or cross-age tutors?
2. Can the student's participation be increased by changing the lesson format?
   Activity-based lessons, games, simulations, role-plays
   Experiential lessons
   Community-based lessons
3. Can the student's participation and understanding be increased by changing the delivery of instruction or teaching style?

Change the Demands of the Task and Criteria for Success

4. Will the student need adapted curricular goals?
   Adjust performance standards
   Adjust pacing
   Same content but less complex
   Similar content with functional/direct applications
5. Will changes be needed in the evaluation system?
   Arrange criterion-referenced or personalized evaluation

Change Elements of the Learning Environment

6. Can changes be made in the classroom environment or lesson location that will facilitate participation?
   Environmental/physical
   Social
   Lesson location

Change the Way the Task Is Done

7. Will different materials be needed to ensure participation?
   Same content but variation in size, number, or format
   Additional or different materials or devices

Change the Support Structure

8. Will personal assistance be needed to ensure participation?
   From peers or general education instructor
   From someone other than the general educator and peers

tive learning. Consequently, each of the seven remaining questions is addressed on the following pages.

Can the Student's Participation Be Increased by Changing the Lesson Format?

Tied closely to instructional arrangements is lesson format. Teachers use a variety of methods to organize an academic task and impart information to students. The traditional and most frequently used lesson format is lecture/demonstration/practice (Callahan & Clark, 1988), also referred to as the expository mode of teaching. With this format, the teacher provides an explanation of a concept or topic, then supports verbal information with an illustration or model. A lecture/demonstration format often is followed by students participating in a class discussion or practicing the concepts covered by the teacher. For example, a second grade teacher introduces the short vowel sound of the letter "O." She models the correct pronunciation and points out the sound as it appears in the weekly spelling words. Several members of the class are called on to select words with the short "O" sound from an array of words. After a 20-minute explanation, the children are directed to complete four pages in their spelling workbooks. This type of lesson format is often textbook guided and relies heavily on the teach-practice-test methodology.

Fortunately, the use of cooperative learning limits the time an instructor can spend in this traditional teaching paradigm as teacher-directed scenarios are kept to a minimum. Yet, there is always the danger that teachers will just impose old lesson formats into cooperative structures. For example, it is possible to structure cooperative lessons so that the teacher demonstrates a skill then provides group time to practice prosaic academic tasks, such as filling out a worksheet, answering comprehension questions, completing a test, or memorizing a list of facts that are suggested in texts and curriculum guides. Teachers must ask themselves if a traditional textbook-driven drill and practice approach is necessary or whether other lesson formats would more fully engage students, including those with disabilities.

Much more in keeping with the spirit of cooperative learning are activity-based, experiential, and community-referenced lessons. Activity-based lessons include games, simulations, role-playing, and presentations. These lessons reinforce or extend the lesson content and encourage students to apply the information that has been previously taught or discussed. This type of lesson is characterized by students: 1) being actively engaged, 2) participating in the planning process, 3) learning by discovery, and 4) constructing their own knowledge. These activities are relatively short in duration, usually one class period or a portion of a class period. For example, after a brief introduction to a science chapter on genetics, the class is divided into cooperative groups. Each group conducts a mini-survey to record and graph the prevalence of certain genetic traits in the sixth grade student population. After surveys are completed, each team presents its findings to the class.

Experiential lessons use real life activities to apply or enhance skills. Activities can take place in the classroom or nonschool environments. These lessons can be as short as one class period, employed during a number of weeks, or occur on a regularly scheduled basis throughout the year. For example, the students in a beginning architectural drawing class must design and build a small storage shed at a local park. In the context of this activity, which lasts for 10 weeks, the students draw a feasible plan, order appropriate materials, and apply construction skills. Experiential lessons are also appropriate in lower grade levels. For instance, in a first grade classroom, students are asked to bring simple recipes for healthy snacks and beverages from home. On a weekly basis during language arts, cooperative groups of students plan and cook a healthy snack that is shared with the class. The students write their own recipe, make a grocery list, calculate the correct amount of money, purchase the groceries, and prepare the snack. As a result of this year-long activity, a student-generated recipe book is developed.

Community-based or community-referenced instruction has been considered a best practice in the education of students with moderate and severe disabilities since the early 1970s (Brown et al., 1979). The value of this teaching format for all students, regardless of disability, is being realized now by many educators (Peterson et al., 1992). Community-referenced instruction is characterized by students applying skills in non-school environments that have some relationship, relevance, and purpose to their lives now or in the future. Instruction may relate to vocational, domestic, community, or recreation curricular domains. This lesson format differs from experiential lessons because it takes place exclusively in the community and occurs on a regularly scheduled basis across the year.

The value of activity-based, experiential, and community-referenced formats for students with disabilities is that learning takes place as a result of a dynamic interaction between the student and the environment. Furthermore, learning is arranged in concrete and applied ways. Sharan and Sharan (1976) state,

> We are most likely to increase the child's chances of gratification from learning experiences by maximizing his role in the planning and carrying out [of] learning tasks. Too much of traditional school teaching is in rote fashion and bears little meaning to students. (p. 4)

If this assumption is true for typical students, it is an even more legitimate consideration for students with disabilities.

Can the Student's Participation and Understanding Be Increased by Changing the Delivery of Instruction or Teaching Style?

Recall that one function of adaptations is to create a match between the student's skills and the lesson content. The solution to creating this match often lies within the teacher's own behavior. A few simple guidelines that educators can follow to alter or adjust their delivery of instruction or teaching style are listed below.

Tell the student exactly what you want him or her to learn or accomplish.
Simplify instructions and demonstrate what you want completed.
Use concrete materials or examples that relate to the student's life.
Reduce irrelevant details and emphasize the essential attributes of concepts.
Divide material to be learned into smaller tasks and sequence learning tasks from
    easy to hard, concrete to abstract.
Provide repeated opportunities to practice the skill(s) of concern.
Provide regular and frequent feedback throughout a lesson when teaching new
    information.
Monitor and provide feedback or intervention *before* errors are made to establish a
    pattern of success.
Incorporate learning games and the use mnemonic devices to recall information.
Desensitize the student to stressful situations by moving through a series of progres-
    sively more demanding steps.

Model and encourage self-advocacy skills (e.g., requesting an alternative presentation style, stating when material is too difficult or confusing).
Back up oral information with alternative methods of input, such as a headset or
tape player, highlighted information, or written directions.
Elaborate or shape a student's response to correspond with the context of the lesson.

In addition to these basic techniques, when cooperative groups are employed the
teacher might provide antecedent coaching to the student with disabilities in needed
collaborative or academic skills (Johnson & Johnson, 1989). The goal, here, is to improve the student's comfort level and develop confidence in contributing to the group.
Teachers must also remember to include more frequent verbal prompts and direct
physical assistance, when necessary, for students with more significant disabilities.

Will the Student Need Adapted Curricular Goals?

To match the unique needs and skills of students with disabilities within the context
of a general education activity, it may be appropriate to individualize learning objectives. Varied outcomes and goals, also referred to as *multilevel* or *flexible* learning
objectives (Giangreco & Putnam, 1991; Stainback et al., 1992) may be needed for one
or several students to experience success in the lesson.

In a heterogeneous classroom, learners acquire and apply knowledge at different levels and rates. Bloom's taxonomy of instructional objectives outlines six levels
of learning (Bloom, 1956). These levels include knowledge, comprehension, application, analysis, synthesis, and evaluation. Educational goals can be individualized
based upon the student's learning priorities at each of these levels. For example, a
cooperative group of three students must create a story about Alaskan wildlife that
will be presented orally to the class. One of the group members has severe intellectual
and dual sensory impairments. The students have the option to develop audiovisual
materials to communicate their story, select music to complement the presentation,
or act out the story line dramatically. This particular group decides to make a diorama to represent Alaskan terrain and clay figures to depict the animals in the
story. The learning objectives for the two students without disabilities relate to applying and synthesizing past information, composing a sensible story, utilizing correct grammar, and employing accurate handwriting skills. The curricular objectives
for the student with disabilities focus on participating in the creation of the diorama
figures, following tactile signs from his classmates, and making choices within the
context of the activity. These objectives represent learning at the knowledge and
comprehension level, whereas the objectives of his teammates represent learning
that requires application, analysis, and synthesis.

All of the students in the group are expected to practice specified cooperative
skills as a social objective. For the two students without disabilities this means using
encouraging statements and gentle physical touch with one another. For the student
with dual sensory impairments, cooperative skills translate to accepting guidance
from a friend without resisting physical touch. Individualizing social and academic
objectives, attending to each student's level of learning, and acknowledging the value
of each child's educational priorities combine to allow the three students to work effectively in a heterogeneous group.

Changes in curricular goals may be significant, as illustrated in the example, or
they can be as minor as allowing one student more time to complete an assignment,
perform fewer test items per page, or master only the highest priority material from

a unit. Curricular goals can be modified to: 1) relate to the same content but be less complex, 2) have functional or direct applications, 3) reduce the performance standards, or 4) adjust the pacing of a lesson. When using a flexible or multilevel orientation with curricular goals, it is also important to remember that academics per se or mastery of skills related to traditional content areas may not be the primary concern or fundamental reason for a student's inclusion in a specific subject area. The social aspects of the activity and the skills that facilitate interpersonal relationships may be considered of equal or greater importance and, therefore, should be regarded as viable learning outcomes (Stainback & Stainback, 1992; York, Vandercook, Caughey, & Heise-Neff, 1988). When determining appropriate learning outcomes for students with disabilities, the selection of curricular goals always should be coordinated with the educational priorities stated in their individualized education programs.

Will Changes Be Needed in the Evaluation System?

Changes in the evaluation criteria and system of assessing performance are often appropriate modifications for students with disabilities. According to Cullen and Pratt (1992), evaluation can serve several purposes: 1) to determine whether objectives have been achieved, 2) to assist in the development and implementation of an education plan, 3) to assist the instructor to identify future teaching directions, and 4) to provide information about the quality of the learning environment.

Reliance on norm-referenced systems defeat these evaluation purposes for students with disabilities because their performance will almost always fall below the scores of the nondisabled comparison group. Norm-referenced systems result in a clear ranking of students by ability, but this information does very little to tell the teacher about the student's learning relative to his or her educational priorities (Shriner, Ysseldyke, & Christenson, 1989).

Criterion-referenced systems are necessary replacements for norm-referenced and standardized measurements when employing cooperative learning. The teacher may select a pre-set standard that reflects the student's abilities and knowledge base. Instructors may still use teacher-made objective tests, essay tests, and oral questioning to assess performance, but personalized criteria may be set for students with unique learning needs.

Given the fact that many students with disabilities will never be able to take a written test or answer complex oral questions, a sensible evaluation alternative is to arrange incidental or situational observations (Wolf, 1984). Incidental observations can occur during the course of regular activities. Students are not singled out to perform, instead they are either demonstrating or not demonstrating the skill(s) of concern when the observation takes place. This technique interfaces nicely with the duties of the teacher to monitor students during cooperative learning sessions. A situational test is a bit more formal, requiring the student to demonstrate the skill under certain conditions or in the context of a real activity. Other methods of evaluation that do not require testing are the use of dossiers and student portfolios, which are particularly effective in showing student improvement over time (Malehorn, 1984; Wolf, 1989).

Within the realm of criterion-referenced systems, teachers may also consider group grades or ratings for products produced collaboratively. The group may be given one performance rating or individual ratings can be averaged for a collective group score. A viable technique noted by Slavin (1990) is to add each student's "gain scores" for a group grade. To calculate a gain score, students come to the group with a base score that represents previous performance. After group work, individual tests are taken and students contribute to the group with the number of points improved from their base score.

When curricular goals differ, should the same letter grades be given to students with disabilities as those given to students without disabilities? The inclusion of students with disabilities often sparks this question about the use of letter grades to represent achievement (Carpenter, 1985). Professionals and parents must first decide *what* the grade is intended to communicate. As long as all parties agree on the intent of the grade and understand that it represents performance with the use of curricular adaptations, then there is no reason to eliminate this method of feedback. For communication purposes, teachers and parents may decide that grades representing effort, improvement, and attitude be assigned separately from academic achievement ratings.

Can Changes Be Made in the Classroom Environment or Lesson Location that Will Facilitate Participation?

Circumstances in the learning environment can affect any student's ability to acquire information. When lessons are designed with students in mind who have sensory impairments, physical disabilities, information processing difficulties, or alternative communication methods, modifications in environmental conditions may be particularly warranted. Environmental conditions refer to such things as lighting, noise level, visual and auditory input, physical arrangement of the room or equipment, and accessibility of materials.

A student who requires adaptive materials or devices may need additional space for an expanded work area. Placing the student's desk next to a large work table or providing a bookshelf that is easily accessible provides a simple accommodation. A student who has difficulty sitting with his cooperative group for any period of time may be equipped with more than one desk or seat in the room, allowing the child to move to different locations when needed without disrupting the class (J.A. Keith, personal communication, April 1991). Other environmental adaptations may include space for maneuvering a wheelchair or a comfortable area for a student to stretch out on the floor when a break from sitting in a wheelchair is required.

Alternative locations for group work may also be appropriate. Using space in the hallway, library, or outdoors may enhance the functioning of the student with disabilities by reducing distractions. Occasionally, changes in the social climate or social rules of the classroom are needed to accommodate a student with disabilities. This might involve allowing a higher noise level in the room for a student who occasionally makes loud vocalizations or allowing partners to read to one another when other students are expected to read silently.

Will Different Instructional Materials Be Needed to Ensure Participation?

Teachers use an assortment of materials for instruction that can include such items as standard curriculum texts, magazines, newspapers, trade books, filmstrips, movies, manipulatives, games, art supplies, computers, and items used in daily life (Callahan & Clark, 1988; Ferguson & Jeanchild, 1992). Students with disabilities may benefit from using the same materials as other students in class, require slight variations, or need alternative materials. Materials may be changed or created to be more manipulable, concrete, tangible, simplified, and matched to the student's learning style or comprehension level. For example, a student in second grade is unable to solve math story problems when the equations are presented only in written form. Yet, when provided with Unifix Cubes (small, interlocking plastic blocks that can be easily manipulated) and allowed to carry out the steps of the mathematical equations with the blocks, she is able to solve the problems. Another student is unable to handle small objects or understand the abstraction of math problems presented in a paper and pencil format; yet, he is able to apply math concepts during attendance by counting the number of cards presented by classmates that represent the choice of hot or cold lunch. The materials required to facilitate his participation and understanding are real, tangible, and contextually based.

Variations in materials must always be age-appropriate and status enhancing. In a high school contemporary affairs class, a syndicated news magazine is used as the primary text. To accommodate a student with disabilities who is unable to read, the class materials were modified in two ways. Classmates without disabilities were enlisted to read selected articles then record themselves on audiotape while paraphrasing the content. These tapes were available for the student with disabilities prior to each class. In addition, the student with disabilities was asked to videotape three airings of CNN news each week. These film clips were shown and discussed in class. Both of these adaptations matched the student's individual learning style without being stigmatizing and illustrated the reciprocal contributions of students with and without disabilities.

Will Personal Assistance Be Needed to Ensure Participation?

In the classroom during cooperative learning, the general education teacher provides direct instruction, facilitates learning among students, or monitors behavior and performance. Spontaneous assistance is provided when it is requested by the student, needed by the student to perform correctly, or required to maintain classroom control. Many students with disabilities need higher levels of assistance or intervention than are provided to typical students. The need for assistance may range from periodic spot checks to close continuous supervision. Assistance may vary from day to day or be required at predictable times. Providing prompts, verbal cues, gestures, or physical assistance can support the student's participation on a temporary or ongoing basis.

Personal assistance can be provided by a variety of individuals in the school environment including peers, cross-age tutors (i.e., coaching from an older student), the general educator, special educator, related services personnel, classroom volunteers, or instructional assistants (Vandercook & York, 1990; York, Giangreco, Vandercook, & Macdonald, 1992). To facilitate inclusion and independence, an implicit goal should be to reduce the need for paid or specialized assistance over time. Consequently, it is preferable that natural supports or support that can be provided by the general education teacher and peers be employed to the greatest extent possible.

Regular prompts, cues, and even physical assistance can often be incorporated as inconspicuous elements of the teaching sequence, which do not interfere with the instruction or the learning of others in the classroom. Assistance and support to a student with disabilities from his teammates are integral parts of cooperative learning when social goals of modeling, helping, and encouraging are promoted. Initially, the teacher must monitor groups closely to check that techniques are employed correctly and assistance does not regress to doing the task for the student. The intervention or assistance from someone outside of the classroom structure can sometimes cause the student to be stigmatized and reduce spontaneous interactions from peers in the environment. Therefore, assignment of a full-time assistant should be assessed cautiously and avoided whenever possible.

PLANNING FOR THE DEVELOPMENT OF CURRICULAR ADAPTATIONS: A SHARED RESPONSIBILITY

There are many ways to categorize and conceptualize curricular adaptations. The curricular adaptations that have been discussed provide a framework from which to make decisions. For any given activity, a student with disabilities may require no modifications beyond the cooperative group structure or a combination of several adaptations. The curricular adaptation planning form shown in Figure 1 has been helpful in facilitating communication and recording decisions among team members as they design adaptations.

Ongoing communication and cooperation between general educators, special educators, and related services personnel are essential to establish useful curricular adaptations (Morsink, Thomas, & Correa, 1991; Vandercook & York, 1990). Without shared responsibility among professionals, adaptations will not be available when they are needed throughout the school day. The planning process most often fails when one professional bears the sole responsibility for designing and implementing the modifications. When a collaborative team approach is used, each professional brings unique expertise to the problem-solving situation, ownership of the problem is shared, and responsibility to implement solutions is distributed fairly among team members (Graden & Bauer, 1992; Thousand & Villa, 1992). When school personnel abide by these basic tenets of collaboration, each member of the student's educational team plays an active role in the planning, design, or implementation of curricular adaptations. The collaborative ethic and the team process to plan cooperative lessons are discussed in detail in Chapter 6, this volume. For a collection of cooperative lesson plans that embody joint efforts between professionals, refer to the Creative Cooperative Group Lesson Plans at the end of Section I.

A commitment to the principles of inclusion brings with it new roles for educators and new expectations for teaching practices. Well-conceived cooperative lesson plans that include curricular adaptations can maximize abilities and minimize disabilities in the general education classroom. Effective adaptations promote opportunities for face-to-face interactions with peers, increase the student's opportunities to be an initiator and active participant, and reduce the level of abstraction of information while making activities more concrete and meaningful to the student's current and future life.

Selecting the right adaptations is still an imprecise science. There are no definitive sources to say, "If you experience this type of disability, then you need this precise adaptation." Good adaptations come from the thoughtful, collective observations and foresight of parents, peers, and professionals. Albert Einstein was quoted as saying, "Imagination is more important than knowledge" (as cited in Farber, 1985, p. 147). This statement rings true when adapting cooperative lessons. Team members must allow themselves to think and create beyond the confines of traditional teaching conventions. When this happens, the result is beneficial for all learners.

GENERAL INSTRUCTIONAL PLAN	DO CHANGES NEED TO BE MADE IN:		
Date:			
Content Area/Subject:	Instructional Arrangement?	Lesson Format?	Delivery of Instruction Teaching Style?
Instructor:			
Estimated Time:			
Activity:			
	Academic & Social Goals? Evaluation System?	Social/Physical Environment Conditions or Lesson Location?	Instructional Materials?
Materials:	Level of Personal Assistance?	Any Other Adaptations or Considerations?	

Figure 1. Curriculum adaptation planning form.

REFERENCES

Aronson, E., Blaney, N., Stephan, C., Sikes, J., & Snapp, M. (1978). *The Jigsaw classroom*. Beverly Hills: Sage Publications.

Baumgart, D., Brown, L., Pumpian, I., Nisbet, J., Ford, A., Sweet, M., Messina, R., & Schroeder, J. (1982). Principle of partial participation and individualized adaptations in educational programs for severely handicapped students. *Journal of The Association for Persons with Severe Handicaps, 7*, 17–43.

Bennett, B., Rolheiser-Bennett, C., & Stevahn, L. (1991). *Cooperative learning: Where heart meets mind*. Toronto: Educational Connections.

Bigge, J. (1988). Modifying student response methods. In J. Bigge (Ed.), *Curriculum-based instruction for special education students* (pp. 64–109). Mountain View, CA: Mayfield Publishing Company.

Biklen, D. (1985). *Achieving the complete school: Effective strategies for mainstreaming*. New York: Teachers College Press.

Bloom, B.S. (1956). *Taxonomy of educational objectives: Handbook I. Cognitive domain*. New York: David McCay Co.

Brown, L., Branston, M., Baumgart, D., Vincent, L., Falvey, M., & Schroeder, J. (1979). Utilizing the characteristics of current and subsequent least restrictive environments as factors in the development of curricular content for severely handicapped students. *AAESPH Review, 4*(4) 407–424.

Callahan, J., & Clark, L. (1988). *Teaching in the middle and secondary schools: Planning for competence* (3rd ed.). New York: Macmillan.

Carpenter, D. (1985). Grading handicapped pupils: Review and position statement. *Remedial and Special Education, 6*(4), 54–59.

Cassella, V., & Bigge, J. (1988). Modifying instructional modalities and conditions for curriculum access. In J. Bigge (Ed.), *Curriculum-based instruction for special education students* (pp. 110–140). Mountain View, CA: Mayfield Publishing Company.

Cullen, B., & Pratt, T. (1992). Measuring and reporting student progress. In S. Stainback & W. Stainback (Eds.), *Curriculum considerations in inclusive classrooms: Facilitating learning for all students* (pp. 175–196). Baltimore: Paul H. Brookes Publishing Co.

DeVries, D.L., & Slavin, R.E. (1978). Teams-Games-Tournament (TGT): A review of ten classroom experiments. *Journal of Research and Development in Education, 12*, 28–38.

Farber, B.E. (1985). *A teacher's treasury of quotations*. Jefferson, NC: McFarland & Co.

Ferguson, D., & Baumgart, D. (1991). *Partial participation revisited*. (Available from Schools Projects, Specialized Training Program, University of Oregon, Eugene, Oregon 97403)

Ferguson, D.L., & Jeanchild, L.A. (1992). It's not a matter of method: Thinking about how to implement curricular decisions. In S. Stainback & W. Stainback (Eds.), *Curriculum considerations in inclusive classrooms: Facilitating learning for all students* (pp. 159–174). Baltimore: Paul H. Brookes Publishing Co.

Ford, A., & Black, J. (1989). The community-referenced curriculum for students with moderate and severe disabilities. In D. Biklen, D. Ferguson, & A. Ford (Eds.), *Schooling and disability* (pp 141–167). Chicago: The University of Chicago Press.

Ford, A., & Davern, L. (1989). Moving forward with school integration: Strategies for involving students with severe handicaps in the life of the school. In R. Gaylord-Ross (Ed.), *Integration strategies for students with handicaps* (pp. 11–33). Baltimore: Paul H. Brookes Publishing Co.

Forest, M. (Ed.). (1987). *More education/integration: A further collection of readings on the integration of children with mental handicaps into regular school systems*. Downsview, Ontario, Canada: G. Allan Roeher Institute.

Giangreco, M.F., & Putnam, J.W. (1991). Supporting the education of students with severe disabilities in regular education environments. In L.H. Meyer, C.A. Peck, & L. Brown (Eds.), *Critical issues in the lives of people with severe disabilities* (pp. 245–270). Baltimore: Paul H. Brookes Publishing Company.

Goldman, J., & Gardner, H. (1989). Multiple paths to educational effectiveness. In D.K. Lipsky & A. Gartner (Eds.), *Beyond separate education: Quality education for all* (pp. 121–139). Baltimore: Paul H. Brookes Publishing Co.

Graden, J.L., & Bauer, A.M. (1992). Using a collaborative approach to support students and teachers in inclusive classrooms. In S. Stainback & W. Stainback (Eds.), *Curriculum considerations in inclusive classrooms: Facilitating learning for all students* (pp. 85–100). Baltimore: Paul H. Brookes Publishing Co.

Hoover, J. (1987). Preparing special educators for mainstreaming: An emphasis upon curriculum. *Teacher Education and Special Education, 10*(2), 58–64.

Johnson, D., & Johnson, R. (1975). *Learning together and alone*. Englewood Cliffs, NJ: Prentice Hall.

Johnson, D., & Johnson, R. (1989). Cooperative learning and mainstreaming. In R. Gaylord-Ross (Ed.), *Integration strategies for students with handicaps* (pp. 213–231). Baltimore: Paul H. Brookes Publishing Co.

Johnson, D., & Johnson, R. (1991). *Learning together and alone* (3rd ed.). Englewood Cliffs, NJ: Prentice Hall.

Kagan, S. (1990). The structural approach to cooperative learning. *Educational Leadership*, 12–15.

Malehorn, H. (1984). Ten better measures than giving grades. *The Clearing House, 57*, 256–257.

Morsink, C., Thomas, C., & Correa, V. (1991). Framework and rationale for interactive teaming. In C. Morsink, C. Thomas, & V. Correa

(Eds.), *Interactive teaming: Consultation and collaboration in special programs* (pp. 3–32). New York: Macmillan.

Nisbet, J., Sweet, M., Ford, A., Shiraga, B., Udvari, A., York, J., Messina, R., & Schroeder, J. (1983). Utilizing adaptive devices with severely handicapped students. In L. Brown, A. Ford, J. Nisbet, M. Sweet, B. Shiraga, J. York, R. Loomis, & P. VanDeventer (Eds.), *Educational programs for severely handicapped students: Volume XIII* (pp. 101–145). Madison, WI: Madison Metropolitan School District.

Oakes, J., & Lipton, M. (1990). *Making the best of schools: A handbook for parents, teachers, and policy makers*. New Haven, CT: Yale University Press.

Peterson, M., LeRoy, B., Field, S., & Wood, P. (1992). Community-referenced learning in inclusive schools: Effective curriculum for all students. In S. Stainback & W. Stainback, (Eds.), *Curriculum considerations in inclusive classrooms: Facilitating learning for all students* (pp. 207–227). Baltimore: Paul H. Brookes Publishing Co.

Piuma, F., & Udvari-Solner, A. (1993). *Materials and process manual: Developing low cost vocational adaptations for individuals with severe disabilities*. University of Wisconsin–Madison & Madison Metropolitan School District.

Rainforth, B., York, J., & Macdonald, C. (1992). *Collaborative teams for students with severe disabilities: Integrating therapy and educational services*. Baltimore: Paul H. Brookes Publishing Co.

Salend, S. (1990). *Effective mainstreaming*. New York: Macmillan.

Sapon-Shevin, M. (1990). Student support through cooperative learning. In W. Stainback & S. Stainback (Eds.), *Support networks for inclusive schooling: Interdependent integrated education* (pp. 65–79). Baltimore: Paul H. Brookes Publishing Co.

Sharan, S., & Sharan Y. (1976). *Small group teaching*. Englewood Cliffs, NJ: Educational Technology Publications.

Shriner, J., Ysseldyke, J., & Christenson, L. (1989). Assessment procedures for use in heterogeneous classrooms. In S. Stainback, W. Stainback, & M. Forest (Eds.), *Educating all students in the mainstream of regular education* (pp. 159–181). Baltimore: Paul H. Brookes Publishing Co.

Slavin, R.E. (1978). Student teams and achievement divisions. *Journal of Research and Development in Education, 12*, 39–49.

Slavin, R.E. (1990). *Cooperative learning: Theory, research, and practice*. Englewood Cliffs, NJ: Prentice Hall.

Slavin, R.E., Leavey, M., & Madden, M.A. (1986). *Team accelerated instruction: Mathematics*. Watertown, MA: Charlesbridge.

Stainback, S., & Stainback, W. (Eds.). (1992). *Curriculum considerations in inclusive classrooms: Facilitating learning for all students*. Baltimore: Paul H. Brookes Publishing Co.

Stainback, W., Stainback, S., & Moravec, J. (1992). Using curriculum to build inclusive classrooms. In S. Stainback & W. Stainback (Eds.), *Curriculum considerations in inclusive classrooms: Facilitating learning for all students* (pp. 65–84). Baltimore: Paul H. Brookes Publishing Co.

Thousand, J.S., & Villa, R.A. (1992). Collaborative teams: A powerful tool in school restructuring. In R.A. Villa, J.S. Thousand, W. Stainback, & S. Stainback (Eds.), *Restructuring for caring and effective education: An administrative guide to creating heterogeneous schools* (pp. 73–108). Baltimore: Paul H. Brookes Publishing Co.

Udvari-Solner, A. (1992). *Curricular adaptations: Accommodating the instructional needs of diverse learners in the context of general education*. Monograph. Kansas State Board of Education—Services for Children and Youth with Deaf-Blindness Project.

Vandercook, T., & York, J. (1990). A team approach to program development and support. In W. Stainback & S. Stainback (Eds.), *Support networks for inclusive schooling: Interdependent integrated education* (pp. 95–122). Baltimore: Paul H. Brookes Publishing Co.

Wolf, D.P. (1989). Portfolio assessment: Sampling student work. *Educational Leadership, 35–39*.

Wolf, R. (1984). *Evaluation in education: Foundations for competency assessment and program review* (2nd ed.). New York: Praeger.

Wood, J., & Aldridge, J. (1985, March). Adapting tests for mainstreamed students. *Academic Therapy, 419–426*.

Wood, J., & Meiderhoff, J. (1988, February). Adapting lesson plans for the mainstreamed student. *The Clearing House, 61*(6), 269–276.

Wood, J., & Rosbe, M. (1985). Adapting the classroom lecture to the mainstreamed student in secondary schools. *The Clearing House, 58*, 354–358.

York, J., Giangreco, M.F., Vandercook, T., & Macdonald, C. (1992). Integrating support personnel in the inclusive classroom. In S. Stainback & W. Stainback (Eds.), *Curriculum considerations in inclusive classrooms: Facilitating learning for all students* (pp. 101–116). Baltimore: Paul H. Brookes Publishing Co.

York, J., Vandercook, T., Caughey, E., & Heise-Neff, C. (1988). Regular class integration: Beyond socialization. In J. York, T. Vandercook, C. Macdonald, & S. Wolff (Eds.), *Strategies for full inclusion* (pp. 117–120). Minneapolis: Institute on Community Integration, University of Minnesota.

ONE DIVIDED BY TWO OR MORE

REDEFINING THE ROLE OF A COOPERATIVE EDUCATION TEAM

*Richard A. Villa
and Jacqueline S. Thousand*

Cooperative group learning models are the most researched educational approach to promote heterogeneous student grouping (Johnson & Johnson, 1987; Slavin, 1984, 1987, 1989). They are gaining increased popularity and acceptance as school personnel simultaneously recognize the need to: 1) address students' social and interpersonal skill development, and 2) create heterogeneous school communities that reflect and prepare students for the "real world" of the 21st century—an ever-changing global community in which diversity (e.g., cultural, racial, ability, ethnic, language, economic) will be the norm.

These authors devote a great deal of time to training administrators, classroom teachers, and support personnel (e.g., special educators, guidance personnel, speech and language specialists, compensatory education personnel) in cooperative learning methods. We have discovered that many school personnel who have a history of working in isolation (e.g., in "self-contained" general education or special class environments) are mystified by the idea of collaborating to educate a more diverse group of learners through interactive processes, such as cooperative learning. They, as well as their students, are full of questions regarding the new role of *partners* in teaching and learning through cooperative structures.

This chapter was simultaneously prepared for publication in this volume and in Putnam, J.W. (Ed.). (1993). *Cooperative learning and strategies for inclusion: Celebrating diversity in the classroom.* Baltimore: Paul H. Brookes Publishing Co., in which it appeared as "Redefining the role of the special educator and other support personnel." It appears here in slightly edited and revised format, by permission of the authors and publisher.

The questions most frequently posed by special educators, who are accustomed to delivering student support primarily through "pull-out" services outside of the general education classroom, include the following:

"What is my role versus the classroom teacher's role during cooperative learning experiences?"

"Do I go into the regular education classroom with the students I serve in order to support them in their cooperative learning groups?"

"How do I ensure that the students I serve are successful members of cooperative learning groups in the general education environment?"

"Do I sit with the students I support as a member of a student-learning group?"

"Am I to interact with other students in the classroom?"

The questions often asked by classroom teachers are:

"How do I most effectively utilize a special education or other support person during cooperative group learning activities?"

"What are the benefits of having another educator in the classroom?"

"Who plans for and evaluates which students?"

"How do the students I support fit into cooperative learning groups?"

Students most often inquire:

"Which one is my teacher?"

"Whom do I ask for help?"

"Whose rules and discipline procedures apply to me?"

"If the special education teacher helps me, will people think that I'm a 'special education' student?"

"Will both teachers want to talk so much we won't have the time we need to work in our groups?"

All of the above questions reflect the confusion of both educators and students regarding their roles when collaborative and cooperative teaching and learning arrangements are introduced to maximize student success.

A primary purpose of this chapter is to illustrate how classroom teachers and support personnel effectively share expertise and responsibility to promote not only the learning and collaborative skill development of their students, but their own professional and interpersonal growth as well. These authors first offer the rationale for professional partnership in the design and delivery of cooperative learning instruction and define a *cooperative education team*. Then they offer strategies to reduce role confusion among classroom teachers and support personnel through teachers' systematic analyses and distributions of instructional responsibilities (i.e., planning, teaching, evaluating student performance). The chapter closes with examples of cooperative education teams in action and offers tips for optimizing team effectiveness.

WHY CREATE COOPERATIVE EDUCATION TEAMS?

Modeling What We Preach

> *The integration of professionals within a school system is a prerequisite to the successful integration of students. We cannot ask our students to do those things which we as professionals are unwilling to do.*
>
> *(Harris, 1987, p. 1)*

Conventional wisdom suggests that a primary learning method for both children and adults is the observation of behaviors displayed by "role models." A critical teacher behavior, therefore, in preparing students for the cooperative workplace and society of the 21st century is to model *cooperative teaching*. With cooperative teaching, students learn through observation how two or more people coordinate instructional, behavior management, and student-evaluation activities. Although students who experience cooperative learning structures acquire the learnings through active participation in the cooperative learning experience, the adult modeling of the same behavior reinforces the message that *cooperative behavior is a norm that extends beyond student life to adult and lifelong success*. Adult modeling increases the likelihood that students will value and cooperate with teachers to create a collaborative classroom culture.

Two Heads Are Better than One

Having worked extensively in public schools with classroom teachers and specialists who regularly partner with each other in instruction and who employ cooperative learning methods in their instructional routines, these authors have found that these educators experience creative thinking and problem-solving outcomes (Thousand & Villa, 1990) similar to those experienced by students who learn in heterogeneous cooperative groups (Johnson & Johnson, 1989). In particular, collaborating teachers are able to generate new conceptualizations and novel solutions to the daily challenges presented by a diverse student population through the synergistic processes of *collective induction* (i.e., inducing general principles together that no one could induce individually) and *process gain* (i.e., generating new ideas through group interaction that are not generated when people work alone).

A primary purpose of assembling a cooperative education team is to increase the potential for individualizing instruction while enabling all students to be educated with their peers. With multiple instructors, the teacher-to-student ratio is higher, which allows for more immediate and accurate diagnosis of and intervention in response to individual student social and academic needs. Instructors also have a greater opportunity to capitalize upon the diverse, unique, and specialized knowledge, skills, and instructional approaches of team members who have different training and experience backgrounds.

Professional Growth and Peer Support

What stereotypic responses are possible to the question, "What do general educators have to offer special educators and vice versa?" One response might be that general education teachers possess content mastery in any number of topical areas from reading and writing to the sciences, whereas special educators have knowledge of specific techniques for remediating or accelerating learning in basic skill areas, such as mathematics or reading. Another response might be that general educators have the experience and skill to manage large numbers of learners whereas special educators have the skill to design individual behavior management plans and to teach social skills that enhance self-management and social acceptability within the classroom. Whatever the response, it is likely that educators will acknowledge that each person in the school community possesses unique talents and perspectives that, when pooled, create a richer *learning environment for adults* as well as for children. In other words, in cooperative education team arrangements, teachers may experience professional growth that cannot be attained in formal coursework.

Research on staff development highlights the importance of educators having frequent opportunities: 1) to observe models of new instructional methods, and 2) to receive coaching and feedback during their efforts to replicate and personalize the new technique (Showers, Joyce, & Bennett, 1987). Cooperative education teams are natural arrangements for modeling and processing to occur. Of course, "peer coaching" (Cummings, 1985, p. 1) both requires and promotes a high level of trust and mutual interdependence among cooperating teachers. Such an interdependent support system for obtaining feedback is necessary to ensure the integrity and continued improvement of teachers' use of cooperative learning and to sustain one another's interest in doing so (Johnson, Johnson, Holubec, & Roy, 1984). Johnson and colleagues (1984) support the *networking* of cooperative education teams through a *schoolwide professional support group* to ensure long-term practice of cooperative methods. In this larger support group, teams may share ideas, lessons, and successes and may solve individual and mutual problems in using cooperative learning methods. They also can structure reciprocal observation and coaching opportunities to improve one another's competence in using cooperative learning procedures.

Support personnel such as special educators who provide technical assistance to several teachers are a very important resource for spreading cooperative learning throughout a school. By offering to teach other teachers' classes, they can model cooperative learning methods for both teachers and students. Support personnel also may "free up" other members of their cooperative education teams so they, too, may model in other classrooms.

WHAT IS A COOPERATIVE EDUCATION TEAM?

A *cooperative education team* is an instructional arrangement of two or more people in the school and greater community who share cooperative learning planning, instructional, and evaluation responsibilities for the same students on a regular basis during an extended period of time. Teams may vary in size from two to six people. They should vary in composition as well, using any possible combination of support personnel (e.g., special educator, speech and language pathologist, guidance counselor, health professional); instructional assistant; student teacher; community volunteer (e.g., parent, member of a local "foster grandparent" program); teacher; and students themselves (Thousand & Villa, 1990).

Members of an effective cooperative education team practice the same critical elements that they structure for their student cooperative learning groups. Specifically, members: 1) have frequent face-to-face interactions, 2) structure a positive "we are all in this together" sense of interdependence, 3) hold one another individually accountable for agreed-upon responsibilities, 4) periodically assess and process their instructional and interpersonal effectiveness, and 5) practice small-group interpersonal skills.

Face-to-Face Interaction

Among the most often posed questions by newly formed cooperative education teams are those that have to do with time for face-to-face interactions. When and how often does the team meet? How much time, during or outside of school hours, will team meetings take? Of the support personnel (e.g., special educators, speech-language pathologists, Chapter 1 instructors, teaching assistants), who will be regular members of the team? When should other people who support students in the classroom (e.g., guidance counselors, health professionals, "outside" consultants, therapists) attend meetings? What means will members of the team use to communicate information quickly among themselves when a formal planning meeting is not scheduled (e.g., a communication log on the classroom teacher's desk, a bulletin board on the classroom computer, "Post-It" notes stuck to the inside of a storage door in the classroom)?

Questions of face-to-face interaction involve team members discussing and collaboratively agreeing on answers. Time must be arranged for team members not only to plan cooperative lessons, but to evaluate the effectiveness of the lessons as well. The need for face-to-face interactions also affects team size. The literature on student cooperative learning arrangements suggests a maximum of five or six group members (Johnson et al., 1984). The same size limitations hold for adult teams to allow each team member adequate "air time" during meetings.

Positive Interdependence

In most North American schools, teachers, whether labeled regular educators or special support personnel, generally are still expected to work alone, independent of one another. This expectation determines not only how teachers behave, but also how they think about the students for whom they have assigned responsibilities. "These students ('general' vs. 'special') are mine and, therefore, my primary or sole responsibility." "Those students ('special' vs. 'general') are not mine, and therefore, of little instructional concern to me."

For cooperative education teams, positive interdependence changes this. Positive interdependence involves the recognition among team members that no one person can effectively address the diverse educational, social, and psychological needs of a heterogeneous group of students (i.e., "your students *and* mine"). It encourages members of the team to *feel* that they *all* are responsible for arranging for the learning of *all* their students through the pooling of their diverse skills and knowledge and material resources. The strategies teams may employ to create feelings of positive interdependence include: 1) distributing and rotating "classroom leadership" and decision-making powers (i.e., the who, what, where, when, why, and how of designing and delivering cooperative lessons) among all members of the team, and 2) regularly celebrating team success in designing and conducting lessons (e.g., including "positive statements" as the first agenda item for all planning and evaluation meetings and sharing lesson outcomes with other teachers, parents, administrators, or the general community).

A cooperative education team "does everything that a 'normal' teacher would do except that now there are two or more people doing it" (N. Keller, personal communication, March 17, 1989). Or, as the title of this chapter suggests, one job is divided by two or more people. What is key here is the implicit recognition that numerous decisions about how the formerly separate "classroom leadership" responsibilities and powers of team members are redistributed and readjusted over time. Some of the questions team members must jointly answer are presented in Table 1. Tough decisions have to be made at times; yet, the professional and personal growth that may result from making such decisions is an invaluable outcome not easily achieved in public schools today.

Individual Accountability

Collaboration, as represented by a cooperative learning teaching team, has the potential to increase teachers' accountability. In a collaborative school, teachers "monitor one another's performance, set limits on one another's behavior, and take respon-

Table 1.   Questions members of a cooperative learning teaching team must answer to distribute leadership responsibilities among team members

1. Who plans for the academic content of the lesson?
2. How will the lesson be presented and explained? Will one person teach the social skills, another the academic material, and other(s) assist in observing, intervening, and processing with student learning groups? Or, will all members share in the instruction, monitoring, and processing?
3. Who adapts the materials, instructional procedures, and performance expectations for individual students?
4. Who evaluates which students? Do team members collaborate in evaluating all students' performances or is each team member primarily responsible for evaluating a group of students?
5. How is the paperwork for students eligible for special education managed?
6. Who decides on the intervention procedures for disruptive student behavior? Who carries out the procedures? How is consistency ensured?
7. How do team members arrange to share and enhance their skills? Do they observe one another and practice "peer coaching"?
8. Do team members rotate teaching and student monitoring and processing responsibilities? How often do these responsibilities rotate? How is the decision made to shift these responsibilities?
9. Who will have the authority to make on-the-spot adjustments in the lesson? How and when during the lesson will decision makers confer to agree upon needed adjustments?
10. Who communicates with parents and administrators?
11. How is the decision made to expand or contract the team membership?
12. How will an equitable balance of work and decision-making power be maintained among team members?

sibility for helping their colleagues to improve" (Smith, 1987, p. 6). The natural consequence of structuring cooperative education teams is the introduction of additional "eyes" to the learning environment and opportunities for team members to observe and assess one another relative to their agreed-upon planning, teaching, monitoring, and evaluation activities.

There is no question that working as a team reduces the autonomy and freedom enjoyed by teachers when they function independently of one another, as in free-standing one-room schools housed under a single roof (Skrtic, 1991). However, a primary purpose of teaming structures is to maximize the instructional performance of each individual through the modeling, coaching, and feedback teammates provide (Johnson et al., 1984). The possible loss of freedom that teaming implies is balanced by the freedom of *not* being solely responsible for students' learning; the potential for power and survival in dealing with an increasingly diverse student population; and the sense of belonging as well as fun that accompanies successful, creative, shared problem solving (Glasser, 1986; Parnes, 1981, 1988).

Small-Group Social Skills

Just because two or more people call themselves a team is no guarantee that they will interact cooperatively. For an adult or student team to collaborate effectively, members must have knowledge of and use small-group interpersonal skills. Unfortunately, few teachers and support personnel who comprise cooperative education teams have had the same opportunity as their students to receive instruction and practice in small-group skills. As a consequence, newly formed teams will include people who were never before required to demonstrate collaborative skills.

The most effective teams are those that are able to maintain equity and parity in decision-making power among their members by arriving at decisions through a *consensual* (i.e., all members agree) rather than a democratic (i.e., the majority of votes wins) process. To behave in a consensual fashion, however, requires the acquisition and mastery of a great many small-group social skills; the mastery of these skills does not occur overnight. The four levels of skills that team members need to demonstrate for group growth to occur are: 1) initial trust-building skills (forming skills); 2) communication and leadership skills that help to manage and organize team activities so that tasks are completed and relationships are maintained (i.e., functioning skills); 3) skills needed to stimulate creative problem solving and decision making and to create deeper comprehension of unfamiliar or confusing information (i.e., formulating skills); and 4) skills needed to manage controversy and conflict of opinions and interest, search for more information (e.g., obtain technical assistance outside the team), and stimulate revision and refinement of ideas (i.e., fermenting skills) (Johnson et al., 1984; Thousand & Villa, 1992).

Of course, small-group interpersonal skills can be learned by adults as well as children. Learning these skills is no different from learning any other skill. It requires opportunities for team members to: 1) see the *need* for the skill, 2) learn how and when to *use* it, 3) *practice* using it, and 4) receive *feedback* on how well they used it (Johnson et al., 1984). A major challenge for beginning cooperative education teams is how to acquire these small-group collaborative skills. One direct method is to arrange for training and guided practice as part of an ongoing inservice agenda. An indirect and natural method, one recommended by David and Roger Johnson, is for teachers simply to begin teaching social skills to students as part of cooperative learning lessons. In this way, teachers acquire the same skills as the students through the process of teaching, and they develop an understanding of the importance of these skills to any team's functioning (Brandt, 1987). A third method is to structure, as a regular component of planning meetings, time for team members to process their instructional and *interpersonal* effectiveness.

Processing Team Effectiveness

As already noted, research on staff development highlights the importance of structuring frequent opportunities for teachers to process and receive feedback regarding the innovative practices they are attempting (Showers et al., 1987). This is particularly true for cooperative education teams in which members are likely to have had little previous experience in co-planning, co-teaching, or exercising small-group interpersonal skills. The final critical element for team success involves the regular structuring of time for team processing of instructional and interpersonal effectiveness and the setting of personal and group social growth goals. Outside observers (e.g., a colleague from another cooperative education team, a supervisor with knowledge and experience in cooperative learning, guidance personnel with knowledge of social skill and group development) may be invited to observe planning meetings or cooperative lessons and to share their observations as part of the team's professional development activities or as an intervention when the team is having trouble functioning.

HOW DO MEMBERS OF THE
TEACHING TEAM PLAN, CONDUCT, AND
EVALUATE COOPERATIVE LEARNING EXPERIENCES?

Cooperative learning may be incorporated into the culture of the classroom in three ways: 1) *formal* lessons and learning groups that are more structured and stay together until a task is done (e.g., a group of four completes a week-long science unit and ensures that all members master the assigned information), 2) *informal* learning groups that are transient and less structured (e.g., "Turn to your neighbor and share with one another your three learnings"), and 3) *base groups* in which students have long-term (e.g., semester- or year-long) responsibility for providing one another with peer support and long-term accountability (Johnson & Johnson, 1991).

Once a cooperative education team understands how to structure formal lessons cooperatively, the other two types of cooperative learning experiences can (and should) be added to the classroom. Clearly, formal cooperative lessons require the greatest degree of coordination and mutual decision making among members of the cooperative education team. Hence, this section addresses the roles and decisions required of members of a cooperative education team as they develop, teach, and evaluate *formal* cooperative learning experiences. Of course, what team members learn through these experiences will influence and better enable them to use informal learning groups and base groups.

The roles that members of a cooperative education team distribute among themselves involve strategies and decisions during the *planning, conduct,* and *evaluation* stages of a cooperative learning experience (Johnson & Johnson, 1991). In planning a lesson, the first team task is to agree upon and to specify clearly *the academic and social skill objectives.* The second is to make certain *decisions* regarding face-to-face interaction (which students will be in which groups, the size of each group, the arrangement of the room), how students will be made interdependent, how academic and social skills will be taught and monitored, and how feedback will be provided to individual students regarding task and social skill performance.

When conducting a formal lesson, one critical role of the cooperative education team is to *clearly explain* to students the *task, the social skills, and the goal structure(s),* that is, whether it is a cooperative, individualistic, and/or a competitive learning structure. Another is to *monitor* the effectiveness of the cooperative learning groups and to intervene to *provide assistance* in the task (e.g., answer questions, clarify or teach parts of the task) or to improve students' interpersonal and group skills. Two final roles of team members are to *evaluate* students' achievements and to *process* with students how well they collaborated with each other.

Evaluation continues following the lesson, with the team's further evaluation of students' performances and the *team's self-evaluation* of the integrity of the lesson's delivery, the effectiveness of the team's instruction, the team's ability to coordinate their actions and to work together, and the team's acquisition or refinement of skills through the teaming process. Evaluation results inform the team on how they may better design and carry out lessons.

Planning a Cooperative Lesson

Like all effective instruction, planning is the key to the successful delivery of a cooperative group lesson. Figure 1 details the diverse factors a cooperative education team must consider when constructing a formal lesson. The team must clearly specify the academic and social skill objectives and make a series of decisions regarding face-to-face interaction, the structuring of positive interdependence among students, social skill instruction and monitoring, and processing with students their task and social skill performance. A great number of these decisions further require the team to agree upon who will do what; for example, how the role of the teacher will be distributed among team members. The questions the team should consider when deciding how the role of teacher should be distributed among team members are presented in Table 1. The following are additional questions that relate to the individualization of instruction for students.

Will there be different academic objectives, materials, or performance criteria for some learners? Who will select the objectives, measure student performance, and process with the students their performance?

Will there be different social skill objectives or performance criteria for some learners? Who will select the objectives, measure student performance, and process with the students their performance?

Will some students receive pre-teaching in academic or social skill areas? When will this pre-teaching occur? Who will conduct the instruction?

Will differences in academic or social objectives be communicated to the class or the group to which the student belongs? When will this communication occur? Who will communicate the information? What is the rationale for communicating or not communicating this information? Is there an issue of confidentiality that should be addressed with families of students eligible for special education?

Creating Positive Interdependence Through a Structured Team Meeting Process   Like student cooperative learning experiences, planning meetings of a cooperative education team must be structured to promote a feeling of *positive interdependence* among team members (Thousand & Villa, 1992). Positive interdependence may be created through a division of labor *during* team meetings as well as during the delivery of a lesson. It is a "best practice" for team members to rotate, from one meeting to the next, different leadership roles that promote either the completion of work or the maintenance of relationships among members. With this structure, the team has as many leaders as members and the message is communicated that no one person has the expertise, authority, or the material or information resources needed to accomplish the team's goals.

Numerous task (e.g., timekeeper, recorder) and relationship (e.g., observer, encourager) roles have been prescribed and defined by various authors (Glickman, 1990; Johnson et al., 1984; Thousand & Villa, 1992). Exactly which roles a team decides to use during a meeting depends upon the nature of the lesson being planned and the level of interpersonal skill development among team members. For example, when conflict and controversy are expected, there may be a need for a "conflict recognizer" to identify emerging conflicts and to signal the team to stop and assess whether the steps of conflict resolution should be initiated. A "harmonizer" role also may be needed to help to conciliate differences by looking for ways to reduce tension through humor and nonjudgmental explanations. A "praiser" role is important when a team has become negligent in regularly affirming the contributions of members. When team discussions become dominated by particular participants, the "equalizer" role can be activated. The equalizer encourages quiet members to participate and regulates the flow of communication by ensuring that all members have equal access to "air time."

Any social skill may be transformed into a role to be practiced by and rotated among team members. Two roles recently invented by school-based collaborative teams are the "but watcher" and "jargon buster" roles. The job of the "but watcher" is to help team members to defer judgment during creative idea-generating or problem-solving periods by monitoring and signaling a member's use of blocking, oppositional, or judgmental language, such as, "Yes, but that won't work because. . . ." A "jargon buster" has the job of signaling whenever a specialized term may not be un-

---

COOPERATIVE GROUP LESSON PLAN

Lesson name: _____ Authors: _____

What is the content area? _____

What are the appropriate age levels for this lesson? _____

ACADEMIC OBJECTIVES

1. What are the prerequisite skills for taking part in the lesson?

2. What are the academic objectives of this lesson? (Remember also to identify the social skills objective in the Establishing Social Skill Performance section.)

3. What, if any, are the modifications of objectives for learner(s) with special needs?

FACE-TO-FACE INTERACTION DECISIONS

1. Group size (2–6)? _____
2. Which students will be in which groups? (Assignments should ensure that students are heterogeneously mixed.)

3. How is the room arranged? (Draw a diagram.)

STRUCTURING POSITIVE INTERDEPENDENCE

(Members get the messages: "We sink or swim together," "Do your work—we're counting on you," "How can I help you to do better?")

1. How will you structure one group goal, a single product, or a shared outcome?

2. Will you structure a group reward (e.g., one group grade, dual grades for individual and group products, dual grades for academic and social skill performance, bonus points if pre-set criterion is exceeded, free time or privileges for meeting criterion)?

3. What student roles will be used to promote positive interdependence? (Define each role, using the words you will use with the students.)

_____
(continued)

Figure 1.   Elements of formal cooperative learning groups that team members need to consider when designing a lesson. (It may be helpful for readers to consult pp. 129–225, Creative Cooperative Group Lesson Plans.)

Figure 1.   (*continued*)

---

4. Will there be division of labor other than roles? Describe.

5. How will materials be arranged to promote positive interdependence (e.g., one set of materials, "jigsaw-ing" of information or materials)?

6. How else will positive interdependence be structured? (Optional)
    a. Will you structure intergroup (between group) cooperation? How?

    b. Will you structure intergroup (between group) competition in order to develop within group cohesion? How?

    c. Will you structure positive fantasy or identity interdependence (e.g., a fantasy mission, selecting a group name)? How?

ESTABLISHING SOCIAL SKILL PERFORMANCE

1. What are the social skills for this lesson?

2. How will the need for each skill be communicated? Who will do this (e.g., After groups have worked for _____ session[s], ask them to brainstorm the behaviors needed to help the group learn and work together well; tell students why the skill[s] is/are important; ask the students why the skill[s] is/are important.)?

3. How will each social skill be explained? Who will do this (e.g., Someone demonstrates the skill, explains each step of skill performance, and redemonstrates the skill; someone structures a role-play of the skill for the whole class, explains each step of skill performance, and structures a second role-play of the skill; a videotape is used to demonstrate and explain the skill.)?

4. How will the social skill(s) be assigned to group members (e.g., Assign the skill[s] generally to the groups, so all group members are responsible for engaging in the social skill[s]; assign the skill[s] to randomly selected students and rotate the skills around the group until all members have performed each skill several times; select target students who need coaching and special training and pretrain them in the skills.)?

(*continued*)

Figure 1.   (*continued*)

SOCIAL SKILL PERFORMANCE:
TEACHER MONITORING AND INTERVENTION

1. How will the groups be observed? Who will observe which groups (e.g., Anecdotal observations and notes are made regarding specific examples of students demonstrating cooperative behaviors; a structured observation form is used and each group is observed for an equal amount of time; a structured observation form is used and only selected group[s] having trouble are observed.)?

2. How will teachers give students feedback if the target social skills are being used (e.g., Interrupt the group and compliment the group on the use of the skill; during processing time, compliment the group on the use of the skill, say nothing.)?

3. How will teachers give students feedback if the target social skills are not being used (e.g., Ask the members of the group what they have done so far to increase the use of the skills; ask the group what it will try next to increase skill use; suggest an action.)?

4. What are likely problems in collaboration? What are interventions to avoid/remedy them (Rules: When you feel like intervening, don't. If you must intervene, do it with a question, not an answer. Move away as soon as you can, even if it is only 3 feet.)?

SOCIAL SKILL PERFORMANCE:
STUDENT MONITORING

1. Will there be student observers?

2. What social skills will the student observers monitor?

3. Will the students observe one or more groups?

4. Will the students observe for the whole lesson?

5. How will student observers be selected?

6. How and when will student observers be trained? Who will train them?

(*continued*)

Figure 1. (*continued*)

7. How and when will student observers share their observations with group members?

STRUCTURING INDIVIDUAL ACCOUNTABILITY

How do teachers determine whether each student learned the material and contributed to the group effort and product (e.g., Roam among groups and randomly question individuals; individually quiz all students; select one paper to represent the group.)?

SETTING THE TASK

1. How will the *academic* task and criterion for success be *explained*? Who will do it?

2. How will the *social* skill(s) and criterion for success be *explained*? Who will do it?

(Always tell the students what the objectives are, give or solicit from the students reasons why it is important to learn this content or perform this task, be specific in your directions, and check for individual student's understanding.)

AFTER THE LESSON:
CLOSURE AND PROCESSING

1. Closure: How will students summarize what they have learned following the lesson (e.g., Teachers randomly "beam" questions to individual students; the entire class gives a choral response or signal; students do a quick "5-minute write" in response to questions.)?

2. How and when will students receive feedback on their academic performance? Who will assess which students and who will provide the feedback?

3. How will teachers' observations be shared? (As a general rule, share negative comments in private and positive comments in public and private.)

4. In addition to hearing observation reports from teacher and peer observers, how will students assess their individual and their group's success in using social skills?

derstood. The jargon user then must define the term or use an analogous term that
everyone knows. This role is very important for cooperative education teams that
include special educators or other support personnel professionals who may use jargon to describe their work and ideas. The jargon buster role prevents team members
who are unfamiliar with particular terms from feeling intimidated or less than
equal. It also establishes the norm that it is perfectly all right not to know something.
Once team members are familiar with the meaning of jargon, the terms may be used
by the group to enhance its efficiency and to promote a feeling of interdependence. A
common language tends to increase communication and to build a team's sense of
identity and spirit.

The Team Meeting Worksheet, presented in Figure 2, has proven to be an effective outline for promoting accountability among team members with regard to meeting attendance and the equitable distribution of work during and after planning
meetings (Thousand & Villa, 1992). The worksheet also ensures attention to the
other elements of the collaborative teaming process (i.e., face-to-face interaction,
positive interdependence, collaborative skill performance, processing).

The worksheet is a valuable guide at team meetings. In order to emphasize individual accountability for meeting attendance and *face-to-face interaction,* names of
present, late, and absent members are recorded on the worksheet. Names of others
who are not at the meeting, but who need to be informed of team outcomes (e.g., extended team members who may be involved in subsequent lessons, administrators or
other teachers in the school interested in cooperative groupings) also are noted; this
alerts the team of who may need information regarding the outcomes of planning.
Accountability for distributing leadership is prompted by the list of possible roles
included on the worksheet and the indication that roles be assigned in advance of the
next meeting. This ensures that the people in such roles (e.g., timekeeper and recorder) will bring with them the materials they need to carry out their roles. Advance
role assignment also prompts team members to rotate roles from one meeting to
the next.

Notice that the team is prompted to create the agenda for the next meeting before it disbands. If all members are alerted (at the meeting and through the minutes)
to the date, location, purpose, and time of the next meeting, *accountability* is ensured. Also, people are motivated to participate in the next meeting; they take an
interest in events and objectives that they have helped to formulate.

Examination of the agenda section of the worksheet in Figure 2 reveals that incorporated into all meetings are: 1) time limits for each agenda item; 2) a time to
celebrate the things that went well in the cooperative lessons just taught and other
positive educationally related events experienced since the last meeting; and 3) a
time, midway and at the end of the meeting, to *process* members' use of collaborative
skills and their progress toward completion of the lesson. The empty numbered
spaces listed on the agenda worksheet represent the actual content of each meeting—the subtasks that contribute to the team's achievement of its overall goals, including successful lesson design. Although the agenda proposed at the end of a meeting *guides* the construction of the actual agenda of the team's next planning meeting,
it must be remembered that many events can occur between meetings. Consequently,
the actual agenda items should be modified at the beginning of each meeting to reflect the intervening events.

Promoting Equity Through the Planning Process   The ultimate outcome of
a planning meeting of a cooperative education team is the actual production of a co-

Team Meeting Worksheet

Persons Present (Note late arrivals)	Absentees	Others Who Need to Know
_____	_____	_____
_____	_____	_____
_____		_____
_____		
_____		
_____		

Roles:	This Meeting	Next Meeting
Timekeeper		
Recorder		
Equalizer		
Other: _____		
Other: _____		

AGENDA

Items	Time Limit
1. Positive Comments	5 minutes
2.	
3.	
4.	
5. Processing (task and relationship)	5 minutes
6.	
7.	
8.	
9. Processing (task and relationship)	5 minutes

MINUTES OF OUTCOMES

Action Items:	Person(s) Responsible
1. Communicate outcomes to absent member and others who need to know by _____	
2.	
3.	
4.	
5.	

AGENDA BUILDING FOR NEXT MEETING

Date: _____   Time: _____   Location: _____

Expected Agenda Items:

1.
2.
3.
4.
5.

Figure 2. Worksheet for promoting effective team meetings. (From Thousand, J.S., & Villa, R.A. [1992]. Collaborative teams: A powerful tool in school restructuring. In R.A. Villa, J.S. Thousand, W. Stainback, & S. Stainback [Eds.], *Restructuring for caring and effective education: An administrative guide to creating heterogeneous schools* [p. 101]. Baltimore: Paul H. Brookes Publishing Co.; reprinted by permission.)

operative lesson, which should be represented in some type of lesson plan format such as that already suggested in Figure 1. The minutes of outcomes section of the Team Meeting Worksheet shown in Figure 2 is intended to prompt equitable distribution of other tasks that should be accomplished in preparation for teaching the lesson. Periodic review of minutes and lesson plans may help to monitor equity in work distribution. If such monitoring reveals that one or two team members regularly assume the majority of tasks, it is a signal of problems with positive interdependence. Team members may be "free loading"—taking advantage of the group's size to avoid work. Some members' interest may be waning. Those doing most of the work may not trust others to carry out assignments. Inequity in the division of labor is an enemy of a team's sense of cohesion and requires the team to explore the causes and possible actions to re-establish balance (e.g., limiting the number of responsibilities for which a single person may volunteer).

These authors offer two final bits of advice regarding the planning of a cooperative lesson. First, *plan together,* face-to-face; do not attempt to "jigsaw" and separately design lesson components. Jigsaw planning inevitably results in duplications, omissions, and a less efficient, effective, enjoyable cooperative experience for students and teachers alike. Face-to-face interaction is as important for collaborating adults as it is for collaborating students. Second, take the time to *identify problem situations* that may arise (e.g., absent students, behavior challenges of individual students, confusion regarding complex directions, attempts to compete rather than cooperate) and, more important, *detail approaches* upon which all team members can agree to prevent the situation from occurring or intervene so as to minimize teacher disruption of group work.

Conducting Cooperative Learning Lessons

Conducting a formal cooperative learning lesson involves the cooperative education team's joint adherence to its lesson plan. Conducting a lesson is not simply the delivery of instruction; it is a time to collect data on several levels and to make adjustments that improve the present and future lessons. During the lesson, designated members of the team provide students with a clear explanation of the academic content, the social skills, and the cooperative activities in which students are to engage. Team members monitor not only the effectiveness of the student learning groups, but also their *own* effectiveness in coordinating actions to deliver the lesson as designed *or* to adjust the objectives, activities, or performance criteria during the lesson if student responses signal this need. Of course, making on-the-spot changes in the lesson requires the team to have a plan for making adjustments. At a minimum, this plan should identify who makes which adjustment decisions as well as how and when the decision makers will confer during the lesson and communicate the changes to the other team members participating in the delivery of the lesson.

During a cooperative group lesson, members of the cooperative education team are responsible for intervening to assist students with task or interpersonal issues and to evaluate and process with students their academic and social skill performance. They are also responsible for *intervening* to assist one another in performing their agreed-upon roles in the lesson (e.g., providing prompts to a team member who forgets or makes an error with an important direction, action, or piece of information). The processing of their own performance evaluations may occur briefly at the end of the lesson and, most certainly, at the team's next planning meeting.

Teaching cooperative lessons on a regular, frequent basis has many benefits. Team members have the opportunity to observe colleagues' demonstrations of new or exemplary instructional approaches and to learn from their colleagues' models. The members also have the opportunity to be observed by trusted colleagues who jointly are acquiring knowledge and competence in using cooperative learning in the classroom. Peer-coaching models, such as that offered by Carol Cummings (1985), provide a structure for teammates to refine their instructional skills by receiving specific constructive feedback. Finally, regular and frequent implementation of cooperative lessons builds a teaching team's cumulative history of successes—examples of strategies that have worked to address various challenges—as well as examples of less effective interventions, all of which inform the team of how to invent more successful future lessons. The cumulative history of successes also builds team confidence and cohesion, which, in turn, influences future success.

Multilevel Evaluation

If conducting a cooperative lesson is an opportunity for data collection, evaluation is an opportunity to use data to improve student and teacher success with cooperative learning structures. Evaluation of student performance occurs during the lesson and continues following the lesson, with the "grading" of student outputs and processing of student social and academic behavior at subsequent planning meetings of the cooperative education team.

One of the first items on the agenda of any planning meeting that follows a cooperative lesson should be an evaluation of the team's performance; that is, the evaluation of the integrity of the lesson's delivery, the effectiveness of the team's instruction, the team members' ability to coordinate their actions and work together, and the team's acquisition or refinement of skills through the teaming process. Evaluation results inform the team of how future lessons may be better designed and conducted.

Table 2 offers a series of evaluation questions that cooperative education teams may wish to address in meetings. Of course, all the questions rely upon observational data collected when the lesson was delivered. Questions that deal with the behavior of team members also require a high level of trust among teammates and skills in giving and receiving negative and positive feedback (Johnson et al., 1984).

The Power of Reward Interdependence in Evaluation   Self-reflection, self-evaluation, processing of successes and failures with others, and the evaluation of others' (student and adult) performances are all evaluative actions that promote professional growth among members of the cooperative education team, as well as improving cooperative learning experiences for students. When members of cooperative education teams are evaluating and providing feedback to one another, it is especially important for them to remember to structure *reward interdependence,* that is, the shared rewards and celebrations for the team's collective work. Reward interdependence means that the recognition of one member's contributions does not overshadow the equally important, but possibly less visible, contributions of another. A norm within effective collaborative education teams is that successes are celebrated collectively—no one person receives special recognition. As a result, when goals are achieved, all members share in the gratification of having contributed to the achievement. A responsibility of cooperative education teams and of the administrators that support their work is to jointly explore and identify what it is that team members view as a reward or incentive for continued collaboration. At a minimum, teams should structure celebration time into every meeting's agenda (see Figure 2). During this time, each member shares at least one positive statement about cooperative lesson-related activities, the students, or other professional accomplishments.

Table 2.   Sample evaluation questions for cooperative learning teaching teams to consider

Integrity of Cooperative Group Learning Lesson Delivery

To what extent was the lesson delivered as designed? Did team members perform their designated roles? What could be done to improve members' role performance?

Did adjustments need to be made? Why? What was learned from making the adjustments?

To what extent were the critical elements of face-to-face interaction, positive interdependence, individual accountability, and social skill development and processing structured into the lesson?

To what extent was attention to academic and social skill objectives balanced?

To what extent did team members successfully anticipate problem areas and employ effective interventions? What are likely future problems and appropriate interventions?

Use of Effective Instructional Methods

Were the academic and social skill objectives appropriate for the learners? What are appropriate objectives for the next lesson? How did or will team members provide additional guided practice or enrichment for those who need it?

Do certain individuals or groups of students require individualized objectives, materials, or performance criteria in the future? If so, what will be done to individualize and measure student success?

Did team members respond to students in a consistent manner?

Was the explanation of the objectives, process, and expected outcomes clear? How might it be improved in subsequent lessons?

How did the team check for students' understanding of the content and the cooperative group task? What are alternative ways of checking for understanding in future lessons.

Modeling of Collaboration

How did the team members provide a model of effective collaboration for their students? How might the team provide an even more effective model of collaboration in future lessons?

Did team members fulfill their agreed upon roles and responsibilities in the design, implementation, and evaluation of the lesson? What is each team member most proud of in designing, implementing, and evaluating the lesson?

Do team members feel that they equitably distributed responsibility for instructing, monitoring, and evaluating the performance of *all* of the students in the class?

Skill Acquisition

What did each team member learn from watching his or her colleague teach?

Do team members want to set individual professional growth objectives for the next lesson? How do team members want their colleagues to support them to monitor and attain the objectives?

Team Membership

Does the team need additional expertise? What resources exist to provide training, modeling, coaching, and feedback?

Is it time for the team to expand or dissolve? If so, for what purpose?

It must be remembered that responsibility comes with joint rewards. There will be times when a lesson goes poorly, a student presents an unexpected exceptional challenge, and things, in general, do not work out as hoped. Teams that swim together also must sink together. When a team faces disappointments or failures, it is the collective "we" and not a single person who accepts responsibility.

CASE STUDIES: EXEMPLIFYING TEACHER ROLES AND DECISIONS

The following are three examples of cooperative education teams in action. Each is a composite of the actual experiences of a number of cooperative education teams functioning in Vermont schools. The descriptions are intended to illustrate the diversity among teams in terms of composition, size, and the way in which they handle the critical elements of cooperative learning structures.

An Elementary Language Arts Team

In a school committed to providing children with heterogeneous learning opportunities, a 15-year veteran teacher of the fourth grade and a novice special educator new to the school system collaborate to meet the needs of all of the students placed in the fourth grade classroom. Fourth graders who are eligible for special education or other special services receive their support within this general education classroom.

The two teachers differed tremendously in training background and experiences. In the past, the fourth grade teacher relied primarily on a basal series to teach her students to read; the special educator was trained to deliver instruction in phonics to individuals or small groups of learners. One commonality was mutual interest in cooperative learning. The fourth grade teacher had recently completed a course in cooperative learning and the special educator had had experience with cooperative groups in his graduate training program. This team decided to use cooperative learning groups in two areas of reading: drill and practice in sound/symbol relations and answering comprehension questions about passages in the basal reading text. They met at least twice a week to plan and every day they co-instructed during the 45-minute reading block.

From the start, the two teachers shared responsibility for selecting objectives and materials. Every lesson included a review of phonetic skills and a set of comprehension questions for student groups to answer. During the first marking period, the fourth grade teacher assumed primary responsibility for the lesson design. She presented the task to the students while the special educator assisted in monitoring student progress in social skill acquisition. The classroom teacher collected anecdotal data for four student groups; the special educator collected data for three groups. Both teachers provided students with feedback regarding their use of collaborative skills. The classroom teacher graded all the papers and provided feedback regarding academic performance to the students and their parents.

During the second marking period, the special educator took on a more active role and co-designed lessons with the classroom teacher. On occasion, he also explained the task and social skill objectives to the students. By the third marking period, the classroom teacher and the special educator were rotating roles and responsibilities on a daily basis. One explained the objectives, the task, and the expected outcomes, while the other assumed primary responsibility for monitoring and processing individual and group performance of the desired social skills. They also took equal responsibility for grading student products, meeting with parents during parent–teacher conferences, and providing one another with feedback regarding their instruction.

Both teachers found this partnership professionally valuable and stimulating. In an effort to further refine their skills and meet student needs, they decided to expand the membership of their cooperative education team. They invited a Chapter 1 teacher, who had expertise in alternative strategies for teaching reading and the development of thematic units, to team teach with them and to attend their Tuesday and Thursday planning meetings. The original two-member team believed the Chapter 1 teacher could help them to develop interdisciplinary units, motivate the students, and breathe new life into the team. The Chapter 1 teacher accepted because she wanted to learn cooperative group instructional methodology so she could meet the needs of her students through a classroom rather than a pull-out service delivery model. She also welcomed the opportunity to develop a closer professional relationship with her colleagues. Two years later, all three instructors continue to meet twice weekly for planning and to team up to deliver language arts instruction a minimum of 4 days per week.

A Middle School Social Studies Team

A sixth grade social studies teacher and a special educator have worked as a cooperative education team for 4 years. They team teach a minimum of 3 days a week. This team does not have a set meeting time for planning; instead, they mutually decide, from week to week, when and where they will conduct the next planning meeting. Neither team member has had "formal" training in cooperative group learning, but both have had the opportunity to team teach extensively with other school personnel who are considered outstanding in the design and delivery of cooperative group learning experiences. In addition, both team members have had training in effective instruction and collaborative teaming (Thousand & Villa, 1992). They try to employ the principles of cooperative teaming when they meet to plan cooperative learning lessons.

This team has chosen to split academic and social instructional responsibilities. Because of his knowledge of social studies content and his enthusiasm for the subject matter, the classroom teacher determines and explains the academic objectives. The special educator, who is familiar with various social skills curricula and is experienced in facilitating social skills groups for middle level students, determines and explains the social skill objectives. Both teachers monitor student progress and intervene to teach academic and social skills. The classroom teacher makes sure that students summarize their learning daily while the special educator guides the processing related to the cooperative skill objectives.

The members of this team recently decided to take a cooperative learning summer graduate course together and to invite colleagues with more experience and expertise in cooperative group learning to observe and provide them with feedback at least once each marking period.

A Secondary School Science Team

A high school science teacher, who relied primarily upon whole-group instruction and lab activities to teach homogeneous groups of high-ability students, decided to try cooperative learning structures. She stated two reasons for taking this new instructional approach. First, she had received strong written negative feedback from her department chair about her continued failure to use a variety of instructional approaches. Second, the school board had adopted a policy that virtually eliminated homogeneous grouping and tracking from the high school. The teacher recognized that soon the composition of her classes would be more diverse and that new instructional strategies, such as cooperative group learning, might enable her to better meet her students' needs and to please her supervisors.

During the previous year, the science teacher had overheard several teachers in the lounge commenting on how a special educator (referred to as a *collaborating teacher* in this school system) with expertise in speech and language had assisted them to acquire or refine their cooperative learning instructional skills. The science teacher thought that this collaborating teacher had a great sense of humor and might be an enjoyable work partner. The science teacher approached the collaborating teacher with an invitation to form a cooperative education team for the class period prior to lunch. The invitation was quickly accepted. The collaborating teacher saw it as an opportunity to acquire content knowledge that would assist him in working with students who are eligible for speech and language services and who struggled with the vocabulary and content of the science classes.

The science teacher (with her expertise in science) and the collaborating teacher (with his expertise in cooperative learning, verbal and nonverbal communication, effective instruction, and individualizing and adapting instruction) formed a cooperative education team 2 years ago. During the first year, they had numerous differences in educational philosophy and approaches to teaching and classroom management. Initially, the collaborating teacher reported feeling more like a teaching assistant than a teacher during the actual instructional period. In retrospect, he identified the primary source of those feelings as his lack of content mastery during the first year of the team relationship. The science teacher noted that she felt very dependent upon the collaborating teacher for the design and presentation of the cooperative learning segments of lessons. She also stated that without the skill and patience of the collaborating teacher, she would have given up using cooperative learning structures.

The science teacher readily acknowledges the many skills she has acquired to design more active student-learning experiences and to accommodate student differences. The collaborating teacher points to the science content he has acquired and the skills in conflict resolution that were refined as he and his teammate developed a classroom-management system that was mutually acceptable. Interestingly, both acknowledged that discipline problems diminished when the students were trained in how to work as a member of a cooperative learning group and given more responsibility for their own and one another's acquisition of academic and social skills.

During the second year of the team relationship, a student with Down syndrome enrolled in the team's "college-level" biology course. She provided the team with the opportunity to refine skills in designing group-learning experiences in which student objectives are individualized. The team wanted this learner both to contribute meaningfully to group activities and to achieve her individualized education program (IEP) objectives. They decided upon several strategies. First, they decided to use a peer tutor to preteach some of the science content to the young woman during her study hall. The science teacher recruited a former student who had demonstrated mastery in the science content of this class as the peer tutor. The collaborating teacher provided initial and ongoing training, support, and evaluative feedback to the peer tutor. Second, they frequently assigned to the student with Down syndrome the role of timekeeper in her group, thus addressing the time-telling and time-keeping needs identified in her IEP. Third, they reduced the amount of content for which this student was held accountable. Fourth, with the permission of the young woman and her parents, the members of her cooperative groups assisted her and her teachers to determine appropriate instructional and social skill objectives, accommodations, and modifications.

The members of this cooperative education team expressed confidence in their ability to design exciting and appropriate group learning experiences. Both are involved in planning the transition of a young man with multiple disabilities to their school. The science teacher has requested that this young man be placed in one of her classes and, with her collaborating teacher teammate, has begun designing cooperative group science lessons to address his IEP goals for increased vocalization, communication board use, and age-appropriate social interactions along with the academic and social skills objectives of the other students in the science class.

DISCUSSION AND ADVICE

We have described how classroom teachers and support personnel can effectively share expertise and responsibility for designing, conducting, and evaluating cooperative learning experiences and, in this way, personalizing curriculum and instruction for students who, by nature, are unique and changing in their needs. As the case studies illustrate, teaching need not be a "lonely profession" (Sarason, Levine, Godenberg, Cherlin, & Bennet, 1966, p. 74), and the traditional pull-out and special class arrangements of compensatory and special education need not be the solution to the challenges of increasing adult-to-student ratios, individualizing instruction, and accommodating student differences. When members of the school community work together to foster the academic and collaborative skill development of students, they offer the students a valuable model of collaboration in action as well as provide opportunities for their own professional and interpersonal growth.

It is important to remember that it may take a cooperative education team some time to become as effective and efficient as it would like. Teams evolve through the forming, functioning, formulating, and fermenting stages of group development, particularly if their members regularly examine the role clarification questions in Table 1 and the evaluation questions in Table 2, and if they process how well they perform small-group social skills. Numerous teams also report that the agenda format presented in Figure 2 is most helpful in alerting them to the critical elements of an effective team (i.e., frequent face-to-face interaction, positive interdependence, individual accountability, social skill performance, periodic assessment, and processing instructional and interpersonal effectiveness).

The task of educating an increasingly diverse student population can be overwhelming. No one teacher is capable of successfully meeting this challenge alone. We propose that collaboration among students (through cooperative learning structures) and adults (through cooperative education teams) is a key to meeting the challenge of educating a heterogeneous student population. We are pleased to report that students now have joined adults as partners in cooperative education teams and have proven to be creative resources in formulating objectives, instructional methods, and accommodations for individual students (Villa & Thousand, 1992). When the work of the traditional teacher is divided between two or more persons, both teachers and students should more fully experience the power of being able to meet increasingly diverse educational and psychological student needs, to free themselves from isolation and the sole responsibility for student learning, and to experience the fun and feeling of belonging that result when people reinvent education together.

REFERENCES

Brandt, R. (1987). On cooperation in schools: A conversation with David and Roger Johnson. *Educational Leadership, 45*(3), 14–19.

Cummings, C. (1985). *Peering in on peers.* Edmonds, WA: Snohomish.

Glasser, W. (1986). *Control theory in the classroom.* New York: Harper & Row.

Glickman, C.D. (1990). *Supervision of instruction: A developmental approach* (2nd ed.). Needham Heights, MA: Allyn & Bacon.

Harris, T. (1987, October). *A speech and language pathologist's perspective on teaming to accom-plish cooperation between and among regular and special educators for the provision of services in the least restrictive environment.* Paper presented at Vermont's Least Restrictive Environment Conference, Burlington.

Johnson, D.W., & Johnson, R.T. (1987). *A meta-analysis of cooperative, competitive and individualistic goal structures.* Hillsdale, NJ: Lawrence Erlbaum Associates.

Johnson, D.W., & Johnson, R.T. (1989). *Cooperation and competition: Theory and research.* Edina, MN: Interaction Book Company.

Johnson, D.W., & Johnson, R.T. (1991). *Learning together and alone: Cooperation, competition, and individualization* (3rd ed.). Englewood Cliffs, NJ: Prentice Hall.

Johnson, D.W., Johnson, R.T., Holubec, E., & Roy, P. (1984). *Circles of learning.* Arlington, VA: Association for Supervision and Curriculum Development.

Parnes, S. (1981). *The magic of your mind.* Buffalo, NY: Creative Education Foundation, Inc., in association with Bearly Limited.

Parnes, S. (1988). *Visionizing: State-of-the-art process for encouraging innovative excellence.* East Aurora, NY: D.O.K. Publishers.

Sarason, S., Levine, M., Godenberg, I., Cherlin, D., & Bennet, E. (1966). *Psychology in community settings: Clinical, educational, vocational, and social aspects.* New York: John Wiley & Sons.

Showers, B., Joyce, B., & Bennett, B. (1987). Synthesis of research on staff development: A framework for future study and a state-of-the-art analysis. *Educational Leadership, 45*(3), 77–87.

Skrtic, T. (1991). *Behind special education: A critical analysis of professional culture and school organization.* Denver: Love Publishing Co.

Slavin, R.E. (1984). Review of cooperative learning research. *Review of Educational Research, 50,* 315–342.

Slavin, R.E. (1987). Ability grouping and student achievement in elementary school: A best-evidence synthesis. *Review of Educational Research, 57,* 293–336.

Slavin, R.E. (1989). Research on cooperative learning: Consensus and controversy. *Educational Leadership, 47*(4), 52–54.

Smith, S.C. (1987). The collaborative school takes shape. *Educational Leadership, 45*(3), 4–6.

Thousand, J., & Villa, R. (1990). Sharing expertise and responsibilities through teaching teams. In W. Stainback & S. Stainback (Eds.), *Support networks for inclusive schooling: Interdependent integrated education* (pp. 151–166). Baltimore: Paul H. Brookes Publishing Co.

Thousand, J.S., & Villa, R.P. (1992). Collaborative teams: A powerful tool in school restructuring. In R.P. Villa, J.S. Thousand, W. Stainback, & S. Stainback (Eds.), *Restructuring for caring and effective education: An administrative guide to creating heterogeneous schools* (pp. 73–108). Baltimore: Paul H. Brookes Publishing Co.

Villa, R.P., & Thousand, J.S. (1992). Student collaboration: An essential for curriculum delivery in the 21st century. In S. Stainback & W. Stainback (Eds.), *Curriculum considerations in inclusive classrooms: Facilitating learning for all students* (pp. 117–142). Baltimore: Paul H. Brookes Publishing Co.

Student Disruptions in the Cooperative Classroom

Experiences in a New Brunswick, Canada, School District

Brian Kelly

During the past decade a number of initiatives prompted significant change in classrooms across New Brunswick, Canada. Two of the most notable initiatives were Bill 85 (1986, June), which supports the inclusion of all children, regardless of their differing abilities, in general education classrooms, and the federal Stay In School Initiative for students who are considered at risk of leaving school. More recently, a New Brunswick provincial government's *Excellence in Education* report (1991, December) critiqued current practices and made recommendations to improve the New Brunswick educational system. The goal of these measures was to promote the capacity of schools to include those once excluded, retain those likely to leave, and be sensitive to those with extenuating life circumstances. Although this may sound like a daunting task, teachers and administrators have risen to the challenge. Within New Brunswick School District #12, teachers have met and discussed how these changes will influence their classrooms and what skills and resources they will need in order to succeed.

SCHOOL DISTRICT #12 INITIATIVES

School District #12 is a small, geographically scattered school system that comprises 300 professional staff members in 14 schools that serve just under 5,000 students. Although limited in resources, the district has a reputation for being innovative. This has come about mainly by restructuring special education services to support all students in regular education classrooms. Method and resource teachers (i.e., the equivalent of American special education consulting teachers or integration facilitators) within the school, guidance counselors, and administrators have a district mandate to help the classroom teacher work through difficulties in a meaningful way that enhances the probability of student success in learning *within* the classroom (Porter & Collicott, 1992). This expectation has led to the implementation of numerous initiatives, which are presented in Table 1.

This chapter examines teachers' perceptions about the instructional strategies that enable them to accommodate a wider range of student behavior in the classroom. Teachers at the elementary and high school level who use cooperative learning were interviewed to gain their insights on how cooperative learning influenced their teaching and how peer-mediated strategies, such as student problem solving and class meetings, assist students with problematic behavior. Peer-influence strategies, including cooperative learning, were identified as procedures that can be used to address, proactively and reactively, students who demonstrate disruptive behavior while promoting academic learning.

At a 1991 District #12 forum on school discipline, teachers noted the need for collaboration among school personnel, parents, and students to resolve discipline is-

Table 1.   Initiatives to support students

Community-level awareness	Targeted student populations	Specific student interventions
School board initiatives • Invitational education • Positive school and classroom climate • Mastery teaching • Building effective schools together	Stay-in-School initiatives • Drop out study • Stay-in-school week • At-risk students sensitization	Conflict resolution
	Workshops • Community partnerships • Stay-in-school teacher teams	Peer influence and mediation strategies
Student services initiatives • Aversives policy • Nonviolent crisis intervention • School organization reform • Suicide intervention training • Psychological maltreatment		Interpersonal/social skills training
	Work orientation workshops	Parenting issues workshops
	Crisis intervention workshops	Behavior management plans
Guidance counselors initiatives • Parenting issues workshops • Conflict resolution training for teachers • Study skills • Peer mediation/facilitators training • Conflict resolution • Personal safety workshops	Peer influence strategies (peer tutoring programs, cooperative learning, peer support groups)	
	Peer-mediation strategies (conflict resolution, peer facilitators)	
Teacher's union initiatives • Forum on school discipline • Classroom management	Literacy tutors	
	Method and resource teacher training (multilevel instruction, literacy training, educational planning, crisis intervention, problem solving, cooperative learning)	
Interested community organizations • Home and school associations • Woodstock Association for Community Living • Early Intervention Services • Rotary Service Club	School mentors	
	School-based student services teams	

sues by empowering students to help one another. Subsequently, teachers met to discuss students at risk of school failure and the obstacles, strategies, and solutions for keeping these students in school through Grade 12. Discussions regarding discipline issues were lengthy. The number one obstacle was dealing with students who did not want help because of what their peers would think. School personnel, therefore, sought intervention techniques that addressed this issue of peer pressure and receiving help.

Teacher Perceptions of Instructional Strategies

In examining classroom strategies, teachers stated that classroom management could not be separated from student learning. They recognized that students actively involved in academic behavior are less likely to engage in disruptive behavior in the classroom. More effective teaching strategies were seen, therefore, as key to teaching all students and appealing to their various learning styles and abilities. Gilstrap and Martin (1976) identified a range of instructional strategies teachers might use to instruct students (see Table 2).

Teachers who were interviewed considered few of these strategies to be purposefully designed to address diverse student needs during a lesson. Only one strategy, cooperative learning, was identified as an instructional strategy to deal with peer pressure concerns, behavior management, and effective instruction in an integrated fashion. Four additional themes, described below, emerged from the teacher interviews.

Most Instructional Strategies Do Not Provide Enough Evidence that They Work   Teachers thought that some of the instructional strategies represented in Table 2 carried assumptions about the type of students they taught. For example, either the classroom was full of well-behaved students, or, if the teacher was having classroom management difficulties, they could simply be addressed by using the right type of motivational technique. Other strategies made only superficial attempts to address classroom management issues. These strategies viewed the classroom in very generic terms and thus showed limited success in specific classroom situations and problems.

Many Classroom Procedures Fail to Be Comprehensive Enough to Solve a Student's Difficulties   Teachers stated that they believe instructional strategies and behavior management procedures fail because they do not complement one another. For example, some schedules of reinforcement, if adhered to specifically, disrupt the flow of teaching. As a result, one type of disruption is replaced by another. Furthermore, some behavior management strategies fail because they require so much time and are too complex for the teaching of a lesson to progress.

Many Classroom Procedures Are Simply Too Ambiguous   Sometimes behavior management advice is unclear; it lacks sufficient detail for complete understanding by the teacher. Procedures often are deployed quickly as immediate responses to crisis situations, rather than planned to fit the overall classroom instruc-

Table 2.   Types of instructional strategies

Lecture	Discussion	Drill and practice
Independent study	Group investigation	Laboratory approach
Discovery	The Learning Centre	Simulation
Cooperative learning	Multilevel instruction	Do-look-learn
Behavior modification	Performance-based learning activity package	

Source: Gilstrap and Martin (1976).

tional design. As a result, errors occur and what was intended is often implemented incorrectly. In summary, the procedures are too ambiguous for a teacher to carry out with a high degree of accuracy.

Many Classroom Procedures Fail Because They Exceed Available Resources Some procedures are not sustained because of the level of effort they require from a teacher; they become just one more thing to be added to a teacher's responsibilities. The extra time required to implement procedures also may exceed a teacher's expectations and that which is available in a school day.

As these themes suggest, teachers want and need integrated strategies that enable them to concentrate on academic instruction and, at the same time, maintain high levels of appropriate behavior in the classroom. Teachers are more likely to implement and maintain an instructional strategy that simultaneously addresses instruction and behavior.

PEER INTERVENTIONS

> The problems shown by our children reflect their search for alternative outlets, for places to release the pressure, for contexts in which they feel efficacious. If children are not "good enough" in academics, and if schools provide few other outlets and pathways to a feeling of effectiveness and accomplishment, students will show that they can be the best at disrupting learning, showing disrespect, and resisting entreaties of teachers and parents to do schoolwork. (Elias, 1989, p. 401)

Elias (1989) suggests that students need to feel they have control or a say in what happens. He further suggests that, academics aside, "school is primarily a social experience" (p. 397). Thus, students need opportunities to interact. Kohler and Strain (1990) coined the term *collaborative interventions* to describe a range of strategies that involve teachers and peers working together to help a particular student by implementing an intervention to increase or decrease certain behaviors. Generally, collaborative intervention strategies have the dual purpose of teaching academic skills and managing certain social skills and behaviors of a specific student. Whereas collaborative interventions are a distinct type of intervention, it is perhaps easier to think of them as falling into one of two categories: peer mediation strategies or peer influence strategies. In peer mediation, peers systematically implement behavior change programs to serve in peer mediation roles. Students are trained and monitored by a teacher or guidance counselor. Within District #12, peer mediation strategies have been incorporated into peer mediation, peer tutoring and peer support group programs, conflict resolution instruction, and classwide meetings. Peer influence strategies, however, take advantage of natural social interactions and consequences that children in groups provide one another when working toward a mutual goal. Peer influence strategies are typified in cooperative learning lessons.

Peer-Mediated Strategies

In this section, two strategies that rely on peer mediation are described: Problem solving and class meetings.

Problem Solving Some students are so consistently challenging or unresponsive that they outlast the usual repertoire of interventions. In these situations, it is good to take a team approach in which a group of people bring their particular perspectives to the meeting. The way to approach problem solving in schools can be on a one-to-one basis or involve large groups, such as a classroom of students (Kelly & den Otter, 1991). Meetings that involve students in structured problem solving take

20–30 minutes and follow six steps (Porter, 1994; Porter, Wilson, Kelly, & den Otter, 1991):

1. Define the problem in specific terms.
2. Brainstorm solutions; write whatever comes into mind.
3. For each possible solution, list what might happen that could help the situation.
4. Select or combine the desired solutions.
5. Plan how to carry out the solution.
6. After a week or two, evaluate how the plan is working.

Problem solving should be viewed as something that is used by students and by teachers.

Class Meetings   Class meetings provide a teacher and students with a forum to discuss how a student's behavior is affecting them and what they can do about it. The intensity of a certain behavior or the fear for the personal safety of members of the classroom may necessitate an adult intervening to defuse a potentially explosive situation and initiating a class meeting. Students and teachers discuss how they feel about the situation and the possible precipitating factors or antecedents that may produce the behavior. They also discuss possible solutions. Consider David, whose life situation and low achievement precipitated a high level of disruption in a sixth grade classroom. This disruptive behavior was being inadvertently reinforced by classmates' responses to his behavior.

Until recently, there had been a lot of violence in David's home. In class he sought attention and approval from his peers by swearing, making loud vocalizations, and throwing objects. In the beginning, classmates reacted with laughter, which caused David's misbehavior to escalate. One morning when David was away from class, the teacher initiated a class meeting to discuss David's behavior and how the class reacted to it. The teacher explained that their laughing was a problem when he was disruptive in learning groups. The teacher drew some parallels to similar situations that might occur at home, such as when a sibling is being silly at the dinner table. The children in the class easily related to the issue and offered appropriate alternatives to solve the dilemma. They decided that ignoring and not laughing at his behavior was the best solution. They also identified and made a list of the cooperative social skills they would encourage.

Clearly, such talks with students should avoid focusing on only negative behaviors and attributes of a student. Rather, the student must be described in a balanced light—as someone who belongs to the class and who has strengths and gifts to contribute to the class, but who at times acts in an unacceptable way. For class meetings to work, the teachers must do at least the following:

1. Demonstrate true concern and empathy for the student during the meeting. If not, students will quickly perceive the discussion as an opportunity to merely slander the student.
2. Model appropriate responses when the child is being disruptive and cue students in the group or class to do likewise.
3. Coach and reinforce appropriate responses to unwanted behavior so that it becomes second nature.

Teachers who have used class meetings identified six advantages of this intervention approach:

1. *Immediacy*   Teachers as well as students have the opportunity to come up with strategies to help the student with problematic behavior.

2. *Ownership*   Students who share the same space with a student who has difficulties have a vested interest in seeing that the situation gets resolved.
3. *Relevance*   Solutions produced through the problem-solving process are tailored to the resources available in the school.
4. *Empowering*   Students involved can feel that they are contributing to a solution for ongoing difficulties.
5. *Assumes a collaborative approach*   None of us is as smart as all of us.
6. *Positive orientation*   Recommendations use positive attributes of the student as the cornerstone for change.

Collaborating with students to generate solutions under nonthreatening conditions is a way to encourage students to own a class problem and demonstrate that they can affect positive change. Class meeting problem solving is premised on the notion that a solution does not necessarily make a problem "go away." Instead, a solution is a temporary accommodation and adjustment in how the school system can meet the needs of the individual child. It requires a positive outlook and confidence that there are ways to resolve a problem.

A Peer-Influence Strategy:
Cooperative Learning as Proactive Management

The general consensus of teachers in School District #12 was that being proactive or preventative with regard to disruptive behavior was better than being reactive. For them, proactive meant to act in advance, to have a plan of action that offered maximum control of a situation. Another aspect of being proactive was combining appropriate student discipline with effective instruction. One teacher noted that most inservice training "examined either effective teaching or classroom management but seldom were examples presented of how the two work together." Also, recommended classroom management strategies tend to focus on individual student behavior without looking at the whole classroom situation, despite agreement that appropriate behavior demonstrated by a student perceived as disruptive often is the by-product of well-managed groups. Cooperative learning structures, when regularly used in a classroom, embody the characteristics of proactive management strategies and clearly demonstrate how good teaching and good classroom management can go hand in hand. Specific proactive strategies of well-designed cooperative group learning classrooms and inservice training opportunities are discussed in the next sections. Experiences of District #12 teachers are used to illustrate each aspect.

Inservice and Follow-Up Training   Most District #12 teachers felt that they learned little in their preservice training programs about a variety of the instructional strategies, including cooperative learning models. When they completed their practice teaching, they had little opportunity to practice and receive coaching on the instructional strategies of which they were aware. Teachers noted that the district's inservice instruction and follow-up coaching on cooperative learning taught them how to: 1) plan lessons more effectively, 2) implement lessons within a cooperative format, and 3) evaluate what they had taught. Teachers reported that more than any other training, this training enabled them to both provide students with academic instruction and prevent off-task, disruptive behavior. Classroom order depends on a teacher's ability to monitor on-task behavior and model high commitment to work—quality instruction maximizes learning and student accountability for doing assigned work. Cooperative learning seems to increase the teacher's capacity to maximize order and quality in teaching.

Teaching Students Appropriate Behaviors Another type of information conveyed to students was appropriate behavior. As most cooperative group learning models emphasize, direct instruction of social skills is crucial to effective group work among students. Teachers of District #12 recognize the power of teaching social skills to curtail the occurrence of disruptive behavior, as well as the importance of beginning the school year by spending time to develop expectations for classroom behavior with students. As one elementary teacher noted:

> We sometimes make real assumptions that students come to school ready to learn and interact with peers. Most of the time when a child gets in trouble it can be attributed to the fact that [he has] not learned an appropriate way of communicating [his] needs. For example, Peter's response to being refused something was to hit other students. I spent a lot of time teaching him simply to say, "That's not fair," or "I'm angry," rather than simply striking out. (S. Langdon, personal communication, November, 1993)

In many elementary classrooms, teachers actively teach social skills. Being able to listen, communicate, and work harmoniously are seen as just as important as learning to read, write, and compute. Teachers noted that their students made noticeable and significant gains when social skills were directly taught. Students in cooperative classrooms were reported to "get along better" than they did in years prior to cooperative learning being introduced into the schools. Teachers also noted that unlike individual social skills programs for students with "poor" social skills, social skills taught to the whole class in the context of classroom activities permitted the socially skilled students to readily serve as strong role models for their less-skilled peers. When students were taught away from the classroom, the skills taught in isolation often did not generalize to the classroom or other school environments. Taking the time to teach socials skills in the classroom context increases the likelihood the skills can and will be used in the classroom now and in the future.

Whenever a teacher teaches social skills, both the teacher and the students learn and experience a common body of information and a common language with which to talk about social skills and expectations. Thus, when a student does something deemed inappropriate, feedback and interventions may be offered in the form of corrective feedback rather than criticism or a threat of punishment. In the words of one teacher:

> Usually students who don't have a lot of self-esteem tend to use put-downs with others in their group. Sometimes other students in the group will have to tell the student to ease up. But there are times when I have felt the need to intervene. Instead of getting on his case, I remind him of why we don't use put-downs and how it makes others feel. (K. Anderson, personal communication, November, 1992)

Some of the District #12 teachers began to directly teach classroom routines and requisite skills to successfully engage in each activity just as academic content was taught. For example, teachers performed a task analysis for each classroom activity. For each task, they identified the social skills (see Table 3) and procedures that were necessary for students to perform as desired. They presented the tasks to students in small steps and with the appropriate level of vocabulary. Finally, students practiced the needed social skills and received feedback on their performance.

By communicating expectations and social skills before each lesson, teachers cued students as to the task demand and, in this way, reduced the likelihood of mis-

Table 3.   Summary of social skills

Self-Disclosure
  Being aware of thoughts, feelings, and needs
  Expressing thoughts, feelings, reactions, and needs to others
  Seeking and giving feedback

Trust
  Responding with acceptance and support when others self-disclose

Communication
  Speaking by using "I" messages when expressing thoughts, feelings, reactions, and needs
  Describing others' actions without making judgments
  Empathy

Responses
  Using appropriately evaluative, interpretive, supportive, and probing responses

Acceptance and Support
  Describing strengths when it is appropriate to do so
  Expressing acceptance of other people when it is appropriate to do so

Influence
  Reinforcing others' actions in order to increase, decrease, or maintain the frequency of their behavior, depend-
    ing on what is in their best interests
  Modeling interpersonal skills for others who wish to acquire them

Conflicts
  Knowing how to define conflict
  Viewing conflict as an opportunity for change
  Taking perspective
  Managing feelings
  Reaching agreement

Stress and Anger
  Following rules for the constructive management of anger
  Asserting anger through descriptions of your behavior, nonverbal messages, and good listening skills

---

Adapted from Johnson (1986).

behavior. Consistent expectations added stability to daily routines, leaving less room for unwelcome disruptions.

Monitoring and Processing Classroom Activity   The ongoing student monitoring that is built into cooperative learning serves as another important means of communicating behavioral expectations to students and allows the teacher to take a more active role in facilitating learning. Once task and social demands of a lesson have been set up, students can begin to work. The teacher's role is to monitor how students work together. Rather than focusing on a specific student, teachers carefully observe what is happening within groups. One teacher stated:

> It's easy sometimes to blame a student if [he is] not working. If the student isn't working, it's [his] problem. But sometimes these students are just the tip of the iceberg. They are the flag wavers who may represent the others who don't understand what is going on. When I ask a group "How are you doing?", I get a feeling of how each student is doing in the context of the others in the group. (L. Purvis, personal communication, November, 1992)

By asking various questions of the group to ensure social skills and academic accountability, the teacher may pinpoint skills in need of more practice or discover problems in groups as they are first emerging. To develop students' behavioral competence, teachers must stimulate self-reflection regarding their social skill and task performance when working with others. The teacher's role of guide or facilitator of this self-reflection (known as group processing) is essential for students' interpersonal and self-control development. Processing does not only occur while the teacher observes how students are working in groups, but at the midway point and sometimes at the end of an activity. Self-reflection occurs as members of the groups themselves evaluate how they did and focus on what they need to change to improve their work in the future. To progress to the point where group processing comes naturally and has an effect on individual behavior requires time and encouragement on the part of the teacher. One teacher commented:

> When groups start processing how they work together, their first attempts seem half-hearted or are token gestures to comply by filling in the sheet. But as time goes on, they get into it. Their comments are more earnest and natural as they talk about their work. (R. Kelly, personal communication, November, 1992)

Dealing with Special Challenges

A goal of peer influence strategies, such as cooperative learning, is to create opportunities for students to work and interact in meaningful and positive ways. However, with every opportunity there are potential drawbacks. Some students, because of their previous learning experiences or particular life situations, will resist working with peers. Johnson and Johnson (1987) identified four types of students who may disrupt group processes: students who do not do their work, students who are withdrawn, students who are low achievers, and students who are disruptive in a group. They then recommended some strategies to deal with these students' behaviors.

Students Who Do Not Do the Work   Thinking of the student who will not do his or her assigned work brings to mind group projects this author was required to complete during his studies. A professor would group together people who were mostly unknown to one another and tell them to prepare a paper, a presentation, or a display. As the deadline date would near, it become apparent that some people were working more than others. Some students would skate along doing little; others would work slavishly and pull up the slack in order to meet the deadline. After such projects, students expressed many negative judgments, such as "I never want to do a group project again" or "I never want to speak to that person." It was and is not enough to assign students to group projects. If students are put in groups without explicit roles and responsibilities, there may be someone who tries to do as little as possible in order to get by. When this appears to be taking place in a group, possible interventions include:

1. Ask the group to discuss the issue with the student and see why he or she is not contributing to the group's work.
2. Take the student aside and ask about the situation to determine his or her perception of it. Problem solve alternative ways in which more commitment or involvement can be obtained.
3. Present a skills lesson on problem solving a situation to be sure that *all* the students have the skills they need to deal with such a situation.
4. Trust the group to resolve the issue.

Another way to change student behavior is to change the way students in the group are evaluated. For example, have part of each student's grade comprise a rating given by each of the other group members. Or, grade the group on the basis of their average performance. If group members are penalized for another student's lack of effort, they are likely to derive strategies for increasing that student's involvement. Another strategy is for teachers to randomly pick one student in the group to represent the group's overall learning for a particular task. This sense of not knowing whose paper will be chosen may motivate most students to help each other be prepared.

Students Who Are Withdrawn   Some children come to school shy and withdrawn. They may have limited opportunities to socialize, no siblings, or live in a rural environment. Other students may become isolated over time; they may lack friendships because of poor interpersonal skills or they may give up on school because of repeated failure, as is the case with many at-risk students. Strategies to help and include these students are discussed below.

Ensure Constructive Teammates   The teacher's decision regarding face-to-face interaction may be to assign students who are likely to be nurturing and supportive to the student's group. Often the key to success is creating opportunities for students to click. One elementary teacher describes such a situation.

> Tom was very withdrawn. He was happy to just sit and watch what was going on in class. At the beginning of the year, his parents told me about this and asked me to keep an eye on things. So I matched him up with Stephanie. She's very outgoing and is good at including others. For instance, I saw Tom sitting and asked Stephanie to go and play with him. Stephanie went and took his hand, brought him to the group, and announced that they were playing house and he was the father. She gave him a helmet and told him what to do. The same thing happens when they are sitting and doing schoolwork. She becomes what I would call an "enabler." (J. Dunnett, personal communication, November, 1992)

Structure Resource Interdependence   Peer interaction may be promoted by having limited materials (e.g., one pair of scissors per group, one set of crayons) available to necessitate sharing and interaction. Assigning different parts of the academic task to each person in the group, similar to a jigsaw puzzle, also may prompt supportive interactions to help the withdrawn student locate and/or prepare his or her unique contribution.

Structure Role Interdependence   Each student has a role with specific responsibilities such as recorder, observer, or speaker. A specific role can be assigned or invented that is low risk to the withdrawn student, but likely to ensure that the student is included (e.g., observer).

Students Who Are Low Achievers   Including students who are low achievers in cooperative learning creates the opportunities for more growth than would be associated with other instructional strategies (e.g., competitive, individualistic). Inclusion of low achievers requires the teacher to adapt lesson requirements so that the student may participate in a way that is valued by the student and the other members of the group. The same suggestions for a withdrawn student may promote active involvement and performance for a low achiever. Coaching the student in advance to make him or her an expert in a specific aspect of the assignment allows the student to be called upon to teach other group members.

Students Who Are Disruptive in a Group   If we consider all behavior to be some form of communication, then we may assume that students who disrupt or students who are actively uninvolved in a lesson are attempting to communicate some underlying message, the source of which may be academic or behavioral. In the academic domain, students may be experiencing difficulty with schoolwork. In the social domain, their social or interpersonal skills may be ineffective. Students who disrupt likely are seeking to avoid school work or be noticed through whatever means possible to them. Some strategies for helping these students are discussed below.

Include Constructive Teammates and Avoid Destructive Teammates   Many children with disruptive behavior have ineffective interpersonal skills and have had negative experiences (e.g., arguments, fights) with other students. When assigning students to groups, try to avoid "deadly combinations" that will exacerbate the situation.

Pretrain Teammates in Procedures for Controlling the Disruption   Create opportunities for classmates to intervene with relevant management strategies that deal with special challenges. It is critical that classmates practice any procedure they are to use consistently (e.g., ignoring, engaging the student in oral planning) with the student when a disruption occurs or is about to occur.

Intervene to Teach Collaborative Skills   When a student disrupts, the teacher may intervene to help group members or the class find ways to influence the disruption. The teacher's role is to guide classmates through problem solving or brainstorming strategies to come up with some ideas that are acceptable and workable in the classroom.

Teach the Disruptive Student Collaborative Skills   Although most cooperative learning models have a significant social skills component, there may be students who require additional time to practice and master social skills. Students may need someone (e.g., the school counselor, special educator, a trained paraprofessional, a peer mediator) to coach them before a group activity takes place and to meet with them again after the lesson to discuss progress.

Reduce the Group Size   Some children who disrupt in groups perform much better in one-to-one situations (e.g., partners or peer tutoring) or in triads. In these situations, they receive a more constant flow of directed attention and feedback that keeps them academically engaged.

CONCLUSION

Student behavior is currently one of the most discussed topics in New Brunswick schools. In search of ways to effectively deal with behavioral challenges, increasing numbers of educators are turning to instructional strategies that rely on peer mediation and peer influence. Cooperative learning has emerged as a preferred, proactive peer-influence strategy that both actively supports the variety of learning styles and abilities that exist within a single classroom and prevents or minimizes disruptive behavior in the classroom.

Teacher interviews revealed a continuum of interventions that address the needs of students with disruptive behavior. One end of the continuum involves *reactive* measures that respond to misbehavior. The other end involves being *proactive* and designing the classroom to *inhibit* the occurrence of disruptions by communicating appropriate behavior through modeling and teaching social skills. The cooperative learning method, for example, increases student interdependence and learning, reduces disruptive behavior, and demonstrates that disruptive behavior is not a random act beyond the teacher's control. Rather, student behavior is a by-product of the way teachers teach and structure their classroom.

A direct relationship exists between classroom management and the need for outside school supports. Teachers who use verbal suppression as a means to stop unwanted behavior typically view continued student misbehavior as a problem innate to the child. They see formal assessments and a trip to a psychologist as the route to purge students of their problems. The teacher sees the student as having to meet the teacher's needs in the classroom and they see no need to change. Thus, they reject the procedures described in this chapter—collaboration, problem solving, restructuring the classroom environment, teaching social skills, and empowering peers. In such a situation, are behavior problems so much a student problem as one of "blaming the victim"? Are discipline problems in some schools as much a reflection of educators' inflexibility as students' behavior characteristics?

As stated earlier, students are an untapped resource. When trained and given the opportunity to act, they can be very effective in mediating their own and their peers' learning and social interactions. When given a voice, even young elementary age students demonstrate a level of maturity and analysis. Cooperative learning is an example of an increasing array of strategies that rely on peers helping peers. When educators and the community support students to run their classrooms, schools become a very different place—a kinder and more meaningful and effective place for everyone.

REFERENCES

Bill 85: An act to amend the Schools Act. (1986, June). 4th session, 5th legislature, Province of New Brunswick.

Elias, M. (1989). School as a source of stress. *Journal of School Psychology, 27,* 393–407.

Excellence in education: Schools for a new century. (1991, December). The Commission on Excellence in Education, Province of New Brunswick.

Gilstrap, R.L., & Martin, W.R. (1976). *Current strategies for teachers: A resource for personalizing materials.* Santa Monica, CA: Goodyear Publishing.

Johnson, D. (1986). *Reaching out: Interpersonal effectiveness and self-actualization.* Englewood Cliffs, NJ: Prentice Hall.

Johnson, D., & Johnson, R. (1987). *Learning together and alone: Cooperative, competitive, and individualistic learning.* Englewood Cliffs, NJ: Prentice Hall.

Kelly, B., & den Otter, J. (1991). Beyond behaviour: A case of social intervention strategies for a student with challenging behaviours. In G.L. Porter & D. Richler (Eds.), *Changing Canadian schools: Perspectives on disability and inclusion* (pp. 257–280). Toronto, Ontario, Canada: The Roeher Institute.

Kohler, F.W., & Strain, P.S. (1990). Peer-assisted interventions: Early promises, notable achievements, and future aspirations. *Clinical Psychology Review, 10,* 411–452.

Porter, G. (Executive Producer). (1994). *Teachers helping teachers: Problem-solving that works* [Video]. Toronto, Ontario, Canada: The Roeher Institute.

Porter, G., & Collicott, J. (1992). New Brunswick School Districts 28 and 29: Mandates and strategies that promote inclusive schooling. In R.A. Villa, J.S. Thousand, W. Stainback, & S. Stainback (Eds.), *Restructuring for caring and effective education: An administrative guide to creating heterogeneous schools* (pp. 187–200). Baltimore: Paul H. Brookes Publishing Co.

Porter, G.L., Wilson, M., Kelly, B., & den Otter, J. (1991). Problem-solving teams: A thirty minute peer-helping model. In G.L. Porter & D. Richler (Eds.), *Changing Canadian schools: Perspectives on disability and inclusion* (pp. 219–238). Toronto, Ontario, Canada: The Roeher Institute.

Salend, S.J., Whittaker, C.R., & Reeder, E. (1993). Group evaluation: A collaborative, peer-mediated behaviour management system. *Exceptional Children, 59,* 203–209.

8

Cooperative Group Learning and Higher Education

*Ann I. Nevin, Karl A. Smith,
and Alice Udvari-Solner*

Interest at the college level in cooperative learning is growing rapidly. Faculty in widely diverse institutions are discovering, often to their surprise, that students learn more, perform at higher levels, develop skills for working with others, and have more fun when learning in cooperative arrangements. The transition to using cooperative learning structures in college classrooms and, thus, actively involving students with fellow students and faculty in the development of their knowledge is one indication of a broader paradigm shift occurring in higher education. Additional features of this shift, as described by Johnson, Johnson, and Smith (1991a), are outlined in Table 1.

This chapter provides a summary of the research base for cooperative learning as an effective instructional method in higher education and teacher education, a description of the basic elements of cooperative learning, and various cooperative learning options professors in all disciplines may use. The benefits of preparing teacher education candidates by having them experience cooperative learning groups is emphasized. Teacher education candidates learn to analyze, evaluate, and refine cooperative lessons they design and conduct in their school-based practicum sites.

RESEARCH BASE FOR COOPERATIVE LEARNING

Cooperation is a very old idea in education. The Talmud, for example, states that three things are needed to learn—a text, a teacher, and a learning partner. The historical

Table 1.   Comparison of old and new paradigms of college teaching

	Old paradigm	New paradigm
Knowledge:	Transferred from faculty to students	Jointly constructed by students and faculty
Students:	Passive vessel to be filled by faculty knowledge	Active constructor, discoverer, transformer of knowledge
Faculty's purpose:	Classify and sort students	Develop students' competencies and talents
Relationships:	Impersonal relationship among students and between faculty and students	Personal transactions among students and between faculty and students
Context:	Competitive/individualistic	Cooperative learning in classrooms Cooperative teams among faculty
Assumption:	Any expert can teach	Teaching is complex and requires considerable training
Ways of knowing:	Logical/scientific	Narrative
Epistemology:	Reductionist	Constructivist
Mode of learning:	Memorizing	Relating
Climate:	Conformity/cultural uniformity	Diversity and personal esteem Cultural diversity and commonality

Adapted with permission from Johnson, D.W., Johnson, R.T., & Smith, K.A. (1991a). *Active learning: Cooperation in the college classroom.* Edina, MN: Interaction Book Company.

roots for the practice of cooperative learning in the United States can be traced to when Joseph Lancaster's idea of the Lancastrian school was brought to America in 1806. The Common School Movement in the 1800s emphasized cooperative learning. Colonel Francis Parker's implementation of cooperative learning procedures in the Quincy, Massachusetts public schools in the late 1880s was probably the first district-wide implementation (Campbell, 1965).

History of the Theory and Research

The history of the theory and research on cooperative learning similarly began in the late 1800s when factors associated with competition were studied. During the 1940s, Morton Deutsch (1949) generated a theory of cooperation and competition that built on the theories of Kurt Lewin (1935). Currently, there are several groups of researchers and practitioners studying the theory and practice of implementing cooperative learning practices, curriculum, and procedures. Theoretically, structuring situations cooperatively results in promotive interactions in contrast to competitive structures that result in oppositional interactions or individualistic structures that result in no interactions. It is the type of interaction pattern that affects such variables as achievement, quality of relationships among students, and students' social competence and psychological adjustment (see, for example, Johnson & Johnson, 1989b). More than 575 experimental and 100 correlational studies have been conducted by researchers in different environments, subject areas, countries, and age groups. The research evidence is clear that cooperative learning promotes higher achievement, higher self-esteem, increased higher-level reasoning, more frequent generation of new ideas and solutions (process gain), and greater transfer or generalization from one situation to another. Other beneficial outcomes include more positive heterogeneous relationships, better attitudes toward subject matter and teachers, greater collaborative skills, and more positive psychological health and social support (see, for example, Johnson, Johnson, Ortiz, & Stanne, 1991).

Cooperative Group Learning in Higher Education

Support for cooperative learning in college classrooms is coming from a variety of perspectives. Astin (1991, 1993) recently completed a study of students at 159 baccalaureate granting institutions. This work represents the first attempt to examine the impact of different general education approaches on student development using a large national sample of undergraduate institutions and a range of student outcomes. Astin was primarily interested in *outcomes*; in particular, how outcomes are affected by *environments*. Eighty-eight environmental factors were investigated to determine which factors influenced students' academic achievement, personal development, and satisfaction with college.

Astin found that the particular manner in which the general education curriculum is structured makes very little difference for most of the outcomes. However, two environmental factors were most predictive of positive change. These two factors— *interaction among students* and *interaction between faculty and students*—carried by far the largest weights and affected more general education outcomes than any other environmental factor studied, including curriculum content factors.

In short, Astin concluded that it appears that *how* students approach their general education and *how* the faculty actually deliver the curriculum is far more important than the formal curricular structure. More specifically, the findings strongly support a growing body of research suggesting that one of the crucial factors in the educational development of an undergraduate is the degree to which the student is *actively engaged* or *involved* in the undergraduate experience. His research findings suggest that curricular planning efforts will reap much greater payoffs in terms of student outcomes if less emphasis is placed on formal structure and content and more is placed on pedagogy and other features of the instructional delivery system as well as the broader interpersonal and institutional context in which learning takes place.

Light (1992) supported Astin's conclusions in his preface to the *Harvard Assessment Seminars: Second Report*. He wrote:

> The biggest challenge for me is to ask what the details all add up to. Do the many suggestions that interviewers get from their long conversations with undergraduates drive toward any broad, overarching principle? Is there any common theme that faculty members can use to help students, and indeed that students can use to help themselves? The answer is a strong yes. All the specific findings point to, and illustrate, one main idea. It is that students who get the most out of college, who grow the most academically, and who are the happiest, organize their time to include interpersonal activities with faculty members, or with fellow students, built around substantive, academic work. (p. 6)

Bouton and Garth (1983) show how cooperative learning can be applied in a variety of college disciplines. Cooper and Mueck (1990), in addition to an overview on cooperative learning, include data on more than 1,000 students enrolled in 18 different courses where cooperative learning is in effect at an urban, multicultural campus. Millis (1991) describes research on cooperative learning at the college level and includes practical applications of cooperative learning across all disciplines. Cooper, McKinney, and Robinson (1991) provide an annotated bibliography of 37 applied and 27 research and theory works related to college level applications of cooperative and collaborative learning published since 1988 in such areas as writing, English as a Second Language, computer science, art, sociology, history, and science.

Another source of support for the use of cooperative learning at the college level comes from businesses and industries where self-managing teams are used. Many companies now emphasize the need for employees at all levels who can participate as members of a team. Finally, the relationship between cooperation and creativity has been researched. A carefully structured cooperative working and/or learning environment helps reduce the devastating effects of the creativity killers. Creativity killers, such as those shown in Table 2, are discussed in detail by Goleman, Kaufman, and Ray (1992), who summarized the research of Teresa Amabile. Dr. Amabile is a research psychologist at Brandeis University who has conducted extensive studies in this area and is a recognized creativity specialist.

ACCOMMODATING STUDENTS WITH
DISABILITIES IN COLLEGE CLASSROOMS

The advent of the Americans with Disabilities Act (ADA) has prompted the faculty of universities and colleges to be more responsive to the needs of students with disabilities who attend their institutions. Signed into law on July 26, 1990, the ADA (PL 101-336) extends and strengthens Section 504, the Rehabilitation Act (as amended in 1992 by PL 102-569). The ADA guarantees equal opportunity for individuals with disabilities in employment, education, public accommodations, transportation, state and local government services, and telecommunications. Although anti-discrimination regulations of Section 504 have applied for years to institutions of higher education receiving federal funds, the passage of the ADA has stimulated organizations to assess whether programs and learning situations truly accommodate students with unique learning needs. There are a number of strategies professors can employ before the course begins, at the beginning of the course, and in the context of cooperative groups to create a supportive learning environment and facilitate success and the inclusion of students with disabilities.

Before the Course Begins

Prior to registration, a detailed course syllabus should be available that outlines course expectations, readings, and the scope of cooperative group work (Equity Action Subcommittee on Disabilities, 1992). Providing a copy of the syllabus to the student advising office and the campus disability resource center may help students prepare in advance for course requirements. The preparation of taped books and braille materials often can take many weeks; therefore, advanced access to the reading list may be essential. Instructors also should include a statement on the syllabus encouraging class members with any special learning needs to set up an appointment at the earliest possible date to discuss necessary accommodations.

The Beginning of the Course

Because it is the student's prerogative to self-disclose any disabling conditions, the instructor should reiterate orally and in written form the commitment to make accommodations in curriculum, instruction, or assessment. This information should be provided to the entire class and assurances made to maintain confidentiality if a student chooses to self-disclose. When the need for accommodations is expressed, schedule a meeting with the student to discuss his or her learning strengths and

Table 2. Creativity killers ameliorated by cooperative learning groups

Surveillance:	Hovering over students stifles their willingness to take risks.
Evaluation:	Too much emphasis on evaluating and grading students' work interferes with their ability to focus.
Rewards:	Rewards can deprive students of the intrinsic pleasure of creative activity.
Competition:	Putting students in a desperate win-lose situation, where only one person can come out on top, tends to cripple creativity.
Over-control:	Too much detail in the directions leaves students feeling that any originality is a mistake and any exploration is a waste of time.
Restricting choice:	Telling students which activities to engage in rather than letting them follow their interests is devastating.
Pressure:	Establishing grandiose expectations for performance can result in students' aversion for the subject being taught.
Time:	The clock-watching compulsion of many teachers is a subtle and deeply culturally rooted barrier to students' creativity.

T. Amabile's research is summarized in *The Creative Spirit* by Dan Goleman, Paul Kaufman, and Michael Ray. Copyright © 1992 by Alvin H. Perlmutter, Inc. Used by permission of Signet, a division of Penguin Books USA Inc.

concerns. Identifying the student's strongest learning modalities will be instrumental in determining appropriate tasks and roles within cooperative groups.

At the onset of the course as well as after the student has an opportunity to experience the instructor's teaching style, the individual should be encouraged to identify any changes needed in instructional delivery. Many accommodations can be incorporated as easily as changing the point size of text and using bold face type for printing the syllabus, lecture notes, class materials, and handouts to accommodate for students with visual impairments. As another example, in a course taught by one of the authors, a student with a hearing impairment discovered only after the course began that she: 1) could only hear the instructor if a microphone was used, 2) could not hear questions from class members unless repeated by the instructor, and 3) lost track of the lecture content if she could not see the instructor's lips. As each of these problems surfaced, the student informed the instructor and changes in the delivery of instruction were made. For individuals who are not as adept at self-advocacy, the professor may need to solicit student feedback at regular intervals. When faculty members demonstrate such receptivity, students become more comfortable sharing information about their learning needs (Siperstein, 1988).

In the Context of Cooperative Groups

Prior to having students form cooperative groups, the instructor typically presents information in a lecture or discussion format. Comprehension can be facilitated by providing a clear written outline of the material to be covered, the sequence of activities, and key terminology (Salend, 1990). Multisensory input, such as the use of overhead transparencies, highlighted key information, and visual or graphic representations, should be incorporated whenever possible (Wood & Meiderhoff, 1988). Providing the student with a duplicate of the instructor's overhead transparencies can significantly reduce the need to copy information as it is delivered. Guided lecture techniques, listening guides, or framed lecture outlines (Lovitt, Rudsitt, Jenkins, Pious, & Bendetti, 1986) that provide a sequential overview of the key terms and main points of the lesson can assist students to focus on the most relevant information. Such guides may comprise incomplete sentences or a rudimentary outline of important lecture elements that the student fills in while listening. Efforts should be made to prepare these same materials in braille or large print for students with visual impairments.

Peer notetakers and taped lectures may be considered when students have significant physical, sensory, or visual-motor difficulties. Using temporary pairs or triads on a regular basis at the end of lectures for the purpose of clarifying and summarizing can be particularly helpful to the student with disabilities to verify understanding of fundamental concepts.

If the student with disabilities has not had previous experience working in cooperative groups, small groups (i.e., pairs or triads) can be used effectively to acclimate members to each other and the expectations of group interaction. Role and task assignments should be planned thoughtfully to capitalize on the student's learning strengths. For example, a student who learns best auditorially may be assigned the role of *checker* in a group so that he or she will have many opportunities to hear and synthesize the information. A student who can express himself or herself better orally than in written form may be assigned the role of the group's *summarizer* or paraphraser. For students who express anxiety about working in a group, nonspeaking roles may be initially assigned (i.e., timekeeper, illustrator). Efforts to engage students in more active roles can be made as the individual adapts to group functioning.

Establishing resource interdependence with a set of shared materials promotes team cohesiveness; however, a second set of materials may be needed for a student with disabilities to aid comprehension. Adaptations to materials should be made wherever possible to enhance the student's stronger learning modalities. As noted for lectures, materials provided to groups may be prepared in large print or braille. For students who need enhancement of their visual perception, the organization of written materials can be altered by reducing the amount of information per page. Perceptual figure-ground discrimination problems (i.e., the inability to focus on one set of stimuli while screening out others) may be reduced by highlighting the most important information both orally and in written form (Cassella & Bigge, 1988). During group work, students with disabilities should be encouraged to use dictionaries, spell checkers, laptop computers, print enlargers, typewriters, braillewriters, or any other tool that expedites gathering or producing information. When a final product (e.g., report, presentation, outline) is an expected outcome of cooperative efforts, examples of previously completed projects can offer guidelines for the desired scope and quality of performance.

To facilitate reflection and self-assessment, a student with disabilities may be offered a written list of questions at the beginning of the session that will foreshadow discussions to occur during group processing. Using cassette recorders or video recorders to document group interactions may be effective tools for use during group processing and feedback sessions as they offer tangible representations of performance that may be reviewed by the group as well as the professor.

When tests are used to assess individual accountability and group performance, a number of simple modifications can be used to decrease test anxiety and secure performance data that are representative of the student's abilities. Consider extending the time allowed to take the exam for the student with disabilities and/or the group in which he or she functions. This allows the instructor to assess mastery of content rather than performance under strict time constraints. The administration of tests may be changed by using taped versions of the test or allowing a group member to read the exam aloud to the student with disabilities. Recording answers to questions with a tape recorder or dictaphone or simply responding orally to questions are alternative options to the written method of expressing knowledge (Bigge, 1988; Wood & Aldredge, 1985). To reduce test anxiety or address endurance issues, frequent breaks can be scheduled or the test can be administered in increments across a number of class sessions. Be sure to examine the purpose of the evaluation and avoid structuring exams with confusing and convoluted questions that measure the ability to take a test rather than knowledge of the subject matter (Salend & Salend, 1985; Wood & Aldredge, 1985).

The use of cooperative learning in college classrooms can establish areas of compatibility between students with and without disabilities, foster sensitivity to different learning styles, and serve as a vehicle to promote students with disabilities as contributing and valued class members. Meeting regularly with a student with disabilities to solicit concerns or needed accommodations and to closely monitor the functioning of the group is a necessary responsibility of the professor to ensure these worthwhile outcomes.

BASIC ELEMENTS OF COOPERATIVE LEARNING GROUPS

Effective implementation of cooperative learning in college classrooms depends on professors who address the five elements that mediate the effectiveness of cooperative efforts: positive interdependence, face-to-face promotive interaction, individual accountability/personal responsibility, interpersonal and small-group skills, and group processing (frequent reflection on how well the group is functioning).

Positive Interdependence

Students working together to accomplish a common goal is at the heart of cooperative learning. Professors can structure positive interdependence (the "sink or swim together" feeling) in a variety of ways, including: 1) establishing mutual goals or products, 2) issuing joint rewards, and 3) assigning shared resources (e.g., expertise or sections of an assignment) and specified roles (e.g., summarizer, encourager, timekeeper).

Face-to-Face Promotive Interaction

Professors ensure that students have *structured time* to support each other's learning by coaching each other, sharing, and encouraging learning efforts. Students sit eye-to-eye, knee-to-knee, and use various means to explain, discuss, and teach what they know about the subject to each other.

Individual Accountability

Professors assess individual students and discuss the results with the group. Clear division of labor on group projects increases personal responsibility. Typical ways to structure individual accountability include giving an individual exam to each student, randomly calling on individual students to present the group's answer, and giving an individual oral exam while monitoring a group's work.

Interpersonal and Small-Group Skills

Professors attend to both the academic content and the social interaction skills that are needed for groups to function effectively. Such collaborative skills as trust-building, communicating, negotiating conflict, and leadership are explicitly addressed.

Group Processing

Professors understand that groups need time to consciously reflect on and describe helpful and unhelpful actions and decide what actions to continue or adjust. The purpose of processing is to improve individual member effectiveness in collaborating so as to ensure achievement of the group's goal.

THE PROFESSOR'S ROLE IN COOPERATIVE GROUPS

Operationalizing the five basic elements of a well-structured cooperative lesson in the college classroom requires skills and strategies that are much different from those most faculty experienced as students. To ensure that professors address the five critical elements described above, the professor's role in planning cooperative lessons (Johnson et al., 1991a) should include the following:

1. Specify objectives.
2. Make decisions about placing students in learning groups to ensure heterogeneity and diversity of student membership.
3. Explain the academic task and the cooperative goal structure (i.e., goal, reward, or resource interdependence).
4. Monitor effectiveness of the cooperative learning groups and intervene when necessary to teach the academic or cooperative skills.
5. Evaluate students' academic achievement and their collaborative skills.

Multiple methods and procedures are available to choose the membership, size, duration, and purposes of cooperative learning groups so as to best serve the purposes professors have at various times during any course. The students in the class can be organized into base groups, formal groups, and informal groups.

Base Groups

The major purpose of base groups is to establish a sense of affiliation with other class members. Base groups are heterogeneously formed; the more diverse the better. Typically, they have four or five members. When students are assigned to a base group, they know they will be meeting with the same students for an extended period of time (e.g., a semester). Johnson and Johnson (1989a) recommend base groups as a way to promote psychological health and social competencies as well as friendships. Indeed, many students do better on their homework assignments because they do not want to disappoint their teammates. The agenda for base group meetings (approximately 5 or 10 minutes of class time) includes: 1) discussing the academic tasks assigned to each member and the strategies for achieving the tasks; and 2) providing personal support, such as listening as each person speaks about their progress on assignments and life at home or in other classes.

Formal Groups

Professors assign students heterogeneously for specified time periods (typically 3–4 weeks) until a task is done. Each formal learning group comprises two or three classmates who stay together to ensure that each achieves the specific learning objectives related to the task. Professors most often use formal learning groups for problem-solving assignments, peer editing of compositions, checking homework accuracy and depth, preparing for a test, classroom presentations, and laboratory or experimental inquiries.

Sabers and Rein (1992) used cooperative learning groups for a performance assessment of students' comprehension of aspects of educational measurement. Students were organized into triads and were assigned the role of a member of a school committee whose task was to select a test for use in their school. The responsibility of the subcommittee was to quantify the differences in reliability between two proposed tests. Each member of the triad received different information on which test to promote as well as specific instructions on which method to use to compute the reliability and why that method was statistically superior, complete with citations from the literature. The task of the subcommittee was to accurately incorporate all three methods into a written and oral report.

Structured academic controversies are another example of how professors can turn any subject, initially judged trivial or boring by students, into a stimulating and energizing learning experience (see the Creative Cooperative Group Lesson Plans at the end of Section I for an example of a structured academic controversy at the college level).

Informal Groups

Professors assign students to partnerships or triads during class periods so they can check each other's understanding and help each other to expand their knowledge of concepts. This technique is especially helpful *following* lectures, films, laboratory experiences, and other activities that have many distractions. Professors may use temporary, informal groups to help *prepare* students for a lecture by posing a focus question and asking student pairs to formulate their best answers. Other assignments can be made *during* a lecture. For example, professors may ask students to discuss with their temporary partner any implications of the first 30 minutes of the lecture. Another important use for informal groups is to evaluate student understanding of concepts related in a *series* of lectures; for example, professors may generate progress checks (similar to a quiz, but not graded). Students work in pairs to complete the progress check, compare answers with a member of each partner's respective base group, and retake the progress check if time permits. Professors also have assigned cooperative note-taking pairs, read-and-explain pairs in which partners clarify concepts in text material, and closure cooperative writing pairs who summarize key learning at the end of the class. Light (1990) used this procedure to identify major unanswered questions at the end of each lecture. Students were asked to write a 1-minute paper describing the major point learned and a main unanswered question. The professor used this information to guide the next lecture session.

Professors can implement cooperative learning activities to fit various class schedules—50-minute class session, 90-minute class session, or 3-hour session. For example, during a typical 50-minute class session, the professor might begin by greeting students and inviting them to meet in their base groups to greet each other, check progress on homework and other class assignments, and provide support. After a few minutes, the professor may lecture for 30–40 minutes using informal cooperative learning groups to guide comprehension. Other options include presentations from formal learning groups, structured academic controversies, or short written assignments. To close the session, base groups meet again briefly to summarize and synthesize the concepts presented in the lecture in order to ensure comprehension on the part of all base group members and to leave the class session with a clear direction of what needs to be accomplished by the next session.

During a 90-minute or 3-hour class session, a similar structure may be used with extended time for base groups to meet or for formal cooperative learning groups to prepare their projects. Progress checks might be implemented, followed by lectures and discussion pairs for clarification of possible misconceptions. Lengthier controversies may be structured and implemented during longer class sessions (see the sample lesson plan in the Creative Cooperative Group Lesson Plans at the end of Section I that illustrates a structured academic controversy in a college classroom).

BENEFITS TO TEACHER EDUCATION CANDIDATES

The major benefit of cooperative learning for college students is increased understanding in any course through their active engagement in the process of discussing and elaborating on assignments. There are added benefits to teacher education candidates.

First, in addition to higher academic achievement, teacher education candidates benefit from the acquisition of social interaction skills while practicing as contributing members of cooperative learning groups. As teachers, they often will be required to use these skills to explain what they do and why they do it to people from diverse backgrounds and with various agendas (e.g., school board members, principals, colleagues, parents, taxpayers, students).

Second, teacher education candidates who collaborate with other college students in cooperative learning activities in various courses (e.g., political science, humanities, sciences, mathematics) gain increased understanding of the thinking and speaking patterns associated with these disciplines that will help them in the preparation and teaching of those disciplines.

Third, teacher education candidates have a direct personal experience of how it feels to learn in a cooperative learning group. They experience the processes of internal self-reflection and conceptual conflict (particularly when faced with others who have different ideas about the course material) that their future students also will experience. Such activities provide important opportunities for teacher education candidates to practice the skills they will be required to perform as teachers.

Finally, it is widely known that the most influential source of competencies in teaching comes from observations of teachers. During 4 or 5 years of exposure to college professors, teacher education candidates observe both positive and negative examples of effective teaching. When the majority of their professors model cooperative learning as a prime method of ensuring active learning in the college classroom, teacher education candidates are more likely to have consciously and unconsciously incorporated this excellent teaching practice into their repertoire.

ADAPTATIONS BY TEACHER EDUCATION PROFESSORS

Teacher education professors can adapt methods courses to increase heterogeneity among students. For example, at the University of Minnesota, elementary science, mathematics, and language arts methods courses (traditionally taught in isolation) were merged and co-instructed by professors in each of these content areas. Similarly, at Arizona State University West, Kathleen Harris and Sharon Moore (personal communication, December, 1992) conducted a common field experience that integrated applications of a language arts assessment and instruction course with a special education assessment and instruction course for elementary and special education students. The use of cooperative learning structures ensured a good mix of students from different disciplines.

When secondary teacher education candidates at Arizona State University West studied cooperative learning strategies during their social studies methods course (L. McGraw, personal communication, February 8, 1993), they requested the option of taking the final examination either as a cooperative group or individuals. The exam focused on infusing academic content (i. e., history, economics, geography) into a variety of graphic organizers (i.e., flow charting, problem-solving frames, forward chaining, back mapping). Of the 23 class participants, 18 chose to take the final as a member of a cooperative team (thereby earning the grade earned by the team product) and 5 took the final as individuals. The six teams earned scores of 83, 85, 89, 90, 92, 97 and the five individuals earned scores of 75, 78, 82, 94, 99. The range of grades (75–99 out of 100 points) for the final compared to the range obtained by previous classes in which students took the final as individuals.

Field experiences and internships are a dynamic component of teacher education programs. Many universities are developing active partnership arrangements with public schools in which university professors and public school teachers cofacilitate the professional development of teams of mentor teachers and interns. Their modeling of cooperative learning methods can enhance the achievement and enjoyment of the acquisition of new teaching practices. Research on staff development highlights the importance of educators having frequent opportunities to observe models of instructional methods and to receive coaching and feedback during their efforts to implement a new practice (Showers, Joyce, & Bennett, 1987).

Finally, when teacher education professors guide their students to implement cooperative learning lessons, teacher education candidates have the opportunity to practice a method that will result in increased achievement and self-esteem for their students, particularly those who have special educational needs. In fact, in order for *all* students to survive successfully in the fast approaching 21st century, they will need to know how to work with people who are *different* in gender, color, ethnicity, culture, and ability. Benjamin (1989) urges that school curricula not only teach students how to communicate, but also how to provide active practice in collaborating with other people who hold different opinions. Cooperative learning has these capacities. Therefore, teacher education candidates need to learn that through the use of cooperative learning groups, they can help *all* students help one another to achieve their academic goals.

CONCLUSION

Johnson et al., (1991a, 1991b) described a new paradigm of college education in which teaching involves helping others construct knowledge in active ways. Cooperative learning groups provide professors with a process that allows students to work together to increase their own and classmates' learning. The research evidence is clear. Cooperative learning promotes higher achievement, more positive student relationships, and healthier psychological adjustment than other classroom methods (i.e., individualistic, competitive).

Professors who successfully implement cooperative learning activities know they must address the five elements that mediate the effectiveness of cooperative efforts: positive interdependence, face-to-face promotive interaction, individual accountability/personal responsibility, interpersonal and small-group skills, and group processing (frequent reflection on how well the group is functioning). The professor's role involves: specifying objectives, making decisions about placing students in learning groups, explaining the academic task and cooperative learning structure, monitoring the effectiveness of cooperative learning groups and intervening to provide assistance in answering academic-related questions or to increase students' collaboration skills, and evaluating students' achievement and helping students discuss how well they collaborated.

Cooperative group learning is a method that enables professors to easily adapt their instruction to meet the needs of students with disabilities while benefiting the other students in the class. In colleges and universities that routinely use cooperative learning structures, professors in teacher education can be ensured that their teacher education candidates benefit by: 1) having direct experiences of cooperatively learning the content of various disciplines as well as education methods classes, 2) increasing their communication and collaboration skills while actively learning with others from various disciplines, and 3) implementing cooperative learning lesson plans with students assigned to them in field experiences and internships.

Professors who practice cooperative learning often find themselves collecting rich data sources: student anecdotes, increased class averages, and changes in the quality as well as quantity of student products. If this data is published, professors integrate two of the four forms of scholarship promoted by Boyer (1990)—the scholarship of teaching and the scholarship of integration. This type of balanced academic life may be the hallmark of professors who actualize the new paradigm of college teaching. Changing college teaching to more active, cooperative learning is not easy. First, faculty must see the need, then they must learn new ways of working with students. Recognizing and promoting three essential aspects of change—an attitude of experimentation, a common goal (positive interdependence), and personal support—is central to making the transition (Smith, Johnson, & Johnson, 1992).

AUTHORS' NOTE

Authors are listed in alphabetical order and authorship is equally divided among the three collaborators. Jacque Thousand and Rich Villa first outlined their thoughts with Ann about what this chapter needed to accomplish. From this initial conversation, Ann generated an outline. Ann enrolled Karl, with his experience and expertise in applying cooperative learning with engineering students at the University of Minnesota, to consider co-authoring the chapter. Subsequently, Ann enrolled Alice as a co-author because of her experience in applying cooperative learning with teacher education students at the University of Wisconsin.

We used a round-robin method of generating the manuscript. Ann wrote the first draft, relying heavily on material from Karl's book *Active Learning in the College Classroom* (Johnson et al., 1991a) and referring to her experiences of implementing cooperative learning for both inservice education of practicing teachers and graduate preparation of educational specialists. This draft was revised independently by both Karl and Alice. Karl elaborated the sections on cooperative learning in college classrooms and creativity; Alice fleshed out the section on adapting cooperative learning to meet the needs of adults with disabilities who are enrolled in college classes. Subsequent drafts reflect the elegant editorial advice of Jacque and Rich.

The outcome is an example of the synergy that can happen in a successful cooperative venture: results that no one person could have generated alone.

REFERENCES

Astin, A. (1991, October). *What really matters in general education: Provocative findings from a national study of student outcomes.* Address presented at the Association of General and Liberal Studies meeting, Seattle.

Astin, A. (1993). *What matters in college: Four critical years revisited.* San Francisco: Jossey-Bass.

Benjamin, S. (1989). An ideascape for education: What futurists recommend. *Educational Leadership, 47*(1), 8–14.

Bigge, J. (1988). Modifying student response methods. In J. Bigge (Ed.), *Curriculum-based instruction for special education students* (pp. 64–109). Mountain View, CA: Mayfield Publishing Company.

Bouton, C., & Garth, R. (1983). *Learning in groups.* San Francisco: Jossey-Bass.

Boyer, E. (1990). *Scholarship reconsidered.* Lawrenceville, NJ: Princeton University Press.

Campbell, J. (1965). *The children's crusader: Colonel Francis W. Parker.* Unpublished doctoral dissertation, Teachers College, Columbia University, New York.

Cassella, V., & Bigge, J. (1988). Modifying instructional modalities and conditions for curriculum access. In J. Bigge (Ed.), *Curriculum-based instruction for special education students* (pp. 110–140). Mountain View, CA: Mayfield Publishing Company.

Cooper, J., McKinney, M., & Robinson, P. (1991). Cooperative/collaborative learning: Part II. *The Journal of Staff, Program, & Organization Development, 9*(4), 241–252.

Cooper, J., & Mueck, R. (1990). Student involvement in learning: Cooperative learning and college instruction. *Journal on Excellence in College Teaching, 1,* 68–76.

Deutsch, M. (1949). A theory of cooperation and competition. *Human Relations, 2,* 129–152.

Equity Action Subcommittee on Disabilities. (1992). *Accommodations for inclusion of all students in teaching and learning activities.* Madison: University of Wisconsin, School of Education.

Goleman, D., Kaufman, P., & Ray, M. (1992). *The creative spirit.* New York: E.P. Dutton.

Johnson, D., & Johnson, R. (1989a). Base groups: What are they? *The Cooperative Link, 6*(1), 2–3. (Newsletter of The Cooperative Learning Center, 202 Pattee Hall, University of Minnesota, Minneapolis, MN 55455)

Johnson, D., & Johnson, R. (1989b). *Cooperation and competition: Theory and research.* Edina, MN: Interaction Book Company.

Johnson, D., Johnson, R., Ortiz, A., & Stanne, M. (1991). Impact of positive goal and resource interdependence on achievement, interaction, and attitudes. *Journal of General Psychology, 118*(4), 341–347.

Johnson, D., Johnson, R., & Smith, K. (1991a). Active learning: Cooperation in the college classroom. Edina, MN: Interaction Book Company.

Johnson, D., Johnson, R., & Smith, K. (1991b). Cooperative learning: Increasing college faculty instructional productivity. *ASHE-ERIC Reports on Higher Education.* Washington, DC: ERIC Document No. ED343465.

Lewin, K. (1935). *A dynamic theory of personality.* New York: McGraw-Hill.

Light, R.J. (1990). *The Harvard assessment seminars: First report.* Cambridge, MA: Harvard University Press.

Light, R.J. (1992). *The Harvard assessment seminars: Second report.* Cambridge, MA: Harvard University Press.

Lovitt, T., Rudsitt, J., Jenkins, J., Pious, C., & Bendetti, D. (1986). Adapting science materials for regular and learning disabled seventh graders. *Remedial and Special Education, 7*(1), 31–39.

Millis, B. (1991). Helping faculty build learning communities through cooperative groups. In L. Hilsen (Ed.), *To improve the academy: Resources for student, faculty, and institutional development* (pp. 43–58). Stillwater, OK: New Forums Press.

Public Law 101-336, Americans with Disabilities Act of 1990. (26 July 1990). *U.S. Statutes at Large, 104,* 327–378.

Sabers, D., & Rein, J. (1992, November). *Performance assessment: An example with content from educational research.* Presentation at Arizona Educational Research Organization, Phoenix.

Salend, S. (1990). *Effective mainstreaming.* New York: Macmillan.

Salend, S., & Salend, S. (1985). Adapting teacher-made tests for mainstreamed students. *Journal of Learning Disabilities, 18*(6), 373–375.

Siperstein, G. (1988). Students with learning disabilities in college: The need for a programmatic approach to critical transitions. *Journal of Learning Disabilities, 21*(7), 431–436.

Showers, B., Joyce, B., & Bennett, B. (1987). Synthesis of research on staff development: A framework for future study and a state-of-the-art analysis. *Educational Leadership, 45*(3), 77–87.

Smith, K., Johnson, D., & Johnson, R. (1992). Cooperative learning and positive change in higher education. In A. Goodsell, M. Maher, & V. Tinto (Eds.), *Collaborative learning: A sourcebook for higher education* (pp. 34–36). University Park, PA: National Center for Postsecondary Teaching, Learning, & Assessment.

Wood, J., & Aldredge, J. (1985, March). Adapting tests for mainstreamed students. *Academic Therapy,* 419–426.

Wood, J., & Meiderhoff, J. (1988, February). Adapting lesson plans for the mainstreamed student. *The Clearing House, 61*(6), 269–276.

CREATIVE COOPERATIVE GROUP LESSON PLANS

Introduction to Creative Cooperative Group Lesson Plans

Ann I. Nevin, Jacqueline S. Thousand, and Richard A. Villa

Cooperative group lesson plans representing preschool, primary, upper elementary, middle, high school, and college levels are featured here. The lesson plans follow the format described in Chapter 6, this volume. A variety of grade levels and curriculum areas (e.g., science, mathematics, language arts, career/vocation, oral expression, art) are featured. The lesson plans emphasize how general and special education teachers have adapted their instruction to meet the unique needs of students with varying abilities (e.g., significant disabilities, gifts and talents, emotional challenges, mild-moderate special education needs). In addition, there are two lesson plans that introduce cooperative learning methods to middle school teachers and other adult learners (e.g., candidates for graduate degrees). The story behind the creation of each lesson plan is provided, followed by an anecdote describing the results of implementing the lesson. The essential elements of cooperative learning lessons are marked with an asterisk (*). At the end of each lesson, the teacher checks that these essential elements were included in the lesson. Readers have permission to photocopy the lesson plans in this section for educational purposes. The range and variety of the lessons are illustrated by their titles:

Elementary Science for a Student with Visual Impairments

Upper Elementary Mathematics for a Student with Gifts and Talents

Introducing Middle School Students to Cooperative Learning Groups: The Fishbowl Technique

Junior High School Language Arts for a Student with Behavior Disorders

COOPERATIVE
GROUP
LESSON
PLAN

ELEMENTARY SCIENCE FOR A STUDENT WITH VISUAL IMPAIRMENTS

Monley (1989), an educational specialist intern, worked with a primary school teacher to adapt a regularly scheduled science lesson for a learner with visual impairments who had no oral language and no formal means of communication.

ACADEMIC OBJECTIVES

What are the prerequisite skills?

Object identification (naming fruits); concepts of "same," "different," and "seed."

What are the academic objectives?

Students learn that different fruits have different kinds of seeds. Students describe and/or compare the seeds by color, size, shape, and number.

How do students demonstrate the academic objectives?

Students demonstrate these objectives by saying and doing the following: When handling a specific fruit, the students say, "This (fruit name) has (number) seeds that look like (shape) and are (color name) and that is similar to/different from this (fruit name), which has (number) seeds that look like (shape) and are (color name)."

What are the criteria for success?

Students are successful if they include at least three fruits and draw shapes that accurately portray the number, size, and shape of the relevant seed(s).

What are the modifications for learner(s) with special education needs?

J. has a visual impairment, is nonverbal, and has no formal means of communication yet. J. explores the different fruits tactually. J. listens to a description of each fruit so as to increase his receptive understanding of these objects. Say, "J., you're holding a banana. It is long and has a peel." Peel it together, feel the peel, and talk about it (e.g., "On the inside, it is squishy.").

How does a learner with special education needs demonstrate the academic objectives?

J. demonstrates these objectives by saying and doing the following: When touching a fruit, J. moves it from hand to hand. When explanations are given, J. is "ear-oriented" to the speaker and demonstrates receptive language by following directions (e.g., when asked to touch the peel, J. touches the peel).

What are the criteria for success for the learner with special needs?

J. is successful if he explores each fruit both independently and with guidance and sits with the group during the entire lesson.

FACE-TO-FACE INTERACTION DECISIONS*

What is the group size?

There are 18 students in the class, three students in each of six groups.

How are students assigned to groups?

To ensure heterogeneity, students are assigned to groups randomly by counting backward from 6 ("6-5-4-3-2-1") with all the "6s" working as a group, all the "5s" working as a group, and so forth.

What is the room arrangement?

The room is arranged so that cut-outs of numbers 1–6 hang from the ceiling. Students move their desks to the area that matches their numbers and then arrange themselves so that they are facing each other.

STRUCTURING POSITIVE INTERDEPENDENCE*

Members get the messages: "We sink or swim together," "Do your work—we're counting on you," "How can I help you to do better?"

What is the structure—a single product, one group goal, or a shared outcome?	There is one collage per group (six for the class). The teacher explains to the group: "Your poster will have at least three fruit and seeds drawings (one for each group member). You decide and agree among yourselves who will draw which fruit and seeds. There will be only one poster and one set of crayons so you will have to decide and agree on how you want to manage the drawing. Your group will have only one fruit at a time and will have to pass the fruit to another group, who will give you theirs, and so forth so that everyone gets a chance to look at all the fruits. So, what should your poster look like?" (Check for understanding by having a student paraphrase.)
Is a group reward structured?	Groups that create posters that meet criteria *and* whose group members can tell about the color, shape, size, and number of seeds receive a colorful sticker for each member of the group.
Are student roles assigned?	No.
What are the other divisions of labor besides roles?	This emerges as the group decides how they will draw their fruits and seeds.
How are materials arranged?	To promote positive interdependence among all groups, various fruits (apples, pears, bananas, oranges, melon, cherries, grapes) are rotated to groups. Poster-size paper (six pieces, one per group) and crayons (six containers, one per group) are distributed.
(Optional) What other ways are used to promote positive interdependence—intergroup cooperation, intergroup competition, positive fantasy mission, or identity interdependence (e.g., group name)?	In this lesson, intergroup cooperation is structured by rotating the fruits among the groups, and at the end, everyone makes a fruit salad by cutting up all the fruit.

ESTABLISHING SOCIAL SKILL PERFORMANCE*

What are the social skills objectives?

Using "Smiley Faces" and "Smiley Face Words," students demonstrate the social skill of giving encouragement by smiling when group members contribute and by saying encouraging statements, such as "Good job!" or "Good idea!" or "The tiny oval seed you drew for an apple looks like it's real!"

The social skill for J. is to sit with his group during the lesson.

How is the need for each social skill communicated?

Ask students what happens when they hear words such as, "good job," "good idea," or "you're right on!" [Acknowledge students' responses—they might say they feel happy inside, they want to work more—or elicit from them ideas; for example, "Do you think you'll feel like talking more if you hear "Good idea!" than if you hear "Your idea is wrong!"?] Say, "That's why we'll be practicing Smiley Faces and Smiley Face Words while you make your posters."

How are social skills explained, demonstrated, role played, or practiced?

Ask students to volunteer how they sound and what their faces look like when they make Smiley Faces and say Smiley Face Words. Praise appropriate demonstrations and give corrective feedback until the students get the idea.

How are social skills assigned to group members?

All group members are responsible for demonstrating the Smiley Faces and Smiley Face Words.

SOCIAL SKILL PERFORMANCE: TEACHER MONITORING AND INTERVENTION*

What is the process (how and who) for monitoring groups?

The teacher rotates to observe and monitor group interactions—approximately 1 minute per group at least three times during the lesson.

What is the process for feedback (how and who) to groups if social skills are being used?

The teacher shares "on the spot" that the group is doing a great job with Smiley Faces and Smiley Face Words.

What is the process
for feedback (how and
who) to groups if so-
cial skills are *not*
being used?

The teacher asks the group, "What does it look like and sound like to practice Smiley Faces and Smiley Face Words? I'll come back in a few minutes and I expect to hear and see you, okay?"

What collaboration
problems are
anticipated?

Arguments about who will draw; one person doing all the drawing.

What are inter-
ventions to avoid
or remedy the antici-
pated problems?

Rules: When you feel like intervening, don't. If you must intervene, do it with questions, not answers. Move away as soon as you can, even if it is only 3 feet. Remind the group that argument is okay as long as Smiley Faces and Smiley Face Words are being used. Ask how the others feel if one person does all the work (e.g., "Does it feel fair?" "What can you do to share the work?").

SOCIAL SKILL
PERFORMANCE: STUDENT MONITORING

What is the student
observer selection
and training process
(what and who)?

Each student is asked to monitor their own use of Smiley Faces and Smiley Face Words.

How are social skills
monitored?

The frequency of Smiley Faces and Smiley Face Words is monitored by the teacher.

Do students observe
more than one group?

No.

Do students observe
for an entire lesson?

Yes.

How and when do
students share their
observations?

As the teacher listens to each group, she can "catch the students" engaging in Smiley Faces and Smiley Face Words and ask them to share. Also, at the end, during the processing, the teacher can randomly select a student from one or two groups to share their examples of Smiley Faces and Smiley Face Words.

STRUCTURING INDIVIDUAL ACCOUNTABILITY*

Are individual quizzes assigned?

No.

Is there a random selection of group members to answer questions?

For social skills practice, students are randomly selected to share their examples of Smiley Faces and Smiley Face Words.

SETTING THE TASK

What is the process for explanation of academic task and criteria for success (when and who)?

"Today you'll work in groups to learn more about these fruits. As a class, please name each of these fruits as I hold them up. Your job is to find out all you can about the seeds inside the fruits. You'll want to look at how they are the same and how they are different. You'll need to look carefully at the size of the different seeds. Are they big, little, tiny? What color are they—red, brown, green? What shape are they—round, oval? How many are there—only one, a few, lots? Your job is for each of you to draw a different fruit and its seeds on the poster paper. Then you'll share with the class what part of the poster your buddy drew. You'll tell the class what you found out about the seeds—color, size, shape, number. If each of you can do this, your poster will receive a sticker!"

How are social skills and criteria for success explained (when and who)?

Just before the students begin their poster preparation, the teacher explains Smiley Faces and Smiley Face Words (see above). "I'll expect each person in the group to practice Smiley Faces and Smiley Face Words and I'll come around to your groups to hear and see you, okay? I expect to hear quiet voices while you discuss your discoveries and decide which fruit and seed you will draw before you start. Make sure each person has a fruit and seed to draw." The teacher checks for understanding: "What will I be checking for?" (Acknowledge students who paraphrase the above directions and give corrective feedback until students understand.)

CLOSURE AND PROCESSING*

What is the process
for closure (students
summarize what they
learned)?

Each group comes to the front of the room to show their poster and to share what they found out about the seeds —color, shape, size, and number. If criteria were met, the poster gets a prize sticker and each student receives a sticker.

What is the process
for feedback on aca-
demic performance
(how, who, and
when)?

If a poster does not meet criteria, ask the group what they can do to fix it. Have the group fix it after all the other groups present their posters. If a group member does not accurately share or know the information about the seeds, ask the group to help provide the answer. They may choose to return as a group and present again after the other presentations are complete.

How are the teacher's
observations shared?

Rule: Share negative comments in private and positive comments in public and private. The teacher shares summary data on frequency and impact of using Smiley Faces and Smiley Face Words.

What is the process
for assessment of in-
dividual and group
success in using so-
cial skills (how and
when)?

After the presentations, the teacher asks each group to take a few minutes to compare how well they did on the poster and how well they used Smiley Faces and Smiley Face Words. Notice any impact. Ask the class as a whole, "What have you liked about working with this group? What didn't you like? What will you do differently when you work together later today?"

AFTER THE LESSON

How does the teacher
evaluate the success
of the lesson?

The teacher checks to see that the essential elements
(noted with an asterisk) of cooperative learning lessons
were included. The next lesson is planned so that the
students can practice student monitoring (Step VI) by
tallying the frequency of their Smiley Face Words. This
integrates the graphing skills they are learning in math
class. In addition, the teacher plans to schedule a written quiz to check individual understanding of the seeds
of fruits.

Anecdote

This lesson was a great success. J. participated for the entire lesson and his group members guided him appropriately to tactually explore each fruit. They came up with
the idea of having J. paste on parts of the fruits and seeds
instead of drawing them. The entire class helped cut up
the fruit and enjoyed a tasty, healthy fruit salad as a class
bonus.

Reference

Monley, M.K. (1989). *Cooperative group lesson plan*. Unpublished manuscript submitted in partial fulfillment of
requirements for the Educational Specialist graduate
program, Professor J. Thousand, University of Vermont,
Department of Special Education, College of Education
and Social Services, Burlington.

UPPER ELEMENTARY MATHEMATICS FOR A STUDENT WITH GIFTS AND TALENTS

Conn-Powers (1988), a special education graduate intern, worked with a sixth grade teacher to implement this lesson. The special features of the lesson included an attention to students' reasoning skills and their interpersonal skills when confronted with different opinions. Math story problems were used to stimulate disagreement, or at least discussion, about different ways of solving the same problem, and to dispel the myth that mathematics is "cut and dried."

LESSON NAME: Math Disagreements
GRADE LEVEL: Fifth to sixth grade
  (Intermediate)

AUTHOR: C. Conn-Powers
CONTENT AREA: Mathematics
TIME: 40 minutes

ACADEMIC OBJECTIVES

What are the prerequisite skills?

Computational skills through fractions and reading skills

What are the academic objectives?

Students solve math story problems requiring reasoning and basic computational skills.

How do students demonstrate the academic objectives?

Students demonstrate these objectives by saying and doing the following: "I think we should go about solving the problem this way because . . . "

What are the criteria for success?

If four problems are assigned, students must show alternative solutions for at least three to receive an A, two for a B, and one for a C.

What are the modifications for learner(s) with special education needs?

D. is a student with gifts and talents and challenging interpersonal behaviors. He tends to advocate only for his ideas as the "right" ones and ridicules his classmates' contributions. His GATE (Gifted and Talented Education) teacher is assisting him to become responsible for the effects of his behaviors on his classmates during two sessions he attends each week. In this lesson, D. will practice one of his new skills by serving as the "encourager" who asks others, in a friendly way, to share their ideas for solutions.

How does a learner with special education needs demonstrate the academic objectives?

D. demonstrates the same academic objectives as his classmates. To incorporate what he has been learning from his GATE teacher, D. demonstrates the skill of encouragement by saying and doing: "Why do you think that's a way to solve it?" or "How about we try it this way?"

What are the criteria for success for the learner with special needs?

D. is successful if he asks at least two encouraging questions of each team member during the 20-minute lesson.

FACE-TO-FACE INTERACTION DECISIONS*

What is the group size?

There are 24 students in the class—four students to each group, six groups total.

How are students assigned to groups?

To ensure heterogeneity, students are assigned to groups by the teacher so that there is equal distribution of boys and girls, high and low achievers, and students who speak Spanish. The teacher prepares name cards for each student using 3 × 5 index cards that are marked with Spanish numbers in words—uno, dos, tres, quatro, cinco, seis.

What is the room arrangement?

The room is arranged so that numbers 1–6 hang from the ceiling. Students move their desks to the area that matches their number and arrange their desks so that they are facing each other.

STRUCTURING POSITIVE INTERDEPENDENCE*

Members get the messages: "We sink or swim together," "Do your work—we're counting on you," "How can I help you to do better?"

What is the struc- ture—a single prod- uct, one group goal, or a shared outcome?

There is one answer sheet per group (six for the class). The teacher explains: "Your group has a large newsprint to make a poster showing two or three ways to solve each problem. You have different color markers to make it easy for us to see your different solutions. You can be as creative as you like—make pictures, diagrams, flow charts, or use words and songs. So, what should your poster look like?" [Acknowledge students' responses or give corrective feedback until they show they understand the directions.]

Is a group reward structured?	"Groups that create posters that meet criteria *and* whose group members can each tell about the reasons why the different solutions work or do not work will have the chance to work at the Math Games table for 10 minutes before the next math class. The music teacher told me that you are learning a special way of using math to harmonize. Any group that can creatively incorporate this skill in one or more of their solutions will earn an extra 5 minutes at the Math Games table."
Are student roles assigned?	Yes. The recorder role will be assigned so that each student practices recording the group's agreed upon solutions on a rotating basis. The decision as to who serves as recorder first is based on whose first name has the *most* number of letters.
What are the other divisions of labor besides roles?	This emerges as the group decides how to draw its solutions.
How are materials arranged?	To promote positive interdependence among all groups, special colored markers (e.g., purple or fluorescent pink) can be *rotated* among groups; poster size paper (six pieces, one per group), water-base magic markers (six containers), and any four math story problems can be used.
(Optional) What other ways to promote positive interdependence are used—intergroup cooperation, intergroup competition, positive fantasy mission, or identity interdependence (e.g., group name)?	Whole class cooperation is structured by having the special markers rotated among the groups. At the end, the class can invite another sixth grade class to come in for a 10 minute Gallery of Solutions demonstration. The music teacher can be invited to comment on the creative applications of her lesson on harmony.

ESTABLISHING SOCIAL SKILL PERFORMANCE*

What are the social skills objectives?

The controversy skills of friendly disagreeing (Brewster, 1990) are practiced. The teacher writes five ways to disagree in a friendly way on the board or on an overhead transparency or a poster to place in a prominent area for students to see while they work on their lesson. (These skills have been introduced and practiced by the class during a previous social studies lesson.)

1. Ask for different opinions: Why do you think that's best? What is your opinion? What is your answer?
2. Ask others to explain why: Explain how you got your answer, please. Explain that last part. Show me how that works. How will that solve the problem?
3. Add on or modify: Could we expand on that answer? How about if we added this? Could we change . . . ?
4. Offer alternatives: What do you think about . . . ? Wouldn't this work also? Here is a different way of looking at things.
5. State disagreement: I have a different idea. My answer is different. Here is why I think this way.

How is the need for each social skill communicated?

Ask students how they feel when they hear words such as "I don't agree with you" said in a friendly tone with a smile or an unfriendly tone with a frown. [Demonstrate. Acknowledge students' responses—they might say how they feel, they might want to work more—or elicit from them those ideas (e.g., "Do you think you'll feel like talking more if you hear a friendly or an unfriendly tone?") Acknowledge contributions and give corrective feedback until students get the idea.] "That's why we'll be practicing friendly disagreeing while you work your math problems today."

How are social skills explained, demonstrated, role-played, or practiced?

Ask students to volunteer to demonstrate how they would sound and what their faces would look like when disagreeing in a friendly manner.

How are social skills assigned to group members?

All group members are responsible for demonstrating at least two of the five ways to disagree in a friendly way.

SOCIAL SKILL PERFORMANCE:
TEACHER MONITORING AND INTERVENTION*

What is the process (how and who) for monitoring groups?

The teacher rotates to observe and monitor group interactions—approximately 1 minute per group, at least three rotations during the lesson.

What is the process for feedback (how and who) to groups if social skills are being used?

The teacher shares "on the spot" those things that the group is doing well.

What is the process for feedback (how and who) to groups if social skills are *not* being used?

Ask the group, "What does it look like and sound like to practice friendly disagreeing?" [Acknowledge student responses.] "That's right! I'll come back in a few minutes and I expect to hear and see you, okay?"

What collaboration problems are anticipated?

Argument over who will write on the poster. One person doing all the writing.

What are interventions to avoid or remedy the anticipated problems?

Rules: When you feel like intervening, don't. If you must intervene, do it with questions, not answers. Move away as soon as you can, even if it is only 3 feet. Remind students that argument is okay as long as friendly disagreeing is being used. Ask how the other's feel if one person does all the work. "Does it feel fair? Remember that the recorder role is to be shared by each person."

SOCIAL SKILL
PERFORMANCE: STUDENT MONITORING

What is the student observer(s) selection and training process (what and who)?

Students use an observation form that they created during social studies class on which each of the five ways to disagree in a friendly manner is listed. Students monitor their own friendly disagreeing.

How are social skills monitored?

Friendly disagreeing is tallied on the student-generated observation form.

Do students observe more than one group?

No.

Do students observe for an entire lesson?

Yes.

How and when do students share their observations?

As the teacher listens to each group, he or she can "catch the students" engaging in friendly disagreeing and ask them to share. Also, during the processing, the teacher can randomly select a student from one or two groups to share his or her examples of friendly disagreeing.

STRUCTURING INDIVIDUAL ACCOUNTABILITY*

Are individual quizzes assigned?

No.

Is there a random selection of group members to answer questions?

Yes. At the end of the lesson when the teacher processes the social skills interactions, students are randomly selected to share their examples of friendly disagreeing.

SETTING THE TASK

What is the process for explanation of academic task and criteria for success (when and who)?

The teacher begins the lesson by talking about math story problems and the math (computational) and thinking skills that are needed to solve them. "How many of you think that mathematicians always agree?" [Acknowledge responses.] "What do you think they do when they don't agree?" [Acknowledge responses.] "Today we're going to find out what you do when you don't agree!"

"I want you to use your reasoning skills to determine which math operation (addition, subtraction, multiplication, or division) to use to solve the problem. I'll be looking for how you use different ways to solve the same problem. You'll need to find at least two different ways for each problem. Your group will make a poster to show the different ways you discover. If three of the four problems have two solutions, then each person in your group earns an A; if two have alternative solutions, your groups earns a B; if one has alternative solutions, your group earns a C; and if your group provides no alternative solutions, then you will have a chance to solve them after recess."

How are social skills and criteria for success explained (when and who)?

"I expect each person in the group to practice friendly disagreeing and I will come around to your groups to hear and see you, okay? I expect to hear quiet voices while you discuss your solutions and decide how you will make your poster before you start. Make sure each person can explain the different solutions. What will I be checking for?" [Acknowledge students who paraphrase the above directions.]

CLOSURE AND PROCESSING*

What is the process for closure (students summarize what they learned)?

Each group comes to the front of the room to show its poster. Buddies share what his or her buddy contributed and what he or she found out about the solutions.

What is the process for feedback on academic performance (how, who, and when)?

If criteria are met, each student in the group receives a ticket to work at the Math Games table for 10 minutes. For groups that incorporate harmony, each student receives a ticket to work at the Math Games table for 5 extra minutes. If a group's poster does not meet criteria, ask the group what they can do to fix it. Have them fix it after all groups share. If a group member does not accurately share or know the information about the solutions, ask the others in the group to help him or her. They may choose to return as a group and present again after the other presentations are complete.

How are the teacher's observations shared?

Rule: Share negative comments in private and positive comments in public and private. The teacher shares summary data on frequency and impact of using friendly disagreeing. If there is time, the teacher shares a story about how a famous mathematician disagreed with an accepted solution and came up with another way.

What is the process for assessment of individual and group success in using social skills (how and when)?

After the presentations, the teacher asks each group to take a few minutes to compare how well they did on the poster and how well they used friendly disagreeing skills. Pass out 3 × 5 index cards for groups to record what skills they practiced very well and what skills they plan to practice the next time. Students sign the card and hand it in for the teacher to review.

Ask the class as a whole, "What did you like about working with this group? What didn't you like? What will you do differently when you work together later today?"

AFTER THE LESSON

How does the teacher evaluate the success of the lesson?

The teacher checks to see that the essential elements (noted with an asterisk) of cooperative learning lessons were included. Both the academic and social skills objectives were met, especially for D. The teacher decided to expand the friendly disagreeing skills to playground activities to ensure maximum generalization.

Anecdote

This lesson was a great success. All six groups met criteria and earned tickets for the Math Games table. Two of the groups (including the one on which D. was a member) incorporated the harmony skills and earned an extra 5 minutes at the Math Games table. D. participated for the entire lesson and his group members told him that they appreciated how he encouraged them to disagree! Later, at recess, the teacher overheard D. practicing one of the friendly disagreeing skills while playing tether ball with another group from his class. In addition, during a science class the next day, the students spontaneously began to use the friendly disagreeing skills to address a challenging series of questions.

References

Brewster, D. (1990). Friendly disagreeing. In D. Johnson & R. Johnson (Eds.). *Creative controversy: Intellectual challenge in the classroom* (pp. 543–547). Edina, MN: Interaction Book Co.

Conn-Powers, C. (1988). *Cooperative group lesson plan.* Unpublished manuscript submitted in partial fulfillment of requirements for the Educational Specialist graduate program, Professor J. Thousand, University of Vermont, Department of Special Education, College of Education and Social Services, Burlington.

**COOPERATIVE
GROUP
LESSON
PLAN**

INTRODUCING MIDDLE SCHOOL STUDENTS TO COOPERATIVE LEARNING GROUPS

THE FISHBOWL TECHNIQUE

Many teachers wonder how to teach the social skills necessary for cooperative groups to be effective. Villa and Thousand (1987) developed this lesson as a demonstration for middle school teachers to observe. Villa was the teacher for a group of 21 middle school students who volunteered to show their teachers how they would behave in classrooms where cooperative learning was being practiced. The 21 students filed into a classroom that was set up with desks in traditionally aligned rows. Their teachers were arranged in the back of the room so as to observe the instruction. The lesson began with a whole-class discussion that was followed by students working in pairs to answer four questions. Volunteers then formed a cooperative group to accomplish a language arts assignment that was observed by their classmates and teachers. The lesson concluded with the entire class working as members of cooperative groups.

LESSON NAME: Introduction to
  Cooperative Learning
GRADE LEVEL: Middle school students

AUTHORS: R. Villa and J. Thousand
CONTENT AREA: Group dynamics
TIME: 50 minutes

ACADEMIC OBJECTIVES

What are the prerequisite skills?

What are the academic objectives?

Be a member of the student body of the middle school

1. Identify what has worked well and what has not worked well when they worked in groups in the past.
2. Identify advantages of working in a group for students and teachers.
3. Identify skills needed to work in a cooperative group, explain why the skills are needed, and give examples of each skill.
4. Identify examples of encouraging and sharing social skills demonstrated by a volunteer group of students.

How do students demonstrate the academic objectives?

After interviewing a classmate, each student contributes the classmate's ideas to the discussion. During the fishbowl demonstration of a cooperative learning lesson, students work with a partner to complete a checklist noting frequencies of cooperative skills.

What are the criteria for success?

For the whole class, at least six publicly shared statements related to each of the four objectives are expected.

What are the modifications for learners with special education needs?

Several middle school students have attention deficit hyperactivity disorders that interfere with their ability to focus. To increase their listening skills, they are assigned to a Study Buddy. Their role with the Study Buddy is to "check for understanding"—to ask specific questions related to the task, to assess understanding, and to answer questions their buddy might have. In this way, they are given added cognitive rehearsal of the material and they have a legitimate way of asking for clarification. During this lesson, all members of the class are paired with a Study Buddy.

How do learners with special education needs demonstrate the academic objectives?

The students with special needs demonstrate the academic objectives in the same way as other students, by participating in the class discussion first by checking answers with his or her Study Buddy and then by sharing answers with the whole class.

What are the criteria for success for learners with special needs?

Each student with special needs offers at least one idea during the discussion of advantages, skills needed for cooperative group work, and things that have and have not worked well in the past.

FACE-TO-FACE INTERACTION DECISIONS*

What is the group size?

There are 21 students in the class. Five students volunteer to practice in "fishbowl" fashion while the other 16 students observe.

How are students assigned to groups?

Random selection of student volunteers.

What is the room arrangement?

Desks are arranged in a circle of five desks with the other 16 students arranged in a semicircle for ease in listening to the volunteer group.

STRUCTURING POSITIVE INTERDEPENDENCE*

Members get the messages: "We sink or swim together," "Do your work—we're counting on you," "How can I help you to do better?"

What is the structure—a single product, one group goal, or a shared outcome?

1. Study Buddies generate a single set of brainstormed lists of advantages, skills needed for cooperative group work, and things that have and have not worked well in the past.
2. Study Buddies share these ideas during the whole-class discussion so that the class lists a set of brainstormed advantages, skills, and things that have and have not worked well in the past.
3. Study Buddies complete an observation sheet during the fishbowl demonstration.

Are student roles assigned?	Students watching the demonstration group are assigned Study Buddies to observe the cooperative skills being practiced in the demonstration group. Students in the demonstration group are assigned cooperative behavior roles (encourager, sharer) as well as leadership roles (observer, timekeeper, recorder).
What are the other divisions of labor besides roles?	None.
How are materials arranged?	One paper containing the story is distributed to the demonstration group. Each Study Buddy pair receives an observer sheet to record their observations of cooperative behaviors shown by the demonstration group.
(Optional) What other ways to promote positive interdependence will be used—intergroup cooperation, intergroup competition, positive fantasy mission, or identity interdependence (e.g., group name)?	None.

ESTABLISHING SOCIAL SKILL PERFORMANCE*

What are the social skills objectives?	Students increase their knowledge and/or practice of the social skills needed for cooperative groups to work effectively.
How is the need for each social skill communicated?	During a class discussion, the teacher elicits from the students their experiences of working in groups in the past with a focus on what worked well and what did not work well and why the skills are needed, giving an example of each skill.
How are social skills explained, demonstrated, role-played, or practiced?	The volunteers are asked to model the behaviors of encouraging and sharing. During the fishbowl demonstration, the demonstration group shows how encouraging and sharing ideas leads to a creative ending to a story.

How are social skills assigned to group members?

Random assignment.

SOCIAL SKILL PERFORMANCE: TEACHER MONITORING AND INTERVENTION*

What is the process (how and who) for monitoring groups?

Monitoring occurs at three levels. The demonstration group has a student observer, classmates observe, and the teacher observes to monitor how well the group members share, encourage, and practice their leadership roles.

What is the process for feedback (how and who) to groups if social skills are being used?

The teacher stops the work at least once to offer specific feedback.

What is the process for feedback (how and who) to groups if social skills are *not* being used?

The teacher may ask the student observer to report to the group his or her results and ask the group to remember to practice the social skills of encouraging and sharing.

What collaboration problems are anticipated?

Lack of volunteers.

What are interventions to avoid or remedy the anticipated problems?

Rules: When you feel like intervening, don't. If you must intervene, do it with questions, not answers. Move away as soon as you can, even if it is only 3 feet. Have all students count off 1–4. Those with the number 4 become the demonstration group.

SOCIAL SKILL
PERFORMANCE: STUDENT MONITORING

What is the student observer(s) selection and training process (what and who)?

1. The teacher models for all students how to use the observation form when giving instructions to the volunteer group.
2. Study Buddy pairs are assigned by the teacher.
3. The teacher selects randomly from the student volunteers one to be a silent observer.

How are social skills monitored?

One student in the demonstration group monitors by completing the observation form (see p. 161). Students observing the demonstration group complete the form with a partner.

Do students observe more than one group?

No.

Do students observe for an entire lesson?

Yes.

How and when do students share their observations?

At the completion of the demonstration, the teacher solicits comments randomly from Study Buddy pairs, and the observer in the demonstration group reports his or her results.

STRUCTURING INDIVIDUAL ACCOUNTABILITY*

Are individual quizzes assigned?

No.

Is there a random selection of group members to answer questions?

Study Buddies are randomly called on to volunteer their observations.

SETTING THE TASK

What is the process for explanation of academic task and criteria for success (when and who)?

The teacher leads a class discussion focusing on cooperation and group work. "How many of you have worked in groups that have been successful?" [Acknowledge those who raise their hands or orally indicate they have.] "And how many of you have worked in groups that have not worked so well?" [Acknowledge those who participate.] "Today we will focus on two key characteristics of what makes groups successful—from Olympic champion teams to business teams to winning football teams—and we will start by making sure you are a winner! First, you will find your Study Buddy—the person who has a championship badge that matches yours. Your job is to be a 'checker for understanding' with your buddy. Throughout this class session, I will stop every once in a while to ask you to ask your buddy if he or she has any questions or ideas to contribute. Your job is to make sure that the question gets answered before we move on and to make sure that your buddy's idea is heard by the class. Raise your buddy's hand now to show that you are partners."

"Good! Now, please check with your buddy to find out three things that have worked well and three things that have not worked well in the groups in which you have been members. You have 3 minutes to do this, so work efficiently." [Pause, circulate to listen to the buddies.] "Thank you. Now, let's get your great ideas on the board. I'll scribe while you tell me what you have come up with. First, let's hear from the buddy with the shortest hair cut." [List as many ideas as you can in about 3 minutes. Print on newsprint with two columns: Things that Work Well and Things that Don't Work Well.] "Thank you! This shows that you all have some great experiences to build upon. Now let's find out from your buddy the advantages to working in groups for yourselves and for your teachers. I'll give you 3 minutes to listen to each other's ideas." [Pause, listen to buddies, and return in about 3 minutes.] "Good work! Now let's hear from the buddy with the longest hair and I'll scribe as you tell me the results of your interviews." [List advantages in two columns: Advantages to Learners and Advantages to Teachers.] "You have certainly identified some key ideas that even executives in businesses have agreed are important for workers and their bosses as advantages for good group members. Now let's see if we can practice what we are preaching."

"Now, please ask your buddy to tell you what he or she thinks are the important skills he or she needs to work in a cooperative group. Be specific and tell why the skill is needed. Think of at least two skills." [Pause, listen to buddies, and return in about 3 minutes.] "You folks are really thinking up some great skills. Let's get them on newsprint real fast. This time let's hear from the person who has on the wildest footwear." [List as many skills as you can and spot check for reasons why they named the skill.] "We'll need five volunteers to show the class how to practice two key roles—encouraging and sharing ideas—as they finish the ending to a short story."

Select five students randomly and arrange them in a circle in the center of the room with the remaining students in a semicircle around them in "fishbowl" fashion. Listen as they complete a short story. Follow the explicit directions below.

INSTRUCTIONS FOR THE
FISHBOWL DEMONSTRATION GROUP

Thank you for agreeing to work as a group today. You will complete one paper that you will sign indicating you agree with the ending to the story that your group has created. Signatures indicate that you agree with the content of the sentences, the sequence of the sentences, and grammatical accuracy. You will each receive the grade that this story earns. (You will receive an A for stories with at least three complete sentences in a logical sequence and with no grammatical errors; a B for stories with at least two complete sentences in a logical sequence with three to five grammatical errors; a C for stories with one sentence and five to seven errors; a D for less than one sentence.) The group will be evaluated for completing the academic task in the assigned time and for practicing: 1) the cooperative behaviors of encouraging and sharing ideas, and 2) the leadership behaviors of timekeeper, recorder, and observer. If your classmates judge that you have met these criteria, they will give you a round of applause!

Role Assignments

Students count off 1–5: 1 serves as the recorder who writes down the group's sentences, 2 is the timekeeper who makes sure the task is completed in the time allotted, 3 is the encourager who lets teammates know their ideas are appreciated and invites contribu-

---

(continued)

tions from everyone, 4 is the observer who completes the cooperative skills observation form (below) and provides feedback to the group, and 5 is the checker who checks to make sure everyone agrees and understands. Each student receives a job card that details each of the roles. The teacher asks each student to read his or her job card out loud. Students are encouraged to remember that they have two jobs to do: one is to practice the social skill of the role and the other job is to thank their teammates when they also practice the role.

Directions for the Academic Task

Read the story below. Brainstorm and record possible ending sentences. Select at least three sentences to finish the story. Agree on grammar, punctuation, and sequence of the sentences. Record the selected sentences on the back of the page. Proofread the three sentences. Make sure all group members sign indicating agreement with the decisions.

The Story

The most unusual things happened to me during the last couple of weeks of school. At the time I was a little nervous about what was going on. Now, when I look back, a lot of it seems funny to me.

_____

Directions to observer: Write the names of your group members in the boxes numbered 1–5. Place a tally mark each time you observe the cooperative skills. If you have time, jot down specific examples of the skills so you can share them later during group processing.

GROUP MEMBERS

	1	2	3	4	5
COOPERATIVE SKILLS					
Sharing Ideas					
Encouraging					

JUNIOR HIGH

How are social skills and criteria for success explained (when and who)?

Encouraging and sharing are focused on as two keys to groups that work well. The brainstormed list of what works well in successful groups is sure to yield both behaviors and the list of what does not work well is sure to yield their opposites (e.g., put-downs, not sharing). The teacher makes a point of connecting these skills to the students' shared experiences.

CLOSURE AND PROCESSING*

What is the process for closure (students summarize what they learned)?

At the end of the demonstration lesson, the teacher solicits comments from the Study Buddies' observations of the strengths and weaknesses of the demonstration group members' performance of the cooperative behaviors (encouraging, sharing) and leadership behaviors (observer, timekeeper, recorder).

What is the process for feedback on academic performance (how, who, and when)?

The teacher comments on the grammatical accuracy of the story ending and the creativity of the ending itself.

How are the teacher's observations shared?

Rule: Share negative comments in private and positive comments in public and private. After the students have shared, the teacher shares his or her observations.

What is the process for assessment of individual and group success in using social skills (how and when)?

The student observer shares results of the observation and makes comments about various team members' participation. The Study Buddies interview each other to find out what behaviors they observed. The teacher randomly calls on a student to report what his or her buddy observed. The teacher tries to show how the behaviors of encouraging and sharing are correlated with the creative process.

AFTER THE LESSON

How does the teacher
evaluate the success
of the lesson?

The teacher checks to make sure the essential elements
(marked by an asterisk) of cooperative learning groups
were completed. The teacher schedules a series of
classes in which students continue to practice working in
cooperative groups.

Anecdote

The students in the fishbowl accomplished their task and
received feedback from their classmates and the teacher.
Immediately following the lesson, the rest of the class was
divided into cooperative groups, and the groups were assigned the same academic task, roles, and social behaviors
as the fishbowl group. Each member of the fishbowl was an
observer in the newly formed groups.

The teachers who observed and the students who participated in the lesson reported that they enjoyed the lesson. The charts that were generated during the class discussion were used for lessons that were subsequently
developed by the middle school teachers. It was clear that
the students enjoyed being consulted about their experiences with group work and that they were committed to
improving the way they worked together.

Reference

Villa, R., & Thousand, J. (1987). *Cooperative group lesson
plan.* Unpublished manuscript developed as part of an inservice staff development activity for A.A. Kingston Middle School faculty (New York), Center for Developmental
Disabilities, University of Vermont, Burlington.

MIDDLE SCHOOL

JUNIOR HIGH SCHOOL LANGUAGE ARTS FOR A STUDENT WITH BEHAVIOR DISORDERS

Conn-Powers (1988), a special education intern, collaborated with a junior high school language arts teacher who wanted to infuse creative writing skills into a reading lesson in a practical way. This was quite a challenge, especially considering the large size of the class, the range of students' reading difficulties, and the inclusion of a student with behavior disorders. The two teachers consciously selected cooperative learning groups as a way to individualize instruction and ensure a high level of accountability for student participation. The social skills and role assignments enabled the language arts teacher to "multiply" himself; he knew many of the students needed to be "coached" in reading and comprehension. The teachers found it easy to adapt the cooperative group lesson for the student with behavior disorders. The guidance counselor met with them in advance to explain the anger management strategy the student used and to update them on the student's progress in using it.

LESSON NAME: Newspaper Ads
GRADE LEVEL: Junior high (grades 7–9)

AUTHOR: C. Conn-Powers
CONTENT AREA: Language arts
TIME: 40 minutes

ACADEMIC OBJECTIVES

What are the prerequisite skills?

Reading skills at least at the fourth to fifth grade level

What are the academic objectives?

Students define classified ads, state the benefits to the community of having classified ads, locate ads according to type of service wanted, and accurately match examples of ads to appropriate categories. Students write a creative story that illustrates the benefits and accurately matches the type of classified ad.

How do students demonstrate the academic objectives?

Students demonstrate these objectives by saying and doing the following: "I need this service or these goods and can find people to help me by looking in this section of the classified ads. The benefits include . . . because. . . . "

What are the criteria for success?

Students who can locate an appropriate classified ad and write and tell a story consisting of at least one paragraph of four or more sentences explaining two benefits of the ad earn an "A" on this assignment; stories with one or two sentences or only one benefit earn a "B"; stories with one or two sentences and no benefits earn a "C."

What are the modifications for learners with special education needs?

No modifications were needed for the academic objectives. L. is an adolescent female with behavior disorders whose IEP includes objectives related to increasing self-control, especially when confronted with difficult or time consuming academic tasks. Instead of throwing a tantrum (throwing her books and materials on the floor, stomping her feet) or withdrawing (leaving the room), L. is practicing "counting to 10 while taking deep inhalations and long slow exhalations" while staying at her seat. This technique has been taught to her by the guidance counselor.

166

How do learners with special education needs demonstrate the academic objectives?

The teacher asks L. privately to show how she practices calming down by deep breathing and counting to 10 and lets her know that today's lesson may be a good time for her to show this skill. The teacher asks L. what kind of support she would like to receive from her group. [Possible requests: "Don't stop talking while I practice breathing because I can still listen," and "Is it OK if I ask for help in reading the small print?"]

What are the criteria for success for the learners with special needs?

L. stays with her group to complete the lesson. She practices "counting to 10 and deep breathing" any and every time she needs to.

FACE-TO-FACE INTERACTION DECISIONS*

What is the group size?

There are 32 students in the class—four students to each group, eight groups total.

How are students assigned to groups?

To ensure heterogeneity, students are assigned to groups by the teacher by classified ad categories: Apartments for Rent, Miscellaneous For Sale, Home Furnishings For Sale, Dogs, Help Wanted (General), Houses For Sale, Personals, Automobiles (Foreign) For Sale. The teacher makes sure that each group has at least one student who can read the material, boys and girls are distributed equally, and so forth.

What is the room arrangement?

Students move their desks into eight clusters so that they are facing each other.

How are materials arranged?

Each group receives one newspaper that includes a classified ad section, one blank piece of paper, and one set of colored pens.

STRUCTURING POSITIVE INTERDEPENDENCE*

Members get the messages: "We sink or swim together," "Do your work—we're counting on you," "How can I help you to do better?"

What is the struc-
ture—a single prod-
uct, one group goal, a
shared outcome, or a
group reward?

Each group selects one ad that accurately reflects its assigned category. Each person reads the ad and explains
what it means. The group then writes a story about the
person who placed the ad and what beneficial things
happen to him or her when the ad is answered.

Are student roles
assigned?

To promote positive interdependence, students are assigned roles by the teacher. The teacher hands out prepared "Role Cards" on 3 × 5 index cards:

Recorder: A person who writes the story the group creates.
Checker: A person who makes sure that everyone in the
     group agrees.
Ad Reader: A person who reads the ad in the assigned
     category.
Encourager: A person who energizes the group by asking
     for or praising ideas.

What are the other
divisions of labor
besides roles?
How are materials
arranged?

This emerges as the group decides the content of its story.

To promote positive interdependence, only one newspaper is given to each group so that team members must
share the paper.

(Optional) What
other ways to pro-
mote positive interde-
pendence are used—
intergroup coopera-
tion, intergroup com-
petition, positive
fantasy mission, or
identity interdepen-
dence (e.g., group
name)?

Intergroup cooperation is encouraged by having groups
listen in on each others' story lines.

ESTABLISHING SOCIAL SKILL PERFORMANCE*

What are the social
skills objectives?

Based on student performance during other group work,
the teacher decides that the social skill of paraphrasing
will be emphasized in this lesson.

How is the need for each social skill communicated?	Ask students what happens when they share an idea and nobody says anything. [Acknowledge student responses along the lines of "I don't think my idea is good." or "I don't feel like saying anything anymore."] "What are some better ways than silence to handle this?" [Acknowledge student contributions (e.g., "Say thanks for the idea," "OK," or "I didn't know that.").] "Another way we can handle it is to restate or paraphrase what that person said. Paraphrasing is saying what someone else said in another way."
How are social skills explained, demonstrated, role-played, or practiced?	Ask students to volunteer to demonstrate how they would sound and what their faces would look like when paraphrasing a statement. Praise appropriate demonstrations and correct until students get the idea. Write on the board or on poster paper some of their examples under two columns: "Paraphrasing sounds like . . . " and "Paraphrasing looks like. . . . "
How are social skills assigned to group members?	All group members are responsible for practicing paraphrasing at least two times during the lesson.

SOCIAL SKILL PERFORMANCE: TEACHER MONITORING AND INTERVENTION

What is the process (how and who) for monitoring groups?	During the lesson, the teacher observes and monitors group interactions for about 1 or 2 minutes per group for at least three rotations.
What is the process for feedback (how and who) to groups if social skills are being used?	The teacher shares "on the spot" when the group is doing a great job at paraphrasing.
What is the process for feedback (how and who) to groups if social skills are not being used?	Ask the group, "What does it look like and sound like to paraphrase?" [Acknowledge student responses.] "That's right! I'll come back in a few minutes and I expect to hear and see you, okay?"

What collaboration problems are anticipated?

One person not contributing to the story; one person taking over the story.

What are interventions to avoid or remedy anticipated problems?

Rules: When you feel like intervening, don't. If you must intervene, do it with a question, not an answer. Move away as soon as you can, even if it is only 3 feet. Ask the group, "How can you rearrange the way you're working to make sure that everyone's ideas are in the story?" [Acknowledge student responses.] "You have some really good ideas. I expect if you use one or two of them, you'll write a more creative story. I'll be back in a few minutes to see how you're doing."

SOCIAL SKILL PERFORMANCE: STUDENT MONITORING

What is the student observer(s) selection and training process (what and who)?

Specifically trained student observers are not used.

How are social skills monitored?

Paraphrasing is tallied by the teacher.

Do students observe more than one group?

No.

Do students observe for an entire lesson?

No.

How and when do the teacher or students share their observations?

Students share during the closure part of the lesson when the teacher randomly calls on students to do so. As the teacher listens in on each group, he or she can "catch the students" engaging in the skill of paraphrasing.

JUNIOR HIGH

STRUCTURING INDIVIDUAL ACCOUNTABILITY

Are individual quizzes assigned?

No.

Is there random selection of group members to answer questions?

Students are randomly selected to read their group's story about the ads. For social skills processing, students are randomly selected to share their examples of paraphrasing.

SETTING THE TASK

What is the process for explanation of academic task and criteria for success (when and who)?

The teacher says, "Today you'll be working as a group to learn more about classified ads. What are classified ads?" [Acknowledge student responses and correct misconceptions.] "Where are they located in the newspaper?" [Acknowledge accurate responses.] "What kind of information are you able to get from the classified ads?" [Acknowledge accurate responses.] "People place ads and others read ads to learn about people in our town. The ads help people get jobs, find housing, and transact business. What are some ads that you or your family might place in the paper?" [Write all responses on the board.] "In what sections of the classified ads would you find these ads?" [Acknowledge or coach accurate responses.] "Ad readers, open your group's paper to the 'For Free' section. Group members, help your ad reader find the section and praise him or her for finding it quickly. Now, read the first ad. Who in the room would like that free item?" [Acknowledge responses.]

"Today you will be reading a specific section of the classified ads. Help your ad reader select one ad that accurately reflects your assigned category. Be sure each person can explain what it means. Your group should then write a story about the person who placed the ad and what beneficial things happen to him or her when the ad is answered. You have 20 minutes to do this. I'll be looking for at least four complete sentences in your story explaining at least two benefits. Groups that meet criteria will have their stories posted on the Young Authors' Award board."

How are social skills and criteria for success explained (when and who)?	"I expect each person in the group to practice paraphrasing at least twice during this 20-minute lesson. I will place a check mark every time I hear your group paraphrase." Teacher checks for understanding by asking, "What will I be checking for?" [Acknowledge students who paraphrase the above directions and give corrective feedback until they get the idea.]

CLOSURE AND PROCESSING*

What is the process for closure (students summarize what they learned)?	One or two randomly selected groups comes to the front of the room to read their stories.
What is the process for feedback on academic performance (how, who, and when)?	If criteria are met, the teacher prominently displays story and authors' names on the Young Authors' Award board.
How are the teacher's observations shared?	*Rule: Share negative comments in private and positive comments in public and private.* The teacher notes exemplary displays of paraphrasing, commenting on how the ideas flowed and explaining the relationship between sharing lots of ideas and "process gain"—how no one person could have come up with what the group did.
What is the process for assessment of individual and group success in using social skills (how and when)?	Pass out one 3 × 5 index card per group for group members to record what went well and what skills they plan to practice the next time. Students sign the card and hand it in. The next time the groups work together, the teacher distributes their commitment cards.

Ask the class as a whole, "What did you like about working with this group? What didn't you like? What will you do differently when you work together next time?"

AFTER THE LESSON

How does the teacher
evaluate the success
of the lesson?

The teacher checks to see that the five elements (marked
by an asterisk) of cooperative learning lessons were included. The next social skill the teacher introduces is
"piggy-backing on ideas," which extends the concept of
paraphrasing to include building on the positive aspects
of ideas that are contributed.

Anecdote

Each group decided on an interesting ad and wrote a one-
page story. This represented many more than four sentences in a 20-minute period—an unexpected outcome.
They cooperated and worked well together. Two groups
had trouble getting started and after sending a team
member to listen to other groups, they managed to get inspired. L. became frustrated twice and used her intervention technique to great advantage. Her group was happy
that she shared her ideas and used them to create a different twist to their story. In their story, the person who
placed the ad needed to know how to deep breathe in order
to use scuba diving gear that was for sale. The scuba gear
did not sell, but it was used to save another person's life.
According to Conn-Powers and her partner teacher, the
most impressive aspect of the lesson was the students
were so eager to hear each other's stories. The class decided to create a composite story using ideas from all eight
stories and send it to the school newspaper. It was published the next month, creating an unexpected whole-
class reward.

Reference

Conn-Powers, C. (1988). *Cooperative group lesson plan.*
Unpublished manuscript submitted in partial fulfillment
of requirements for the Educational Specialist graduate
program, Professor J. Thousand, University of Vermont,
Department of Special Education, College of Education
and Social Services, Burlington.

JUNIOR HIGH

SECONDARY LESSON RELATED TO CAREER DEVELOPMENT FOR A YOUNG MAN WITH A LEARNING DISABILITY AND MEMORY IMPAIRMENT

Remeika (1990), a high school employment specialist, collaborated with an experienced vocational educator of a regional vocational education center. They creatively adapted this lesson to successfully include a teenager challenged by memory and learning disabilities.

LESSON NAME: Interviewing for a Job
GRADE LEVEL: High school students
16–19 years old

AUTHOR: S. Remeika
CONTENT AREA: Employment
(vocation/career preparation)
TIME: 43 minutes (1 period or module)

ACADEMIC OBJECTIVES

What are the prerequisite skills?

Reading and writing skills at approximately sixth grade level; following directions, asking for clarification; previous experience with role playing in small groups; some practice with saying or hearing positive "I" statements.

What are the academic objectives?

1. Using the information gathered from a previous lesson plan in which groups identified employment organizations of interest to them. Each group member uses one of the identified organizations to describe a brief job interview situation.
2. Using the handout shown below, each group member identifies three items from the list (or generates additional items) that they can talk about in role-playing a job interview.
3. Each group designs a mnemonic to help members recall the items they include in their interviews.

Employer Expectation Handout

Employers look for workers who can accomplish the goals they have in mind. There are some universal characteristics that every employer seeks to ensure that every prospective worker has. They include, but are not limited to:

Regular attendance
Being on time
Productivity
Ability to get along with others: Supervisor, fellow employees
Willingness to accept responsibilities for duties
Willingness to accept advancement within the business
Willingness to help
Maintaining personal hygiene and grooming on the job
Good moral character

(continued)

> It is your job to convince the employer that you are this kind of person, and, if there have been some lapses in the past, that you have recognized the problem(s) and have resolved them. It is the employer's job to convince himself or herself, based on your answers, that you will be a good employee for the business.
>
> It is not enough to be able to demonstrate that you have the skills. By recounting past employment history and other situations, you will demonstrate that you have those personal attributes employers are looking for.

How do students demonstrate the academic objectives?

Each group member will be able to say: "My organization of interest is . . . ," "The three items that I will discuss in my role play interview are . . . " Each member role plays an interview with his or her team members.

What are the criteria for success?

Four items from the list in the Employer Expectation Handout above initiated by each team member, one organization for each group member, one written description of each person's role play situation, and a mnemonic to help remember the key skills to practice in an interview.

What are the modifications for learners with special education needs?

S. is a young man with a learning disability and memory impairment. This lesson is designed for maximum cognitive rehearsal of information and minimum reliance on written and printed information through oral interviewing. Although S.'s reading and writing skills are less than the sixth grade level, S. can perform the role of observer (checking off behaviors as they occur) as he has been previously trained to do so for himself. The mnemonic requirement is particularly helpful for S. For example, S. might choose being on time, ability to get along with others, and willingness to pitch in as important to cover in his interview, with a mnemonic of "BAW."

What are the criteria for success for the learner with special needs?

S. develops and uses his own mnemonic.

VOCATIONAL SCHOOL

FACE-TO-FACE INTERACTION DECISIONS*

What is the group size?

How are students assigned to groups?

There are seven groups of three students for this session.

To ensure heterogeneity, the students form random groups of three. They count off by 7s in the French language ("Une," "Deux," "Trois" . . .). All the "unes" work in a group, "deuxs" in a group, and so forth. (French was chosen because many students in this school have French Canadian heritage.)

What is the room arrangement?

Students arrange their chairs to ensure face-to-face interactions. One group is clustered by the windows, another by the back of the room, and a third in front of the chalkboard, and so forth.

STRUCTURING POSITIVE INTERDEPENDENCE*

Members get the messages: "We sink or swim together," "Do your work—we're counting on you," "How can I help you to do better?"

What is the structure—one group goal, a single product, or shared outcome?

Is a group reward structured?

There is one paper from each group.

The teacher has a point system in place for appropriate academic and social classroom interactions. Groups that achieve criteria for the academic task receive 10 points and those that achieve the social objective receive 10 points. Groups that achieve both receive 25 points.

Are student roles assigned?

To promote positive interdependence, each group member is assigned a role as follows:

Recorder: Writes the name of one organization per team member and writes a brief description of the role play the team will enact.

Reader: Reads the handout aloud.

Observer: Uses the observer form below to tally when the group members say positive "I" statements and seek clarification.

Observation Form

Directions to observer: Write the names of your group members. Place a tally mark whenever you hear the person make an "I" statement about themselves or whenever they make a clarifying statement.

GROUP MEMBERS

	1	2	3
COOPERATIVE SKILLS			
"I" Statements			
Clarifying Statements			

What are the other division of labor besides roles?

Division of labor may emerge as a result of enacting the role plays. For example, someone may emerge as the employer, another as the secretary who greets the candidate, and so forth.

How are materials arranged?

To promote positive interdependence: one handout per group, one extra piece of paper per group, one pen(cil) for each group, and one observer form for each group.

(Optional) What other ways to promote positive interdependence are used—intergroup cooperation, intergroup competition, positive fantasy mission, or identity interdependence (e.g., group name)?

Groups create a group name representing a mnemonic of their selected organizations. If all seven groups meet both academic and social objectives, the entire class receives bonus points (which they have been accumulating for a class reward).

VOCATIONAL SCHOOL

ESTABLISHING SOCIAL SKILL PERFORMANCE*

What are the social
skills objectives?

Students ask for clarification. Students use positive "I" statements.

How are social skills
demonstrated?

Students say the following: "Would you please explain what you mean when you say that?", "I know that one of my strengths is my ability to get along with others; for example, . . . "

What are the criteria
for success?

The observer notes at least one clarifying statement from each member and two positive "I" statements.

How is the need for
each social skill
communicated?

The teacher asks, "What do you think your chances are of making a good impression on an employer if you ask for clarification about his or her expectations, or if you say something positive instead of negative about yourself by giving specific examples about what you do?" [The teacher acknowledges students' responses to these questions, or elicits them, along the lines of "good impression" or "The boss will think I can figure things out."]

How are social skills
explained, demon-
strated, role-played,
or practiced?

Ask students to brainstorm some possible "I" and clarifying statements related to the list on the Employer Expectation Handout. Write them on the board for students to refer to later. The teacher ensures that each group has at least one "model" oral and written response for each skill.

How are social skills
assigned to group
members?

Each group member is responsible for demonstrating each skill.

SOCIAL SKILL PERFORMANCE:
TEACHER MONITORING AND INTERVENTION*

What is the process
(how and who) for
monitoring groups?

The teacher and the student observer monitor concurrently for frequency of "I" and clarifying statements.

What is the process for feedback (how and who) to groups if social skills are being used?

As the teacher circulates to listen to group performance, he or she gives feedback "on the spot" when he or she hears "I" and clarifying statements. The teacher also checks to make sure the observer is accurately tallying "I" and clarifying statements.

What is the process for feedback (how and who) to groups if social skills are *not* being used?

The teacher privately asks the group, "What social skills are you practicing today?" [Acknowledge students responses or elicit them—"I" and clarifying statements.] "Right! Now what might I hear you saying or see you doing?" [Acknowledge students' responses or remind them to check the board for models.] "Right again! You guys are hot! Now, I'm going to step aside a few minutes and when I return I'll expect to hear and see you practicing "I" and clarifying statements, okay?"

What collaboration problems are anticipated?

1. Groups getting stuck on making up role-plays.
2. One member balks at having to participate in role-play.
3. Recorder having too much to write.

What are interventions to avoid or remedy the anticipated problems?

Rules: When you feel like intervening, don't. If you must intervene, do it with questions, not answers. Move away as soon as you can, even if it is only 3 feet.

1. Suggest creative ways to get unstuck—suggest they change where they are sitting or consider another perspective (e.g., "What if you were a fly on the ceiling?").
2. Ask the group to brainstorm creative ways to include the student who is balking (e.g., "Why not let him or her pretend to be the boss's desk?").
3. Watch for how other groups handle the recorder role, maybe students take turns writing or they develop a creative shorthand system. Encourage the group to observe another group.

VOCATIONAL SCHOOL

SOCIAL SKILL
PERFORMANCE: STUDENT MONITORING

What is the student observer(s) selection and training process (what and who)?

Students have had some previous experiences monitoring their own behaviors.

How are social skills monitored?

The students assigned the role of observer within their group are monitoring the social skills of using "I" statements and clarifying statements using the observation form shown earlier.

Do students observe more than one group?

No.

Do students observe for the entire lesson?

Yes.

How and when do students share their observations?

At the end of the lesson, observers orally describe their results.

STRUCTURING INDIVIDUAL ACCOUNTABILITY*

Are individual quizzes assigned?

Initials by items selected by each group member and observations and listening in on role plays provide evidence of achievement.

Is there a random selection of group members to answer questions?

At the end of the lesson, the teacher asks students to share what it was like to be in groups where they were supported to make "I" and clarifying statements.

SETTING THE TASK

What is the process for explanation of the academic task and criteria for success (when and who)?

At the beginning of the class period, the teacher greets the students pleasantly, and rather formally, as candidates for jobs in various organizations. The teacher says: "I'm happy you've come to my organization to interview for a job today! To help you be successful in getting the job you would be best at, I'm asking you to practice with some of the other candidates here. This also gives me a chance to watch you as you work in a group, which is an important part of working at this place, as you know! You can use the Employee Expectation Handout (see pp. 176–177) I'm giving you to identify three things for each of you that you want to talk about with me later during your interview. I will know the ones you are interested in because you will put your initials by the items you select. I'm also looking forward to seeing how you will use your creative minds to come up with clever mnemonics— memory tricks—to help each other remember the skills you have that employers want."

"In our organization, it is more important for people to understand information, not just read it or write about it. So one person on each of your teams should be the reader. It is also important for people to share the labor, so another person should be the recorder. I am more interested in your ideas than complete sentences or good spelling, so be sure to get as many ideas down as you can."

"Your recorder will write the name of the organization you are interested in and your ideas for a practice interview. You will be given time (about 10 minutes each) to practice your role play interviews so that you will be as well prepared as you can be for your interview with me."

"I care a lot about how people treat each other in our organization by what they say and do when they work together. So each group will have an observer who will check off whenever you make a clarifying or positive 'I' statement about yourself. Can someone tell me some of the things you think I, as an employer, might want in a person interviewing for a job? What are some reasons for saying positive things about yourself in a job interview? How do you think you could turn something negative to your benefit? For instance, what if the employer knows that you were fired from your last job? Or that you were late 9 times out of 10?"

"You could do these things: Be honest, but brief about your experience, pointing out the positive lessons you learned. Do not blame your negative experience on anyone else, no matter how justified you feel about it. Then ask the employer a clarifying question to redirect the interview. For example, you might say, 'Would you please tell me what makes an employee successful in your business?' In summary, I expect each group to hand in one handout with these things written on it: three initialed items for each team member, the name of one organization written down for each member, one written

VOCATIONAL SCHOOL

description of each person's role-play situation, and a mnemonic to help you remember the key skills you want to practice in your interview. I will be observing to be sure the role-plays take place and to make sure the observer accurately indicates participation on the social skills and in the role-play."

"Now, to make sure you understand, what are we going to do today?" [Teacher acknowledges any paraphrases and gives corrective feedback if necessary.]

How are social skills and criteria for success explained (when and who)?

The teacher says, "I care a lot about how people treat each other in our organization by what they say and do when they work together. What do you think your chances are of making a good impression on an employer if you ask for clarification about their expectations, or if you say something positive instead of negative about yourself by giving specific examples about what you do?" [Acknowledge students' responses to these questions or elicit them, along the lines of "good impression" or "The boss will think I can figure things out."]

What is the check for understanding?

The teacher asks for and acknowledges students' paraphrasing of directions.

CLOSURE AND PROCESSING*

What is the process for closure (students summarize what they learned)?

Students summarize what they learned. At the end of the lesson, the teacher collects the written handout, the observers' checklists, and asks the entire class to create a positive "we" statement for the whole class to give in choral response by saying something such as, "We all participated in our role play." The teacher calls on students and lists mnemonics they designed for helping each other to remember key employability skills on newsprint to preserve for the next session. If all seven groups meet criteria, the class receives a bonus of 25 extra points.

What is the process for feedback on academic performance (how, who, and when)?

The teacher evaluates each group and decides whether or not they meet criteria; if so, he or she awards 10 points for meeting academic criteria.

How are the teacher's observations shared?

Rule: Share negative comments in private and positive comments in public and private. The teacher shares observations of clarifying or positive "I" statements that he or she heard students express. For each group that meets criteria, he or she awards 10 points for meeting the academic criteria, 10 points for meeting the social criteria, and 25 points for meeting both academic and social criteria.

What is the process for assessment of individual and group success in using social skills (how and when)?

At the end of the processing of academic success, the teacher conducts a brief "communications whip" (each team member shares a comment about his or her participation in 5 seconds).

AFTER THE LESSON

How does the teacher evaluate the success of the lesson?

The teacher checks to ensure that he or she included all parts of the lesson plan, particularly the essential elements of successful cooperative learning groups (marked with an asterisk). The teacher forms new heterogeneous groups so that students can teach each other their mnemonics.

Anecdote

The cognitive rehearsal embedded in this lesson provided students with lots of practice in stating what employers expect from employees. They wanted to find out if what they were learning was "real." So, as a follow-up lesson, the teachers located a local business personnel manager who agreed to have the entire class come to her office. Students experienced a real interview and reported being much more confident about going out on their own to interview for jobs.

The personnel manager was impressed with the students' understanding of employer expectations and asked for the Employer Expectation Handout used in class. She appreciated the mnemonics and acronyms the students had generated and decided to post them for the benefit of her own employees and the prospective employees she interviews.

Reference

Remeika, S. (1990). *Cooperative group lesson plan.* Unpublished manuscript submitted in partial fulfillment of requirements for the Educational Specialist graduate program, Professor J. Thousand, University of Vermont, Department of Special Education, College of Education and Social Services, Burlington.

HIGH SCHOOL SCULPTURE CLASS FOR A STUDENT WITH INTELLECTUAL DISABILITIES AND VISUAL IMPAIRMENT

This lesson was developed collaboratively by Alice Udvari-Solner, a professor in the area of inclusive schooling, Nancy Caldwell-Korpela, a special education support facilitator, Don Hunt, an art teacher, and 12 students enrolled in a high school sculpture class. Students were required to complete projects that ranged from making South American rain sticks and realistic masks to free-form sculpture. Projects were designed and fashioned by each student, with flexibly negotiated timelines for completion and self-paced monitoring of progress. Such an individualistic learning model, common to many art classes, does not necessarily facilitate spontaneous natural support among the students. Although the atmosphere of the classroom was relaxed and congenial, due to the individualized nature of assignments, most students worked alone. The social climate was particularly conducive to facilitating the inclusion of J., a student with disabilities. Because J. often required physical assistance and frequent encouragement to maintain participation, the art teacher asked a small group of class members, "How can we ensure that everyone in this class is involved? Is there any way we can change the way we do our projects to include J. more effectively?" J.'s classmates made three unique and viable proposals that were used in the lesson plan: 1) form a collective mural of ceramic tiles with each cooperative group selecting a feature of the human face on which to concentrate (e.g., a panel of all noses, all lips, or all eyes); 2) work in cooperative groups in the creation of a progressive sculpture where the group would start with a lump of clay and each group member would add a dimension to the piece and pass it on to the next group member; and 3) draw a collective design for a free-form sculpture for which each class member takes responsibility to complete one or more components.

LESSON NAME: Oaxacan Style Animal
  Sculptures
GRADE LEVEL: Middle school or high
  school (ages 12–18)

AUTHORS: A. Udvari-Solner,
  N. Caldwell-Korpela, D. Hunt, and
  sculpture class members
CONTENT AREA: Art/Sculpture I
TIME: Eight periods (50 minutes each)

ACADEMIC OBJECTIVES

What are the prerequisite skills?

Experience with slab pottery construction (i.e., kneading clay to remove air bubbles, rolling clay to a uniform flatness, and use of modeling tools). Exposure to traditional Oaxacan wooden animal sculpture through readings and examples on slides

What are the academic objectives?

1. Students complete a sculpture in the traditional Oaxacan folk art style within eight 50-minute class periods.
2. Students prepare a one-page typed description of the religious or cultural symbolism the figure holds in Oaxacan society.
3. Students prepare and give a 5-minute presentation to describe the construction process and significance of the figure in the Oaxacan culture.

What are the criteria for success?

Satisfactory completion of the sculpture requires accurate slab construction, bisque firing, and painting with acrylic paint within the eight periods. Sculptures are graded on a 25-point scale for creativity, finishing techniques, correspondence with traditional Oaxacan construction, and paint detail. The written description is graded using a 10-point scale for correct grammar, spelling, and accurate citation of one reference to the literature.

What are the modifications for learners with special needs?

J. is a student with intellectual disabilities, cerebral palsy, and visual impairment. The lesson is designed to provide J. with opportunities for making choices and using fine motor skills to prepare selected parts of the sculpture with adapted materials and tools. J. contributes to group decision making by selecting the type of figure to be constructed and the colors used for decoration. An adapted crank-operated rolling device enables J. to place the clay in the device and grasp and turn the handle to flatten the clay into a slab. J.'s peers were taught to give a verbal cue and light physical assistance at the wrist to enable J. to push a metal template into clay slabs to form the ears, wings, and horns of the figure.

What are the criteria for success for the learner with special needs?

J. points to items he prefers to work on within 15 seconds. J. uses the crank-operated rolling device on 7 of 10 opportunities. J. pushes the template on 4 of 5 opportunities.

FACE-TO-FACE INTERACTION DECISIONS

What is the group size?

There are 12 students in the class—three groups of four members.

How are students assigned to groups?

The teacher assigns students to groups to ensure heterogeneity in gender, ethnicity, and experience or ability in pottery skills.

What is the room arrangement?

Large work tables with stools are standard furniture in the art classroom. Each group is assigned to a table. During decision-making times and constructive feedback sessions, students move away from the table to arrange their stools in a close-knit circle for face-to-face interactions.

HIGH SCHOOL

STRUCTURING POSITIVE INTERDEPENDENCE*

Members get the messages: "We sink or swim together," "Do your work—we're counting on you," "How can I help you to do better?"

What is the structure—a single product, a shared outcome, or a group reward?

Each group submits one sculpture and one written report. Each group completes one observation sheet for each class session. Groups that meet the academic and social goal criteria assist in preparing a display of the sculptures in the high school art gallery during one class period.

Are student roles assigned?

Due to the complex nature of the project, each group member has more than one role. J. has the roles of clay preparer, appendage technician, and base painter. Clay preparers obtain clay from storage bins daily and roll them into slabs; template designers design the metal template forms that are used to cut out the appendages (ears, horns, wings, etc.) of the sculpture; detailers use modeling tools to apply textured designs to sculpture elements and complete fine finishing work on attachments to the sculpture (smoothing and shaping edges); body technicians use a potter's wheel to throw the base shape of the figure; limb technicians use slab construction techniques to fashion the arms, legs, and head of the sculpture; appendage technicians use metal templates to prepare figure appendages; base painters apply a uniform base color to the figure; the presenter is the spokesperson for the group when the sculpture and report are exhibited to the class; researchers find written resources on Oaxacan culture and folk art; recorders/report writers summarize group findings in written form; and observers attend to and record evidence of effective constructive criticism between group members.

What are the other divisions of labor besides roles?

Material set-up and clean-up is shared by each member of the group on a rotating basis. Other roles may surface based upon how detailed the sculpture becomes. Groups are encouraged to identify and assign new roles as the need emerges while being aware of ensuring an equitable distribution of responsibility.

How are materials arranged?	To promote intergroup cooperation, each group uses one set of tools, one piece of paper and one pencil for report writing and designing ideas, and one observation form per session. The group begins with one portion of clay that is prepared and shared among the team members.
How else is positive interdependence structured?	Students develop identity interdependence by selecting a group name. The group name is based on the Spanish word for the selected figure (i.e., the group designing a wolf sculpture would refer to themselves as "Los Lobos"). The teacher refers to the groups by these names during the project.

ESTABLISHING SOCIAL SKILL PERFORMANCE*

What are the social skills objectives?	Students give constructive feedback to each other on a daily basis. Students provide constructive feedback to other groups at a final critique. Students in J.'s group provide models, prompts, cues, and physical assistance to give feedback to J. as he completes his responsibilities.
How are social skills demonstrated?	Students provide constructive feedback using the following six guidelines:

1. Sandwich a critique between two positive comments.
2. Use a friendly and supportive tone of voice.
3. Suggest or recommend an action (e.g., "To get a smoother edge, try . . . ").
4. Be concise and specific rather than global (e.g., Instead of saying "the color looks nice," say, "I like the way you've made the colors blend from soft to bold.").
5. Acknowledge and give credit to others for their contributions.
6. Criticize ideas, not people.

How is the need for each social skill communicated?	The teacher explains to the class that a common procedure in artistic circles is to engage in collegial critiques so as to improve each other's work. Honesty in giving and receiving feedback about technique, form, and impact through critiques is emphasized.

What are the modifications for learners with special needs?	Students in the same group as J. critique by providing: 1) spontaneous physical prompts, 2) encouraging verbal statements, and 3) models of the desired skill. During each session, J. greets his group members by name through two vocalizations or a vocalization and a sign or gesture. J. initiates a conversation with group members at least once per class session by vocalizing, signing, or pointing to conversational pictures on his communication board.
How are social skills explained, demonstrated, role-played, or practiced?	The teacher shows a videotape of past classes engaged in constructive feedback, pointing out the critical elements. After observing the tape, a volunteer student role-plays with the teacher to further model the essential features. The teacher makes a distinction that feedback can be provided in many forms based upon how each person learns best. Students volunteer to share how they prefer to receive feedback from others. The discussion is guided so that students understand that feedback can also be provided in the form of physical prompts, as is true for J.
How are social skills assigned to group members?	Each student is assigned the responsibility of demonstrating the social skill of constructive feedback.
What are the criteria for success?	Each member of the group uses two or more constructive feedback techniques with other group members during each class session.

SOCIAL SKILL PERFORMANCE: TEACHER MONITORING AND INTERVENTION*

What is the process (how and when) for monitoring groups?	The student observer in each group tallies the frequency of constructive feedback techniques. The teacher monitors the quality and accuracy of the statements via listening during 5–7 minute time samples of each group.
What is the process for feedback (how and when) to groups if social skills are being used?	While circulating during each class session, the teacher notices and acknowledges acceptable techniques as they occur.

What is the process for feedback (how and when) to groups if social skills are *not* being used?

The teacher sits with each group for brief portions of the daily feedback sessions. If skills are not being used, he or she may model one or two comments and then ask the group to analyze why the comments did or did not fit the guidelines for constructive feedback. He or she asks the students to rehearse and practice the guidelines for a few minutes after he or she leaves the group. The teacher returns to verify that they followed through.

What collaboration problems are anticipated?

Students may try to work individually without input from the group. One student may want his or her ideas to have priority.

What are the interventions to avoid or remedy the anticipated problems?

The teacher schedules a constructive feedback session midway through the class period. The teacher assigns periodic checks with all group members to ensure all components of the sculpture interface. The teacher can distribute decision making among all group members by having them count off randomly (1s select the color of the base shape, 2s select the shape of the figure, etc.). The teacher can distribute tasks in such a way that each member has personal control over one or two elements, thereby diffusing conflict over every decision.

SOCIAL SKILL
PERFORMANCE: STUDENT MONITORING

What is the student observer(s) selection and training process (what and who)?

The teacher assists the entire class to generate the social skills checklist shown on the next page. The list may be modified as the class identifies other skills it finds helpful and as the students become skilled at critiquing each other's work. Different students assume the observer role for each class.

How are social skills monitored?

Observers record frequencies during the designated critique sessions, using a class-generated observation form shown on the next page.

HIGH SCHOOL

GROUP MEMBERS

SOCIAL SKILL	Name	Name	Name	Name
Sandwiches feedback				
Uses positive voice tone				
Uses specific terms				
Gives credit to contributions				
Gives recommended actions				
Provides assistance by modeling or prompting				
Modifications for J.'s specific social skills				
Greets class members				
Initiates conversations				

How and when do students share their observations?

At the end of each feedback session, observers share data with the group.

STRUCTURING INDIVIDUAL ACCOUNTABILITY*

How is student learning assessed? How are contributions to the group product assessed?

Students sign their initials to the written report indicating they have provided input to the report. The teacher assesses mastery of the academic task by observing each student during the construction process. The daily observation records serve as data for the demonstration of social skills objectives. Students complete an evaluation of themselves and their group using the self-evaluation form on page 196.

HIGH SCHOOL

Self-Evaluation Form

Name: _____ Group Name: _____

My tasks for the group project were:

_____

_____

_____

What I did included:

_____

_____

_____

How I think my contribution added to the overall quality of the project:

_____

_____

_____

What my group was particularly effective in doing:

_____

_____

_____

What my group should do differently next time:

_____

_____

_____

SETTING THE TASK

What is the process for explanation of the task and criteria for success (when and who)?

The classroom teacher greets the students, encourages them to take 5 minutes to look at the art work on display (there will be two real Oaxacan animal figures as well as three different enlarged pictures of the figures). The teacher begins a discussion by saying, "Remember to study this artwork from the critical eye of an artist. By this I mean, try to identify some of the characteristics of each piece so that we can understand the construction and meaning behind this work." Next, the teacher refers the students to the board that lists key characteristics (materials, tools, construction techniques, detail of design, paint, finish, and cultural significance). These items remain prominently displayed throughout the project. Allowing 5 minutes for this exploration, the teacher circulates and listens to the students.

"Now, let's generate a list of your observations to the various aspects of this artwork. To begin, talk with two of your neighbors to find out the name of the culture from which this art is created." [Pause while students discuss. Listen in and hopefully hear the word "Oaxacan."] "Yes, that's right! It's called Oaxacan ("wa-ha-kon") and you'll be talking more about the Oaxacan culture. Now, let's focus our attention on some of the other characteristics of this work." The teacher allows for spontaneous and free-flow comments to be generated from the students. He or she guides the group to include input with regard to each of the listed characteristics. If J. does not spontaneously offer input, the teacher asks him at a natural point in the discussion, "J., will you point to the figure you like the most?"

"It is wonderful to hear and see each of you beginning to view art with an artist's eye. You are looking at the detail and construction techniques involved in each creative piece. As we have discussed before, we need to learn of and begin to understand the benefits that a multicultural society brings to each of us. As you noticed, each piece is very unique even though all of them come from the same culture! Your discussion showed that those characteristics can be similar and yet we can respect how each piece is different. This is very much like it is with human beings. In order for us to build and live as a community, we must first learn of our similarities and show respect and understanding for our differences.

The challenge for each of you over the next seven class sessions is to work cooperatively with people who are different from you, respecting their differences. The four of you in each group should design, create, and share with each other your own Oaxacan style animals. Let's go over some of the expectations for this project."

"You will be divided into three groups of four students with each group being responsible for outcomes that require viewing, reading, and listening. To *view*, you will create a Oaxacan style animal for your classmates to examine, incorporating the characteristics discussed. The sculpture will be graded on a 25-point scale based on creativity, finishing techniques, correspondence with traditional Oaxacan style construction, and the paint detail. To *read*, you will write a one-page, typed description of the religious or cultural symbolism the figure holds in Oaxacan society. The report will be graded on a 10-point scale based on correct grammar, spelling, and citation of at least one reference to the literature. To *listen*, you will give a 5-minute presentation to your classmates, describing the construction process and significance of the figure in Oaxacan culture. The final grading aspect of your project focuses on social skills that are characteristic of effective groups: community building and cooperation. These skills include *respect* for one another and the strengths each person brings to the project, *cooperative effort* as it shows up in the division of labor to create an equal level of participation and responsibility throughout the project, and *constructive feedback* to each other on a daily basis and during the final critique sessions on the 'gallery day' when all projects are displayed and examined."

The teacher shows a videotape of methods to provide constructive feedback, including strategies appropriate when J. is a member of the group.

"At the conclusion of the eight sessions for this project, the groups that meet the academic and social skills objectives will prepare a display of their sculptures in the high school gallery."

The teacher checks for understanding of the expectations by asking students to paraphrase and to rehearse the meaning behind *view, read, listen,* and *respect, cooperative effort,* and *constructive feedback.*

The teacher asks an identified member of each group to pick up an information packet and to convene his or her group. The packet includes names of the group members and their assigned roles and responsibilities, a blank space for the group name to be entered, a suggested timeline of events, and the grading criteria. The students then begin their cooperative group project.

The teacher explains the bonus point system. The intent behind offering groups an additional means of earning points is two-fold: to encourage and extend students time together outside of class and to offer supplemental strategies for achieving the social skills objectives. Groups can earn 5 bonus points if the group members (as a group) tour the local art gallery that is showing a folk art display outside of school hours. Groups can earn 5 bonus points if the group agrees to be videotaped on the day of the whole-class critique.

In subsequent classes, in addition to the responsibilities J. has been assigned as part of his participation in the group project, J. is responsible for bringing in and playing on a tape player music representative of the Oaxacan culture. The tapes can be checked out from the local public library or school library during J.'s nonschool and study hall instructional time periods. If J.'s group elects to go with him for this responsibility, the group can earn 5 bonus points.

The role and responsibilities of the special education support facilitator include collaborating with the classroom teacher regarding specific academic and social objectives for J., identifying and creating curricular and material adaptations, and assisting in the coordination of various resources that students may need to access for information to complete their projects (e.g., school library books, Oaxacan animal sculptures, filmstrips and audiotapes, periodicals, local art gallery folk art displays, videos, find and interview an "artist in residence," interview a high school history teacher with background knowledge in Oaxacan culture so as to coordinate and interface with other academic classes).

How are social skills and criteria for success explained (when and who)?

The teacher shows a videotape of past classes engaged in constructive feedback, pointing out the critical elements. After observing the tape, a volunteer student role-plays with the teacher to further model the essential features. The teacher makes a distinction that feedback can be provided in many forms based upon how each person learns best. Students volunteer to share how they prefer to receive feedback from others. The discussion is guided so that students understand that feedback can also be provided in the form of physical prompts, as is true for J.

HIGH SCHOOL

CLOSURE AND PROCESSING*

What is the process for closure (students summarize what they learned)?

Students meet individually with the teacher in a debriefing session before the initiation of the next project to discuss their self-evaluations and to set personal goals for future participation.

What is the process for feedback on academic performance (how, who, and when)?

The teacher provides group scores for each sculpture and written report. (A total of 35 points is possible.)

How are teacher's observations shared?

At the end of the eight sessions, the teacher shares the positive aspects of each group's performance with the whole class. Students' strengths and growth in providing constructive feedback, critiquing, and support are emphasized and connected to the development of unique and creative ideas for sculpture design. Any negative comments or concerns about performance are shared individually with each student during the individual debriefing sessions when students develop their performance contracts for the next project.

What is the process for assessment of individual and group success in using social skills (how and when)?

Students hear reports from the teacher and peer observers on a daily basis and during structured critique sessions as well as during the gallery session on the last day.

AFTER THE LESSON

How does the teacher evaluate the success of the lesson?

The teacher checks to see that the essential elements (marked by an asterisk) of cooperative learning lessons were included. Based on the success of this series of lessons, the teacher decides to expand the cooperative group learning options for his other art classes.

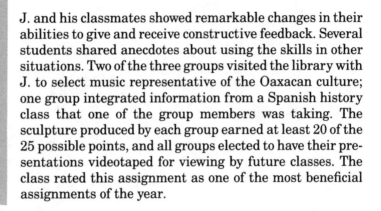

Anecdote

J. and his classmates showed remarkable changes in their abilities to give and receive constructive feedback. Several students shared anecdotes about using the skills in other situations. Two of the three groups visited the library with J. to select music representative of the Oaxacan culture; one group integrated information from a Spanish history class that one of the group members was taking. The sculpture produced by each group earned at least 20 of the 25 possible points, and all groups elected to have their presentations videotaped for viewing by future classes. The class rated this assignment as one of the most beneficial assignments of the year.

COOPERATIVE LEARNING AT THE COLLEGE LEVEL

Ann I. Nevin and Jacqueline S. Thousand have adapted cooperative learning for their undergraduate and graduate personnel preparation programs for more than a decade. Recently, they began to incorporate structured academic controversies to enable their students to become more skilled at negotiating conflict. This lesson plan was originally developed and implemented in a graduate seminar for educational specialists. Ann Nevin adapted it to meet the needs of an undergraduate class for special education teacher candidates.

COLLEGE

LESSON NAME: Full Inclusion of
  Students with Disabilities:
  A Structured Academic Controversy
GRADE LEVEL: College undergraduates
  (juniors/seniors) and graduate
  students

AUTHORS: A. Nevin, J. Thousand,
  S. Dominque, K. Fillioe, V. Gasco-
  Wiggin, M.K. Monley, L. Mulley,
  K. Noone, and K. White
CONTENT AREA: Teacher education
TIME: One or two 90-minute sessions

LESSON SUMMARY: Students summarize pro and con positions with citations from the literature related to: 1) full inclusion (FI) or heterogeneous schooling (HS) for students with all levels of disabilities, also known as the regular education initiative (REI) or mainstreaming (Jenkins, Pious, & Jewell, 1990; Lipsky & Gartner, 1989); and 2) recent efforts for restructuring the special and general education systems to meet several requirements of the Individuals with Disabilities Education Act Amendments of 1991 (IDEA) (PL 102-119) and the Americans with Disabilities Act (ADA) of 1990 (PL 101-336) (Villa & Thousand, 1988).

ACADEMIC OBJECTIVES

What are the prerequisite skills?

Knowledge of current exemplary practices in general and special education; understanding of values driving FI, HS, REI, and mainstreaming movements (gained through experiences and completion of readings and written exercises prior to the controversy)

What are the instructional objectives?

Higher-order thinking skills of analysis, evaluation, and synthesis are emphasized in this lesson. Students understand the roles and relative influences of best practices, values, and research to current movements in education. The goal is not to "win," but to comprehend, which is why this controversy is conducted within a cooperative context (Johnson & Johnson, 1991). Each student writes his or her personal views regarding FI by completing the statement "Full inclusion is . . . because . . . " and citing at least three current exemplary practices, values, or research results to support the position.

How do students demonstrate objectives?

Students demonstrate these objectives by saying and doing the following: "The best practice of (or value, or research result) . . . indicates that . . . " Each student actively speaks and writes during the controversy.

FACE-TO-FACE INTERACTION DECISIONS*

What is the group size?

There are 24 students in the class—six groups of four members.

How are students assigned to groups?

Structured pairs in quartets: Students are randomly assigned to groups of four. When groups are formed, members count off "1" and "2," 1s and 2s each being a structured pair. (Check to see that gender, ethnicity, experience, and ability are distributed among the pairs and quartets.)

What is the room arrangement?

Arrange desks and chairs so that quartets are separate and that structured pairs are seated so they can see each other comfortably (e.g., knee-to-knee).

STRUCTURING POSITIVE INTERDEPENDENCE*

Members get the messages: "We sink or swim together," "Do your work—we're counting on you," "How can I help you to do better?"

What is the structure?

There is one written and oral report from each group representing the best possible resolution, given current knowledge and practice.

Are student roles assigned?

1s take the Pro FI position; 2s take the Con FI position. During the Reverse Perspective phase, they switch positions.

How are materials arranged?

Each structured pair receives one handout (below) summarizing the research on their position. They brainstorm additional evidence (i.e., research results, best practices, values, and personal experiences), noting their mutually decided best evidences on a large newsprint to be presented to the opposing pair. Each pair receives two magic markers and two large pieces of newsprint.

COLLEGE

Full Inclusion Is the Best Policy for Students with Special Needs

Pro Position

Having students with special needs in regular classes increases the quality of education for all students. Current exemplary practices in special education include systematic data-based instruction on curriculum objectives that are age-appropriate and delivery of instructions in public school placements in neighborhood schools to ensure social interaction with same-age peers without disabilities. Integrated delivery of services and community-based training allows students with severe challenges to experience friendships as well as services available to all citizens. Dozens of North American school systems are providing heterogeneous schooling successfully through collaborative teams of educators, specialized personnel, parents, volunteers, and students. Values related to treating individuals with respect (independent of gender, sexual preference, race, ethnicity, and socioeconomic background) are now extended to individuals with disabilities.

Con Position

Having students with special needs in regular classes interferes with the quality of education for students without disabilities. The scientific evidence related to integrated, regular education services compared to segregated special services is mixed and inconclusive; we should continue with current practices of separate special education. The provisions of IDEA regarding the least restrictive environment (LRE) do not require integration into regular classes or schools. Besides, the law clearly states that a continuum of services should be available for students who display severe forms of maladaptive behavior or for those who lack the ability and skills to succeed in the mainstream. Not only do students without disabilities suffer, but students with special needs are often rejected or ridiculed by other students. The reality is that public schools are a long way from doing a good job and should wait until they are ready to integrate.

What are other ways to promote positive interdependence?

Quartets are invited to select a popular song that reflects their resolution.

ESTABLISHING SOCIAL SKILL PERFORMANCE*

What are the social skills objectives?

Students demonstrate effective controversy skills:

1. Be critical of ideas (not people) by challenging and refuting ideas while accepting the people.
2. Encourage participation to master all of the information by asking for opinions.

3. Add on or modify ideas.
4. Ask for explanations to bring out all ideas and facts for all sides *before* trying to integrate.
5. Change positions when evidence indicates the need by suggesting alternatives.

How is the need for controversy skills communicated?

Ask students how comfortable they feel when their opinions are challenged. Acknowledge their contributions and elaborate by saying that during this controversy they will focus on challenging and refuting ideas while simultaneously accepting the person stating the ideas. By focusing on the best resolution possible, encouraging participation, listening and restating ideas, and asking for explanations to bring out all ideas and facts before integrating, it is more likely that the best resolution is forthcoming.

How are social skills explained, demonstrated, role-played, or practiced?

Ask students to volunteer how they would sound and what their faces or body language would look like while challenging and refuting ideas while accepting the person. Write the "looks like" and "sounds like" ideas on the chalkboard so that students words are reflected. Acknowledge student demonstrations and give corrective feedback. For example, a student might say, "The person leans forward and touches my hand in a friendly way and says, 'I'm glad you're my partner and I disagree with what you said about. . . . , I would say, 'Will you please tell me more about why you think that way?' "

How are social skills assigned to group members?

For this lesson, each group member is accountable to demonstrate at least three of the controversy skills, monitoring his or her own performance.

SOCIAL SKILL PERFORMANCE: MONITORING AND INTERVENTION*

What is the process for monitoring groups?

Using the following observation form, the professor rotates to observe and monitor group interactions, approximately 1–2 minutes per group. Frequency of occurrence of the five controversy skills are noted for individual students who ask for opinions, ask for explanations, add on or modify ideas, suggest alternatives, and disagree in a friendly manner (being critical of ideas, not people).

COLLEGE

Directions to observer: Write in the names of group members. Tally the frequency of occurrence for each skill. Note specific examples to share during group processing.

GROUP MEMBERS

	1	2	3	4
CONTROVERSY SKILLS				
1. Criticizes ideas				
2. Asks for opinions				
3. Adds on or modifies				
4. Asks for explanations				
5. Suggests alternatives				

What is the process for feedback to groups if social skills are being used?

The professor gives nonverbal cues (e.g., thumbs up signal) or verbal feedback regarding appropriate use of controversy skills.

What is the process for feedback to groups if social skills are *not* being used?

The professor asks the group, "What does it look like and sound like to practice controversy skills?" Acknowledge accurate representations of the controversy skills by saying, "I'll come back in a few minutes and I expect to hear and see you practice these, OK?"

What collaboration problems are anticipated?

What are the interventions to avoid or to remedy the anticipated problems?

Arguments about accuracy of information and validity of sources.

Rule: When you feel like intervening, don't. If you must intervene, do it with a question, not an answer. Move away as soon as you can, even if it is only 3 feet! Remind the group that argument is okay as long as it is tempered with the five controversy skills. If there is disagreement about validity of sources, you may need to use one of the skills to balance the less valid source with a fact from a mutually acceptable source.

SOCIAL SKILL
PERFORMANCE: STUDENT MONITORING

What is the student observer(s) selection and training process?

How are social skills monitored?

Students monitor their own use of controversy skills by completing the controversy checklist shown above.

Students indicate their use of "I ask for opinions; I ask for explanations; I add on or modify ideas; I suggest alternatives; I disagree in a friendly manner; I'm critical of ideas not people."

STRUCTURING INDIVIDUAL ACCOUNTABILITY*

Are individual quizzes assigned?

Is there random selection of group members to answer questions?

Each student hands in written pro and con positions.

Periodically during the controversy, the professor may stop the class to ask randomly selected partners to publicly state their positions.

COLLEGE

SETTING THE TASK

What is the process
for explanation of the
task and criteria for
success?

The task is to understand as fully as possible the multiple contexts for full inclusion, heterogeneous schooling,
regular education initiative, or mainstreaming movements. In addition to the empirical context, there is an
ethical or moral context as well as a current best practice context. The basic objective is to attest to all sides of
an issue and to generate resolutions that are meaningful
to all sides. Each position (pro, con, and resolution) must
be supported by at least three relevant best practices,
values, or research results. There are no winners or
losers in this controversy. Remember that the goal is to
be able to attest to all sides of the issue. There are five
parts to the lesson, as shown below.

STRUCTURED ACADEMIC CONTROVERSY PROCESS

Prepare Position:	Each structured pair (the 1s and the 2s) works together to prepare the best case for their position (1s prepare pro; 2s prepare con). They complete the sentence stem, "Our best ideas are. . . . " They organize a reasoned position and use persuasive argument by stating a claim and arranging supportive facts, values, experiences, and practices into a rationale that leads to their (inescapable) conclusion.
Present Position:	Structured pairs then partner with a member of the opposing position (1 with a 2). They each present their best case for their position by completing the sentence, "The answer is . . . because . . . ," making eye contact, keeping within time limits, using more than one media (e.g., written and oral), and show-ing enthusiasm or feeling for the position. The listener takes notes so as to prepare a paraphrase of the position and to more inci-sively refute it.
Discuss Issues:	Each 1 and 2 continues to advocate for his or her position, completing the sentence, "My position is right because . . . ," emphasizing facts, evidence, and rationale while trying to win with fallacious arguments and add hu-mor and interest. Each person refutes the opposing argument by completing the sen-tence stem "The opposing position is wrong because . . . "

(continued)

Reverse Position:	Reverse perspectives and tell the best case for the opposing side by completing the sentence, "Your position is right because. . . . " See the issue from both perspectives simultaneously. Change seats, be forceful and persuasive, and add new facts and evidence if possible. Listen to how the other person presents your position, correcting any errors or omissions.
Reach a Resolution:	Synthesize to reach a resolution among the four of you. See any new patterns or perspectives that might even be more powerful than the arguments you identified. Summarize the best evidence and reasoning into a joint position to which all members can agree. Create a new position that subsumes the previous ones or unites their best features at a higher level of reasoning. Complete the sentence, "Our best reasoned judgment is . . . because. . . . " Prepare a written summary and be ready to orally present your resolution as a team.

Note: Adapted with permission from Johnson, D.W., & Johnson, R.T. (1992). *Creative controversy: Intellectual challenge in the classroom.* Edina, MN: Interaction Book Company.

What is the process for explanation of social skills and criteria for success?

The skills of controversy are the focus of this lesson. Each student is expected to demonstrate as many controversy skills as possible, with a minimum of at least three. The professor asks students to paraphrase, making any necessary adjustments.

CLOSURE AND PROCESSING*

What is the process for closure (students summarize what they learned)?

Each quartet comes to the front of the classroom to state their resolution and to display their supporting evidence (prepared on an overhead transparency or newsprint).

What is the process for feedback on academic performance?

The professor provides explicit feedback on relative accuracy and perspicacity of student resolutions and supporting evidence.

COLLEGE

How are the professor's observations shared?	The professor shares anecdotes with specific examples of how various partners and quartets demonstrated the controversy skills.
What is the process for assessment of individual and group success in using social skills?	The professor asks students to complete the following for each group member: "Two things I appreciate about how you helped me gain a new perspective are. . . . " Students also discuss how well they did on stating research results, values, and best practices. As a group they decide on two controversy skills they will focus on during the next controversy lesson.

AFTER THE LESSON

How does the professor evaluate the success of the controversy?	The professor checks to see that the essential elements (marked with an asterisk) of cooperative learning lessons were included. The professor is also interested in noticing the accuracy of arguments cited for pro, con, and resolution positions to plan for future lessons (e.g., readings, lectures, activities) to correct any misconceptions or errors in logical presentation of arguments.

Anecdote

This is one of the most highly rated activities for both graduate and undergraduate students. The educational specialists often used the controversy they developed to introduce administrators, parents, teachers, and advocates to the major issues involved in changing from a segregated special class model for delivering special education to more inclusive models. All participants agreed that having the opportunity to experience controversy of ideas in a structured, planned way helped everyone develop a more comprehensive understanding of both sides of a potentially divisive issue.

The undergraduate students reported similar reactions and began to look at how to incorporate controversy as part of the lesson plans they might use. They expressed commitment to teaching students with special needs how to handle themselves in a conflict. An unexpected outcome was the realization that controversy might be a great way to structure lessons in subjects that might otherwise seem boring.

References

Americans with Disabilities Act of 1990, PL 101-336. (July 26, 1990). Title 42, USC 12101: *U.S. Statutes at Large, 104,* 327–378.

Individuals with Disabilities Education Act Amendments of 1990 (IDEA), PL 102-119. (October 7, 1991). Title 20, USC 1400 et seq: *U.S. Statutes at Large, 105,* 587–608.

Jenkins, J., Pious, C., & Jewell, M. (1990). Special education and the regular education initiative. *Exceptional Children, 56,* 479–491.

Lipsky, D.K., & Gartner, A. (Eds.). (1989). *Beyond separate education: Quality education for all.* Baltimore: Paul H. Brookes Publishing Co.

Johnson, D.W., & Johnson, R.T. (1991). *Creative Controversy: Intellectual challenge in the classroom.* Edina, MN: Interaction Book Co.

Villa, R., & Thousand, J. (1988). Enhancing success in heterogeneous classrooms and schools. *Teacher Education and Special Education, 11*(4), 144–154.

COLLEGE

INTRODUCING ADULTS TO COOPERATIVE LEARNING AS A STRATEGY FOR INTEGRATING STUDENTS WITH DISABILITIES

Jacqueline S. Thousand developed this lesson plan for teachers and other adults who want to make sure that students with disabilities are meaningfully included in cooperative learning groups. The role-play embedded in the lesson enables the adults to empathize with students who might have the sensory, intellectual, psychological, or learning challenges that they simulate. Teachers have enthusiastically embraced both the simulation and the task of reading and sharing their reactions to one of the poems from Silverstein's (1981) classic story, *A Light in the Attic*. The excerpt is likely to evoke strong feelings and empathy for the alienation that comes when people feel incompetent.

LESSON NAME: Cooperative Learning for Adults   AUTHOR: J. Thousand
GRADE LEVEL: Grade 3 through college   CONTENT AREA: Language
arts and appreciating
diversity
TIME: 55 minutes

ACADEMIC OBJECTIVES

What are the prereq-
uisite skills?

Membership in the class (i.e., selecting this session to attend during the inservice); in each group, someone must
be able to read the poem and write, and there must be
comprehension of the language used in the poem

What are the aca-
demic objectives?

Group members interpret the poem about diversity and
feelings.

How do students
demonstrate the aca-
demic objectives?

Group members are observed to be saying the following:
Giving at least one answer per question and individually
answering one of the three questions with the answer
that matches the group's answer. They are observed
doing the following: Producing at least five answers per
question, selecting and circling the agreed upon answer,
and initialing to indicate agreement with answers.

What are the criteria
for success?

Contributing at least one answer per question and initialing to indicate agreement.

What are the modi-
fications for learners
with special educa-
tion needs?

Participants are assigned role cards that instruct them
to simulate students with various challenges. Modifications for the challenges are also described on the cards.
A student with visual impairments needs a fellow student to serve as a reader; a student who does not read
needs a fellow student to serve as a reader; a student
with cerebral palsy who uses a computer to write is assigned the role of recorder for the group; a student who
likes to get the group "off task" needs an engaging role
such as "checker for understanding"; and a student who
is academically gifted, likes to work alone, and sees little
value in others' contributions needs a supportive role
such as "encourager."

FACE-TO-FACE INTERACTION DECISIONS*

What is the group size?

Participants work in groups of five.

How are students assigned to groups?

There must be at least one person who can read the poem and one who can write. Otherwise, the group is heterogeneously mixed according to gender, culture, ethnic background or race, gifts, challenges, and achievement (such as one high-achieving, three average-achieving, and one low-achieving student in each group). The teacher, not the students, decides who is in each group.

What is the room arrangement?

Participants arrange their seats in a circle with or without a table so they may be seated face-to-face, close enough to have eye contact, hear one another, and do their work jointly. There should be enough space for the teacher to move from group to group.

STRUCTURING POSITIVE INTERDEPENDENCE*

Members get the messages: "We sink or swim together," "Do your work—we're counting on you," "How can I help you to do better?"

What is the structure—a single product, a group goal, a shared outcome, or a group reward?

The teacher says, "I want one set of answers from each group that all members agree to, as indicated by the signature of your initials on the group product. Initialing indicates that you have participated and that you understand and agree to the answers."

"Each group can earn up to 100 points. Your group can earn a total of 100 points for the group answer sheet. There are 20 points for each of your four answers and an additional 20 points if all members sign their initials on the answer sheet within 20 minutes."

Are student roles assigned?

Role cards with definitions, as shown below, for each role are prepared and distributed as follows: The encourager role is assigned to the "gifted" learner; the timekeeper role to a nonreader who knows how to tell time; the checker role to the student with visual impairment; the reader role to the student who gets the group off task; and the recorder role to the student who uses a computer to write.

Role Definitions	
Role	Definition
Encourager/Equalizer	Watch to make certain all group members are contributing. Invite silent members by asking them for their opinions and help.
Timekeeper	Notify the group of approaching time limits (e.g., 5 or 10 minutes). Move the group along to the next step in the assignment. Allot no more than 5 minutes for each question. Make sure signatures (initials) are secured within the time limit.
Checker	Check to make certain each member can state each answer. Check to make sure members agree on reasons for the answers. Check at any time during the discussion. Try a "quiz" for each of the group members.
Recorder	Summarize answers until the group is satisfied. Record all answers. Secure signatures (initials) within the time limit.
Reader	Read aloud to the group as often as requested.

What are the other divisions of labor besides roles?

This may emerge as the students participate in the lesson. The role of "jargon buster" may be needed if the adults begin discussing the interventions for students with various disabilities. The jargon buster signals when a specialized term that might not be understood by everyone is used; the jargon user is then asked to define the term.

How is material arranged to promote positive interdependence?

Each group shares two copies of the Silverstein poem "The Little Boy and the Old Man" that includes a set of four questions for the group to answer (see next page). One copy is for the reader; the other is for the recorder to record the group's answers on the computer.

THE LITTLE BOY AND THE OLD MAN

Said the little boy, "Sometimes I drop my spoon."
Said the old man, "I do that too."
The little boy whispered, "I wet my pants."
"I do that too," laughed the little old man.
Said the little boy, "I often cry."
The old man nodded, "So do I."
"But worst of all," said the boy, "it seems
Grown-ups don't pay attention to me."
And he felt the warmth of a wrinkled old hand.
"I know what you mean," said the old man.

(Silverstein, 1981, p. 95)

Instructions: Please share your answers to each question. Recorders list all answers given.

As a group, circle the favorite answer for each question.

1. What is the poem saying?

2. What emotion(s) does the poem evoke in you? (How does this poem make you feel?)

3. What are two key words in the poem? Why did you select these words?

4. How does the content of this poem relate to your feelings about people with disabilities?

INSERVICE

Sign your initials indicating you have participated and you understand and agree to the answers.

ESTABLISHING SOCIAL SKILL PERFORMANCE*

What are the social skills objectives?

Group members contribute at least one idea for each question. Group members praise each other's contributions at least once.

How is the need for each social skill communicated?

The instructor asks the group, "What do you think is the least used social skill in adult groups?" [List all answers on newsprint.] "Thank you! Yes, it's true. Adults rarely praise each other's contributions, especially adults in the helping professions. Today we'll be focusing on the use of praise or encouragement particularly because the poem is likely to evoke strong feelings that may result in reluctance to share."

How are social skills explained, demonstrated, role-played, or practiced?

The instructor says, "Please check with the two people next to you to find out their favorite, most authentic praise statements. I'll check back with you in 2 minutes to list them on the newsprint." [Wait for 2 minutes and then list the responses on newsprint so that the participants can easily see them.] "Thank you! Now these are visible to all encouragers and remember that the encourager's role is two-fold: Modeling how to praise by actually praising your team members' contributions and monitoring your team members to ensure that they are praising also! I'll be coming around to each of your groups to listen for these important social skills."

SOCIAL SKILL PERFORMANCE: MONITORING AND INTERVENTION*

What is the process (how and when) for monitoring groups?

The instructor systematically visits each group to listen in for 3–5 minutes to: 1) ensure that group members understand and are following the directions, 2) ensure that the social skills of contributing and praising are being practiced, 3) check that group members are performing assigned roles, and 4) intervene if necessary. Use the observation form shown below to take note of significant examples of cooperative behaviors to share during the closure part of the lesson.

GROUP MEMBERS

COLLABORATIVE SKILLS	TEAM A					TEAM B					TEAM C				
	1	2	3	4	5	1	2	3	4	5	1	2	3	4	5
Contributing															
Praising															
Asking questions															
Checking for understanding															
Encouraging others															

What is the process for feedback (how and when) to groups if social skills are being used?

During processing at the end of the lesson, provide examples to each group on their use of the social skills. Be specific by giving verbatim phrases and describing the situation and, if possible, the result (e.g., the impact on the group's creativity, attitude, or cohesiveness).

What is the process for feedback (how and when) to groups if social skills are *not* being used?

If an interaction problem is observed, encourage the group to stop and solve it before continuing. Ensure that the encourager is facing the board where the list of praise statements can be seen. Ask the group to brainstorm other statements that might be more authentic or believable to the group.

What collaboration problems are anticipated?

Due to the emotional sensitivity of the poem, some adults may be reluctant to share. In some cases, loss of a child or older family member may be remembered. Another likely problem is superficial answers.

What are the interventions to avoid or remedy the anticipated problems?

Rule: When you feel like intervening, don't. If you must intervene, do it with questions, not answers. Move away as soon as you can, even if it is only 3 feet. Encourage the group to allow "space" for deep emotions by letting each person experience whatever emotions may surface. Do not try to stop the flow of emotions or soothe or mask them. Instead, let them be. It may be helpful for each person to write about his or her feelings. Invite each person to share and allow an individual to "pass" if he or she prefers.

If superficial answers are surfacing, interrupt the group and gently challenge the participants to explore interesting answers or elaborate on the superficial ones.

SOCIAL SKILL PERFORMANCE: STUDENT MONITORING

What is the student observer(s) selection and training process? (what and who)?

In this lesson, there are no student observers.

How are social skills monitored?

The teacher monitors with an observation form as shown earlier.

Do students observe more than one group?

No.

Do students observe for the entire lesson?

No.

How do students share their observations?

Participants are asked to share their reactions to the process.

STRUCTURING INDIVIDUAL ACCOUNTABILITY*

Are individual
quizzes assigned?

Is there random
selection of group
members to answer
questions?

No.

The instructor tells the class, "After the lesson, I will collect your group papers and ask each group member to
answer in writing one of the four major questions. You
won't know ahead of time which of the questions I will
ask you, so be prepared to answer them all. Remember
that you will need to generate some creative alternatives
to writing for the student who is visually impaired and
for the nonwriter so that they too can give their individual answers. Remember that when you sign your initials
on the group product, it means that you have participated and that you understand and agree to the answers."

SETTING THE TASK

What is the process
for explanation of
academic task and
criteria for success
(when and who)?

"Remember what the objectives for this lesson are—I've
printed them on newsprint for you. For the last 3 weeks
we've been reading the poems of various American poets.
Each of you has composed a number of poems with
themes you have selected yourselves. You may find yourself wanting to compose a poem today! Poetry is a way
for each of us to express our feelings and ideas in a creative way. Poetry is a form of literature that some people
enjoy reading; similar to music, poetry is rhythm and
rhyme can be quite beautiful. The poem for today deals
with emotions. Your task, as a group, is to read or listen
to the poem, "The Little Boy and the Old Man," and answer some questions. I want your group to generate at
least five possible answers for each question and then
circle your group's favorite answer."

"Each group can earn up to 100 points. Your group
can earn a total of 100 points for the group answer
sheet—20 points for each of your four answers and an
additional 20 points if all members initial the answer
sheet within 20 minutes. Signing your initials indicates
that you have participated and that you understand and
agree to the answers."

INSERVICE

How are social skills and criteria for success explained (when and who)?

The instructor says, "I expect each of you to contribute at least one idea for each of the questions. I expect to see and hear you as you listen and praise other team members' ideas. I'll be looking for at least one praise statement to someone else. Finally, I want to see you pushing for many possible answers (at least five) before deciding on one answer. Also, each group member has a role. I'll be counting on the checkers to share how well you performed your roles and the social skills of contributing, praising, and pushing for more answers."

CLOSURE AND PROCESSING*

What is the process for closure (students summarize what they learned)?

The instructor randomly "beams" questions to individuals in each group and asks them to share the group's answer.

What is the process for feedback on academic performance (when and who)?

The instructor scores group and individual responses and returns the work at the start of the next day's class period.

How are the instructor's observations shared?

Rule: Share negative comments in private and positive comments both in public and private. The instructor shares examples of observations of group members performing their assigned roles and examples of contributing, listening, and praising.

What is the process for assessment of individual and group success in using social skills (how and when)?

The instructor asks each group to huddle for 3 minutes to write their answers as a group to these questions:

1. What social skills did we do well?
2. What do we need to improve?
3. How well did we perform our roles?
4. What do we need to perform them better?

The checker facilitates the discussion, and the encourager records the group's answers and hands them in to the instructor. The instructor solicits one answer from each group as a class closure.

AFTER THE LESSON

How does the instructor evaluate the success of the lesson?

The instructor checks to see that the essential elements (marked with an asterisk) of effective cooperative learning lessons were included.

Anecdote

Those who participated in this lesson realized their group's performance depended on each individual member's contribution *and* the group's ability to accommodate for the individual differences among the group members. They experienced the importance of achieving the academic task (i.e., understanding the poem) and maintaining positive interactions with group members (i.e., engaging in specific interpersonal skills such as encourager). This combination yielded an appreciation for the feelings their own students may experience when working in cooperative learning groups.

Reference

Silverstein, S. (1981). *A light in the attic*. New York: Harper & Row.

INSERVICE

Partner Learning, Peer Tutoring, and Peer Mediation

THE POWER OF PEER-MEDIATED INSTRUCTION

HOW AND WHY IT PROMOTES ACADEMIC SUCCESS FOR ALL STUDENTS

Gregory F. Harper,
Larry Maheady, and Barbara Mallette

Peer-mediated instruction refers to an alternative teaching arrangement in which students serve as instructional agents (e.g., tutors, models, encouragers) for their classmates and/or other students (Strain, 1981). Peer-mediated instruction, therefore, includes cooperative learning strategies (e.g., Johnson & Johnson, 1989) and peer tutoring. This chapter discusses three peer-mediated strategies effective in promoting both academic and social integration of children with disabilities: Classwide Peer Tutoring (CWPT), Classwide Student Tutoring Teams (CSTT), and Numbered Heads Together (NHT). For each, we provide a description of the instructional procedures and a review of research relevant to its use with children with disabilities. It is important that practitioners understand why certain instructional practices work, as well as how they work. Thus, this chapter includes an examination of potential barriers to successful integration of children with disabilities and some of the essential elements of effective classroom instruction. The select peer-mediated strategies succeed because they help to overcome barriers and include many elements of successful instruction. Each of the three sections that describe the peer-mediated strategies concludes with "Power Pointers" that guide the use of the strategy and suggest possible applications, modifications, and ways of avoiding some common problem areas.

PERSISTENT BARRIERS TO SUCCESSFUL INTEGRATION

Salend (1990) defines mainstreaming as the carefully planned and monitored placement of children with disabilities into regular classrooms for the majority of their academic and social education programs. He notes that the academic component of this definition requires that the classroom environment be adapted to address the specific needs of students with disabilities, whereas the social component requires that the children be assimilated into the classroom environment and be accepted by peers without disabilities (see also Kaufman, Gottlieb, Agard, & Kukic, 1975).

But how does one promote the academic and social integration of children with disabilities into inclusive environments? One way this can be done is through the development and/or identification of more powerful instructional interventions for classroom teachers to use. Classroom interventions must be: 1) *effective* for heterogeneous learning groups, 2) *feasible* to implement on a classwide basis, and 3) *socially acceptable* to the primary consumers of the program (i.e., classroom teachers, students, parents). Peer-mediated instructional techniques are among the interventions that appear to meet these criteria.

Reynolds and Birch (1988) delineate three aspects of mainstreaming: physical, social, and instructional. One can easily conceive situations in which a child with a disability is physically integrated into a regular classroom, but where social integration (prosocial interaction among children with and without disabilities) and instructional mainstreaming (the provision of appropriate academic content for all pupils in a common environment) may not occur. While the legal, and to a certain degree the physical and attitudinal, barriers to inclusion have been overcome, it is far less certain that children with disabilities have been socially or instructionally integrated. The vigor with which the regular education initiative (REI) has been debated in recent years suggests that many of the concerns raised about mainstreaming in 1975 have not yet been resolved. For example, Salend (1990) delineated at least five problems that continue to impede the successful integration of children with disabilities into inclusive environments. These problems, and the role peer-mediated instruction may play in overcoming them, are presented in Table 1.

Many of these concerns are supported by research that suggests that mainstreamed children do not always benefit academically or socially from instruction in regular education classes (see, for example, Zigmond & Baker, 1990). Similarly, additional evidence suggests that many regular classroom teachers *perceive* themselves as unable to meet the instructional and social needs of children with disabilities (e.g., Hannah, 1988; Nader, 1984; Winzer, 1985). This does not mean that such concerns, as well as the attitudinal and practical barriers they represent, cannot be successfully overcome with effective and efficient classroom-based instructional practices.

The needs of children with disabilities are rarely *qualitatively* different than those of their peers without disabilities. For both groups to succeed, the instructional environments must be restructured in such a way as to ensure all students equal opportunities to respond to critical academic content. Furthermore, these equal response opportunities must be provided within a supportive, mutually assistive environment. Only in such an environment can the attitudinal barriers to social acceptance of children with disabilities be overcome.

Table 1.   Barriers to mainstreaming and possible peer-mediated solutions

Barrier	Solution
Lack of teacher training to meet the needs of exceptional learners	Powerful, easy-to-use instructional practices for use by the whole class
Exceptional learners require excessive teacher time	Use of peers as instructional agents
Negative attitudes toward exceptional learners	Increased social- and task-oriented interaction with a high probability of success
Regular classrooms are not structured to meet the needs of all students	Simple restructuring strategies that are successful for all students
Research has not demonstrated the efficacy of inclusive environments	Use of strategies with demonstrated effectiveness in inclusive environments

ESSENTIAL INGREDIENTS OF EFFECTIVE AND SUPPORTIVE CLASSROOM ENVIRONMENTS

Truly effective and supportive learning environments are characterized by high rates of active student involvement; sufficiently high levels of success for all; clear instructional purpose; close congruence between what is taught and what is assessed; and goal and reward structures that promote cooperative, rather than competitive, responding among pupils within the classroom (Kameenui & Simmons, 1991).

Student Involvement

Academic achievement is related *directly* to the amount of time students spend actually thinking about and working with important instructional content. Student involvement, in turn, is influenced by at least three instructional variables over which teachers exert some control: 1) allocated time—amount of time scheduled for a particular subject, topic, or skill; 2) engaged time—amount of time students are actively engaged with academic content; and 3) academic learning time—amount of time students are engaged successfully in relevant instructional pursuits (Fisher et al., 1978).

High Rates of Accurate Practice

Findings from research on teaching indicate that students need repeated practice on material, to the point of overlearning (Rosenshine & Stevens, 1986). Furthermore, they need to perform learning tasks successfully, that is, with 80%–90% accuracy if they are to benefit instructionally (Brophy & Good, 1986). New content should be introduced only when prior mastery criteria are reached (Keller, 1968), and the rate or pacing of instruction must be high to maintain student engagement (Carnine, 1976).

Clear Instructional Purpose

Many classroom teachers believe that their primary task is to ensure that course content is covered; that is, it is presented in lectures, films, demonstrations, workbook pages, and/or discussions. There are, however, barriers to successful content coverage. For example, some teachers may be ineffective in communicating the intent or purpose of the content being presented, confusing students about what they must learn and why. Students with specific learning difficulties may be particularly prone to academic failure when instructional purpose is not clearly articulated.

Testing What Is Taught

The amount of content covered and the content over which students are tested varies widely. In one study, it was found that some teachers presented as little as 4% of the content tested, whereas other teachers tested 95% of the same content (Kindsvatter, Wilen, & Ishler, 1988). Obviously, pupils are likely to perform well on exams if the content upon which they are being assessed is taught explicitly by their classroom teachers. This does not mean that teachers should only test what is taught and vice versa. It does suggest, however, that unless there is sufficient overlap between instructed and tested knowledge, it is difficult to obtain truly accurate measures of instructional effectiveness. Teachers may use tests to measure students' ability to generalize, apply, or analyze acquired instructional content. Although demonstrations of these advanced cognitive activities may be worthwhile goals, they may be impeded by students' failure to master the critical knowledge, ideas, and skills upon which advanced cognitive activities are based.

Classroom Reward Structures

Johnson and Johnson (1989; see also chap. 3, this volume) identified three common goal and reward structures used in most classrooms: individualized, competitive, and cooperative. Although it is beyond the scope of this discussion to describe each of these, classrooms traditionally have been characterized by individualized and/or competitive goal and reward structures. Whereas these structures have certain beneficial outcomes, only cooperative structures directly promote the type of friendly, mutually assistive, and supportive social environment in which every child may experience social acceptance. Results of these authors' investigations suggest that even brief exposures to cooperative learning contingencies promote improved students' perceptions of social acceptance and friendship (Maheady & Harper, 1987; Maheady, Harper, & Mallette, 1991; Maheady, Harper, & Sacca, 1988).

PEER-MEDIATED INSTRUCTION

In this section, we describe three specific peer teaching methods effective in promoting the academic and social integration of children with disabilities: Classwide Peer Tutoring, Classwide Student Tutoring Teams, and Numbered Heads Together.

Classwide Peer Tutoring

Classwide Peer Tutoring (CWPT) was developed by researchers at the Juniper Gardens Children's Project in Kansas City, Kansas, to improve the acquisition and retention of basic academic skills by low-achieving pupils (Delquadri, Greenwood, Whorton, Carta, & Hall, 1986). CWPT consists of four major components: 1) weekly competing teams, 2) highly structured teaching procedures, 3) daily point earning and public posting of scores, and 4) direct practice of functional academic skills. Each week the class is divided randomly into two competing teams. Typically, students draw colored slips of paper from a covered box to determine team membership. The teacher then assigns students *within each team* to tutoring pairs. One student in each pair serves as the tutor for 10–15 minutes, while the other child is the tutee.

After the established time limit has expired, the tutoring pairs reverse roles for an equivalent amount of time.

While students work in tutoring dyads, they must follow prescribed teaching procedures. That is, the tutor presents an instructional item (e.g., spelling word, math problem, social studies question) and the tutee must "say and write" the response. If the answer is correct, the tutor awards two points. However, if the tutee responds incorrectly, the tutor: 1) provides the correct response, 2) requires the tutee to write the answer three times, and 3) awards one point if the tutee corrects the mistake. If the tutee refuses or fails to correct the answer, no points are awarded. The object of the tutoring game is to complete as many items as possible in the allotted time. The more items that students complete, the more points they earn for themselves and their team.

While peer tutoring is in effect, the teacher moves about the classroom and awards bonus points for "good" tutor and tutee behavior. Behaviors that may be reinforced include: 1) clear and succinct presentation of materials, 2) appropriate use of points, 3) correct use of the error correction procedure, and 4) supportive comments and assistance. Immediately after the tutoring session, students total their daily points and record them on a laminated scoreboard in the front of the classroom. Tutoring sessions typically occur two to four times per week and are followed by a weekly quiz (e.g., Friday spelling test, math facts review, chapter test). Students take tests *individually*, however, and earn five points for each correct answer. At the end of the week all points, including bonus and test points, are totaled and the "Winning Team of the Week" is announced. Weekly results, as well as outstanding individual efforts, are posted in classroom or school bulletins and through achievement certificates.

Classwide Peer Tutoring has been shown to be effective across subject areas (e.g., reading, spelling, math, social studies) (Greenwood et al., 1984; Maheady, Harper, & Sacca, 1988); age levels (Delquadri, Greenwood, Stretton, & Hall, 1983; Maheady, Sacca, & Harper, 1988); and instructional environments (i.e., general, compensatory, and special education classrooms) (Delquadri et al., 1983; Maheady & Harper, 1987). It is significant to note that *all* CWPT studies have been conducted with students who possess characteristics commonly associated with at-risk status (i.e., low socioeconomic status, mild disabilities, domestic conflict) in both inclusive and segregated classrooms. The most comprehensive CWPT investigation thus far (Greenwood, Delquadri, & Hall, 1989) reported data from more than 400 low income students enrolled in four separate schools across 4 years of implementation. Results indicated that students made significantly greater gains in spelling, reading, and math with CWPT than with teacher-led instruction. Moreover, after 4 years of CWPT instruction, low SES students who were "at-risk for academic delay exceeded or approached the national norm in all three academic domains" (Greenwood et al., 1989, p. 380).

Recently, a series of three studies assessed the effectiveness of CWPT procedures within self-contained, special classes for primary age children with mild disabilities. Harper, Mallette, and colleagues (Harper, Mallette, & Moore 1991; Mallette, Harper, Maheady, & Dempsey, 1991) demonstrated that CWPT consistently improved the spelling test performance of these children. In the Mallette et al. (1991) study, CWPT was used daily with nine students with mild disabilities to practice five spelling words per week. During a 12-week intervention period, students' short-term, intermediate-term, and long-term retention of words practiced was assessed. Stu-

dent retention of words practiced the prior week (short-term retention) averaged between 73% and 79% correct. Intermediate retention (i.e., correct spelling of words
practiced 2 weeks prior) averaged 85% correct; whereas long-term retention (i.e., a
posttest of 25 randomly selected words taken from all previously practiced spelling
lists) averaged 88% correct for the entire class. Particularly impressive was the fact
that, prior to CWPT, these youngsters had received no formal instruction in spelling.
Harper, Mallette, Maheady, Parkes, and Moore (1993) replicated this study using 10-
word lists and also assessed students' ability to use newly acquired words in a structured writing exercise (i.e., transcribing sentences from teacher dictation). Students
spelled more than 76% of the dictated words correctly, and short- and long-term retention rates were comparable to those described above.

All three studies also assessed student satisfaction with various components of
the CWPT program. Students consistently rated all tutoring components favorably.
Furthermore, they reported positive social and self-esteem outcomes as a result of
CWPT. Outcomes included improved friendship patterns within the classroom and a
general perception on the part of students that their classmates thought they were
"smarter" as a result of the tutoring experience. Negative side effects associated with
the use of mildly competitive situations or the public posting of individual point totals did not appear.

Why Does CWPT Work?

CWPT is successful because: 1) it ensures high rates of accurate responding, 2) it
includes both massed and distributed practice, 3) it requires active engagement of
the tutor and tutee, and 4) the practice task matches the criterion task (e.g., a weekly
spelling test). CWPT incorporates many of the elements of effective instruction and
it provides all students with ample opportunity to practice. The immediate error correction provided by the tutors ensures that correct responses are practiced. Often
traditional instructional practices, such as workbooks and individual seat work, do
not require that students practice a task everyday or more than a few times. Correc-
tions, even when reasonably prompt, come long after the response has been made,
and practice of the correct response is not always required. Finally, the practice material often does not resemble the test on that material. For example, having students
individually write spelling words several times increases practice, but copying is not
the same task as hearing the word pronounced and writing it down. As is true of most
peer-mediated strategies, CWPT allows students who otherwise might never interact
socially to work together on a common task and succeed together.

Power Pointers for Using CWPT

In addition to reviewing the articles referenced in this chapter, teachers are encouraged to write for materials on CWPT identified at the end of this chapter in the Resources section to obtain more detailed information on planning, implementing, and
evaluating the use of CWPT. The following are some pointers to consider when using
CWPT in your classroom:

Teaching Students to Use CWPT All students with whom we have worked
(i.e., students with and without disabilities) have learned to use CWPT effectively in
no more than two 30-minute training sessions. In Session 1, the teacher models appropriate tutoring procedures by serving as "tutor" while a student serves as "tutee."
Other class members are instructed to watch. Then roles are reversed with the student partner. The teacher should make some "mistakes" so students can see how the

error correction procedure works. Next, dyads are formed with the remaining class members and pairs are given practice tutoring and role reversing. It is essential to monitor dyads closely to ensure that appropriate procedures are being followed. During the second session, CWPT procedures are reviewed and students are provided with additional, supervised practice opportunities. Teams are formed and students practice obtaining materials and moving quietly to their partner's desk. Regular tutoring may begin the next day.

Monitor and Award Bonus Points Teachers must move around the room during CWPT. Research shows that students may fail to benefit from CWPT if some procedural components (e.g., the error correction procedure) are not used correctly by students. Close monitoring also provides the teacher with ample opportunities to identify and recognize successful student performance.

Use CWPT Often Students must use CWPT *at least* twice per week to have sufficient practice opportunities and sessions should last approximately 25–30 minutes. Teachers must regularly check student papers to ensure that all children, especially those with learning difficulties, have several opportunities to practice each item correctly.

Monitor Student and Class Progress and Adjust the CWPT Program Some students may not progress adequately under CWPT instruction, signaling the need for change in the CWPT program. Diagnosis may reveal too few practice sessions, insufficient length of tutoring sessions, inappropriate use of tutoring procedures, excessive student absenteeism, or students' inadequate prior knowledge of course content.

Classwide Student Tutoring Teams

Given initial success with CWPT, these authors were encouraged to try other peer teaching systems with pupils who experienced academic and/or behavioral difficulties in school. Elements of the CWPT program (i.e., structured tutoring procedures, daily point earning, public posting of scores, group rewards) were combined with specific facets of the Teams-Games-Tournaments (TGT) program developed by Slavin and colleagues at The Johns Hopkins University (Slavin, 1985, 1986, 1990, 1991). This "hybrid" intervention is called Classwide Student Tutoring Teams (CSTT).

CSTT actively engages students in content-related discussions and review. First, new instructional content is introduced, reviewed, and discussed by the teacher. Students then are given the opportunity to interact with the material during two or more 30-minute CSTT sessions per week. Typically, these practice sessions take the place of independent seat work activities.

CSTT operates as follows. First, the class is divided into groups of three- to five-member heterogeneous learning teams. Students are assigned systematically to learning teams according to the procedures outlined by Slavin (1986). Specifically, teachers *privately* rank order their students according to levels of academic competence. The highest ranked student is assigned to Team 1, the second highest to Team 2, and so on until all students are placed. This systematic assignment procedure results in student learning teams that include high-, low- and intermediate-achieving students and "fairness" in weekly competitions among teams. Students are encouraged to name their own teams and decorate their respective work folders. Teams remain the same for 4–6 weeks.

After teams are formed, teachers tell students that their responsibility is to help each of their teammates learn weekly content previously introduced by the teacher.

The teacher's main responsibility in CSTT is to develop a series of 10–30 questions and answers for weekly study guides. Each team receives one study guide, a deck of numbered cards that correspond to the number of questions on the study guide, and pieces of blank writing paper. CSTT sessions begin with the teacher setting a timer for 30 minutes. One student on each team begins the session by selecting the top card from the shuffled deck. The number on the card designates which item or question on the study guide is presented. The student seated directly across from the card selector serves as tutor and reads the designated item to his or her teammates. Each team member (except the tutor) writes his or her own answer. When finished, each shows his or her response to the tutor who checks it against the answer on the study guide. If an individual's answer is correct, the tutor awards the tutee five points. However, if a student responds incorrectly, the tutor presents the correct answer, asks the teammate to write it one or two times, and awards two points for a successful correction of the error. No points are given to a teammate who refuses or fails to correct a mistake. After all points are assigned for an item, the procedure is repeated with a new "tutor," the student seated to the left of the first tutor. The teammate seated directly across from the new tutor selects a new card. Students continue through the study guide as many times as possible before the time expires, rotating tutor roles on each successive item. They quickly learn that the more items they complete, the more points they earn for themselves and their respective teams. Bonus points and public posting of students' scores are also used. Pupils are tested individually on material practiced during CSTT to demonstrate personal competence. However, individual test points are added to a team's cumulative total and "Winning Teams of the Week" are recognized based upon the total number of test and CSTT points.

The effects of CSTT were compared to teacher-led instruction with regard to math test performance of six classes of low-achieving ninth and tenth grade pupils enrolled in a special district program for potential dropouts (Maheady, Sacca, & Harper, 1987). With CSTT, students' weekly math quiz scores increased by approximately 20 percentage points (i.e., from 62% to 82%). Moreover, mainstreamed pupils with learning and behavior challenges performed as well or better than their non-disabled peers. All but one of 93 students received passing grades on report cards when CSTT was in effect. In contrast, 45% of the students failed under teacher-led instruction.

More recently, CSTT and Direct Instruction teaching procedures were combined to help students solve math word problems. Sixty second graders, including eight students with mild disabilities, used CSTT procedures to solve a predetermined series of math word problems. One student in each team read the problem; another student reviewed the problem-solving checklist. All students were required to solve the problem. Accurate problem solving and appropriate use of the problem-solving checklist were required to earn team points. Results suggest considerable improvements in children's problem-solving skills with more modest gains in strategy acquisition and generalization (Harper, Mallette, Maheady, & Brennan, in press).

Why Does CSTT Work?

CSTT works because it contains all of the elements of successful instruction contained in CWPT. Some additional benefits accrue from a team-based versus a dyadic model. Often the natural desire for students to affiliate, which gets stronger as students mature, is seen as an obstacle to keeping students focused on their tasks. In CSTT, this affiliation is accommodated and focused on learning. Team-based approaches also have unique benefits for both high and low achievers. High achievers, who otherwise might be considered show-offs or competitors for teacher and peer approval, are valued by teammates for their contribution to team success. Low achieving students have the opportunity and the motivation to demonstrate their competence. Roberts and Zubrick (1992) report that social acceptance of children with disabilities in the regular classroom is significantly related to peers' perception of their academic behavior. In a CSTT group all students must participate and interact; all students have the chance to serve as both teacher and tutee. Peer pressure, which otherwise might support antiachievement norms, now supports achievement.

Part of the success of CSTT can be attributed to teachers' development and use of study guides that identify the most important or relevant ideas, concepts, principles, or facts contained in each unit of instruction and that focus student attention, which eliminates guesswork about what must be learned. Finally, tests are based on the study guide, which improves the correspondence between the material studied in CSTT sessions and the material tested. As students recognize the necessary correlation of study and academic achievement, their motivation increases.

Power Pointers for Using CSTT

CSTT is relatively easy to use in most academic environments. The videotape and manual listed in the Resources section at the end of this chapter provide detailed instructions on how to use CSTT. Students usually enjoy CSTT and view it as a motivating and rewarding alternative to traditional teaching methods. Many of the power pointers for CWPT apply to CSTT as well; however, there are a few other pointers to consider.

CSTT Is a Review Procedure CSTT should be used only after important instructional material has been presented and students have had an opportunity to discuss and assimilate the content. It is recommended that CSTT study guides be distributed when teacher-led instruction begins to help focus students on important information in lectures and discussions and to serve as advance organizers for subsequent reading assignments.

Limit the Number of Study Guide Items If too many items are included in the study guide, students may not have an opportunity to practice each item often enough to ensure mastery. Likewise, CSTT sessions should occur often enough and for sufficiently long periods of time to allow students to get through study guides several times before taking a test.

Test What You Teach Students will not find CSTT a useful or valuable activity unless it results in better grades. Mastery of the items on the study guide, therefore, must ensure a good chance of success on the test. This can only happen if there is close correspondence among course content, study guide material, and the test on which that content will be assessed. If teachers want students to apply, generalize, or give multiple examples of a concept, then they must provide appropriate study guide items.

Numbered Heads Together

Numbered Heads Together (Kagan, 1985, 1989–90) is an alternative teacher questioning strategy designed to actively engage *all* students during adult-led instruction and discussion. Numbered Heads Together (NHT) works as follows. First, students are placed into four-member heterogeneous learning teams consisting of one high-achieving, two average-achieving, and one low-achieving pupil(s). Students number themselves 1–4 and sit together during teacher-directed lessons. After the teacher directs a question to the entire class, pupils are instructed to "put their heads together," come up with their best answer, and make sure that everyone on the team knows the answer. The teacher then asks, "Which number 1s (or 2s, 3s, 4s) know the answer?" After a randomly selected student responds, the teacher asks, "Which other number 1s (2s, 3s, 4s) agree with that answer?" or "Which number 1s (2s, 3s, 4s) can expand upon the answer?" The teacher then recognizes and rewards students who provided or agreed with correct answers and who offered meaningful expansions. Students are given time to discuss possible answers prior to responding, making it more likely that everyone, including low achievers, will know and give the correct responses. Moreover, because team members cannot predict which group member will be called upon to respond, they are more likely to coach one another to ensure that everyone knows the answer. (For a more complete discussion see Kagan, 1989–90.)

In a recent empirical study (Maheady, Mallette, Harper, & Sacca, 1991), NHT was compared to a whole-group questioning strategy by examining social studies test performance and "on task" rates of a group of 30 culturally diverse third graders. Over the course of the study, student performance on teacher made tests under NHT conditions exceeded that under the whole-group questioning condition by 2–30 percentage points or an average of nearly 16% (i.e., whole group x = 68.50% vs. NHT x = 84.29%). Under NHT conditions no student had a failing average and six pupils maintained averages above 90%. In contrast, when whole-group questioning was used, six students had failing averages and only one child maintained an average above 90%. Furthermore, students were far more likely to be on task and to pay attention to the teacher during NHT lessons.

Why Does NHT Work?

Numbered Heads Together is not intended to be a strategy to promote mastery, retention, or generalization. Thus, it includes fewer of the elements of learning found in CWPT or CSTT. NHT is primarily intended to improve student *cooperation* and to promote informal sharing of ideas. Although the authors have no direct observational data on student activities during NHT, informal observations suggest that several direct and indirect benefits accrue to students. Because team success in responding to teachers' questions requires that everyone on the team know the answer, NHT students engage in informal peer teaching. Students who may know an answer share information with others. Students who may not have responded in a whole-group situation because of uncertainty, shyness, or reluctance to risk making a mistake gain increased confidence by comparing answers with teammates and contributing to their NHT group discussions. Questions posed by teachers during NHT are more likely to accomplish their intent—to focus student attention on important information, maintain student interest and involvement, and assess student understanding of the material presented. Finally, and perhaps most importantly, NHT allows "think time" (Kameenui & Simmons, 1991, p. 98) between the question and student response, making it less likely that students will respond impulsively or that the teacher will only call on students who are the most energetic hand wavers. When NHT works well, all students are more likely to succeed; no one need fail.

Power Pointers for Using NHT

Numbered Heads Together is one of several peer-mediated or cooperative learning structures developed by Spencer Kagan, from whom the materials identified in the Resources section at the end of this chapter are available.

Create Heterogeneous Teams Numbered Heads Together works best when students are placed in heterogeneous groups that include at least one high-achieving child. This arrangement facilitates peer teaching, allows higher-achieving students to serve as instructional models for others, and increases the probability that everyone on each team knows the answer as a result of putting their heads together.

Ask Different Kinds of Questions Be sure to ask questions that require various kinds of knowledge: recall, application, implications, integration, synthesis, and evaluation. Some questions may even require that students consult readily available reference materials such as texts, notes, or library books.

Be Sure All Teams Have Equal Opportunity By keeping a record of which teams have answered, it is possible to discreetly give low-scoring teams additional chances to answer. In general, however, attempt to distribute opportunities to respond equitably among all groups.

SUMMARY

The purpose of this chapter is to introduce readers to three relatively new peer-mediated teaching systems that have been used successfully with students at risk for academic failure. We hope to encourage others to try peer-mediated instructional approaches with students who have been hard to teach. The authors have found that the three procedures not only work, but are feasible to implement. They also are *preferred* by both teachers and students over traditional teaching methods.

Each of the procedures has certain desirable aspects. They increase students' involvement in learning and shift responsibility and empowerment to the learner. They combine group and individual accountability and they provide an opportunity for *all* students to be both teachers and learners. They also include individual, cooperative, and mildly competitive teaching arrangements. Competition has caused some practitioners to avoid peer-mediated methods. To date, no detrimental effects have been associated with these mildly competitive situations. In fact, satisfaction surveys indicate that students like being on teams, earning points, *and* publicly posting their points. In any event, if competition is a real or perceived problem, students can compete against their own scores from previous weeks or an absolute criterion (e.g., a preset average on the quiz, total class points). The *entire* class could also work for both individual and group awards.

Empowering students means giving them both the opportunity *and* the means to become successfully involved in their own achievement. Typically this has not occurred within traditional instructional arrangements. Peer-mediated instruction is simply *one* set of instructional options. Surely, many more educational interventions will be needed if we are to meet successfully the instructional challenges of the 21st century. The basic instructional principles upon which such interventions may be created are well established. Our challenge is to empower ourselves, as teachers, to develop more effective instructional strategies and to adopt those that have been shown to be effective.

REFERENCES

Brophy, J., & Good, T. (1986). Teacher behavior and student achievement. In M.C. Wittrock (Ed.), *Handbook of research on teaching* (3rd ed.) (pp. 328–375). New York: Macmillan.

Carnine, D. (1976). Effects of two teacher presenta-

tion rates on off-task behavior, answering correctly, and participation. *Journal of Applied Behavior Analysis, 9,* 199–206.

Delquadri, J.C., Greenwood, C.R., Stretton, K., & Hall, R.V. (1983). The peer tutoring game: A classroom procedure for increasing opportunity to respond and spelling performance. *Education and Treatment of Children, 6,* 225–239.

Delquadri, J.C., Greenwood, C.R., Whorton, D., Carta, J.J., & Hall, R.V. (1986). Classwide peer tutoring. *Exceptional Children, 52,* 535–542.

Fisher, C.W., Felby, W., Marliane, R., Cahen, L., Dishaw, M., Moore, J., & Berline, D. (1978). *Teaching behaviors, academic learning time and student achievement: Final report of phase 111-13. Beginning teacher evaluation study.* San Francisco: Far West Laboratory for Educational Research and Development

Greenwood, C.R., Delquadri, J.C., & Hall, R.V. (1989). Longitudinal effects of classwide peer tutoring. *Journal of Educational Psychology, 81,* 371–383.

Greenwood, C.R., Dinwiddie, G., Terry, B., Wade, L., Stanley, S.O., Thibadeau, S., & Delquadri, J.C. (1984). Teacher- versus peer-mediated instruction: An ecobehavioral analysis of achievement outcomes. *Journal of Applied Behavior Analysis, 17,* 521–538.

Hannah, M.E. (1988). Teacher attitudes toward children with disabilities: An ecological analysis. In H.E. Yuker (Ed.), *Attitudes toward persons with disabilities* (pp. 154–170). New York: Springer-Verlag.

Harper, G.F., Mallette, B., Maheady, L., & Brennan, G. (in press). Classwide student tutoring teams and direct instruction as a combined strategy to teach generalizable strategies for mathematics word problems. *Education and Treatment of Children.*

Harper, G.F., Mallette, B., Maheady, L., Parkes, V., & Moore, J. (1993). Retention and generalization of spelling words acquired using a peer-mediated instructional procedure by children with mild handicapping conditions. *Journal of Behavioral Education, 3,* 25–38.

Harper, G.F., Mallette, B., & Moore, J. (1991). Peer mediated instruction: Teaching spelling to primary aged children with mild handicaps. *Reading, Writing, and Learning Disabilities International, 7,* 139–154.

Johnson, D.W., & Johnson, R.T. (1989). *Cooperation and competition: Theory and research.* Edina, MN: Interaction Book Company.

Kagan, S. (1985). *Cooperative learning.* Riverside: University of California-Riverside.

Kagan, S. (1989–90). The structural approach to cooperative learning. *Educational Leadership, 47*(4), 12–15.

Kameenui, E., & Simmons, D. (1991). *Designing instructional strategies: The prevention of academic learning problems.* Columbus, OH: Charles E. Merrill.

Kaufman, M., Gottlieb, J., Agard, J., & Kukic, M. (1975). Mainstreaming: Toward an explanation of the concept. In E. Meyen, G. Vergason, & R. Whelan (Eds.), *Alternatives for teaching exceptional children* (pp. 35–54). Denver: Love Publishing Co.

Keller, F. (1968). "Goodbye, teacher . . ." *Journal of Applied Behavior Analysis, 1,* 79–89.

Kindsvatter, R., Wilen, W., & Ishler, M. (1988). *Dynamics of effective teaching.* New York: Longman.

Maheady, L., & Harper, G.F. (1987). A classwide peer tutoring program to improve the spelling test performance of low income, third and fourth grade students. *Education and Treatment of Children, 10,* 27–36.

Maheady, L., Harper, G.F., & Mallette, B. (1991). Peer-mediated instruction: An illustrative review with potential applications for learning disabled students. *Reading, Writing, and Learning Disabilities International, 7,* 75–103.

Maheady, L., Harper, G.F., & Sacca, M.K. (1988). Classwide peer tutoring programs in secondary self-contained programs for the mildly handicapped. *Journal of Research and Development in Education, 21*(3), 76–83.

Maheady, L., Mallette, B., Harper, G.F., & Sacca, M.K. (1991). Heads Together: A peer-mediated option for improving the academic achievement of heterogeneous learning groups. *Remedial and Special Education, 12*(2), 25–33.

Maheady, L., Sacca, M.K., & Harper, G.F. (1987). Classwide student tutoring teams: Effects on the academic performance of secondary students. *Journal of Special Education, 21*(3) 107–121.

Maheady, L., Sacca, M.K., & Harper, G.F. (1988). Classwide peer tutoring with mildly handicapped high school students. *Exceptional Children, 55,* 52–59.

Mallette, B., Harper, G.F., Maheady, L., & Dempsey, M. (1991). Retention of spelling words acquired using a peer-mediated instructional procedure. *Education and Training in Mental Retardation, 26,* 156–164.

Nader, A. (1984). Teacher attitude toward the elementary exceptional child. *International Journal of Rehabilitation Research, 7,* 37–46.

Reynolds, M., & Birch, J. (1988). *Adaptive mainstreaming* (3rd ed.). New York: Longman.

Roberts, C., & Zubrick, S. (1992). Factors influencing the social status of children with mild disabilities in the regular classroom. *Exceptional Children, 59,* 192–202.

Rosenshine, B., & Stevens, R. (1986). Teaching functions. In M.C. Wittrock (Ed.), *Handbook of research on teaching* (3rd ed.) (pp. 376–391). New York: Macmillan.

Salend, S. (1990). *Effective mainstreaming.* New York: Macmillan

Slavin, R.E. (1985). An introduction to cooperative learning research. In R. Slavin, S. Sharan, S. Kagan, R. Lazarowitz, C. Webb, & R. Schmuck (Eds.), *Learning to cooperate, cooperating to learn.* New York: Plenum.

Slavin, R.E. (1986). *Using student team learning* (3rd. ed.). Baltimore: The Johns Hopkins University Press.

Slavin, R.E. (1990). *Cooperative learning: Theory, research, and practice.* Englewood Cliffs, NJ: Prentice Hall.

Slavin, R.E. (1991). *Educational psychology* (3rd ed.). Englewood Cliffs, NJ: Prentice Hall.

Strain, P.S. (1981). *The utilization of peers as behavior change agents.* New York: Plenum.

Winzer, M. (1985). Teacher attitudes toward mainstreaming: An appraisal of the research. *British Columbia Journal of Special Education, 9,* 149–161.

Zigmond, N., & Baker, J. (1990). Mainstream experiences for learning disabled students (Project MELD): Preliminary report. *Exceptional Children, 57,* 176–185.

RESOURCES FOR PEER-MEDIATED INSTRUCTION

Classwide Peer Tutoring Manual, Educational Achievement Systems, 319 Nickerson, Suite 112, Seattle, Washington 98109

Classwide Student Tutoring Teams Video and Manual, Classwide Student Tutoring Teams, Department of Education, State University of New York, College at Fredonia, Fredonia, New York 14063

Heads Together Manual and Video and **Cooperative Learning** (Kagan, 1985), Resources for Teachers, 27128 Paseo Espada, Suite 622, San Juan Capistrano, California 92675

CREATING POWERFUL PARTNERSHIPS THROUGH PARTNER LEARNING

Mary McNeil

During the 1980s, educational research has produced a wealth of information regarding schools and teaching practice. For example, in classrooms where the teacher does all of the teaching, it has been documented that students' opportunities to respond academically in key subject areas tend to be very low (Delquadri, Greenwood, Whorton, Carta, & Hall, 1986; Greenwood, Delquadri, & Hall as cited in Delquadri, Greenwood, Stretton, & Hall, 1983). Researchers found that while 75% of the day was allocated for academic instruction, only 25% of the day was actually spent in engaged learning time, that is, students interacting with materials or actively responding.

Today, many classroom teachers are confronted with larger class sizes, cutbacks in materials and resource personnel, and increasing demands to produce better results with an increasing population of diverse abilities and needs (McAllister, 1990; National Commission on Excellence in Education, 1983). The essence of the matter is that teachers are being asked to deliver far more services without additional resources. Considering current educational practices, this appears to be an unrealistic request. However, it does allow for an interesting challenge that can be attained only through the development of new ways of dealing with resources available to the classroom teacher (Pierce & Van Houten, 1984b; Thousand & McNeil, 1990).

One alternative to the traditional model, and one that is often overlooked, is to design structured partnerships between students. Such arrangements are often referred to as partner learning or peer tutoring programs (Greenfield & McNeil, 1987; McNeil, Stahlbrand, & Armstrong, 1989; Pierce & Van Houten, 1984a). Partner learning is a powerful approach for which evidence of instructional, social, and cost effectiveness (Gartner & Lipsky, 1990; Thousand & Villa, 1990) is mounting. The many benefits for the tutor and the tutee have been summarized in research reviews and a meta-analysis of research (Cohen, Kulik, & Kulik, 1982; Good & Brophy, 1987; Madden & Slavin, 1987; McNeil et al., 1989; Thousand & Villa, 1990). The documented benefits to students receiving instruction (i.e., learning gains, the development of positive social interaction skills with another student, and heightened self-esteem) are typical areas of concern for educators and families of all children.

According to Madden, Slavin, Karweit, Dolan, and Wasik (1991), as many as 20% of the first grade children in several urban school districts are held back each year. Children who began the year in September with great enthusiasm become failures at their "full-time jobs" within a matter of months. In a Chapter 1 program referred to as Success for All, emphasis is placed on preventing academic deficits from occurring and/or intervening in a highly intensive manner to provide students with a rich educational experience and a firm foundation for future study. Although a combination of approaches is advocated by the Success for All Program, a very important component is that of tutoring. "One-to-one tutoring is the most effective form of instruction known" (Madden et al., 1991, p. 594). Priority is given to first graders when assigning reading tutors because of the assumption that it is best for children to be successful in reading when they are beginning to learn how to read.

While students are working in a one-to-one situation with other students, the teacher is free to serve as an instructional manager, checking procedures and assisting tutors when necessary. Creative teachers have found a variety of ways to structure partnerships to maximize the learning process in any subject area (Greenfield & McNeil, 1987; McNeil et al., 1989; Pierce & Van Houten, 1984b). Similar to other instructional and peer support strategies that incorporate peer power (Villa & Thousand, 1988), peer-tutoring partnerships are a cost effective way for teachers to increase the amount of individualized instructional attention available to their students (Armstrong, Stahlbrand, Conlon, & Pierson, 1979; Villa & Thousand, 1988). "Good and Brophy (1987) suggest that peers trained as tutors may be more effective than adults—they use more age-appropriate and meaningful vocabulary and examples; as recent learners of material being taught, they are familiar with the tutee's potential frustrations and problems; and they tend to be more direct than adults" (Thousand & McNeil, 1990, p. 8).

Partner learning is an eminent example of individualized instruction in which students work together to achieve educational objectives. If the curriculum used is designed as a system—a skills sequence that provides for regular assessment—the teacher can identify exactly those skills that each student needs to learn next. Tutoring can then focus directly on critical outcomes of instruction for each child, thus "individualizing" an entire classroom (McNeil et al., 1989). Teachers who have availed themselves of these partner learning arrangements in their classrooms have discovered that their students receive more individualized instruction, tend to learn at an accelerated rate, enjoy the exciting opportunity of working cooperatively with classmates, demonstrate heightened responsibility for their learning and that of their partners, relish the association with the teacher as a member of the instructional team, and are found to be more actively involved in creating a positive classroom learning environment (McAllister, 1990; Pierce & Van Houten, 1984a).

The case studies presented in the next section of this chapter were selected to demonstrate the essential elements for successful tutoring programs. They serve as exemplars of the areas in which teachers can apply this powerful technique to enhance the learning of all children and youth. Each of the case studies includes a description of the tutors and tutees, the program design, the method of data collection, the monitoring and evaluation procedures, and a discussion of results. They represent the work of teachers and teachers-in-the-making (student teachers) and were carried out in public schools. Taken as a collective, they demonstrate the power of partnerships through which each child may have the opportunity to become a "competent, caring, productive, responsible individual and citizen who is committed to learning throughout life" (Vermont Department of Education, 1990, p. 1).

Case studies such as these point to the importance and possibilities of teachers assuming the role of researcher in educational environments. Nevin, Thousand, and McNeil (1990) discussed ways in which teachers and teacher trainers can collaborate to design and implement research in schools. Results of such endeavors have had an impact on the university training programs as well as the educational practices of schools.

CASE STUDY 1: INCREASING THE COMPLETION RATE AND ACCURACY OF BASIC MULTIPLICATION FACTS THROUGH A PEER TUTORING PROGRAM

This study (Sherwin, Hurtubise, & McNeil Pierce described in McNeil et al., 1989) describes the initiation of a peer tutoring program by a student teacher. It illustrates how educators may function as action researchers while benefiting a student experiencing academic difficulty. The student teacher was the tutor-trainer and peer tutoring program manager.

The learner in this study was a third grade student named Ira. Peer tutoring sessions were held Monday through Thursday for approximately 20 minutes of the math period.

Ira was observed by the student intern as experiencing much difficulty learning the basic multiplication facts expected of children in his grade. He used a multiplication grid and other multiplication manipulatives to derive answers to the multiplication problems assigned to him.

A mathematics pretest previously given to Ira revealed a score of 57% on the multiplication facts section. Additional testing revealed similar results (i.e., an average score of 46% on multiplication facts). The classroom teacher and the intern decided that Ira would benefit from participation in a peer tutoring program. A parental permission slip explaining the program designed for Ira (see Figure 1) was sent home to Ira's parents. The parents readily agreed to the program.

Choosing the Partners

A classmate, Ellen, was chosen as Ira's tutor because she displayed to the intern a strong desire to work with classmates. She was very helpful and assisted many times with correcting tasks. When a peer tutoring program was mentioned to the class, Ellen asked if she could help a classmate by tutoring.

Like Ira, Ellen also needed practice learning her multiplication facts. On the entry level test, Ellen scored 57%; on baseline tests, her score averaged 82%. Her knowledge of multiplication facts was, therefore, somewhat higher than Ira's. The teacher believed that Ellen would benefit from participation in the program and the data suggested that Ellen was an excellent candidate for the job as Ira's tutor.

Dear Mr. and Mrs. _____ :

Your son, _____, has been selected to participate in our peer tutoring program so he can obtain a firmer base in mathematical skills. _____ has expressed a strong desire to participate in this program so that he can learn his multiplication tables.

    If you agree that _____ should be a part of our program, please sign the attached permission slip and return it to school with _____.

    If you have any questions, feel free to call one of us at Shelburne Village School (985-2541) any morning except Friday.

Sincerely,

Mrs. Smith
Mr. Jones

Teacher Interns

I give permission for _____ to participate in a peer tutoring program.
Signature _____
Date _____

Figure 1.   Sample permission slip for tutees.

Figure 2 presents the parental permission form used with Ellen and other tutor volunteers.

Program Design and Tutor Training

The training program for the tutor was completed in five 20-minute sessions. During Session 1, the intern met with the tutor and explained the objectives of the program. Materials were introduced and the tutor was informed of her responsibilities as a tutor.

    Session 2 began with a review of materials and procedures. The tutor was introduced to the steps for the tutoring session sheet, shown in Figure 3, that describes in detail the procedure that would take place during each session. A "Things to Remember" sheet that outlines praising techniques, shown in Figure 4, was reviewed with the tutor. These sheets were laminated and kept at the beginning of a peer tutoring notebook that included the materials listed in Table 1. Session 2 also consisted of the student intern modeling the roles of the tutor and the tutee and then role-playing the tutoring session with the student.

    In Session 3, the intern and student switched roles and practiced the procedure twice. In Session 4, the tutee was introduced to the materials and procedures. At this time, he was informed of his responsibilities as a tutee and he practiced the procedure with the intern. In the fifth and final training session, the tutor and the tutee carried out an entire session while the intern observed and offered comments and praise as they continued through the session.

    At the end of the tutoring training program, Ellen was presented with the badge shown in Figure 5 that certified her as a "Super Tutor" in her school.

Teaching/Learning Procedures

During the assigned math period, Ellen retrieved the peer tutoring notebook and went to her desk. She looked at the flash cards for the day to make certain that she

Dear Mr. and Mrs. _____:

Your daughter, _____, has been selected to participate in our peer tutoring program as a tutor for another student working with multiplication skills. The daily tutoring sessions will last 15–20 minutes and will not be a substitute for _____ regular math program. If you agree that _____ should be a part of our program, please sign the attached permission slip and return it to school with _____.

    If you have any questions, feel free to call one of us at Shelburne Village School (985-2541) any morning except Friday.

Sincerely,

Mrs. Smith
Mr. Jones
Teacher Interns

I give permission for _____ to participate in a peer tutoring program.
Signature _____
Date _____

Figure 2.   Sample permission slip for tutors.

Before the session begins:

1. Look over flash cards for session.
2. Fill out recording sheet and daily worksheet with student's name, date, and session number.
3. Write the multiplication facts for the day on the recording sheet and the daily worksheet.
4. If you have any questions, ask Mrs. Smith or Mr. Jones.

Begin session:

1. Meet your partner and take him or her to the table in the hall outside the classroom. Smile and be friendly. Make your partner feel comfortable.
2. Go over flash cards with answer side showing. Say "$2 \times 3 = 6$" and have student repeat after you. Go through all 10 flash cards.
3. Give student a piece of scrap paper. Go through the cards again with the answer side showing. Say "$2 \times 3 = 6$" and have student write the fact on the piece of paper. Go through all 10 flash cards.
4. Trial #1: Go through each flash card. Have the student give the answer. If the answer is wrong, say "$2 \times 3 = 6$" and have the student repeat after you. Put the card in a separate pile and go on with the rest of the cards.
5. Fill out a recording sheet. Mark a plus sign (+) for right answers and a zero for wrong answers.
6. Give the student a fact quiz. Give him or her 2 minutes to complete it. Use a stopwatch.
7. Correct quiz. Go over the quiz with the student so that he or she knows how he or she did.
8. Mark the recording sheet.
9. Trial #2: If an answer is wrong, say "$2 \times 3 = 6$", and have the student repeat after you. Have him or her write "$2 \times 3 = 6$." Say "$2 \times 3 = ?$" Have the student say the answer.
10. Mark the recording sheet.
11. Check over the recording sheet. If the student received three plus signs on one problem, give the cards to him or her to put on the "learned word" ring. $2 \times 3 = 6$ + + +
12. Give the student a "feelings" card to fill out.
13. Send the student back into the classroom.
14. Set out new cards for the next session. Remember to include cards the student has received a zero on and then take cards from the new card pile to make 10 new cards. Fill in the bar graph.
15. Fill out the bottom of the recording sheet. Staple the worksheet and the recording sheet together. Put all materials away.
16. See Mrs. Smith or Mr. Jones to let them know the session is over.

Figure 3.   Steps for tutor to follow during sessions.

Things to remember

1. Smile and be friendly at all times.
2. Ask your partner friendly questions before each session.
3. Always remember to praise your partner. Never criticize.
4. Say things such as:

Very good	Right
You are doing very well	Nice job
That's right	

5. Try using other words to praise your partner so that you do not always say the same thing.
6. Never say "That's wrong" or "No."
7. Never do or say anything that will make your partner feel bad.
8. Say things that will make your partner feel that he or she is doing well so that he or she will enjoy being tutored.
9. Feel free to ask Mrs. Smith or Mr. Jones any questions, even during the tutoring session.
10. Have fun!

Figure 4.   Praising techniques for a tutor—"Things To Remember" sheet.

understood them. She filled out the recording sheet (see Figure 6) and the daily fact quiz (see Figure 7) with the specific multiplication problems for that day. Ellen wrote the multiplication problem to the right of the X. The box was left blank so that Ira could fill in the answer to the problem. (This provided a permanent product for the teacher to review.) Ellen then informed Ira that it was time to work with her and they went to the table.

The flash card procedure for each session consisted of the five component parts presented in Table 2. For components 3, 4, and 5, the data were collected by the tutor. If the tutee responded correctly, praise was given and a plus sign ($+$) was placed in the designated area on the recording sheet. If an incorrect response was given, a zero was placed in that area. The procedure for correcting an incorrect response followed the script:

Tutor: $2 \times 3 = ?$
Tutee: 7
Tutor: $2 \times 3 = 6$
Tutee: $2 \times 3 = 6$
Tutor: please write it
Tutee: writes problem
Tutor: $2 \times 3 = ?$
Tutee: $2 \times 3 = 6$

For the daily fact quiz, the tutee corrected his own paper using the data sheet. He also recorded on the top of the quiz sheet the time that it took him to finish the test. The tutor kept track of the time using a stopwatch.

Table 1.   Materials included in a peer tutoring notebook

Daily recording sheet	Things to remember sheet
Daily fact quiz sheet	Steps for session sheet
Flash cards	Quick reference sheet
Two pencils	35-problem fact test
Scrap paper	Tutor graph
Stopwatch for RTI	Tutee graph
Crayons	Tutor bar graph

Figure 5.   Sample tutor achievement badge.

At the end of the daily sessions, Ira was given the cards for which he had received three plus marks and Ira placed these cards on his "learned word ring," which he was allowed to keep in his desk or take home if he wished.

Also, at the end of the session, the tutee was asked to complete a "feelings card" (see Figure 8). The tutor summarized the results of the session using the bottom part of the recording sheet (see Figure 6) and filled in a bar graph that summarized the number of correct responses for the session. She ended the session by stapling all papers for the session together, placing them in the designated area in the peer tutoring notebook, and setting out the next 10 flash cards to be used in the next tutorial session. She put all materials away and informed the intern that the session had ended.

Name:			
Date:			
Session number:			
Problem	Trial #1	Peer quiz	Trial #2
1.			
2.			
3.			
4.			
5.			
6.			
7.			
8.			
9.			
10.			
How do you feel about today's session? _____ Happy _____ OK _____ Sad			

Figure 6.   Daily recording sheet for facts.

Name: _____

Date: _____

Session number: _____

X _____   X _____   X _____

[ ]   [ ]   [ ]

X _____   X _____   X _____   X _____

[ ]   [ ]   [ ]   [ ]

X _____   X _____   X _____

[ ]   [ ]   [ ]

Figure 7.   Format for daily fact quiz.

To ensure retention of these facts, a quiz consisting of (oral and/or written) facts was given at least twice a week. The test, administered by an intern, consisted of problems that were on the tutee's learned word ring. If Ira missed a fact, it was placed back into the flash card pile for future practice. This same test was also given to the tutor during the same time unit.

Evaluation Results

Figure 9 shows a significant increase in Ira's completion rate and accuracy with basic multiplication facts. His scores increased from a baseline measurement of 46% to an average score of 94% during the intervention procedure. The scores also indicate that he maintained his new knowledge of the basic facts.

Figure 10 shows that Ellen's multiplication fact scores also increased through participation in the peer tutoring program. Ellen's scores increased from 82% during baseline to an average of 96% during the intervention.

Table 2.   Flash card procedure for the tutor

Components	Behavior
1. Say	Given a fact ($2 \times 3 = 6$), the tutee will repeat after the tutor.
2. Write	Given a fact ($? \times 3 = 6$), the tutee will repeat after the tutor and write the fact on scrap paper.
3. Trial 1	Given a fact ($2 \times 3 = ?$), the tutee will write the answers to 10 fact problems.
4. Fact quiz	Given 2 minutes, the tutee will write the answers to 10 fact problems.
5. Trial 2	Given a fact ($2 \times 3 = ?$), the tutee will give the answer.

What happened in today's session?

Date _____

Figure 8.   Sample feelings card.

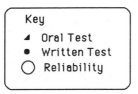

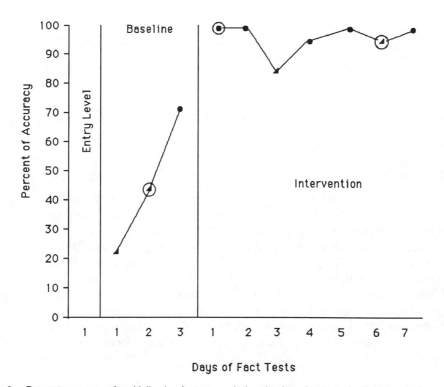

Days of Fact Tests

Figure 9.   Percent accuracy of multiplication facts on verbal and written fact tests for the tutee (Ira).

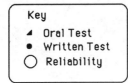

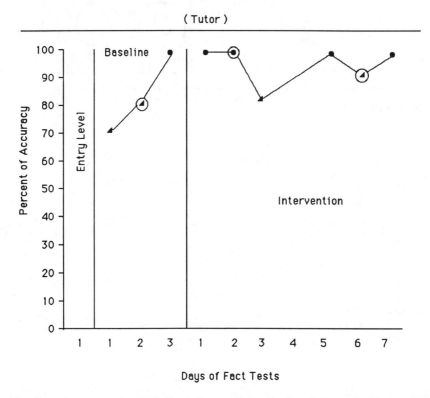

Figure 10.   Percent accuracy of multiplication facts on verbal and written fact tests for the tutor (Ellen).

DISCUSSION

The peer tutoring program was extremely successful. Ira and Ellen both increased their knowledge of multiplication facts over their baseline rates and the benefits of the program transferred to their regular math assignments. It was observed by the teacher that Ira and Ellen increased their scores and accuracy on their other multiplication math facts. The students no longer had to refer to multiplication grids and manipulatives to complete problems that required facts.

Clearly, many students in the regular classroom could benefit from a program such as this partner learning program. When carefully planned, the procedure takes a minimal amount of time to prepare and gives the teacher a greater amount of valuable teaching time. As the data suggest, it was an effective program for these students.

CASE STUDY 2: A PEER TUTORING
SPELLING PROGRAM FOR CHILDREN WITH AUTISM

Although it has been known for many years that children learn from teaching each other, most of our teaching procedures have relied on the teacher as the only instructor (Franca, Kerr, Reitz, & Lambert, 1990). One of the biggest problems that arises with a teacher-directed instruction style is that the teacher often does not have enough time or "hands" to teach each child in a personalized way (Kamps, Locke, Delquadri, & Hall, 1989).

This study (Dahlquist as cited in Casey, Dahlquist, Roberts, & McNeil, 1992) was designed to increase spelling accuracy by providing a child with autism a one-to-one learning experience with a peer. Not only was the tutee able to learn from his peer, but he was also provided with an increased number of opportunities to interact with another person. This study was based upon one reported by Delquadri et al. (1983), which was conducted in an inner-city third grade classroom. Prior to the tutoring program, the classroom teacher used only a teacher-directed style and the children worked independently in workbooks. With this teaching method, students with "learning disabilities" averaged 9.0 spelling errors. With a tutoring game, their errors decreased to a mean of 2.5. The next year, the teacher continued the spelling peer tutoring game and started a similar one for math instruction.

Method

Subject   Two males diagnosed with autism participated in this peer tutoring study. John was 13 years old and verbal; Ron was 9 years old and verbal. Both boys engage occasionally in noncompliant and self-injurious behavior.

Measurement and Reliability Procedures   For this study, one session consisted of 10 trials with a list of 10 spelling words. The dependent variable was the percent correct in 10 trials. A correct response was recorded as a "2." An incorrect trial was scored with a "0." A practice trial was recorded as a "1." This method of recording was intended to make the program seem more like a game; the scoring of trials is very similar to scoring points for a basketball game.

Each trial began by John giving Ron a verbal cue or stimulus, such as "Ron, spell the word car." A trial ended after 10 seconds of noncompliance, 1 minute of an actual attempt, or 2 seconds after the word was correctly spelled.

Reliability was taken every session by a student teacher and John, the peer tutor. Inter-observer agreement for reliability and to prevent any bias was determined by dividing the number of agreements observed by the number of agreements plus the number of disagreements observed and multiplying by 100. The inter-observer agreement was always 100%.

Baseline Procedure   A multiple baseline—experimental design—was employed and data were collected on both the tutor's and the tutee's spelling performance. Three lists of 10 three-letter spelling words were used. During baseline, the tutor, John, presented the 10 spelling words one at a time to Ron. Ron either spelled the word correctly or incorrectly using magnetic letters placed in front of him. John recorded a "2" for correctly spelled words and a "0" for those incorrectly spelled. No praise, prompting, or correction was offered during baseline.

Peer Tutoring Procedure   John praised Ron each time he spelled a word correctly and recorded a score of "2." If Ron spelled the word incorrectly, John would say, "Ron, car is spelled C A R. Spell car." Ron then had a second chance to spell the word correctly. If he did so, he received a score of "1" for his success. If he was still unsuccessful, John prompted Ron, using the letters, until Ron spelled the word correctly. John then praised him and recorded a score of "0."

Results

Figure 11 presents the percentage of correct trials for each session during baseline and intervention periods with the three word lists. For the first list, the percent correct baseline scores ranged from 0% to 20%, an average of 6.67%. During the peer tutoring intervention, the scores ranged from 50% to 100%, an average of 88.89%. For the second list, baseline percentages ranged from 0% to 40%, an average of 14%. During peer tutoring the range was 50%–60%, an average of 55%. Baseline percentages for the third list ranged between 0% and 40%, an average of 14%. The range for peer tutoring was 60%–70%.

Discussion

Results indicate that the peer tutoring spelling program was effective. There was an increase in the percentage of correctly spelled words concurrent with the introduction of the peer tutoring procedure. Ron seemed to enjoy the sessions and was able to learn the spelling words much faster with the increased opportunities to respond and the consistent positive feedback. Ron continued this program with another peer, Jason, and proceeded to four-letter words.

CASE STUDY 3: SPELLING PROGRAM USING PEER TUTORING

In a fourth grade class, 4 weeks of spelling scores revealed the necessity for an intervention to enhance the learning of the children. Encouraging students to study and use spelling words at home had not been enough to improve the spelling of a large number of the students in the class. A peer tutoring intervention was selected for a number of anticipated consequences. First, peer tutoring would increase individualized attention, give tutees a positive role model, and increase the likelihood of increased self-esteem on the part of tutors and tutees. There also was the possibility that through the tutoring experience, the tutors' knowledge level of the subject matter (spelling) would be enhanced and they would take pride in engaging in a helping relationship. Cooperative learning was a predominant instructional approach in the classroom; the program built upon and expanded this approach.

The partner learning program involved 17 students. Each student was *both* a tutor *and* a tutee. Spellers of differing performance levels were paired with one another. In pairing students, consideration also was given to who needed and who could offer a positive role model in the areas of motivation, self-esteem, and social skills. After careful consideration, pairs were established with the condition that these partnerships were not necessarily permanent.

Teaching Students to Be Peer Tutors

After a baseline of 4 weeks of spelling test scores, the peer tutoring program was introduced. The tutoring procedure was discussed and modeled by two teachers as the script in Table 3 describes. Several examples were practiced with the students.

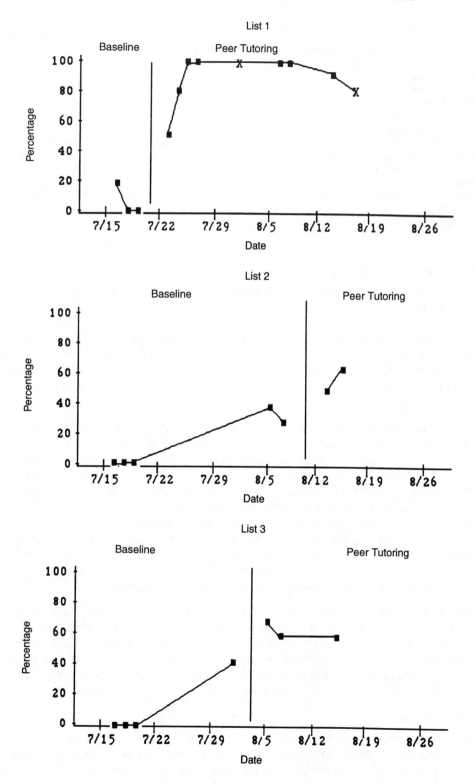

Figure 11. Percentage of correct trials for each session between John and Ron on three word lists.

Table 3.   Directions for an instructional sequence

After writing each partner's words on an index card, do the following:
1. Tutor, tell your partner the word.
    Tutor: "The word is *cat*."
2. Tutee, spell the word.
    Tutee: "C-A-T"
3. Tutor, give positive feedback.
    Tutor: "Very good! Nice job!"
4. If a word is misspelled, tell and show the tutee the word and how it is spelled. Then have the tutee write the word, while looking at it, three times. Do not forget to praise when the tutee finishes.
    Tutor: "The next word is climb."
    Tutee: (makes an error) "C-L-I-M-E"
    Tutor: (showing the tutee the word, says) "The word is climb and it is spelled C-L-I-M-B. Write the word three times (while looking at the card). How do you spell it? That's right, good!"
5. After one person goes through all of the words, switch partners.

Motivation System for the Peer Tutor Program

To motivate children, group and individual goals were incorporated into the program.

Group Goal   A point system of 100 maximum points was established. Whenever a pair earned 100 points, they received a dolphin stamp mark, which was displayed on a poster board entitled "Dolphins Are Us." The students' collective stamps climbed the poster board in a vertical fashion. Whenever stamp marks reached the top of the poster board paper, the class was rewarded with a "spelling party" in which snacks, punch, special activities, and music were provided for approximately 15 minutes. Students could earn 100 points in two ways:

1. During a tutorial session, if the tutee spelled a word correctly on the first trial, the tutee earned two points. If the tutee misspelled the word, he or she could write the word three times correctly to earn one point. The teacher also walked around the room and gave out extra points to pairs of students when she heard a tutor deliver positive feedback to a partner. When a pair accumulated 100 points, a dolphin stamp mark was added to the goal chart.
2. Partners earned 100 points if the tutee scored 100% on the weekly spelling test. A dolphin stamp was given for every perfect (100%) test score. If, however, a student did not get 100% correct, he or she was still given one point for every word spelled correctly. Therefore, every word counted for something and it was the pair's effort in learning words that contributed to earning a party.

Individual Goal   Each student was given a piece of manila construction paper posted on the classroom wall for monitoring individual versus partner performance. Students created a sticker collage from stickers received every time they scored 100% on a test or each time they increased by three or more the number of words spelled correctly as compared to the previous test. By having a group goal along with an individual goal, competition did not become an issue. Everyone was a winner!

Accommodations

For one student, the word list was divided into two smaller lists. This idea, which was generated by the student's parent, enabled the student to take a test on half of the spelling word list at the beginning of the week and the second half at the end of the week.

Another accommodation for two students was the use of a tape recorder. Two students were unable to read their partner's words so they presented a tape-recorded list of words to their partner. The tutor wore headphones and listened for the word while looking at the card. The tutee spelled the word after hearing it on the tape. In this way, these two tutors were able to present their partner with their more difficult spelling lists and experience a higher level sight/sound vocabulary. It should be noted that none of the students reacted adversely to modifications in the program.

Evaluation

Each of the 17 students were assigned a number appearing on the horizontal axis shown in Figure 12. The vertical axis represents the range of test scores. Figure 12 shows two scores for each student. Each score represents the average of pair spelling test scores during a 4-week period. The 4-week baseline results are represented by the solid diamond. The score averages from the second 4-week period during which partner learning occurred are represented by the triangle. Improvement in each child's scores with the tutoring intervention can be assessed by reading the scores above each student number.

As Figure 12 illustrates, for all students (except number 12, who switched grade levels during this study), spelling performance improved with the introduction of re-ciprocal partner learning.

SUMMARY

Following a review of research related to the tutoring process, this chapter presents three examples of partner learning programs designed and implemented by teachers

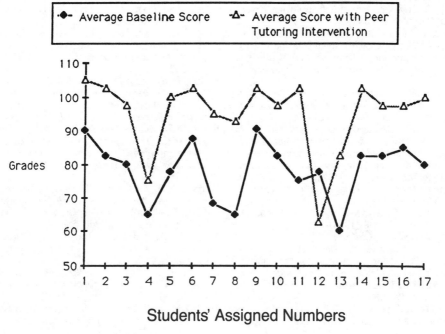

Figure 12.   Peer tutoring spelling results.

and student teachers to show the power of student partnerships on the learning process of children. Peer teaching promotes the individualization of instruction by increasing students' time on task and their opportunities to respond and receive coaching and feedback.

There is a growing, impressive database recognizing partner learning programs as effective approaches to addressing student heterogeneity in classrooms (e.g., Good & Brophy, 1987; Greenwood, Delquadri, & Hall, 1989; Harper, Maheady, & Mallette, chap. 9, this volume; McAllister, 1990; McNeil et al., 1989). With such programs readily available, extra assistance for students struggling with their learning becomes an integral part of the classroom.

If we take seriously the challenge to promote creative, collaborative learning models that empower students and teachers, continual refinement of partner learning approaches is essential. As teachers become involved in designing and implementing such programs, their enthusiasm and expertise can propel them into a new role—*action researcher*—that enables teachers and university teacher learners to collaborate to determine exemplary educational practice (Nevin et al., 1990; Villa, Thousand, Paolucci-Whitcomb, & Nevin, 1990). "Teachers who explore the world of peer teaching gain new perspectives about their effectiveness as teachers. They generate fresh energy and enthusiasm about their profession" (McAllister, 1990, p. 59).

REFERENCES

Armstrong, S.B., Stahlbrand, K., Conlon, M.F., & Pierson, P.M. (1979, April). *The cost effectiveness of peer and cross-age tutoring*. Paper presented at the international convention of the Council for Exceptional Children. (ERIC Document Reproduction Service No. ED 171 058)

Beirne-Smith, M. (1991). Peer tutoring in arithmetic for children with learning disabilities. *Exceptional Children, 57*, 330–337.

Casey, D., Dahlquist, K., Roberts, D., & McNeil, M. (Eds.). (1992). Successful strategies for full inclusion. *Center for Developmental Disabilities Monograph Series*. Burlington: University of Vermont.

Cohen, P.A., Kulik, J.A., & Kulik, C.C. (1982). Educational outcomes of tutoring. *American Educational Research Journal, 19*, 237–248.

Delquadri, J.C., Greenwood, C.R., Stretton, K., & Hall, R.V. (1983). Code for instructional structure and student academic response reported in the peer tutoring spelling game: A classroom procedure for increasing opportunity to respond and spelling performance. *Education and Treatment of Children, 6*, 225–239.

Delquadri, J., Greenwood, C.R., Whorton, D., Carta, J., & Hall, R.V. (1986). Classwide peer tutoring. *Exceptional Children, 52* 535–542.

Franca, V.M., Kerr, M.M., Reitz, A.L., & Lambert, D. (1990). Peer tutoring among behaviorally disordered students: Academic and social benefits to tutor and tutee. *Education and Treatment of Children, 13*, 109–128.

Gartner, A., & Lipsky, D. (1990). Students as instructional agents. In W. Stainback & S. Stain-

back (Eds.), *Support networks for inclusive schooling: Interdependent integrated education* (pp 81–93). Baltimore: Paul H. Brookes Publishing Co.

Good, T.L., & Brophy, J.E. (1987). *Looking into classrooms* (4th ed.). New York: Harper & Row.

Greenfield, S.D., & McNeil, M.M. (1987). The effects of an intensive tutor training component on a peer tutoring program. *The Pointer, 31*, 31–36.

Greenwood, C.R., Delquadri, J.C., & Hall, R.V. (1989). Longitudinal effects of class wide peer tutoring. *Journal of Educational Psychology, 81*, 371–383.

Kamps, D., Locke, J.D., Delquadri, J., & Hall, R.V. (1989). Increasing academic skills of students with autism using fifth grade peers as tutors. *Education and Treatment of Children, 12*, 38–51.

Kohler, F.W., Schwartz, I.S., Cross, J.A., & Fowler, S.A. (1989). The effects of two alternating peer intervention roles on independent work skills. *Education and Treatment of Children, 12*, 205–218.

Madden, N.A., & Slavin, R.E. (1987). *Effective pullout programs for students at risk*. Baltimore: The Johns Hopkins University, Center for Research on Elementary and Middle Schools.

Madden, N.A., Slavin, R.E., Karweit, N.L., Dolan, L., & Wasik, B.A. (1991). Success for all. *Phi Delta Kappan, 72*, 593–599.

McAllister, E. (1990). *Peer teaching and collaborative learning in the language arts*. Bloomington, IN: EDINFO Press, ERIC, and CRLS.

McNeil, M., Stahlbrand, K., & Armstrong, S. (1989). *Increasing student progress through peer tutor-

ing programs (Monograph No. 9-1). Burlington: University of Vermont, Center for Developmental Disabilities.

National Commission on Excellence in Education. (1983). *A nation at risk: The imperative for educational reform*. Washington, DC: Author.

Nevin, A., Thousand, J., & McNeil, M. (1990, June). *Methods of applied research for classroom teachers: Cooperation among teacher education researchers to accommodate students with diverse educational needs*. Paper presented at the Central Institute for Education of Teachers, Bratislava, Czechoslovakia.

Pierce, M.M., & Van Houten, R. (1984a). Preparing materials for peer tutoring. *The Directive Teacher*, *6*, 24–25.

Pierce, M.M., & Van Houten, R. (1984b). Involving your students in the educational process: Partnerships in the classroom. *The Pointer*, *29*, 38–45.

Thousand, J.S., & McNeil, M. (1990, October). *Current research in peer power: Teachers and students working together to provide quality schooling*. Paper presented at the Contemporary State and Future of Education Research International Seminar, Smolenice, Czechoslovakia.

Thousand, J., & Villa, R. (1990). Sharing expertise and responsibilities through teaching teams. In W. Stainback & S. Stainback (Eds.), *Support networks for inclusive schooling: Interdependent integrated education* (pp. 151–166). Baltimore: Paul H. Brookes Publishing Co.

Vermont Department of Education. (1990). *Vermont's education goals*. Montpelier: Author.

Villa, R., & Thousand, J. (1988). Enhancing success in heterogeneous classrooms and schools: The power of partnerships. *Teacher Education and Special Education*, *11*, 144–154.

Villa, R.A., Thousand, J.S., Paolucci-Whitcomb, P., & Nevin, A. (1990). In search of new paradigms for collaborative consultation. *Journal of Educational and Psychological Consultation*, *1*, 279–292.

CHAPTER

11

PARTNER LEARNING SYSTEMS

Laurie LaPlant and Nadine Zane

Partner learning systems are not new. One-room school houses often utilized the knowledge and skills of all the students attending school. Children and adolescents are continually teaching each other informally when playing games and sports. Students' instructional influence not only occurs in school, but also at home through interactions in the community among friends, siblings, and neighbors. Schools today need to capitalize upon students as resources. This can be accomplished, at least in part, by developing and implementing partner learning systems.

Partner learning systems build relationships between students. They involve students who are of the same or different ages. They can occur within a class, between classes, or across a school or district. The design of partner learning systems can be for academic or non-academic purposes and can be one-on-one, in small groups, or as whole classes.

COMPONENTS OF EFFECTIVE PARTNER LEARNING SYSTEMS

These authors have developed a six-component model for creating an effective partner learning system. Those components include identification, recruitment, training, supervision, evaluation, and reinforcement. This chapter explains each component in detail and provides examples of systems that have been successfully established.

Identification

The first consideration in developing a partner learning system is to identify who will participate. A student may need a partner to tutor him or her to acquire a skill or more actively participate in a classroom activity. Conversely, a student may be identified to be in a tutor role because of a need to develop skills and be in a leadership role. For example, Kevin, a fifth grader who might be labeled as having a moderate mental disability, needed frequent adaptations, accommodations, and specific resources for him to have successful participation in general education activities. His program called for support from a paraprofessional and teacher, as well as peers. His team established a peer tutor program in which Kevin assumed the role of tutor with a second grader who needed to learn sight words similar to the words Kevin was learning in his own program. Serving as a peer tutor helped to reinforce sight word skills for Kevin while providing him with a leadership role and enabling him to be a contributor in his school community.

A parent, teacher, or other staff member may initiate the request for a partner learning system. In many schools there are collaborative teams (Villa & Thousand, 1992) that work together to support a student or that team teach to support a classroom of students. Teams may be particularly effective in identifying who would benefit from being an instructor or learner in a partner learning program.

Recruitment

Recruitment involves considering: 1) the various sources of potential student participants, 2) methods for informing participants, and 3) the skills (both technical and interpersonal) students need or will acquire by participating in a partner learning program.

Sources of Tutors and Tutees   Sources for recruiting tutors and tutees are as varied as the children in a school. Sources may include in-school or after-school clubs, classes, or other community organizations. At the Mary S. Babcock Elementary School in Swanton, Vermont, classes of older students teamed with kindergarten age students to assist them in their reading development. On the opposite end of the age spectrum, classroom teachers of a multi-age second/third grade class recruited residents of a nursing home to listen to their students practice oral reading once a week. In this relationship, students benefited in many ways, including receiving encouragement and nurturing from caring and appreciative older adults.

Methods for Informing Potential Participants   Methods to inform potential participants include flyers; class presentations; direct contact; or referral from a teacher, guidance personnel, or family member. An illustration of class presentations for information giving involved a fifth grade student named Melissa who was labeled as having severe mental and physical disabilities. To facilitate Melissa's transition to a new school, teachers and students discussed her strengths and needs with her future classmates. As a result of these sessions, students were asked to volunteer for tutoring or "buddy" systems that oriented Melissa to her new school prior to her transition. These initial partner learning relationships helped classmates to make informed decisions about whether they wanted to participate in other partner learning programs with Melissa when she began to attend her new school on a full time basis.

Who Has or Needs to Acquire Teaching Skills?   Students who serve as tutors need to acquire certain effective *technical* instructional skills, such as direct questioning, checking for understanding, giving feedback, and evaluating another person's performance. Equally important are the affective *interpersonal* partner skills, such as giving praise and eye contact, assessing another student's willingness to participate, and problem solving. Furthermore, it is important that students develop the skill to make adjustments during the sessions, just as classroom teachers do whenever they teach a lesson. Thus, in recruiting potential tutors, a teacher wishing to maximize initial success may choose to seek out students who possess or are more likely to grasp some of these skills quickly. Another teacher may wish to do just the opposite—recruit students in the greatest need of learning interpersonal skills.

The deliberate recruitment of a particular student for a partner learning program is illustrated by Alex, a fourth grader at the J.F.K. Elementary School in Winooski, Vermont. Alex received support because he was identified as gifted and talented. He had advanced understanding and application of a broad range of academic concepts. However, Alex had a difficult time relating to peers in social situations, often resulting in arguing and physically fighting with schoolmates. His support team designed a partner learning program to specifically address his interpersonal needs. A major objective of the program was to intentionally teach Alex how to adjust his language when talking about a content area to a level appropriate for the student he was tutoring. A second objective was to teach Alex to use praise, correction language, and other social skills in accord with the age and experience of his tutee.

Training Partners

Training is the heart of partner learning programs. Decisions must be made regarding: 1) who will conduct the training of partners, 2) where training will occur, and 3) the number and length of training sessions. For example, there may be a member of a teaching team who has the skill to conduct the training, but who has limited time in his or her schedule to carry out the training. Another team member might provide coverage to allow for release time for the training to occur. Trainers can include classroom teachers, special educators, paraprofessionals, secretaries, custodians, administrators, and most importantly, other students who have participated in prior partner learning programs.

Another issue to address in training partners is what and how to teach, the actual content, and methods needed to teach the lesson effectively (McNeil, Stahlbrand, & Armstrong, 1989). The trainer needs to work with the tutors to set the objective, use the materials, and evaluate the effectiveness of their procedures. To illustrate a training procedure, a collaborating teacher at the JFK Elementary School in Winooski, Vermont, designed a partner learning program for a third grade classroom teacher to give her students practice in math facts. The objective of the program was for each tutee to practice facts for the operation they were learning (e.g., addition, subtraction). The materials included sets of flash cards with a problem written on one side and the problem and the correct answer written on the other side, and recording sheets with a space for tutors to record the problem and for students to respond. The evaluation procedure involved tutors summarizing the lesson by writing the total number of correct responses over the number of facts presented.

The trainer guides tutors to learn and develop their own teaching methods that match their skill and age levels. Instructional methods include procedures as basic as establishing eye contact with the tutee, stating instructions clearly, and using age-appropriate verbal and nonverbal praise. Methods also include procedures as complex as giving corrective feedback in a respectful way and monitoring and then adjusting a lesson's sequence or content. In one third grade classroom, the instructional methods taught to all tutors were how to present flash cards in a neutral manner, praise correct responding, and neutrally state a correct response when an incorrect response was given.

Supervision of Partner Learning Systems

Planning for ongoing supervision of partners requires teachers to discuss and answer at least the following questions: Who is responsible for supervision? How frequently does supervision need to occur? What should be the intensity of the interaction between the supervisor and the partners? This, of course, requires direct observation of partner learning experiences. Supervisors should examine both the technical (effective) and interpersonal (affective) aspects of a partner learning program. As with trainers, anyone in the school community may supervise. Supervision may occur as infrequently as once a month or as often as daily, depending on the goals of the program (e.g., daily social skills practiced in the context of a classroom in which cooperative learning is the norm) and the intervention needed to validate program success or make changes in the program. Ultimately, supervision should result in validating what partners are doing well and initiate changes to improve the partner learning program as needed.

An example of collaborative supervision involved sixth graders at the Swanton Schools who regularly tutored younger students. Initially, the special educator took on the training and supervisory role. She then gradually reduced the amount of time she spent with the tutors as the classroom teacher assumed a more active supervisory role, monitoring the program and initiating needed changes when necessary. The special educator and teacher continued to check with each other on a regular basis to communicate any issues that arose related to the partner learning program.

Evaluation

Every day, Kaitlyn a fifth grade student, worked with Tyler, a second grade student, in the area of reading. Kaitlyn read story books to Tyler, questioning him about story elements such as characters, plot, and setting. She kept a daily record of the stories she read to Tyler and logged his responses to questions. Kaitlyn and the special educator met periodically to analyze Kaitlyn's records and logs to determine if changes were needed in the objectives or methods of instruction. The special educator met with both Kaitlyn and Tyler to assess their overall working relationship and ongoing interest in continuing as partners in the program.

As the example of Tyler and Kaitlyn illustrates, evaluation involves assessing: 1) the content relevance, 2) the effectiveness of methodology, 3) the frequency of teacher evaluation sessions, and 4) the need for changes in any aspect of a partner relationship. Evaluation of content involves assessing whether the learner's objectives are being met and determining the next steps of the instructional program. Evaluation of methodology involves the assessment of the interpersonal relationship between the partners. Frequency of teacher evaluations concern formative (i.e., daily, weekly, monthly) and summative (i.e., semester, annual) evaluation. Finally, changes should be based on the information gathered during the evaluation process. Change may relate to the content of the lesson, the delivery of instruction, the partners' relationship, location of tutoring sessions, the time of the sessions, or any other variables related to a program. The change should revitalize a program by providing it with a booster shot of something new that, in turn, will need to be reflected upon in future evaluations.

Reinforcement for Participating in Partner Learning

Designing and implementing ways of reinforcing children for participating in a partner learning relationship is the last component of a comprehensive partner learning program. Reinforcement systems may be formal or informal. Formal systems may take the form of ceremonies and awards, parties (e.g., tutors and tutees having a pizza party together during lunch hour at the end of a program), and recognition in print (e.g., classroom or school newsletters).

Informal reinforcement systems arise in tutoring programs and sometimes arise unpredictably. For example, two students from a fifth/sixth grade multi-age classroom in Swanton, Vermont, were after-school peer tutors for Nick, a kindergarten student who was labeled as having autism. Nick stayed after school while his mother attended weekly collaborative meetings. The tutors engaged Nick in playful learning activities at a sand table or block area. At the end of the year, Nick's mother wrote unsolicited letters of gratitude to each student's parents expressing thanks for the assistance her son received and the opportunity provided for Nick to develop a peer network. The tutors continued their relationship with Nick throughout the summer. Nick's friendship with the tutors was particularly important to his parents because they had only recently moved into the community and had not yet established many friendship links for Nick.

Another example of informal reinforcement occurred in a partner learning program with Murphy. Murphy had participated in a variety of partner learning programs throughout his elementary school years as both a tutor and a tutee. One day his class was working through a very difficult math concept. At one point in the lesson, students were required to independently work on the application of the concept. Murphy raised his hand and, when called upon, stated that he would be happy to do his work if he could have a peer tutor. Murphy's request was rewarding for everyone. Murphy received help and was successful; it spoke to the success in his past experiences as tutor and tutee. His classmates were validated because it acknowledged the effectiveness and importance of their partner learning relationships with Murphy. For the teacher, his request validated the use of partner learning programs in the class and demonstrated the ultimate goal of students taking a proactive role in their own learning. His parents were pleased to know that Murphy was becoming more interdependent. Finally, visitors who happened to be observing the class that day had the opportunity to witness a student spontaneously initiate a request for a technique they had come to observe.

EXAMPLES OF PARTNER LEARNING PROGRAMS

The six components of partner learning (identification, recruitment, training, supervision, evaluation, and reinforcement) are illustrated in the following case studies of partner learning. Variations include within-class, between-class, schoolwide, and district-wide arrangements, as well as same-age and cross-age relationships.

Cross-Age Partner Learning for a Tutor with Unique Needs

An initial and crucial first step when considering a partner learning relationship is to identify how each student participant is expected to benefit. A team (at times including the student) can activate its creative powers to design unique, powerful partner learning programs. At the Mary S. Babcock School in Swanton, Vermont, a team concerned with a second grade student, Stephen, followed steps similar to the creative problem-solving model of Sidney Parnes (1988) described in detail in Chapter 15, this volume. In brief, the process involves fact-finding, problem-finding, idea-finding, and solution-finding steps to arrive at an acceptable idea that is subsequently put into action.

Through fact-finding (i.e., observing and analyzing Stephen's behavior patterns throughout the day), the team identified that transitions from activity to activity were particularly difficult for Stephen. The team speculated that at the end of the day Stephen was fatigued, irritable, and anxious about the transition from school to home. Stephen also hesitated to engage in activities at which he perceived himself to be less than competent. Ignoring undesirable behaviors was not effective in engaging Stephen to participate appropriately in class activities. The team agreed that adaptations were needed for end-of-the-day activities and companions. Without exception, Stephen demonstrated his most challenging behaviors (e.g., resistance to and defiance toward adults) during the last half hour of each school day, prior to boarding the school bus to go home. However, he displayed a range of challenging behaviors throughout the day that were chronic in nature. His challenging behaviors included resistance to authority figures, difficulty with perceiving another person's perspective appropriate to his age level, a strong tendency to dominate and control the outcomes of student-centered activities, extreme difficulty relating to and interacting with other children, poor social skills in team and group activities, and an unusually competitive spirit for his age level. During fact-finding, the team examined resources and identified that it was difficult to provide additional support for Stephen in the classroom on a consistent basis at the end of the day due to scheduling conflicts.

Stephen had not yet been identified under any special education labels during the second grade (he has since been labeled with Tourette syndrome and attention deficit hyperactivity disorder). The school he attended provided a noncategorical service delivery model in which all children received supported services and planning as needed, whether they were identified as eligible for special education or not (Schattman, 1992). Stephen's needs were intensive enough to receive the ongoing support of a collaborative team and the presence of special education support in the classroom.

The team framed the challenge as: "In what ways might we restructure the last 30 minutes of the school day prior to his boarding the school bus home to reduce or eliminate power struggles with adults?" When the team moved to an idea-finding stage, many ideas regarding accommodations of current activities and environment were generated, one of which was to explore bringing an older peer into the last activity of each school day.

During solution-finding, the team refined the idea of having older peers tutor Stephen (with the sustained presence of an adult due to the unpredictability and the potential for unsafe behaviors from Stephen).

Putting a Program in Place for Stephen   In acceptance-finding, the team cycled back to facts critical to the consideration of a partner learning relationship and established that:

The tutor would need to have an air of confidence when interacting with Stephen.
Given training, the tutor would need to be able to demonstrate skills of ignoring, staying focused on the task, and engaging in a high rate of praise in his or her interactions with Stephen.
The tutor would need to be able to initiate "judgment calls" during an interaction with Stephen that required negotiating and a "give and take" in a situation that might arise.

Avoiding "burn out" also was considered in designing the tutor program. Because of Stephen's challenging behaviors, it was speculated that one tutor might quickly become overwhelmed and lose interest in continuing a partner learning relationship. A team member suggested a "tag team" approach, in which two tutors are trained in the program. The two tutors also shared in the responsibility of tutoring other students in the classroom as well. While one tutor worked with Stephen, the other worked with another student the teacher identified as needing help for that day. The tutors were given responsibility for how they would share the two jobs. If one tutor was absent, the session was not interrupted, because the other tutor present in school on that day would "substitute" teach with Stephen.

The remaining job of the team was to identify two tutors and establish the partner learning program. Team members shared responsibilities for this. The collaborating special educator recruited and trained two tutors. The classroom teacher selected educational activities that Stephen enjoyed. She took responsibility for organizing lesson plans for the tutors, gathering materials, and ensuring space for each session. The principal contacted the parents of the tutors for explanation and permission, Stephen's parents explained and encouraged Stephen to participate in the program, and a special education paraprofessional who supported the classroom on an occasional basis shared with the special educator the adult "supervisor" role in the tutoring sessions.

Evaluation Leading to Change   Shared responsibility among team members for the establishment and implementation of this partner learning program was critical to its success. The program was "do-able" because each team member contributed to some aspect of the program. Also critical was the teacher's willingness to individualize for Stephen during this activity time each day. Furthermore, she chose to have primary responsibility for monitoring Stephen's accomplishments during tutoring sessions. When the other team members "picked up" other responsibilities, the teacher was able to focus on ensuring academic outcomes for Stephen's tutorial sessions.

After several sessions in this partner learning relationship, Stephen began to request "to be the tutor." The team recognized that the communicative intent of Stephen's requests was a need to serve in a leadership role as teacher. Not only did Stephen enjoy being helped, but he wanted to experience being a helper as well.

Throughout the teaming process, a second partner learning program was initiated for Stephen. On alternate days from his tutoring sessions with older tutors, Stephen began tutoring a first grade student who needed to practice oral reading. This partner learning program required more vigorous supervision; anticipating this, the team planned proactively. The team took the time to plan for the second program carefully because of their strong belief that Stephen, being in a caring type leadership role, would have short- and long-term positive outcomes in terms of behavioral self-management, self-esteem, a sense of belonging, mastery, and independence (Brendtro, Brokenleg, & Van Bockern, 1990).

A Schoolwide, Cross-Age Tutoring Program

In a fourth grade classroom, there were two students who presented significant challenges. As part of the students' educational programs, a variety of same-age support programs of both an academic (peer tutoring) and nonacademic (peer buddy) nature were developed for the classroom. The classroom tutors performed their responsibilities so magnificently that the classroom teacher wanted the skills of the tutors to extend beyond their classroom. The class of tutors eventually became cross-age math tutors in a first grade classroom for the remainder of the school year. This was the beginning of a schoolwide, cross-age tutor program. The Winooski cross-age tutoring program evolved to include 75% of the student population at JFK Elementary School. Students in five upper elementary classrooms tutor five lower elementary classrooms in the areas of math and language. Initially, a collaborating teacher (special educator) matched classrooms and facilitated the scheduling, planning, delivery, evaluation, and reinforcement components of the program. Over time, each cross-age tutoring match developed its own unique approach to implementing the cross-age tutoring program.

Identification Initially, only a few involved students were identified as likely to benefit from a tutoring situation for either academic or nonacademic reasons. Over time, it became obvious that each individual student could benefit in a partner learning relationship. Any student in the upper and lower elementary classrooms were potential tutors and tutees.

Recruitment At the start of each school year, upper elementary students are introduced to the cross-age tutoring program through a class discussion about past student experiences as tutors and tutees, including students' perceptions of the art and science of teaching. Following the discussion, students receive a letter to be shared with their parents that explains the program. Also included with the letter is a sample contract stipulating their responsibilities should they choose to participate as a tutor in the program. All students who return their contracts with appropriate signatures are allowed to participate in the cross-age tutoring program. In general, 95% or more of the students in each class elect to become tutors. The few students who do not choose to do so often change their minds during the school year.

Training Generally, training sessions of 30–45 minutes occur either once or twice a month, alternating with bimonthly or biweekly tutorial sessions. Students are required to identify the critical elements of the concept they will teach in their next tutoring session. Then, students either develop their own lesson plan for their tutees or learn how to deliver a previously developed plan. Necessary materials for the tutoring session are prepared and the lesson is rehearsed. Students usually ask many questions related to lesson development, material preparation, lesson delivery, or behavior management at the training sessions. Students' questions and issues are addressed as they bring them up.

Supervision Each upper or lower elementary classroom determines its own supervision arrangement. Usually the upper elementary classroom teacher participates in planning sessions with a collaborating teacher (special educator). The lower elementary teacher usually supervises the delivery of the tutoring in the classrooms with the support of a collaborating teacher. All teachers share in monitoring tutors to make sure their contractual responsibilities are being met. This is necessary because tutoring is a privilege contingent upon adequate work completion and social responsibility.

Evaluation At the end of each tutorial session, tutors and tutees alike are asked to evaluate the session. In 3–5 minutes of discussion, students identify "what went well with the lesson" and "what could be done better" for the upcoming sessions. The upper elementary students use this information to develop lessons in their next planning session. Periodically, evaluation occurs to determine if major changes need to occur across the entire elementary school partner learning program. Surveys with open-ended questions, checklists, or class meetings are used to gather information for this summative evaluation. As a result of program evaluations, the cross-age tutor program was changed from a small group of students as tutors to whole classes of tutors and from twice a month tutoring sessions to once a month tutoring sessions in a couple of classrooms.

Reinforcement   Reinforcement in the Winooski, Vermont, cross-age tutor program is structured for everyone. Tutors reinforce the tutees at the end of each tutor session with tangible reinforcers or fun activities. Classroom teachers are reinforced through observations of their students in responsible teaching and active learning. They gain information from observations to improve their own work with their students. The school community is reinforced by stories told by students about experiences and the emerging interest of a number of students in becoming a teacher. At the end of each school year, all tutors are publicly applauded for their service to their school through a tutor recognition ceremony.

In summary, the Winooski cross-age tutoring program is one way the school community is attempting to structure the opportunity for students to become active participants in their own education and the education of others, help tutors better learn content through learning about the metacognitive aspects of teaching information to another, and give students the opportunity to contribute to a community to which they belong (Brendtro et al., 1990; Villa & Thousand, 1992).

Partner Learning as a Community Service

Each year at the Swanton (Vermont) Central School, Linda Pearo and Joan Lumbra's fifth/sixth multi-age program develops their classroom culture and ethos, identifying themselves as the "Songadeewin Family" (meaning "strong heart" in one Native American language) through which children demonstrate how they may be "keepers of the earth through mind and spirit." The class is structured to provide services to others in the belief that one way to help students define who they are is to have them decide how they will contribute to others.

To achieve the goal of generosity for the Songadeewin family, the 50 students in the class are subdivided into groups of six to eight children and one adult advisor. The adults include teachers, teaching assistants, the principal, special educators, parent volunteers, and student teachers. Each group, called a Council Circle, meets twice weekly for approximately 30 minutes to develop and implement service projects in the four areas of Songadeewin—family, school, community, and the earth.

One year, Council Circles developed a service project called "Songadeewin Family Tutees." The advisor of this particular group trained students in essential technical and interpersonal tutoring skills. Linda utilized many of the suggestions and followed tutor training strategies such as those described by McNeil in Chapter 10, this volume. Students role-played partner learning situations to develop and practice the tutoring skills as well as behavior management strategies.

Each student created a folder that included materials they would need for a partner learning program. They had an index card that "introduced" them to their potential tutees. For example, Kyle's card stated, "My name is Kyle. I am in grade six. My teachers are Ms. Pearo and Mrs. Lumbra. I am good at spelling and English. The subject I am not good in is math." On the opposite side of the card, Kyle listed "conversation starter" questions to ask his tutee to help them become acquainted, such as "What are you good at?" and "How old are you?" The folder included a list of teaching skills the tutor had learned that served as a prompt to use the skills in an actual partner learning session. Each tutor also generated a list of positive words and statements that could be used to encourage tutees to respond. A personalized "praise list" was developed. For example, Kyle listed 17 statements, such as "Good," "Nice job,"

"Fantastic work," and "You're doing fine." Stickers and awards selected or made by tutors were in the folders, along with a Tutor Log Book. The log was used to record tutee's answers and any information from a tutorial session that could help a tutor reflect on the session. The information was intended to help tutors improve as teachers through self-reflection.

When Council Circle members completed their training and tutoring folders were assembled, each prospective tutor created a brochure advertising the program and the services the student could provide. Brochures were distributed and the Council Circle advisor promoted the program to other adults in the school community. Teachers "employed" the students and reported that they made excellent teachers in partner learning programs; they needed minimal teacher time in orientation or supervision because of the prior training they received in their Council Circle groups.

The tutoring program subsequently expanded to a "Songadeewin Day Care" program. The same group of students learned child-care skills through a process similar to the partner learning training. They developed materials and activities for younger children and performed child-care duties during and after school for parents and teachers who needed to attend a variety of school meetings. The Songadeewin Day Care providers were a valuable asset to the school, keeping younger children meaningfully engaged and supervised during adult meeting times. In keeping with the Songadeewin community service ethic, the child-care providers volunteered their services.

A Partner Learning Program to Acquire Math Facts

This example of a partner learning program for two students of the same age in a third grade classroom illustrates how supervision may need to intensify at points during a partner learning relationship. Barbara Trushaw, a third grade teacher, was concerned with two students who were not mastering addition and subtraction math facts at a satisfactory rate. The teacher described both students as having difficulty attending and working independently. They both were frustrated in math, voicing a lack of confidence about their abilities.

Barbara's collaborating teacher (special educator) developed a reciprocal peer tutoring program for math fact acquisition that had sequential steps that incorporated auditory, verbal, and writing components in a repeated rehearsal format (Harper, Maheady, & Mallette, chap. 9, this volume). The teacher ensured that the students had at least one opportunity a day for reciprocal tutoring. Each tutorial took approximately 10 minutes each day that allowed for each partner to play the role of tutor and tutee. The students concentrated on six math facts per session (four "known" and two "unknown," or yet unmastered), practicing them until mastery using an auditory, kinesthetic, and visual program.

It was hoped that once the two students were trained in the procedure and in tutoring, only intermittent supervision would be needed to monitor the program and provide students with reinforcement and feedback. The students did, in fact, master the program steps quickly and demonstrated mastery of the teaching-learning procedure. Once the students demonstrated consistent behaviors during tutoring, the collaborating teacher who supervised the program arranged to visit weekly to monitor the program.

Before the first supervisory visitation, Barbara approached the collaborating teacher with concerns over the way in which the two students were treating each other during tutoring sessions. She observed the students frequently using "put-down" statements and abandoning reinforcement, feedback, and other skills in which they had been trained. They also fought over materials. Nevertheless, the feedback sheets the students filled out after each session indicated they perceived the sessions to be going well. When the collaborating teacher queried the students, they did not take responsibility for what was happening and made strong accusations toward each other.

There was a clear need for more training, modeling, and supervision of the tutoring sessions. Both teachers hoped that the students eventually would not require constant supervision to carry out the program. The collaborating teacher arranged to increase her supervision time daily on a flexible schedule when her presence would not interrupt direct instruction or another critical activity. This resulted in a "win-win" situation for everyone. The teacher was pleased the students were able to continue the tutoring, the special educator was able to meet her training and supervision obligations, and the students received intensified intervention.

The students did need reinforcement and reminders of the steps of the program, but the emphasis of supervision was to develop the students' skills in making positive statements and sustaining positive interactions with one another while gradually removing adult supervision. The supervising teacher developed a data sheet that included each step of the teaching sequence, adding the steps of "saying nice things" and "saying thank you." As she supervised, she checked off each step as the tutor performed it, particularly noting examples of partners saying "nice things" and "thank you."

Prior to introducing the data collection system to the partners, she observed them collecting baseline data on their performance. She then shared the data and her observations with the students and set goals with them to improve their performance. The students could collect "points" based on the number of checkmarks they jointly accrued that later could be traded for activity-based reinforcers (e.g., lunch with the supervisor, games, free time).

With this intervention, the students quickly improved in all areas of the partner learning program. Yet, the goal of reducing supervision was slow to be achieved. Supervision was reduced, but only to every other day. Nevertheless, the teacher and collaborating teacher agreed to continue the program because the students did show consistent gains in acquiring math fact and interpersonal skills. Although supervision in this case remained somewhat intensive, it was seen as a necessary support to the partner learning program. Adult intervention was needed to prompt, guide, and reinforce cooperative behavior rather than teaching actual math skills.

Adam's Positive Experiences as a Classroom Tutor

Several years ago, Michelle Steady, a second grade teacher, was working in her school's Resource Center while her student teacher did her "solo week." She met Adam, a fifth grader with severe emotional challenges, who was in the Resource Center working while he "cooled down" following a disruption in his regular classroom. On this day, Michelle observed Adam as he patiently helped another student who was struggling with a particular concept. She was amazed with his teaching skills and impressed with how well he related to the younger child. This was the beginning of Adam's experience as a classroom tutor in Michelle's second grade classroom that would continue for almost 3 years. Michelle quickly identified Adam as a student who had developed and was able to apply good tutoring skills. Adam's educational support team had identified Adam's needs for opportunities to practice identified social skills in a normalized environment and to improve his perceptions of himself and his school experiences in general. Collaborating teachers (special educators) in the school brought Michelle and Adam's team together and encouraged them to develop a tutoring program for Adam.

At the time, Adam had a behavior contract to support him in maintaining appropriate school behavior. Recruiting Adam to become a tutor was easy, as Adam had come to like Michelle and wanted to work in her classroom. The educational team ultimately decided to use Adam's strong desire to tutor as a reinforcement when he met his obligations on his behavior contract.

Training and supervision of Adam as a tutor was Michelle's responsibility. Because Adam was a tutor for any student in the class, he had the chance to deliver many types of lessons in different content areas. Initially, someone needed to spend time explaining and modeling lessons to Adam; Adam's collaborating teacher helped Michelle with this. Over time, as Adam became familiar with the various programs and content areas in Michelle's classroom, the amount of training and supervision decreased dramatically.

Michelle's and Adam's collaborating teacher met regularly to evaluate Adam's performance as a tutor; sometimes Adam participated in these meetings. Adam also was observed to determine the degree to which he generalized to other children the positive social interactions he showed with students in Michelle's second grade classroom.

Participating as a classroom tutor was very reinforcing to Adam. He rarely failed to meet the requirements of his behavioral contract, thus earning his time to serve as a tutor. One school year at Christmas time, Adam came to a tutoring session with a bag filled with small stuffed animals that he had won at various fairs and carnivals. He gave each student in the class a stuffed animal, surprising everyone including the teacher. Becoming a classroom tutor empowered Adam to expand his social interactions in an atmosphere of acceptance.

CONCLUSION

Partner learning systems can be uniquely tailored to meet the existing needs of an individual student, a classroom, or a school community to achieve both social and academic goals. *Intentional* planning of the partner learning programs increases the likelihood that the student partnerships will be successful. These authors have seen, first hand, the benefits of partner learning and learned that instruction may come from people other than adults with a "teacher" label. For students who have few positive outside connections, partner learning may be a source of positive relationships. By instilling a sense of responsibility for others in a student community, it is our hope that an ethic of generosity will develop, transcend the walls of the school, and follow children into adulthood.

Partner learning relationships offer educators much, including a fresh look at learning, as they observe their students teaching and learning from each other. However, to initiate a partner learning system requires change in the attitudes of educators, students, and communities about the roles of teacher and learner and how adults and children interact in school. Change is always difficult, but attitudes can affect outcomes, as Winnie the Pooh points out.

"We're all going on an expotition with Christopher Robin!"
"What is it when we're on it?"

"A sort of boat, I think," said Pooh.
"Oh! That sort."
"Yes, and we're going to discover a Pole or something. Or was it a mole? Anyhow, we're going to discover it." (Milne, 1957, pp. 106–107)

REFERENCES

Brendtro, L., Brokenleg, M., & Van Bockern, S. (1990). *Reclaiming youth at risk*. Bloomington, IN: National Educational Service.

Milne, A.A. (1957). *The world of Pooh*. New York: E.P. Dutton.

McNeil, M., Stahlbrand, K., & Armstrong, S. (1989). *Increasing student productivity through peer tutoring programs*. (Monograph No. 9-1). Burlington: University of Vermont, Center for Developmental Disabilities.

Parnes, S. (1988). *Visionizing: State-of-the-art processes for encouraging innovative excellence*. East Aurora, NY: D.O.K. Publishing.

Schattman, R. (1992). The Franklin Northwest Supervisory Union: A case study of an inclusive school system. In R.A. Villa, J.S. Thousand, W. Stainback, & S. Stainback (Eds.), *Restructuring for caring and effective education: An administrative guide to creating heterogenous schools* (pp. 143–159). Baltimore: Paul H. Brookes Publishing Co.

Villa, R.A., & Thousand, J.S. (1992). Student collaboration: An essential for curriculum delivery in the 21st century. In S. Stainback & W. Stainback (Eds.), *Curriculum considerations in inclusive classrooms: Facilitating learning for all students* (pp. 117–142). Baltimore: Paul H. Brookes Publishing Co.

THE ROLE OF STUDENTS IN RESOLVING CONFLICTS IN SCHOOLS

Fred Schrumpf

"That's not fair," "You're cheating," "I'm going to get you after school," "Did you hear what she said about you?", "Your momma. . . . " These or similar statements are heard in every school each day of the year. They are the beginning or continuation of unresolved student conflicts. David and Roger Johnson (1991a, 1991b) suggest there are at least four types of conflict that teachers encounter in their classrooms: controversies, conceptual conflicts, conflicts of interest, and developmental conflicts. A controversy exists when one student's ideas, information, conclusions, and opinions are incompatible with those of another student and the two seek an agreement. A conceptual conflict occurs when incompatible ideas exist at the same time in a student's understanding or when new information does not seem to fit with what the student already knows. A conflict of interest occurs when the actions of one student who is trying to maximize his or her wants and benefits prevents, blocks, or interferes with another student who is also trying to maximize his or her wants and benefits. Peer mediation is specifically focused on helping students learn how to resolve conflicts of interest. A developmental conflict exists when cognitive and social imperatives demand that a student behave in a certain way (e.g., dependence and independence, autonomy and belonging).

Conflicts are part of everyday life for most children in school. Unresolved conflicts, however, can hurt a school climate and can result in violence, absenteeism, and vandalism. Knowledge of how to handle conflicts in an appropriate way is a life skill that can be learned cooperatively with peers; its application will benefit students beyond the school environment and school years.

When students bring peer conflict issues to teachers, adult advice may be to "ignore it" or "walk away." When friends are asked for advice, their response often is to "get 'em back." When student conflicts reach a principal's desk, the consequence often is detention or suspension. With all of these responses, the conflict fails to get resolved and often increases.

Many North American schools attempting to handle student conflicts in a proactive and positive way have turned to conflict resolution programs that employ students as peer mediators. Students who serve as mediators sometimes are called *peacemakers* or *conflict managers*. Peer mediation assumes that: 1) conflicts are a normal part of growing up, 2) conflicts can be treated as learning opportunities, and 3) conflict resolution skills are positive forces for personal growth and social change.

A peer mediation approach may be initiated on a schoolwide basis or within a classroom at the elementary through high school levels. A small number of students may be selected and trained in the mediation process. The students then are available during the school day to conduct mediations as requested by teachers, principals, or peers. Requests for mediations frequently come from students themselves. In elementary schools, mediators also may frequently be assigned to playground areas to settle disputes on the spot.

At some schools, *all* students are trained in the conflict resolution skills of negotiation and mediation (Johnson, Johnson, Dudley, & Burnett, 1992). They may be part of an elementary curriculum or at the secondary level in subjects such as social studies, language arts, or health/wellness classes. Students receive instruction in the nature of conflict, communication skills, problem solving, and the steps of negotiation and mediation. Whenever a peer conflict arises, students first are asked to negotiate their differences. If the disputants cannot reach an agreement on their own, the teacher selects a peer mediator to assist. Only if the peer mediator cannot help resolve the conflict does the teacher become mediator. Such an approach in an elementary school in Minnesota resulted in an 80% decrease in the frequency of student–student conflicts that teachers had to manage and a reduction in principal referrals to zero (Johnson et al., 1992).

Evaluations of peer mediation programs at the secondary level have shown a reduction in the drop-out rate (Millhauser, 1989) and suspension rate (McDonald & Moriarty, 1990). A high school peer mediation program in New York City resulted in a 46%–70% drop in suspensions for fighting by the end of the first year of the program (Cheatham, 1989). An elementary principal in Lancaster, Pennsylvania, reported a 75% drop in the number of incidents referred to his office with the introduction of peer mediation (Sadalla, Holmberg, & Halligan, 1990). In a middle school in Illinois, more than 200 disputes were resolved a year with a 96%–100% success rate, and overall school attendance increased (Schrumpf, Crawford, & Usadel, 1991). In Charlotte, North Carolina, school officials credit peer mediation with helping to reduce the number of student assaults by 50% between 1989 and 1990 (Meek, 1992).

Common to all peer mediation programs are trained peer (student) mediators who respond to student conflict by facilitating a process of communication and problem solving. The mediation process is voluntary and enables two disputants to talk face-to-face and come to some common understanding. Solutions are generated and evaluated and agreed-upon solutions become a written agreement on the part of the disputants. The remainder of this chapter offers a rationale for peer mediation, discusses the nature of conflict, describes in detail the mediation process and strategies for training students and establishing mediation within a school, and concludes with an example of peer mediation in action.

WHY PEER MEDIATION?

Why develop peer mediation in a school? First, schools today reflect the problems and conflicts with which students live in their larger environments. Many educators include the teaching of life skills and coping skills as an essential curriculum domain so that daily conflicts experienced by students become teachable moments and opportunities for cooperative learning. Second, mediation is a life skill that empowers students to solve their own problems through clear communications, applied decision making, and critical thinking. Peer mediation can reduce the time that teachers, principals, or counselors spend dealing with discipline problems. It can help reduce absenteeism, vandalism, and violence, and it can be more effective than detentions or suspensions to teach responsible behaviors. Finally, resolving conflict promotes peace and understanding of individual differences in a multicultural world.

UNDERSTANDING CONFLICT

It is easy to come up with examples of conflicts in school. At almost every grade level, when students are asked to give examples of conflicts, their responses include teasing, put-downs, being left out, rumors, problems with sharing, lost or damaged property, threats, and aggression.

Some schools have more conflicts than others; this often has to do with how the school staff handles conflict and the atmosphere of each classroom. Kreidler (1984) identified some common causes for classroom conflicts.

1. Competitive atmosphere: students work against each other and are compelled to win.
2. Intolerant atmosphere: there is mistrust and intolerance of different ideas or lifestyles, including racial prejudice.
3. Poor communication: students have misunderstandings, poor listening skills or cannot express their needs.
4. Misuse of power by the teacher: rigid and inflexible rules, authoritarian, uses fear and threats. (pp. 4–5)

Glasser (1986, 1990), examining the origins of conflict, explained how people are not controlled by external events, but, instead, are motivated by the desire to satisfy internal basic psychological needs:

1. The need to *belong:* loving, sharing, and cooperating
2. The need for *power:* being recognized, achieving, and respected
3. The need for *freedom:* making choices in life
4. The need for *fun:* laughing and playing

Students want and try to satisfy these needs in the classroom. When students feel excluded or discriminated against, go unrecognized, have no freedom to make classroom decisions, or stop having fun, there will be conflicts in the classroom.

Limited resources can be a source of school conflict. For example, when students need to share materials, equipment, or teacher time, conflict may arise. It is harder for students to have their basic needs met when school resources are in short supply.

Furthermore, conflicts may arise because of *different values*. People have different convictions and when they interact their values are represented in their words and actions. When students say, "It's not fair," or "I'm right and you're wrong," or "He's not telling the truth," it is often because the concepts of honesty, equality, and fairness are viewed differently by different people.

Conflicts due to different values also may be bias based and expressed as racism, classism, sexism, and homophobia (Woolner, 1992). Because people bring learned biases and ethnocentric views of the world to the negotiating table, prejudice reduction and cross-cultural sensitivity must be part of conflict resolution training. In summary, it takes communication and understanding to discover differing values; it takes negotiation skills to create shared sets of values.

An important first step in conflict resolution involves awareness of one's response to conflict. The conflict diagram presented in Figure 1 illustrates sources and responses to conflict. An obvious response to conflict is *confrontation*. Confrontation involves threats, aggression, and anger. Another response to confrontation is *avoidance*. Sometimes it seems easier to withdraw from, ignore, or deny a conflict. Although resentment or internalized anger or depression results in avoidance, a preferred way to handle conflict that leads toward resolution is *communication* that includes understanding, respect, and resolution.

PHASES OF PROGRAM ORGANIZATION AND IMPLEMENTATION

An effective peer mediation program requires schoolwide interest. Teachers, administrators, and students all need information and training on peaceful conflict resolution. The four organizational phases to establishing a successful program are discussed below.

Phase I: Develop Awareness and Interest

The first phase is to interest a group of staff and parents to form a committee that familiarizes itself with resource materials that teach conflict resolution and with any available materials on peer mediation programs in other schools in the area. The committee also may research and document conflict situations in the school. After such a study, a proposal is developed that describes how peer mediation could be initiated and how it would benefit the school.

Phase II: Establish Schoolwide Support

Phase II involves educating staff and students about what peer mediation is and how it operates. Staff may be informed via orientations at regular staff meetings, or better yet, through inservice training on conflict resolution strategies. Students may be informed through classroom presentations, grade level assemblies, daily announcements, and informational brochures. All orientations should answer questions such as: What is mediation? Who is a student mediator? Are there any rules to mediation? How do I get a conflict mediated? Why should I try mediation? Figure 2 offers suggestions for questions and responses that might be included in a student brochure.

Next, those who have developed an interest will need to develop the program, adapt materials for the program, arrange for more in-depth training for teachers who want to implement a classroom curriculum, and select students to become mediators. Student mediators should be representative of the student body with regard to race, gender, grade point average, extracurricular interests, and clique membership. They

CONFLICT DIAGRAM

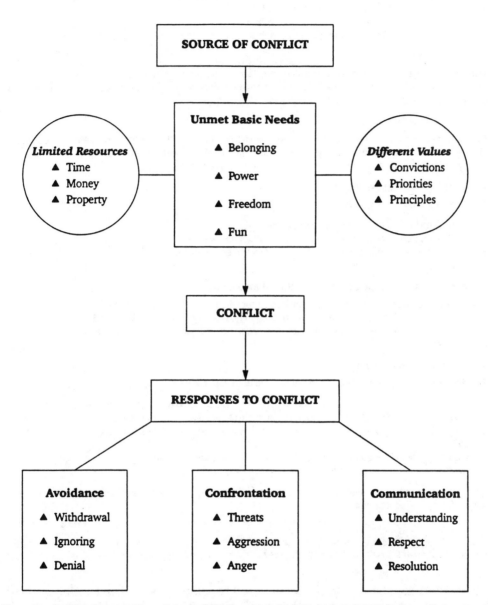

Figure 1.   Conflict diagram. (From Schrumpf, F., Crawford, D., & Usadel, C. [1991]. *Peer mediation: Conflict resolution in schools.* Champaign, IL: Research Press Company. Reprinted by permission.)

also should be judged as good listeners, respectful of others, trusted by peers, and motivated to help people work together.

Phase III: Provide Mediation Training

Mediation is like any other skill. It can be learned and it improves with practice. Between 6 and 12 hours of training is needed for students and teachers to learn and practice the basic skills of negotiation and mediation. To implement this phase, one

---

Having a conflict?

- Has someone made fun of you or teased you?
- Did someone say, "Just wait and I'll get you after school?"
- Did "he say" that "she said" that "you said," and a rumor is going around the school?

What is mediation?

Mediation is a chance for you to sit face-to-face and talk, uninterrupted, so each side of the dispute is heard. After the problem is defined, solutions are created and then evaluated. When an agreement is reached, it is written and signed.

What is a student mediator?

A student mediator is one of your peers who has been trained to conduct the mediation meeting. The student mediator makes sure the mediation session is helpful and fair. Your fellow students were selected to help you resolve differences because they might better understand your point of view.

Are there any rules in mediation?

To make the process work, there are a few simple rules.

1. Mediation is a process that both students choose.
2. Everything said during a mediation is kept confidential; what is said in the room stays in the room.
3. In mediation, students take turns talking and no one can interrupt.
4. The student mediator does not take sides.

If I have a conflict, how do I go about getting it mediated?

It is very easy to request a mediation. Just pick up a mediation request form from a counselor or social worker. Take 2 minutes to fill it out and return it to any counselor or social worker. Within a day you will receive notification of the time and place of mediation. Mediations will be scheduled when the least amount of class time is missed.

Why should I try mediation?

There are many reasons why mediation will be helpful to you. Here are a few.

1. Conflicts that do not get resolved often end in fights, which could result in suspension.
2. Conflicts that do not get resolved often result in hurt feelings, which could cause you to lose friends.
3. You will learn to choose a peaceful, responsible way to solve your own problems without an adult doing it for you.
4. Mediation will help you develop mutual respect and clear communication.
5. Mediation will make school a more positive place to learn and grow.

If you answered yes to any of the questions at the top of this brochure, check out Common Ground, Urbana Middle School's student mediation center.

Figure 2.   Sample student brochure. (From Schrumpf, F., Crawford, D., & Usadel, C. [1991]. *Peer mediation: Conflict resolution in schools.* Champaign, IL: Research Press Company. Reprinted by permission.)

or more staff members from the school need to complete additional training in conflict resolution in order to train other staff. Alternatively, an outside trainer may be used to provide the instruction. Details of a model 2-day workshop that would prepare a trainer for this phase are presented later in this chapter.

Phase IV: Implement and Evaluate the Program

Peer mediation should have high visibility among teachers and students and be promoted through schoolwide announcements and materials that inform everyone of the program and how it can help. Posters that encourage peace and talking out problems may be designed and placed throughout the school. T-shirts, hats, or buttons worn by mediators can help build a positive image of mediation. The goals of promotion should be to encourage student participation and increase the likelihood of requests for mediation from teachers, principals, and students.

It is critical that student mediators receive ongoing training and support for their efforts. Monthly or more frequent meetings allow peer mediators an opportunity to discuss any problems they have had as mediators, receive more advanced training, and learn that skills improve over time with practice.

Finally, data collection is a critical part of any peer mediation program. A Peer Mediation Request form, such as that shown in Figure 3, may be used to gather information about a conflict (who was involved, where the conflict happened, a description of the events) and show the types of mediation requested.

A summary of agreements (type of conflict, agreement reached, length of mediation) may be compiled by analyzing the information included on a Peer Mediation Agreement form, such as that shown in Figure 4. To give the program committee and the school community overall data regarding student conflict, additional data should be collected regarding individual students and overall detentions, suspensions, fights, or absenteeism.

TRAINING MEDIATORS

Conflict resolution skills can be taught at all grade levels. Classroom curricula have been developed for the elementary grades by Drew (1987), Kreidler (1984, 1990), and Johnson and Johnson (1991b). Training materials for student mediators in grades 4–12 were developed by Schrumpf et al. (1991) and Sadalla et al. (1990). These materials build on natural leadership and communication skills that students bring with them. The materials include problem-solving techniques to assist others to resolve their conflicts.

A workshop to train elementary-age student mediators generally involves two half-day sessions that total 6–8 hours of instruction. At the secondary level, a 2-day workshop of 10–12 hours is recommended. At both levels, students learn the definition of conflict, the goal of mediation, the role of the mediator, and communication skills. Students also learn each step of the mediation process through role-plays of conflict situations. The following is a brief overview of how training is conducted.

Section 1: Understanding Conflict

Students are introduced to the nature of conflict by being asked to brainstorm a list of words that come to mind when the word conflict is stated. The list usually includes many words with negative meaning such as fight, disagreement, argument, yelling, problem, threat, and war. Students then are challenged to think of conflict as positive with the introduction of words such as: opportunity, change, talk, challenge, risk, and problem solving.

The desired outcome of such an exercise is that students acquire a new and positive understanding of conflict as: 1) a natural part of everyday life, 2) capable of being handled in positive or negative ways, 3) having either creative or destructive results, and 4) a positive force for personal growth and social change.

Students learn that in order to resolve a conflict, the conflict's source must be identified, as shown in Figure 1. Students learn that almost every dispute between people involves attempts to meet basic human needs for belonging, power, freedom, and fun (Glasser, 1986, 1990). Needs are discussed by asking students to give per-

Peer Mediation Request

Date _____

Names of students in conflict:

_____ Grade _____

_____ Grade _____

_____ Grade _____

_____ Grade _____

Where conflict occurred (check one)

☐ Bus   ☐ Classroom   ☐ Hallway   ☐ Cafeteria   ☐ Outdoors

☐ Other (specify) _____

Briefly describe the problem:

_____

_____

_____

_____

_____

_____

_____

Mediation requested by (check one)

☐ Student   ☐ Teacher   ☐ Counselor   ☐ Administrator

☐ Other (specify) _____

Signature of person requesting mediation _____

Figure 3.   Sample peer mediation request form. (From Schrumpf, F., Crawford, D., & Usadel, C. [1991]. *Peer mediation: Conflict resolution in schools.* Champaign, IL: Research Press Company. Reprinted by permission.)

Peer Mediation Agreement

Peer mediator _____ Date _____

Briefly describe the conflict: _____

_____

_____

_____

_____

_____

Type of conflict (check one) ☐ Rumor ☐ Threat ☐ Name-calling ☐ Fighting

☐ Loss of property   ☐ Other (specify) _____

The students whose signatures appear below met with a peer mediator and with the assistance of the mediator reached the following agreement.

Disputant _____

Agrees to _____

_____

_____

Disputant _____

Agrees to _____

_____

_____

We have made and signed this agreement because we believe it resolves the issue(s) between us.

_____   _____
Disputant signature   Disputant signature

_____   _____
Peer mediator signature   Length of mediation (minutes)

Figure 4. Sample peer mediation agreement form. (From Schrumpf, F., Crawford, D., & Usadel, C. [1991]. *Peer mediation: Conflict resolution in schools.* Champaign, IL: Research Press Company. Reprinted by permission.)

sonal examples of how they have each of their needs met and clarifying those conflicts that arise because of limited resources or differing values or cultures.

Next, responses to conflict are explained. Students are asked to think of various conflict situations and formulate possible responses (e.g., avoidance, confrontation, communication).

Section 2: Goal of Mediation and Role of Mediators

The goals of peer mediation are discussed. Mediators learn that disputants need to: 1) learn to understand and respect different views, 2) open and improve communications, 3) develop cooperation in solving a common problem, and 4) reach agreements that address the interests of both sides.

Students become familiar with peer mediation as a noncompetitive approach to solving differences. They learn how trained peer mediators facilitate cooperative (vs. competitive) processes by helping disputants to state honestly what they want and how they feel. The approach is to focus on the problem without blaming the other person.

Roles and qualities of mediators are also taught. Students learn that in all cases peer mediators remain unbiased; they are neutral and do not take sides. Peer mediators are empathic listeners; they listen for understanding of thoughts and feelings. The mediator is respectful and does not judge or show prejudice. The mediator helps people work together and cooperate in order to find their own solutions. Finally, the peer mediator keeps information confidential in order to build trust and confidence in the process. The mediation is not discussed with other students in the school.

Section 3: Communication Skills

The basic communication skills used in mediation are presented in Figure 5. The first skill, active listening, emphasizes the use of nonverbal behaviors (e.g., eye contact, nodding, facial expressions, not interrupting) to show understanding. The second skill, summarizing, involves the mediator restating the main facts and feelings described by the disputants. Summarizing information ensures facts and feelings are heard correctly; it also shows that the mediator listens. The third skill, clarifying, includes asking open-ended questions to gain more information. Because an open-ended question cannot be answered with a "yes" or "no" response, it serves to help all parties better define the problem and develop understanding. Mediators are instructed to avoid giving advice, interrupting, judging, criticizing, or sharing their own conflicts.

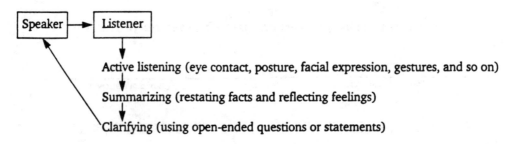

Figure 5.   Communication skills diagram.

Section 4: The Mediation Process

There are six steps to the mediation process, each of which is practiced using role-play situations. Students may generate conflict situations to role-play and/or the trainers may prepare scenarios in advance. Students work in groups of three: two students play disputants and the third is the mediator. Figure 6 summarizes each of the six steps to mediation (Schrumpf et al., 1991). The next section explains each step in more detail.

THE MEDIATION PROCESS

The six-step mediation process employs the problem-solving and communication skills in which peer mediators already have been coached and facilitates students' and teachers' learning of the process.

Mediation Process Summary

Step 1   Open the session

Make introductions
State the ground rules
    1. Mediators remain neutral
    2. Everything said is confidential
    3. No interruptions
    4. Agree to solve the conflict
Get a commitment to the ground rules.

Step 2   Gather information

Ask each person, "Please tell me what happened."
    (Listen and summarize.)
Ask each person, "Do you want to add anything?"
    (Listen, summarize, clarify with questions.)
Repeat until the problem is understood. Summarize.

Step 3   Focus on interests

Determine interests, ask each person:
    "What do you really want?" "Why?"
    "What might happen if you don't reach an agreement?"
    "What do each of you have in common?"
      (Listen, summarize, question.)
Summarize shared interests.
State what disputants have in common.

Step 4   Create options

Brainstorm solutions, ask disputants:
    "What could be done to resolve the problem?"

Step 5   Evaluate options and decide on a solution

Choose a solution; ask each person:
    "Which of these options are you willing to do?"
Restate: "You both agree to . . ."

Step 6   Write an agreement and close

Write the agreement and sign it.
Shake hands.

Figure 6.   Mediation process summary.

Step 1: Open the Session

The mediator sits between the two disputants at a table, makes introductions, and states the ground rules:

"As mediator I remain neutral and do not take sides."
"Each person takes a turn talking with no interruptions."
"Everything said is kept confidential; meaning, what's said in this room stays in this room."

Each person is then asked to agree to the ground rules and commit to try to solve the problem. Once they agree, the mediation begins. If they do not agree, the dispute is referred to an adult.

Step 2: Gather Information

The purpose of this step is to get "the story" from each of the disputant's point of view. The mediator asks each party to tell what happened. The mediator first listens to one person and summarizes what was stated. Next, the other party is asked to tell his or her side of the story. Again, the mediator listens and summarizes relevant information stated. Active listening is very important so each disputant believes he or she is heard and understood. The mediator gives each disputant another chance to clarify and share additional information until the problem is clearly understood and well defined. Many times the mediator will ask clarifying questions such as:

"Is this a long-lasting conflict?"
"Is it a recent problem?"
"Was there a difference in beliefs?"
"Were you friends before?"

The mediator finishes this step by stating the problem.

Step 3: Focus on Interests

The mediator invites the disputants to identify what they want to happen so that the conflict will be resolved. The mediator tries to find common ground by asking questions to each participant, such as:

"What do you really want to happen?" "Why?"
"What might happen if you don't reach an agreement?"
"Is fighting getting you what you really want?"

The mediator listens and summarizes the shared interests and states what the disputants have in common.

Step 4: Create Options

This step involves brainstorming possible solutions. The mediator asks disputants to work together to list as many ideas as possible to solve the conflict. The mediator explains this step as a brainstorming session where ideas are not to be evaluated at that time. The process is to generate a list of new possibilities. It is helpful for the mediator to list the ideas as they are generated. Each party is encouraged to make at least three suggestions. The mediator refrains from making suggestions, as it is important for the disputants to "own" the solution as well as the problem.

Step 5: Evaluate Options and Decide on a Solution

Solutions are evaluated in this step. The mediator asks each disputant which of the listed solutions are acceptable. Often a disputant will say what he or she wants the *other* person to do. When this occurs, the mediator points out that the agreement states what each person is willing to do, not what the other person should do.

Agreed-upon options should be mutually satisfactory to both parties because a balanced agreement is important for a lasting resolution. The solutions should be specific and realistic and include a time frame. Questions that the mediator may ask at this step are:

"Which option is most fair for both of you?"
"Does this help the interests of everyone involved?"
"Can it be done?"
"What will be the results?"

Step 6: Write an Agreement and Close

A mutual agreement is written using a Mediation Agreement form as shown in Figure 4. A written and signed agreement increases the disputants' commitment. In some cases, a written agreement might not be used if mediations are being conducted more informally, such as on a playground. The agreement is signed by both disputants and the mediator. The mediator shakes hands with each person and congratulates them for their efforts. Both parties are then asked to shake hands.

Of course, there are times when an agreement will not be reached. In such cases, an effort is made to get the parties to meet again the next day to continue. In the meantime, a truce to the conflict is called. If an impasse is reached, it may be helpful to talk to each disputant separately. This is called caucusing and the same ground rules apply as for the mediation. A caucus is confidential, so the disputant must agree whether what is discussed may be shared outside of the private session.

CONFLICT RESOLUTION IN ACTION

The following example shows how a peer mediator used the six-step process to cooperatively help two seventh grade students reach an agreement. In this situation, James and Victor were engaged in a loud, threatening argument in the hallway. When a teacher referred them to Jack, a peer mediator, they both agreed to go.

Step 1: Open the Session

Mediator: Hello, my name is Jack and I am the mediator assigned to hold this session. James and Victor, welcome to mediation. Let me explain the ground rules. First, I remain neutral—I do not take sides. Everything said in the mediation is kept confidential. That means what is said in mediation is not discussed outside this room. Each person takes turns talking without interruption. You are expected to do your best to reach an agreement that satisfies both of you. James, do you agree to the rules?
James: Yes.
Mediator: Victor, do you agree to the rules?
Victor: Yeah.

Step 2: Gather Information

Mediator:	James, can you tell what happened?
James:	Victor and I were arguing in the hallway. I am mad at him because he borrowed my basketball during lunch yesterday. When he brought it into school, he was dribbling it in the hallway and a teacher took it from him. Now it's lost and he says he can't get it back.
Mediator:	You're mad at Victor because he lost your basketball and you want it back.
James:	That's right. He was responsible for the ball.
Mediator:	Victor, can you tell what happened?
Victor:	It's true that I borrowed his basketball yesterday during lunch. We all like to shoot baskets after we eat. I was bringing the ball back to his locker after lunch when somebody hit the ball out of my hands and it bounced on the floor until Mr. Thomas picked it up. It wasn't my fault it was lost.
Mediator:	You borrowed the ball and when returning it, someone hit it from your hands. That's when Mr. Thomas took it.
Victor:	Yeah, and Mr. Thomas is very strict and he says we won't get it until the end of the year.
Mediator:	James, do you have anything to add?
James:	That was a new ball and I thought we were friends, but now he is just ignoring me.
Mediator:	So, you and Victor are friends and you don't want to be ignored when there's a problem.
James:	Right.
Mediator:	Victor, do you have anything to add?
Victor:	I don't mean to ignore James, but I don't like to be yelled at in the hallways.
Mediator:	So you are willing to talk to James to work this out?
Victor:	Sure.

Step 3: Focus on Interests

Mediator:	James, what do you really want to happen here?
James:	I want my ball back.
Mediator:	Beyond your ball, is there anything else?
James:	Yeah, I want to be friends with Victor.

The conversation continues until it is clear that both boys want to be friends and that they both have a common interest (e.g., they want the ball back so they can use it at lunch). At first the source of the conflict seems to be over a limited resource (the basketball); however, at closer look, it really is over trying to meet the basic psychological needs of "belonging" and "fun." When the mediator identifies this common ground, Step 3 is complete.

Step 4: Create Options

Mediator:	What are possible ways to solve the problem with the ball and keep your friendship?

Victor and James brainstormed a list that includes:

Both boys going to Mr. Thomas to explain what happened.
Both boys going to the principal to explain what happened.
Victor giving James his ball until school is out.
Victor giving Mr. Thomas his ball to hold until the end of the year.
James accepting an apology and forgetting the ball for now.

Step 5: Evaluate Options and Decide on a Solution

Mediator: Which of these ideas will probably work best for you?

Victor and James both respond with ideas they believe are the best solutions to the conflict. The boys agree to talk first to Mr. Thomas. After their explanation, if he does not return the ball, Victor agrees to offer his ball to James.

Step 6: Write an Agreement and Close

The mediator writes an agreement to be as specific, realistic, and balanced as possible. The mediator signs it and shakes hands with both Victor and James. Finally, the mediator asks both boys to sign and to shake hands.

This process took about 20 minutes. The boys made a plan and did not lose their friendship. The mediator assisted with the plan, but it was really generated by the two disputants and the process was cooperative and structured.

PROGRAM EVALUATION AND EFFECTIVENESS

How do we evaluate peer mediation? How might it make an educational environment more peaceful? Clearly, program evaluation is critical to sustaining support for a peer mediation program. Communication, negotiation, and compromise are life skills people practice and improve over years and learn through the mediation process in the classroom. Use of these skills outside the classroom may be reported by students, parents, and friends.

As already mentioned, records that indicate the type of conflict, location of conflict, names of students, and agreement reached for each dispute should be shared quarterly and annually with staff and other interested school community members. Schrumpf et al. (1991) described a middle school in Illinois with a population of approximately 1,000 students (25% African-American, 70% white, 5% Asian) that collected some important and interesting data. During the 1989–1990 school year, 245 conflicts were resolved through peer mediation. Slightly more than half (51%) of the requests for mediation were from students, with other referrals from teachers (27%) and administrators (22%). Of the disputes resolved, 31% were between males, 43% were between females, and 26% were conflicts between males and females. Disputes between white students accounted for 47% of the total, whereas disputes between African-American students accounted for 26%. A total of 27% of the conflicts were between different races. One in every 10 disputants were interviewed 1 month after an agreement was reached and asked if the process had been satisfactory and if the agreement had held. As Figure 7 shows, the results of the evaluations were extremely positive. The number of requests for mediation increased by approximately 25% from the initial semester to the next and referrals from administrators doubled.

Common Ground, the peer mediation program at the Urbana, Illinois, Middle School, began in September 1989 and operated through May 1990. During that time, peer mediators resolved 245 conflicts between students.

Records were kept and the information totaled. Information was tallied from school records and from Peer Mediation Request and Peer Mediation Agreement forms. Disputants from 1 in every 10 cases were interviewed a month after the agreement and asked if the process had been satisfactory and if the agreement had held.

Slightly over half of the requests for peer mediation (51 percent) were from students. Other referrals came from teachers (27 percent) and principals (22 percent). Of the disputes resolved, 31 percent were between males and 43 percent were between females. A total of 26 percent were conflicts between males and females. Disputes between white students accounted for 47 percent of the total, while disputes between black students accounted for 26 percent. A total of 27 percent of the conflicts were between students of different races.

The causes of conflict and their resolutions were reported as follows.

Name-calling	26 percent	Resolved at a 98 percent success rate
Rumors	23 percent	Resolved at a 100 percent success rate
Hitting/fighting	16 percent	Resolved at a 100 percent success rate
Other (lost or damaged property, relationship problems, etc.)	35 percent	Resolved at a 93 percent success rate

The number of requests for mediation increased approximately 25 percent from the previous semester. Referrals from administrators almost doubled from the previous year. Both these figures suggest increased support for and perception of the effectiveness of the program.

Figure 7.   Annual evaluation summary. (From Schrumpf, F., Crawford, D., & Usadel, C. [1991]. *Peer mediation: Conflict resolution in schools.* Champaign, IL: Research Press Company. Reprinted by permission.)

In New York City, where students were trained in conflict resolution skills (Meek, 1992), the program was rated as effective on a survey conducted of 130 teachers. Of the classroom teachers, 71% reported a reduction of physical violence in the classroom, 66% heard less name-calling and verbal put-downs, and 69% saw increased student willingness to cooperate with each other.

Some schools also were able to correlate the peer mediation program with improved school attendance and a decrease in fights, student suspensions, and vandalism. A commitment to resolve conflicts in a different way clearly resulted in positive schoolwide changes.

PEACEMAKING IN A GLOBAL CONTEXT

Conflicts will always occur as long as people live, work, and play together. That is good because conflicts are teachable moments—opportunities to better understand differences that exist between people and the common ground that they share. Peer mediation is a democratic, cooperative approach for resolving conflicts that appears to be effective in getting students to become more invested in their learning environment.

Through peer mediation, students learn how to resolve their own conflicts—a responsible and empowering action that may be generalized from two individuals to the world of nations. Learning to resolve conflicts with peers has the potential of promoting peace today and in future generations.

REFERENCES

Cheatham, A. (1989). Peaceful playgrounds. *Woman of Power, 10,* 24–29.

Drew, N. (1987). *Learning the skills of peacemaking.* Rolling Hills Estates, CA: Jalmar Press.

Glasser, W. (1986). *Control theory in the classroom.* New York: Harper & Row.

Glasser, W. (1990). *The quality school.* New York: Harper & Row.

Johnson, D., Johnson, R., Dudley, B., & Burnett, R. (1992). Teaching students to be peer mediators. *Educational Leadership, 50*(1), 10–13.

Johnson, D.W., & Johnson, R. (1991a). *Creative controversy: Intellectual challenge in the classroom.* Edina, MN: Interaction Book Company.

Johnson, D.W., & Johnson, R. (1991b). *Teaching students to be peacemakers.* Edina, MN: Interaction Book Company.

Kreidler, W. (1984). *Creative conflict resolution.* Glenview, IL: Scott, Foresman.

Kreidler, W. (1990). *Teaching concepts of peace and conflict.* Cambridge, MA: Educators for Social Responsibility.

McDonald, S., & Moriarty, A. (1990). The Rich East High School mediation project. *School Social Work Journal, 14,* 25–32.

Meek, M. (1992, Fall). The peacekeepers. *Teaching Tolerance,* 46–52.

Millhauser, M. (1989). Gladiators and conciliators. *The Legal Reformer, 9*(2), 17–20.

Sadalla, G., Holmberg, M., & Halligan, J. (1990). *Conflict resolution: An elementary school curriculum.* San Francisco: Community Boards, Inc.

Schrumpf, F., Crawford D., & Usadel, C. (1991). *Peer mediation: Conflict resolution in schools.* Champaign, IL: Research Press.

Woolner, C. (1992). *Rethinking mediation: Living peacefully in a multicultural world.* Amherst, MA: National Association of Mediation in Education.

CHRISTINE'S INCLUSION

AN EXAMPLE OF PEERS SUPPORTING ONE ANOTHER

Tracy Harris

When Christine made a presentation before 200 parents, teachers, and administrators, she stumbled slightly. The stumble came as she read something she had written 3 years earlier and decided to make a modification. "I have . . . *nothing* . . . and I'm not handicapped," the 19-year-old proclaimed and immediately received a well-earned round of applause.

The applause came when the audience read the 3-year-old article, projected overhead on a screen, that Christine had written in her school newspaper. In that article, she explained, "I have Down syndrome, but I'm not handicapped." The adaptation described above represents Christine's anger at the labels placed upon her and her own refusal to accept the limitations that some labels imply.

This chapter describes some of the highlights of Christine's 4-year journey through high school. An emphasis is placed upon the peer supports that made her full inclusion into a public high school possible. More specifically, the relationships between Christine and those who became her tutors, tutees, friends, advocates, and recipients of her advocacy are described.

FRESHMAN YEAR

Christine enrolled as a freshman at Winooski High School shortly before the start of the 1988–1989 school year. Christine, her mother, and several teachers had 6 days to nervously plan for her transition from a segregated special education class in a public school in a neighboring town. What that group soon realized was that Christine's future classmates would play a critical role in making her transition to Winooski a successful one.

Christine's story opens 2 days before the 1988–1989 school year following a meeting of Christine's mother, former teachers, and a team of Winooski teachers. What was learned at that point was that Christine was a 14-year-old student with Down syndrome who had been educated in segregated public school environments for all of her previous public school years. Christine's mother described her as outgoing, but stubborn. She further explained that she intended to have her daughter graduate with a high school diploma so that she could go on to college. Christine's former teachers described her as a student with academic skills at approximately the second to third grade level. They also described a variety of motor, speech, and behavioral challenges that they had addressed throughout Christine's elementary school years. As a team of Winooski teachers reviewed this information and designed a ninth grade schedule to fit her needs, Christine toured the campus.

Christine's tour ended when she happened to notice several girls engaged in cheerleading practice. After stopping dead in her tracks and watching for a few moments, Christine announced, "I want to do that." One day and several telephone calls later, Christine was to learn that cheerleading try-outs had already occurred and the team had been selected. There was, however, an opening for the position of manager; Christine eagerly accepted the opportunity to fill that slot.

Christine's role as manager for the cheerleading squad included attending practices and "cheering on" the cheerleaders. She assisted in making posters for the hallways, announcing upcoming games, and spreading "school spirit." Christine also attended each varsity game, wearing the same sweater as the rest of the squad and keeping close watch over each girl's personal belongings. When the squad entered a statewide competition, Christine accompanied them to the finals and shared in their pride by walking away with the state championship title. The key ring that she and each team member received as their trophies remains one of Christine's most valued possessions.

According to other members of the cheerleading team, Christine's role was invaluable. "Even on the most dreary of days, when I felt like skipping out of practice, Christine picked me up," stated Jen. "She's that kind of person who can make you smile" (J. Dion, personal communication, October, 1989). Stephanie, another member of the squad, said, "Christine has taught me that nothing's too far out of reach. When I think that I'll never be able to do the splits or ace an English test, I think of her. Just walking up the stairs is a challenge to her and she faces that with determination day after day" (S. Picard, personal communication, October, 1989). Christine's coach remarked that Christine's presence on the squad added an extra element of sportsmanship and unity.

Likewise, becoming a member of a cheerleading squad has had innumerable payoffs for Christine. As a newcomer to our school who looked, talked, learned, and acted differently than many, Christine might easily have been forced *apart* from her peers. Her membership with this group served to make her *a part* of our school community. This is not to say that Christine was widely accepted by all members of our student body. Indeed, several students delighted in calling her names, mocking her idiosyncratic behavior, and enticing her to behave inappropriately. This rarely occurred, however, without one member of the cheerleading squad coming to Christine's defense and chastising those who criticized her. As in most schools, the members of the cheerleading squad were generally deemed to have "high social status" and a large group of friends. As Christine became more familiar to the friends of her new friends, her social support network widened and incidences of teasing decreased. By the end of her freshman year, it was not at all uncommon to hear numerous greetings and exchanges of "high fives" whenever Christine walked through the hallways.

At the close of Christine's freshman year at Winooski High School, she carried with her six credits toward graduation and a delightful group of friends. Her articulation had improved as a result of repetitive drill and practice of the cheers bellowed by her teammates, all of whom concentrated on proper enunciation. Fine motor needs had been targeted in keyboarding and home economics classes; gross motor activities had been addressed in the freshman physical education class. Modifications and accommodations to the regular science curriculum had enabled Christine to acquire personal safety and health skills in inclusive classes. Also, her reading, writing, and math skills had been addressed through a variety of community-based activities. By extending our classroom walls to the community, Christine's social network had expanded to include local merchants, postal clerks, and bus drivers.

Christine's "acting-out" behaviors, although decreased, were still considered in need of improvement. Her behavior had been managed through a written contract implemented by all of her ninth grade teachers and reinforced by classmates. They all learned to ignore what was considered inappropriate, to respectfully address that which was intolerable, and to praise the desired behaviors targeted on her individualized education program (IEP).

At the annual IEP review meeting, Christine's mother took interest in what teachers had to say about progress relative to the goals targeted in the IEP document, but her measure of progress extended beyond what was cited in this document. The goals for which she measured progress during the freshman year took the form of conversations with familiar faces in the grocery store, telephone calls from classmates reminding Christine of upcoming dances and other events, vocabulary growth that included the current slang and jargon of most teens, a surge of self-esteem promoted by warming the bench at each varsity game, and a better understanding of the "natural consequences" for her daughter's "stubborn streak" that included detentions and comments on report cards.

SOPHOMORE YEAR

Christine faced a difficult decision at the start of her second year at Winooski High School. She, along with other members of her IEP team, was exploring employment opportunities. When she was offered a job at a nearby pizza house, she discovered that her hours on the job would conflict with cheerleading practice. After much consideration, she chose to pursue the job and leave her position as manager of the cheerleading squad. It did not take long, however, for Christine to find group membership—and a voice—through other channels.

To earn an English credit toward graduation, Christine participated in a journalism course that year. The members of this class were responsible for the production of the weekly school newspaper. This activity involved a great deal of team work during and beyond the regular class meeting time, where two or more students "paired up" on assignments. Because it took Christine up to five times longer to complete an assignment than other students, her teachers and the student editor sought a full-time "partner" for her. Cathryn, a fellow journalist who also happened to have study hall the same period as Christine, volunteered to fill that need. The two worked together during class twice each week and in the computer lab every day during their study hall to produce "Christine's Corner," a weekly column featuring the unique accomplishments of various students in the school. Each Thursday, the entire class came together in a frenzy to meet deadlines and put the finishing touches on the paper before it went to press. Fridays, too, demanded unity in the form of critiques and celebration following distribution of the paper. The tasks and arrangements from this class paved the way for naturally occurring friendships.

Bubba, a gregarious junior and key player for the school's football, hockey, and baseball teams, was among those who formed an especially strong bond with Christine. As a result of his fondness for Christine, Bubba opened his eyes to others in the school who faced challenges and volunteered his time to serve as a "peer buddy" and "peer tutor" for several younger students.

Bubba's affiliation with Christine and other students helped him in much the same way as it helped the cheerleader who put her own challenges into perspective. "I sweat and bleed on the field, but the work I do in athletics can't even come close to the realities that they face doing everyday tasks," Bubba remarked (C. Ritchie, personal communication, July, 1989). Bubba's coaches observed a newfound tolerance and acceptance on his part for teammates not as gifted as himself. Other teachers recognized a change as well. "I used to see him as a jock who never looked past Friday's game," explained one teacher. "Now I notice a young man with empathy and a sense of responsibility for others" (J. DeFilippi, personal communication, September, 1989). Bubba's father was, perhaps, the most delighted with his son's actions and insights. "Bubba's never had a direction in his life and now, for the first time ever, he's talking about college and a career in special education. No touchdown, hat trick, or home run could make me prouder," he said (C. Ritchie, personal communication, May, 1990).

Later that year, Bubba was asked to speak to a gathering of people in Canada. His talk was made in support of a young woman named Becky who was forbidden from entering public school because she was considered to be too disabled. When Christine learned of Bubba's actions and Becky's plight, she decided to highlight Becky in that week's edition of "Christine's Corner."

Becky Belongs

By Christine Durovich

Knock it off! Knock it off! Becky is a girl who has cerebral palsy and lives near Toronto. She's not allowed in school because of her handicaps. I think her school should just knock it off and let her in.

She needs an education. Just because she is handicapped doesn't mean she can't learn. She's just got to do what she can do, which can be just about anything.

Becky is smart enough to fight back, just like I would if I wasn't allowed in school. I have Down Syndrome and I can still do anything I want to do. If I wasn't allowed in school, I wouldn't have learned to do all the things I do now. *I have Down Syndrome, but I'm not handicapped.*

I say Becky belongs in school, so knock it off and let her learn. (Durovich, 1990)

Christine's article represents not only her first public acknowledgment of her own strengths and challenges, but a courageous act of advocacy. Her article was well received by students and teachers, who then felt more comfortable discussing her range of abilities openly. Because of Christine's article, several people asked how they might help Becky or others like her.

Christine's sophomore year represented continued academic, behavioral, and social growth. She maintained relationships with the cheerleaders she had befriended the year before and continued to attend varsity games as a spectator. The new friends she met in journalism class joined her widening circle of friends and Cathryn, her writing partner, joined her IEP team as a peer advocate.

Christine's speech goals were incorporated into her behavioral contract, which was again managed by her classroom teachers. When her hours on the job and, consequently, her paycheck were tied to appropriate speech and behavior, gradual improvement was noted. Christine's fine and gross motor programs were incorporated into her job and were addressed also during art and computer classes. As Christine's computer literacy and motivation to get published each week increased, her written language skills soared. Her math program was tied to the banking, budgeting, and spending of her paychecks.

Christine's self-esteem continued to grow with successful paid employment and the notoriety attained with having one's byline read by others each week.

JUNIOR YEAR

During her junior year at Winooski High School, Christine chose, as some upperclassmen do, to enroll in a half-day vocational program. Her mornings were spent in classes at school and, rather than entering one of the area vocational-technical centers, Christine spent her afternoons at a work site in the community. It became important for those planning her educational program to maintain a sense of belonging for Christine in high school while building a network outside of school in environments to which she would transition after graduation. With the input of Christine and her friends, a process for planning Christine's transition to "post high school" life was initiated.

In addition to Christine's IEP team, a transition team was formed and met quarterly to begin planning for Christine's life beyond graduation. Christine, her mother, her special education support services coordinator, the school's employment specialist, and Cathryn (Christine's journalism partner and peer advocate) were core members of the transition team. Extended team members included various adult service providers who were routinely invited to attend meetings. After a series of goal-setting exercises, the team began to plan for Christine's transition to adulthood. Positive outcomes of the team's work included the completion of the application process for vocational rehabilitation services, Christine's placement on the waiting lists for several adult programs (e.g., independent living services), and increased awareness of programs and services available in the community.

As the transition process evolved, it became clear that leaving high school and "letting go" of the familiar was very frightening to Christine. Cathryn was the one to communicate to the team just how threatening that process was for Christine, as well as for herself. Cathryn played a critical role in bringing a student's perspective to issues, voicing the concerns that Christine might not have been able to articulate herself, preparing Christine for these meetings ahead of time, and processing with her afterward. She suggested strategies that adults might not have considered. Cathryn, who was equally threatened about applying to colleges and universities, also benefited from participation on Christine's transition team. "I face different challenges than Christine," explained Cathryn, "but I realized that to achieve our goals, we both have to do a lot of planning. I might have waited until it was too late if I hadn't seen the planning required for Christine's program" (C. Blanchard, personal communication, December, 1992).

Academically, Christine and Cathryn enrolled as second-year journalism students and resumed their collaboration. Cathryn had also arranged to receive credit as a peer tutor for Christine during her study hall. Cathryn's responsibilities included planning, implementing, and evaluating daily lessons designed to assist Christine in completing her health, journalism, and history assignments. She met weekly with her supervisor (a special educator who coordinated Christine's educational services), kept a journal, and learned Madeline Hunter's model of effective teaching (Hunter, 1988a, 1988b, 1988c, 1988d, 1988e). With Christine as her "tutee," Cathryn embarked on what would be her future career as a teacher. Cathryn reported, "Not many kids my age get to sample the job that they hope to have five or six years down the road. Thanks to Christine, I get to do that. My transcript and portfolio will show that I've chosen this as an individualized course of study and that should help me to get into the college I want" (C. Blanchard, personal communication, June, 1991).

Christine was extremely appreciative of Cathryn's support. She stated, "It's boring having my teachers all day. I like having Cathryn as my tutor because we're friends and she is fun." In reference to Cathryn's role on her transition team, Christine explained, "I get scared. I don't know all those people and sometimes I cry. That's why Cathryn helps me. She tells me it's okay and she will stick up for me. After those meetings, we go to McDonald's and talk it over" (C. Durovich, personal communication, June, 1991).

As much as Christine enjoyed her tutor–tutee relationship with Cathryn, she also wanted to reverse that arrangement so that she, too, was in the helping role. Christine did not have the content knowledge to assist Cathryn in all of her academic courses, so we looked for opportunities elsewhere. What resulted was a weekly health lesson that Christine team-taught with a third grade teacher. Christine applied the knowledge she was acquiring in her eleventh grade health course to the personal safety unit offered to this class of 8-year-olds. Christine then evaluated her own performance by summarizing the lessons and their outcomes to Cathryn, who planned to be an elementary school teacher. "I learned from Christine what worked and didn't work for little kids," Cathryn relayed. "By sharing her experiences with me, she helped me to see that younger students have shorter attention spans. I'll remember that some day when I have a class of my own" (C. Blanchard, personal communication, June, 1991).

Christine's junior year at Winooski High School represented a fermentation of old relationships combined with the scary process of meeting new people who helped her to explore her future. Her speech and behavioral goals were tied again to her employment. Christine made extra efforts to improve her articulation and model appropriate behavior for the third graders that she taught each week. Her skills in all academic areas progressed steadily.

SENIOR YEAR

Christine concluded her career at Winooski High School with a senior year marked by intensive transition planning, continued employment, and cementing of friendships. Her school days resembled those of her junior year, with morning classes and afternoon employment.

Christine's academic classes included two courses required by the district for all seniors (i.e., government and life issues), another computer course, and her "structured study hall" with Cathryn. Christine continued to benefit from Cathryn's instruction and Cathryn's teaching skills advanced to higher levels. The year was unique for Cathryn, who was 1 year behind Christine in school, in that she was reinforcing concepts from classes that she had not yet taken. "I learn things so thoroughly when I have to teach them. The two senior classes that Christine took were difficult for all kids and I feel lucky because next year I'll have already been exposed to the material," she said (C. Blanchard, personal communication, April, 1992).

Christine's transition team now met monthly in an effort to realize the dream of college that her mother had articulated a few days prior to Christine's start at Winooski in 1988. Christine was certain to earn her diploma in June. Therefore, the transition team began pursuing her application to and enrollment in Trinity College, a small, 4-year college in nearby Burlington. Trinity's Enhance Program offered Christine an opportunity to enroll in courses suited to her skills, to audit any other courses in which she was interested, and to pair her with another coed on campus who would include her in various aspects of residential life. When Christine was accepted into this program midway through her senior year at Winooski High School, she was immediately paired with Gail, the Trinity student who would serve as her advocate on campus. Christine and Cathryn met Gail, who then began to attend the monthly transition meetings. Any hesitation Christine felt regarding her decision to pursue postsecondary education dissolved when she visited Gail's dormitory. Reminiscent of her proclamation when observing the cheerleading practice, Christine took in the atmosphere of dorm life and claimed, "I want to live here!"

As graduation day approached, Christine, her mother, Cathryn, and many others began to feel a mix of emotions. Christine frequently became emotional and there was a regression in her social behavior. Like many students stricken with "senioritis," Christine was having a difficult time accepting her departure from the place she'd grown to love. Of particular concern was the graduation ceremony itself; the fear was that Christine might become overwhelmed with emotion and disrupt the ceremony. The transition team convened and brainstormed strategies to support Christine in the situation and to identify peers who could provide Christine with the extra support she might need. Bubba had graduated during Christine's junior year, Cathryn was still a junior, and several of Christine's fellow seniors had extra roles and responsibilities during commencement exercises. When Josh's name was suggested, several team members raised their eyebrows questioningly. Josh, a "class clown," had faced many challenges himself. He had fallen short in credits, had faced several disciplinary actions, and was earning his diploma by the skin of his teeth. He also was one of Christine's dearest friends. As freshmen, it was he and Christine who initiated the "high five" greetings between classes. His penchant for writing rock lyrics earned him his own spot on the school newspaper staff, and they shared that interest. When Christine stayed after school for detentions, she and Josh formed a bond there as well.

After much discussion, the transition team approached Josh and the senior class advisor about having Christine and him sit together at the graduation ceremony. Josh was happy to sit with his friend and many people felt that his lighthearted and humorous personality was ideally suited to combat any overwhelming emotions Christine might feel. The strategy worked well. On graduation day, Christine did cry a bit; however, she found a willing shoulder to lean upon and a few hushed comments that put a smile back on her face. In the end, Christine received her diploma with the same mix of joy, pride, sadness, and trepidation as the other members of her class.

CONCLUSION

It has been said that what goes around comes around, and I feel extremely fortunate to have coordinated Christine's educational services throughout her 4-year journey through Winooski High School. Christine, in my opinion, is a remarkable woman who has freely shared her thoughts and feelings with others. In return, she has been the recipient of support, respect, and unabashed admiration from some of the most unsuspecting and extraordinary adolescents I have known. She and her friends have taught me that camaraderie and common sense are far more useful than a master's degree and that some of the best educational resources come free of charge.

I welcome the opportunity each June to engage in reflective thought as I attend commencement exercises and bid another class of students farewell. I think I was in good company during the 1992 commencement exercises at Winooski High School when I felt more than the usual mix of emotion watching one woman cross the threshold to adulthood.

Just before the band readied themselves for a final round of *Pomp and Circumstance*, the senior class advisor rose to address Winooski High School's Class of 1992 one last time. Her gift was an *a cappella* version of a popular rock song lamenting farewells. As I scanned the crowd of green and white gowns, I noticed Josh's hand resting in Christine's lap, their fists clenched together as if to ward off the tears threatening to stream down each of their faces. It was not at all clear to me at that moment who was supporting whom.

COLCHESTER—Christine Durovich, 21, of Westward Drive passed away Friday, Dec. 10, 1993, at the Medical Center Hospital of Vermont following a brief illness.

Christine was born Oct. 5, 1972, in Burlington, the beloved daughter of Peter and Lorraine (Chicoine) Durovich. Christine was a remarkable young woman who had a profound impact on the lives of everyone with whom she interacted. Although her life was short, she lived it like a bright comet racing across the sky. In many ways, Christine was a pioneer. She was one of the first young people with Down syndrome to be totally integrated into school, community and family life. Regardless of the activity in which she was involved—as a cheerleader, student at Trinity College, employee, or as a volunteer in Winooski School District's preschool program—Christine brought enthusiasm, humor, curiosity, advocacy and a love of others to all that she did. Through her life and actions, Christine brought many gifts to her family, friends, teachers and students with differing abilities as well as their families. She presented at educational conferences across the United States and Canada and inspired many people to see beyond disabilities and to see and realize the possibilities. Christine will live in the hearts and minds of all who knew and admired her and some of the lessons that she taught will be featured in an upcoming book for educators. Thank you, Christine, for being a part of our lives and making the world a better place.

Christine is survived by her mother, Lorraine Durovich of Colchester; her father, Peter Durovich of Stowe; two very loving and caring brothers, John Durovich of

Salt Lake City, Utah, and David Durovich of Colchester; her special grandmother and best buddy, Mrs. Alice Chicoine of Winooski; several aunts, uncles, cousins, and a great many beautiful friends.

Christine's determination, spirit, humor and caring for others will live on and on. We will dearly miss her, as will all who have had the privilege to know her.

—Richard A. Villa

This picture was taken in July of 1993. Christine with her colleagues and friends presented at the McGill Summer Institute in Integrated Community and School, McGill University, Montreal, Quebec, Canada. First Row: Cathryn Blanchard, Christine Durovich, Conrad "Bubba" Ritchie. Second Row: Jacque Thousand, Rich Villa, Lorraine Durovich.

REFERENCES

Durovich, C. (1990, February 9). Becky belongs. *Spartan Warrior*, p. 2.

Hunter, M. (1988a). *Motivation theory for teachers*. El Segundo, CA: Theory into Practice Publications.

Hunter, M. (1988b). *Reinforcement theory for teachers*. El Segundo, CA: Theory into Practice Publications.

Hunter, M. (1988c). *Retention theory for teachers*. El Segundo, CA: Theory into Practice Publications.

Hunter, M. (1988d). *Teach for transfer*. El Segundo, CA: Theory into Practice Publications.

Hunter, M. (1988e). *Teach more—faster!* El Segundo, CA: Theory into Practice Publications.

COOPERATIVELY CREATING NEW RESPONSES AND NEW BEHAVIORS

AWARENESS PLANS FOR FACILITATING CREATIVE THINKING

Herbert L. Leff,
Jacqueline S. Thousand,
and Ann I. Nevin

Our school has made a commitment to serving *all* children regardless of their needs and gifts through teaching teams of educators who used to work apart from one another (e.g., classroom teachers, special educators, guidance personnel). Our challenge is that we have no time scheduled for us to meet so that we can plan and evaluate our students' and our own performance.

Johnnie doesn't seem to be motivated by anything I am doing in my classroom. I am concerned that he will start acting out or simply choose to stop coming to school. In what ways might I adapt the curriculum, change my instructional approach, or engage Johnnie's classmates in idea finding so that Johnnie becomes more involved in class? It is critical that whatever we do, Johnnie does not stand out from the rest of the kids.

Our new teaching team has been meeting regularly every other day for 6 weeks now. We are having a number of problems with the behavior of team members. One member, for example, dominates the discussions and fails to listen carefully to the needs and concerns of the other teachers. Another member is chronically late for meetings. And most of the members seem to shoot down every suggestion before we can figure out how to make it feasible. What can we do to deal with these small-group interpersonal issues and make our team more effective?

These are but three of the many challenges encountered by teams and individuals attempting to create caring and effective educational experiences for children and adults. Left unsolved, any of these situations could lead those involved to throw in the towel—to give up on a student or a promising innovation. The good news is that there are numerous strategies for enhancing the creative spirit, thinking, and developing actions of an individual or a team so that effective solutions to challenges such as these can be more readily found. This chapter is about how to promote creativity in human imagination and actions, with creativity defined simply as the process of being "productive, . . . imaginative" (*Webster's New Collegiate Dictionary*, 1973, p. 276), and inventive.

Throughout this chapter, these authors will rely upon a conceptual tool called an *awareness plan* (Leff, 1984) to discuss creative thinking strategies. An awareness plan is simply one's mental procedure for selecting and processing information. Clearly, any thinking activity uses some awareness plan. However, people usually do not consciously think about or deliberately select the way in which to process information, examine issues, or explore possible actions in response to a problem (see also Leff, 1978).

Leff and Nevin (1990; Nevin & Leff, 1991) emphasized that children and adults can increase their creative thinking capacity by learning and practicing a variety of new awareness plans. To illustrate this point, several different awareness plans from the book *Playful Perception* (Leff, 1984) can be applied to Johnnie's challenging situation described at the beginning of this chapter. In response to the motivational concerns expressed by Johnnie's teacher, the awareness plan of *viewing everything in school and the classroom as alive* could be tried. Thinking of school in this way certainly would add fun and flexibility to the search for ideas. Another awareness plan— *searching for the most boring* things in the classroom and then identifying what is interesting about them—might help Johnnie's teacher to more closely tune into what *is* happening in her educational environment and to discover untapped possibilities. As for the third scenario described earlier about team difficulties (i.e., members quickly judging and discarding suggestions), it might be enlightening for them to exaggerate even further their tendency to judge by engaging in an *orgy of evaluation* (using many different criteria for judging) and, afterward, discussing the potential negative effects of judgment on team productivity.

Barriers to creative thinking and action abound, particularly in group situations. Summarized in Table 1 are thoughts and actions identified by Adams (1986) as common barriers to the creativity of teams. Clearly, learning new ways of thinking takes commitment and energy. In fact, a subtle, but pervasive, barrier to creativity *is* the amount of mental effort and intellectual commitment it takes to learn and practice anything new or unfamiliar.

A TOOLBOX FOR CREATIVE THINKING AND ACTION

What follows is a toolbox with tools that break down the barriers to creativity. All of the awareness plans are drawn from *Playful Perception* (Leff, 1984) and the discussion builds directly on the presentation in that book. The first dozen tools presented are awareness plans for *imagining an improvement* and formulating actions to accomplish the improvement. Following these are awareness plans that capitalize upon the "two heads are better than one" phenomenon known as *synergy*, in which contributions reinforce each other to create a "total effect [that] is greater than the sum of the effects taken independently" (*Webster's New Collegiate Dictionary*, 1973, p. 1183). This second set of tools is intended for use by teams of people. The third and last set of

Table 1. Actions and thoughts that discourage creativity

Insisting on early precision and being correct	Supporting confusion, ambiguity, or uncertainty
Cross examining	Pointing out only the flaws
Misinterpreting, arguing, or challenging	Not listening
Reacting negatively, discounting, or putting down	Being dominant and in command
Being cynical, skeptical, or noncommittal	Ordering, directing, threatening, or warning
Disapproving, preaching, or moralizing	Taking the "ball away from" another
Being critical, judgmental, or pessimistic	Correcting
Blaming, name-calling	Getting angry, scaring others
Being competitive, making fun of others	Demanding
Acting distant, not joining in, or using silence to work against others	Assuming it cannot be done
	Putting the burden of proof on "others"
Setting up win-lose conflicts	

Adapted from Adams (1986).

tools includes *basic enlightenment* awareness plans that may be employed by teams or individuals. "Basic enlightenment," as defined by Leff (1984, p. 103), refers to a way of experiencing events (including problems) so as to maximize personal fulfillment and joy, which, in turn, should enhance outcomes of the experience (including the solutions to problems).

A Dozen Awareness Plans for Imagining Improvements and Planning for Change

Throughout every day, each one of us imagines improvements in our lives and surroundings. We imagine improving our personal relationships, making our homes more comfortable and attractive places to live, and creating a more harmonious country and world. Educators and others concerned with education and student learning are asked and expected to imagine beneficial changes in curriculum, instruction, classroom management, school governance, individual student programs, teacher collaboration, and many other organizational and instructional issues. It is common to imagine improvements. What is not common is to deliberately use awareness plans to stimulate new and novel ideas that lead to action.

The power of the dozen awareness plans for imagining improvement, represented in Figure 1, is that they address some common barriers to creative thinking by helping to:

Break traditional and usual assumptions about what is and is not possible (e.g., #2: Ask, "What if . . .?" questions; #4: Think of unusual, nutty things; #6: Use magic-wand wishes as guides to feasible ideas).

Take on new and different perspectives (e.g., #7: Take on different roles of people, animals, things; #8: Use all senses and emotions).

Think of unusual and new combinations (e.g., #3: Reverse goals, #11: Form new mental connections; #12: Invent games that inspire your thinking).

Generate lots of ideas (e.g., #5: Force yourself to think of many alternative ideas; #10: Break the problem into subproblems).

Go beyond merely correcting a problem to thinking of potential positive possibilities (e.g., #9: Define the goal in different ways).

Remember, the more quickly these aids are incorporated into your automatic thinking and problem-solving repertoire, the sooner and more often you can try them out. Although a dozen awareness plans are offered, even one can be enough to help

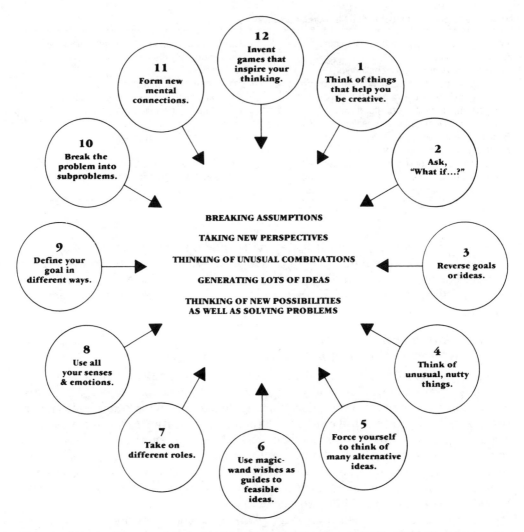

Figure 1.   A dozen awareness plans for imagining improvements. (From Leff, H.L. [1984]. *Playful perception: Choosing how to experience your world.* Burlington, VT: Waterfront Books; Copyright © by Waterfront Books, Inc., and Herbert L. Leff; reprinted by permission.)

with a problem. Experimentation will inform you as to which works best for you and which works best with the adults and students with whom you collaborate.

   1. Think of Everything that Helps You to Be Creative   When is your creativity boosted? During what activities are you most inventive in your thinking? What feelings, which people, and what states of mind help you to be creative? After you have made a list, your awareness plan is to put yourself into a creative frame of mind for imagining improvements by either: 1) vividly imagining experiencing each of these things, or 2) actually doing the things that prompt your creative spirit. Things that may enhance creativity are:

Exercising	Sailing	Running
Falling asleep	Waking up	Meditating
Sitting by the ocean	Reading poetry	Listening to classical music

Feeling independent	Feeling confident	Being playful
Thinking out loud	Not straining	Not fearing criticism
Becoming immersed in the problem	Acting and talking crazy with a "best" friend or colleague	

2. Use "What if . . . ?" Questions to Challenge Usual Assumptions and Expectations One purpose of the "What if . . .?" awareness plan is to remove limitations and expectations that we consciously or unconsciously assume must be in operation in situations we are trying to change. This strategy is particularly effective and energizing when used with a group of people. Suppose, for example, that you are a member of a team charged with imagining improvements in the community's school building and playground. Questions that might help the team to abandon the usual assumptions of what a school "looks like" are:

What if nothing could touch the floor?
What if rooms had three or four levels?
What if the building and rooms allowed for dancing, leaping, jumping, and running to occur at a moment's notice?
What if only people with no sight (or no hearing) were to use the building and the playground?
What if infants and toddlers attended school daily?
What if senior citizens, some of whom use wheelchairs, were part of the school staff or student body?

Each of the questions should trigger ideas for new "What if . . .?" questions as well as novel and nontraditional changes—hanging ornamentation and furnishings from the ceiling, having furniture fold out of the walls, having all furniture on wheels, having walls that recede into the ceiling, relying primarily on soft furniture, having wide doors that automatically recede into the walls when people and objects approach, having the playground indoors as an integral part of the school.

"What if . . .?" questions can be particularly useful in coming up with alternative *actions* for carrying out a change. For example, consider the different possible actions regarding school design suggested by these questions:

What if this change were the most important thing in our lives?
What if we did not need to spend money to accomplish this change?
What if we could wait twice (or half) as long for the change?
What if everything we did to get this done had to be fun?

3. Reverse Goals or Ideas Interpreting things as the reverse of what we normally think they are is an awareness plan intended to stretch mental flexibility as well as stimulate constructive alternatives. Let's use the school redesign challenge discussed above to illustrate how reversing works. Suppose, for example, your team thought of replacing the old window blinds with new colored blinds. Reverse the idea by taking away all window coverings and thinking of ways to decorate windows that would never block light. Imagine the ceiling used as the floor, the walls as the ceiling, and the floor as the walls. Reverse your view of what is inside and what is outside, so that bushes, flowers, and trees become interior furniture and blackboards, computers, and televisions become play equipment. Or try mentally reversing the relative values of things—things in trash cans and left on shelves unused for years are priceless, whereas the school building, property, and money are worthless junk.

Thinking of possible actions for improving education, we might reverse cause-and-effect relationships and think of children's learning as causing teachers' instructional behaviors. We also might imagine working against our goals. For example, imagine a school as the most physically and psychologically uninviting environment in which to spend time (e.g., as a prison camp, as a place where physical and emotional garbage is dumped on children). Does such imagining offer deeper insight into current problems with schooling and how to deal with them constructively? Suppose that the goal of a sixth grade teaching team is to have a more harmonious relationship with a new principal with whom team members have numerous conflicts. Reversing the goal, think of ways the team could decrease harmonious relationships (e.g., as a group, storm into the principal's office to present written documentation of her failings and call her names in front of the superintendent and school board chairperson). Now, imagine reversing these actions to achieve your goal (e.g., send flowers to the office, drop in one by one to develop more personal relationships, deliver public praise for positive actions concerning students, write a note to the superintendent and school board praising the principal for actions that represent more effective communication with the team).

There is no limit to the reversals we can perform in our minds. At the very least, reversal awareness plans can provide users with endless possibilities for free entertainment while contemplating the usually "unthought of" or the "unthinkable."

   4. Deliberately Think of Unusual, Nutty Things   How ridiculous, strange, and crazy can we be in our thinking? The awareness plan of deliberately thinking in unusual and nutty ways is a starting place for genuinely useful ideas that nonetheless depart from old assumptions of what is possible or appropriate. For example, in imagining improvements to classrooms, in how many ridiculous ways can we cover the floors, the walls, and the ceilings? What are the most bizarre furnishings (from history, other cultures, the future) imaginable? What unexpected activities (e.g., wrestling, shopping, ballet, opera, art show, space travel, moon walking) can be envisioned for classrooms?

Off-the-wall notions can be called upon to suggest feasible *actions* as well. Let's focus upon making the school's playground more interesting. What are some wild ideas for action? Teachers could quit teaching and work full time on the playground; so could the students. The school could be sold to pay for the playground or the faculty could apply for a federal grant. Finally, the children could be brainwashed to think the playground already has been made more interesting. Assuming none of these ideas are feasible, how could they be massaged to become feasible? Perhaps teachers, parents, community members, and students could work after school, on weekends, or on a special community project day to renovate the playground. This has been done in many communities. Maybe parts of the school building could be rented out for meetings or classes at night or over the summer, thus raising money for improvements. Perhaps a special physical fitness project that would merit a federal grant could be proposed and written with the help of community college faculty. Perhaps the children might really be encouraged to play more imaginative games and make more imaginative use of existing equipment and facilities.

   5. Force Yourself to Think of Many Alternative Ideas   *Brainstorming* is now a commonly used term describing the awareness plan of forcing yourself or a group to generate a large number of alternative ideas. The procedure initially was described more than 40 years ago by Alex Osborn (1953) in *Applied Imagination: Principles and Procedures of Creative Thinking*. Application of the brainstorming awareness plan, illustrated in more depth in Chapter 15, this volume, requires adherence to at least five essential rules.

1. No negative reactions to comments are allowed. A judgment may interrupt the flow of ideas or stop the next idea from being expressed.
2. Freewheeling is welcomed. Wild ideas are desired. Ideas will be critically examined later.
3. Quantity is the desired outcome; the more the better. Skip talking about details, as it slows down the process. Details come later.
4. The time limit must be short. Several minutes usually is about as long as the mind can stay intensely creative in a group.
5. Assign a recorder, but do not let the recording slow down the idea-generating. The job of the recorder is to quickly jot down a key word or phrase to represent each idea and to move on.

The importance of quantity is that the first run of ideas that usually represent the "same old ideas" clear out the cobwebs, so to speak, and pave the way for more novel, imagined improvements. One aid for envisioning actions is to make each new action as *different* as possible from the previous one. Thus, if your team already imagined five ways to make money to improve the school's playground, try for a sixth and seventh way that have nothing to do with money. For example, work to change community members' attitudes so they will volunteer time or materials to construct the playground; or perhaps recycle materials—tires, railroad ties, old barn board—already on hand.

6. *Imagine Having a Magic Wand* If you had a magic wand that could allow all things to be possible and remove all barriers, how fanciful could you be in dreaming up changes or actions? The magic-wand awareness plan is intended to help an individual or team to temporarily forget about the genuine barriers to change and defer judgment, so that the imagination can run wild.

After thinking of magical wishes, the next step is to identify the specific features of the wishes that are particularly appealing and to figure out feasible ways to embody some of these features. Suppose the goal is to come up with actions for getting the school's administrators to be more open to teachers' suggestions. You might imagine spiking their morning coffee with a magical potion that prevents people from being closed-minded for up to 8 hours. Appealing features of this magic-wand inspired idea are that it is simple, fast, effortless, and nonthreatening to everyone concerned. What are some real actions that share some of these features? As a faculty, you might send each administrator a holiday gift of an audio tape or a book that conveys the advantages and skills of open-mindedness, such as David Johnson's (1986) *Reaching Out: Interpersonal Effectiveness and Self-Actualization*. Anonymously, distribute to all administrators and teachers a current article that deals with the same topic. Gift wrap suggestions and slip them in with the morning coffee as presents. What other actions resemble a "magic pill" in effect? Given the magic wand, what more can you think of?

7. *Take on Different Roles While Imagining Improvements* Taking on the role of other people, creatures, or things has the magical power of expanding our capacity for viewing a situation and imagining actions from points of view other than our own. The basic idea is to switch among different roles. As you switch among different roles and values, notice how your thoughts change. This sort of self-observation while taking on new mental roles is a powerful technique for helping people to develop empathy with others.

To illustrate this awareness plan, suppose several educators are meeting to plan instructional accommodations for a student with intensive educational needs. The team's creativity might be boosted by a *role reversal* awareness plan. The classroom teacher might take the student's perspective, the special educator might take the perspective of the student's classmates and friends, the teaching assistant might take the role of a parent, and the parent might take the role of the classroom teacher. Team members could switch roles several times as they explore alternative actions for accommodating instruction, materials, and classroom arrangements. When these authors tried this technique with teaching teams in inclusion-oriented schools, accommodations tended to be more fun, less disruptive to daily routines, and more reliant upon classmate support than when the adults stayed in their usual roles.

Academic roles also can be used to broaden thinking. Leff and Nevin (in press) encourage teachers to instruct students to take on the thinking patterns associated with specialists in various academic subject areas and fields of work. How would you think and act if you had the role and values of the following people?

Historian
Mathematician
Daredevil race car driver
Teacher who is blind
Ornithologist
Environmental activist
Bomb defuser

As you try out each role, intensify the values associated with it. As a mathematician, nothing is more important than logic combined with tentativeness and tenacity. A mathematician values sticking with a problem until it is solved, even if it takes years. Therefore, time is of little importance. As a daredevil racer, however, time and speed as well as excitement and competition are all that count.

To maximize flexibility in perspective taking, try using the reversal awareness plan to switch between the values, likely ideas, and actions of a particular role and its *opposite*. For instance, first think like the race car driver who values competition as the spice of life, then shift to regarding cooperation as the most crucial value. In what ways might you act differently in a team meeting when in either of these opposing roles? Next, adopt the values of a historian (e.g., preservation of the past), then switch to the values of a futurist (e.g., accurate prediction of the yet undone). What ideas and actions for restructuring a school's physical plant or reorganizing the people who work within it are suggested by the opposing values of these two roles?

Finally, viewing the world as an animal or even a thing can not only shift thinking away from the usual, but be entertaining and emotionally enriching as well. For example, what kinds of things in school would be important if you, the teachers and the learners, were dogs? What would dogs need or want to learn? How would dogs teach? What would be important to know about a dog's home environment? Now, imagine that you are an object or thing. For example, you are a school building and all of the school's contents, material and human, are part of you. The parts of the school and the school community are cells in your body. Imagine the emotions, sensations, and thoughts you would experience and how you would react to what's going on "inside of you." Now, use this information to think of ways in which to restructure a school organization to be maximally responsive to the emotions, sensations, and thoughts you experienced.

8. Use Different Senses and Emotions to Suggest New Possibilities In Western culture, we are schooled to process information using our senses of sight and hearing. In redesigning a school building, what if you focused on the sense of touch to guide your design. Touch might suggest the use of new textures or it might suggest creating a closer atmosphere where children and adults could more easily connect with one another. Taste sensations (e.g., hot, spicy, sweet, cool) might suggest a more exciting, ethnic-oriented lunch menu or lunch room design, or different tastes might suggest different color schemes throughout the building—hot and spicy reds and oranges in one section, cool blues in another. As for emotions, anger might suggest more flamboyant, vibrant colors and arrangements, while joy might suggest a more open, flowing Eastern decor with movable partitions.

Turning to the domain of actions, suppose your school has a goal of increasing harmony and excitement among staff. The sense of smell might suggest the scent of roses or the aroma of fresh-brewed coffee and fresh-baked cookies, which, in turn, might suggest having floral arrangements and home-made snacks at meetings, in the teachers' room, or throughout the school.

Again, the full range of human emotions—from humor and joy to anger and sadness—can be used in awareness plans. What if everyone in the school were engaged in thinking of the funniest ways to increase harmony, infuse excitement, or achieve any other change? How might the "positive qualities" of anger (e.g., intensity, focus) be constructively channeled into an attack on a problem rather than on a person?

Even the active expression of sadness might be used to forward a beneficial goal, as was the sorrow of the classmates of a young man with disabilities after his sudden and unexpected death. These students learned of a girl with disabilities similar to those of their friend who was being denied access to her local school, which was in another city. Amazed that any community would do this to a child, they wrote newspaper articles and letters to the school board and the superintendent advocating for her admission into regular classes. Three students even traveled to her community and, in front of several hundred people, presented the benefits of all children being educated together. These actions helped to speed the healing process for the young man's classmates and heightened the public's awareness of the many contributions that a student with disabilities can make to the lives of others.

9. Define Your Problem or Goal in Many Different Ways For example, with regard to the problem of teachers not having enough time to meet, the starter phrase, "In what ways might we . . . ," could be used to brainstorm positive restatements of the problem. Actual alternative problem statements generated by teachers include: In what ways might we . . .

Use community volunteers to free up teachers so they can meet?
Rearrange the master schedule so teachers who need to meet have common preparation periods?
Use some inservice training days as planning days?
Have a "floating" permanent substitute to cover for teachers who need to meet?
Build up a store of student contact hours by lengthening the school day by 20 minutes and, through a biweekly early release of students, exchange the earned hours for a half-day time block for collaboration?

Whether the objective is to restate a goal or envision alternative means to achieve a goal, each new definition points thinking toward different possibilities.

10. Break the Problem into Subproblems   If it is hard to think of where to begin with a seemingly massive or complex problem or goal (e.g., school restructuring), try to focus on just one part of the problem at a time (e.g., student empowerment) and list the various actions you personally could take that conceivably could contribute to solving the problem (e.g., involving students as instructors, advocates, and decision makers). Once you have thought of potential actions or improvements, mentally follow through by imagining the consequences each action or improvement might have. Select the most promising approaches and break them down into subparts (e.g., implementing cooperative learning and partner learning in daily lessons). Then, try them. The key to creating change is to search until you find a way that *you* can enter the process of working for a final goal.

11. Form New Mental Connections   Awareness plans in this category link thoughts about a thing, event, idea, or feeling together with another, with the goal of jogging novel ideas. The simplest of the awareness plans is to think of things or situations that in some ways are similar to what you want to change or do and use them to jog thinking. In improving a school building, you might think of a famous hotel and hotel lobby or an architectural gem, such as a home designed by Frank Lloyd Wright, and use it as a model. Going farther afield, try deriving ideas from museums, parks, or the "homes" of animals and birds. Try picking decidedly unattractive or repulsive things (e.g., a bus terminal, a prison) and, using the *reversal* awareness plan, reverse their features as your source of inspiration.

New mental connections also can be used to think of new actions. If you are trying to come up with ways to increase the amount of laughter and play among the adults in your school, try thinking of the people with whom you have had the most fun and laughs and recall how that fun and laughter was created. Or, think of analogies from the animal kingdom—how do various animals play and "have fun"?

To push thinking further, connect things to your goal that have no logical reason to be connected. Connect the first thing that you sense or think of to your goal. What, for instance, does a deck of cards suggest for the goal of making the school grounds safer at night? Perhaps a bridge tournament or a casino night could be organized to raise money for improving lighting of the grounds, or safety tips might be printed onto cards and made into an educational game.

12. Invent Imaginative Games to Inspire Thinking   Inventing games is an awareness plan that can be employed to help groups more easily or enjoyably reach a goal, learn a task or concept, or solve a problem. Leff and Nevin (in press), for instance, propose that teachers use the inventing games awareness plan to liven up academic content previously considered mundane. Games can increase students' motivation, achievement, and appreciation of subject matter. As an example, Susan Underhill (personal communication, April, 1991), a fifth grade teacher in an inner-city elementary school, developed a "Preposition Game" for grammar exercises. As an overnight game assignment, she challenged the students to notice and list every preposition they heard or used as they talked with family members, neighbors, friends, and so forth. All 32 students—including those with chaotic home lives or special education needs—brought in a list of three or more examples. Working in groups, students checked to be sure the examples actually did represent prepositions. They wrote each example on a 3 × 5 card and posted the cards around the room. Within 15 minutes, hundreds of accurate examples lined the walls. The students' competence in using and labeling the examples of prepositions was publicly displayed for all to see and celebrate. Over time, other grammar exercises turned into games, and students began to state that grammar was fun and easy.

Games also can be used to make it fun to apply *several* awareness plans (e.g., the ones presented thus far) to the same problem or goal. Here, for instance is a possible game for imagining improvements in a school library.

Step 1.   Gather a few members of the school community into the library and briefly explain the procedure.

Step 2.   Ask one another "What if. . .?" questions for 5 minutes to loosen up assumptions about what can be done in and with a library.

Step 3.   Spend some time taking on various animal roles. From each animal's perspective, discuss how each animal would most like the library to change.

Step 4.   Translate the animal suggestions into feasible ideas for improving the library for children and adults.

Step 5.   Ask the group to invent yet another *new game* and use it to come up with creative *actions* to achieve the improvements identified in Step 4. For instance, a new game might use the "magic wand" and the "form new mental connections" awareness plans to come up with creative actions.

Thus far, these authors have presented techniques for teams and individuals to be more creative in envisioning improvements and inventing strategies for accomplishing the improvements. The next two sections offer awareness plans for harnessing the synergistic potential of human interaction and making any situation in life more fulfilling.

Thinking for Synergistic (Team) Outcomes

Synergy refers to combined action in which individual contributions reinforce one another. It is an exciting phenomenon of human interaction that relies upon the ongoing interchange of thoughts and actions of members of a group. Synergy connotes creativity, inventiveness, and excitement in human exchange and requires (as well as develops) honest communication, inviting rather than manipulating others to consider ideas, and mutual problem solving rather than competitive approaches to conflicts. In these authors' view, synergistic thinking is highly related to valuing the well-being of all people.

The awareness plans presented in this section are particularly useful for *teams*. They are intended to illustrate ways of thinking and perceiving to enhance the "two heads are better than one" phenomenon of synergy. Four synergistic awareness plans are explored in depth; five additional plans are presented in Table 2.

Look for Points in Other People's Ideas on Which to Build   The next time you are in the middle of a disagreement, stop and deliberately focus on as many good points as you can find in the other person's ideas and *build on them to generate even better ideas*. Let's say you are in a discussion about discipline and someone says that punishment through suspension or expulsion is the best way to handle a student's violation of school rules. If you disagree, rather than immediately trying to shoot down the other person's position, see if you can find *something* in the idea that you can genuinely agree with or use as a place to start generating better ideas. For instance, you might think suspension is a mistake, but agree with the idea of letting students know when their behavior violates rules. You could then build on this positive aspect of suspension and start suggesting alternative, nonpunitive ways of

Table 2.   Additional synergistic awareness plans

1. Carefully consider how the feelings or emotional states of others (e.g., teammates) affect your feelings and vice versa.
2. Consciously take the points of view of others; imagine you *are* the other people.
3. Think of advantages of sharing power and decision making with others.
4. Identify and question the underlying assumptions about your goal or situation.
5. Imagine being openly cooperative, creative, and synergistic; then tackle a troubling situation while in that state of mind.

Adapted from Leff (1984).

achieving the same effect (e.g., developing an oral plan or written contract for improved behavior with the student).

This awareness plan is based on the *spectrum policy* described by George Prince (1970) in his book *The Practice of Creativity*. The policy is to always pick out the best part of the total spectrum of a person's ideas and think of the weaker parts as challenges to address, rather than as points to reject or attack. The net effect of this constructive orientation is that it both stimulates one's own creativity and promotes a productive and more friendly social atmosphere.

Think of People's Ideas as Gifts or Invitations   What if disagreements were considered celebrations or parties of diverse ideas rather than a kind of war or competition? What if members of a group thought of themselves as living in a shared pool of thoughts rather than each person being the "owner" or originator of unique ideas? What if, rather than judging a thought or idea as "wrong," we viewed it as an opportunity to teach or learn something new? What if we thought of our own proposals as *invitations* to others to propose and explore even better ideas? If awareness plans like these were routinely used within groups, it would not be much of a struggle at all to find exciting, shared goals and the means to achieving them.

Define Conflicts in Terms of Underlying Needs Rather than Incompatible Solutions   This awareness plan involves thinking of a conflict with others and imagining how it might be handled if first everyone determined ways to satisfy one another's underlying needs or desires. For example, imagine two teachers, attempting to team teach, embroiled in an argument over how high of a noise level was acceptable in the room. One teacher likes to hear the "hum" of children talking and making noise; the other wants it quiet. If the two teachers define the problem strictly in terms of preconceived solutions—having it either noisy or quiet in the room—the conflict likely will be difficult to resolve to both teachers' satisfaction.

What if, instead, the teachers began their discussion by determining what basic needs or desires underlie their preferences and then framed the problem as finding a way to meet both of their needs or desires? They might discover that one teacher's need is to structure cooperative learning groups where students' dialogue is a part of the classroom routine; the other teacher's need is to have relative silence in order to run focused reading comprehension groups with selected students. If both were committed to finding a resolution that satisfied each of these needs, they might come up with possibilities such as finding mutually agreeable times of the days for quiet work versus more noisy group work, or searching out alternative places in the school building to do reading or cooperative groups. The net result should be satisfied needs and a strengthened partnership.

Focusing first on needs rather than preconceived solutions can do wonders for resolving many educational issues. Just think of the possibilities for issues such as inclusive educational practices, student empowerment, teacher empowerment, school busing, and school choice. The key to success in using an awareness plan that focuses on underlying needs is for all parties to enter the process with a firm commitment to divulging *real* needs and taking the *time* to find solutions that work for everyone.

Think of Superordinate Goals that Could Resolve Conflicts and Foster Excitement A *superordinate goal* is one that is so big, important, or exciting that people who previously were either apathetic or in conflict enthusiastically unite to pursue it. Survival often provides the basis for superordinate goals; for example, a polarized community pulls together to rebuild after a hurricane or tornado, or unites to save a small rural school from being closed in a school-consolidation drive. Superordinate goals also may be based upon seeking creative improvements. For example, a group of students energize and mobilize themselves to raise money for new athletic facilities and equipment. In numerous communities, formerly unconnected families have united in the highly cooperative, superordinate effort of designing and building a community recreation area. As with the awareness plan that focuses on underlying needs, discovering goals that are truly superordinate requires people to communicate honestly about what they really value and want.

Employing Basic Enlightenment to Enhance Individual and Team Experiences

The purpose of this final section is to present a few awareness plans that help make any situation in life more fulfilling, including work with students and colleagues in school. The underlying disposition to develop is referred to as "basic enlightenment" (Leff, 1984, p. 103). Enlightenment has many meanings, most of which involve a spiritual connotation. *Basic enlightenment* refers to a way of experiencing events (including problems) so as to maximize personal fulfillment or joy, which, in turn, should enhance any outcomes of the experience (including the solutions to problems). What follows is advice on how to immediately experience each moment in richer ways. The four awareness plans for basic enlightenment presented are useful for both individuals and teams.

Think of Every Moment as an Opportunity A powerful way to bring choice to life is to view each moment as an *opportunity* for choosing how to experience or act. Regardless of the situation, try thinking or saying out loud, "Well, here I am. This is all I have to work with. I commit myself to treating this situation as an opportunity for a constructive and fulfilling experience." It is important to recognize that feelings and thoughts are as much a part of a situation as external circumstances. So, suppose you are facing a stressful event. The "opportunity" involves not only how you treat the event itself, but also how you treat the *feelings* of stress. For example, one of these authors, faced with the stress of several impending writing deadlines and intensive job and family responsibilities, used the feeling of stress as an opportunity to identify stress-reducing activities. This, in turn, led to the re-introduction into the author's life of two favorite calming and fulfilling activities—piano playing and weight lifting—activities that had been lost in the rush of a too busy life.

Although this awareness plan may be applied to any situation, it is especially useful for "reframing" problematic or disturbing circumstances. What positive opportunities are provided by an otherwise disappointing cold and rainy weekend, an automobile breakdown, or having to stay home because of illness? How could an argument with a supervisor be turned into an opportunity for personal growth by coming up with creative ways to resolve conflict? As an exercise in the use of this awareness plan, take a single problem that particularly bothers you and spend 30 minutes exploring opportunities it might offer for enriching your life.

Regard Everything as If It Were Your Hobby   Imagine that you are doing some required paperwork for school that you really hate doing. Now, see if you can change your feeling about paperwork by regarding it as a long-standing favorite hobby. To do this, however, first you need to think about how it *feels* to engage in a hobby you genuinely like. Picture the activities and feelings associated with hobbies. You may experience aesthetic pleasure, intense attention to detail, feelings of having chosen to do what you are doing, loving the activity involved, enjoying the people who also have the same hobby, and so forth. Now, transfer these thoughts and feelings to the activity of doing paperwork.

Is it possible to think of paperwork as a hobby, something to look forward to and savor, take pride in, and do for recreation? Do "hobby feelings" change your experience when you actually do paperwork? If it is hard for you to imagine paperwork as an enjoyable pastime because you dislike it so much, perhaps you could regard *hating paperwork* as a hobby and think: "Yeah! Another opportunity to hate paperwork. Let's think up all of the reasons why and ways in which to hate it today." The value of the awareness plan of treating a feeling of dislike as a genuine hobby is that it reminds us that we can always choose to welcome our feelings.

Focus on What You Can Do   For any problematic situation, focus on what you are doing and especially on what *you can do,* rather than focusing on what you might see as being done to you. In your most creative frame of mind, imagine possible actions to *change* the situation or even to *get out of it.* Or, if the situation cannot be changed or you cannot get out of it, think of new ways to experience it so that it feels better. For example, instead of struggling or resisting, treat the whole thing as an educational experience, a game, or as unimportant and silly.

The trick to effectively using this awareness plan in a situation that you truly want to change is to start by committing yourself to finding something—*anything*—that you actually can do to make a difference. In some cases, it simply may be to choose to experience the situation differently, perhaps with a playful awareness plan.

Learn from Whatever You Encounter   Regarding all things and experiences as having something important to teach is the last and possibly the most powerful awareness plan offered in this chapter. This awareness plan works best if you actively seek ways to identify possible lessons rather than waiting for the lessons to appear. In the search, be sure to use any of the other awareness plans presented in this chapter to: 1) help you suspend your assumptions about what is important, 2) look for new connections, and 3) learn from unexpected or overlooked sources (e.g., discarded materials, outdated texts, the most troubled or troubling children in the school, senior citizens). Finally, be sure to attend to your own feelings, emotions, thoughts, and actions as well as those of others as sources of information. In summary, just about everything in life offers a lesson, even though it may take some mental digging to find it.

AN INVITATION TO INVENT THE EXTRAORDINARY

A main message of this chapter is that there are many strategies for individuals and teams of people to employ to overcome traditional barriers to creativity. In these authors' experience, when collaborative teams (Thousand & Villa, 1992) have employed the awareness plans presented in this chapter, they have successfully created time for collaboration, developed meaningful accommodations and modifications to curriculum and instruction, and redefined the roles of educator and student so that all children, regardless of their needs and gifts, experience quality education in schools that are both caring and effective.

A second message of this chapter is that each person can choose how to experience the world at each moment by trying out new and different awareness plans. While the awareness plans in this chapter should prove useful and enjoyable, coming up with *your own* will allow you to personalize new plans to the specifics of your life— your work; your relationships; and your interests, goals, and pleasures. And so, the authors end this chapter with an invitation to invent the extraordinary—to devise your own awareness plans, try them out, and share them with others through your actions. Finally, we invite you to directly teach them to children. It is, after all, the imagination and creativity of our children that represent the future of this planet.

REFERENCES

Adams, J. (1986). *Conceptual blockbusting: A guide to better ideas* (3rd ed.). Reading, MA: Addison-Wesley.

Johnson, D. (1986). *Reaching out: Interpersonal effectiveness and self-actualization.* Englewood Cliffs, NJ: Prentice Hall.

Leff, H. (1978). *Experience, environment, and human potentials.* New York: Oxford University Press.

Leff, H.L. (1984). *Playful perception: Choosing how to experience your world.* Burlington, VT: Waterfront Books.

Leff, H., & Nevin, A. (1990). Dissolving barriers to teaching creative thinking (and meta-thinking). *Teacher Education and Special Education, 13*(1), 36–39.

Leff, H., & Nevin, A. (in press). *Turning learning inside out.* Tucson: Zephyr Press.

Nevin, A., & Leff, H. (1991). Is there room for playfulness? *Teaching Exceptional Children, 22*(2), 71–73.

Osborn, A. (1953). *Applied imagination: Principles and procedures of creative thinking.* New York: Charles Scribner & Sons.

Prince G. (1970). *The practice of creativity.* New York: Macmillan.

Thousand, J.S., & Villa, R.P. (1992). Collaborative teams: A powerful tool in school restructuring. In R.P. Villa, J.S. Thousand, W. Stainback, & S. Stainback (Eds.), *Restructuring for caring and effective education: An administrative guide to creating heterogeneous schools* (pp. 73–108). Baltimore: Paul H. Brookes Publishing Co.

Webster's new collegiate dictionary. (1973). Springfield, MA: G & C Merriman Company.

Problem-Solving Methods to Facilitate Inclusive Education

Michael F. Giangreco,
Chigee J. Cloninger,
Ruth E. Dennis, and Susan W. Edelman

Inclusive educational practices require people to work together to invent opportunities and solutions that maximize learning experiences of all children. This chapter presents ways of planning, adapting, and implementing inclusive educational experiences for students of varying abilities. It is a *how to* chapter that is based on the assumption that inclusive educational experiences are desirable for children with and without disabilities. As pointed out by Giangreco and Putnam (1991), when people use terms such as *inclusion*, they may mean different things. To assist the reader to understand what the authors mean, a five-point definition of *inclusive education* is presented in Table 1. Inclusive education is in place *only when all five features occur on an ongoing, daily basis.*

An inclusive school, therefore, is "a place where everyone belongs, is accepted, supports, and is supported by his or her peers and other members of the school community in the course of having his or her educational needs met" (Stainback & Stainback, 1990, p. 3). It is designed to benefit everyone—students of varying characteristics (including those with disabilities) as well as teachers and other

Support for the preparation of this manuscript was provided by the United States Department of Education, Office of Special Education and Rehabilitative Services, Innovations for Educating Children with Deaf-Blindness in General Education Settings, CFDA 84.025F (#H025F10008), awarded to the Center for Developmental Disabilities at the University of Vermont. The content of this manuscript reflects the ideas and opinions of the authors and does not necessarily reflect the ideas or positions of the U.S. Department of Education; therefore, no official endorsement should be inferred.

Table 1. Basic components of inclusive education

Inclusive education is in place when each of these five features occur on an ongoing, daily basis.
1. *Heterogeneous Grouping* All students are educated *together* in groups where the number of those with and without disabilities approximates the *natural proportion*. The premise is that "students develop most when in the physical, social, emotional, and intellectual presence of nonhandicapped persons in reasonable approximations to the natural proportions" (Brown, Ford, Nisbet, Sweet, Donnellan, & Gruenewald, 1983, p. 17). Thus, in a class of 25 students, perhaps there is one student with significant disabilities, a couple of others with less significant disabilities, and many students without identified disabilities working at various levels.
2. *A Sense of Belonging to a Group* All students are considered members of the class rather than visitors, guests, or outsiders. Within these groups, students who have disabilities are welcomed, as are students without disabilities.
3. *Shared Activities with Individualized Outcomes* Students share educational experiences (e.g., lessons, labs, field studies, group learning) at the same time (Schnorr, 1990). Even though students are involved in the same activities, their learning objectives are individualized and, therefore, may be different. Students may have different objectives in the same curriculum area (e.g., language arts) during a shared activity. This is referred to as *multi-level instruction* (Campbell, Campbell, Collicott, Perner, & Stone, 1988; Collicott, 1991; Giangreco & Meyer, 1988; Giangreco & Putnam, 1991). Within a shared activity, a student also may have individualized objectives from a curriculum area (e.g., social skills) other than that on which other students are focused (e.g., science). This practice is referred to as *curriculum overlapping* (Giangreco & Meyer, 1988; Giangreco & Putnam, 1991).
4. *Use of Environments Frequented by Persons without Disabilities* Shared educational experiences take place in environments predominantly frequented by people without disabilities (e.g., general education classroom, community worksites).
5. *A Balanced Educational Experience* Inclusive education seeks an individualized balance between the academic/functional and social/personal aspects of schooling (Giangreco, 1992). For example, teachers in inclusion-oriented schools would be as concerned about students' self-image and social network as they would be about developing literacy competencies or learning vocational skills.

school personnel. Readers interested in the philosophical rationale for inclusive education are referred to the wide variety of resources (e.g., Forest, 1987; Giangreco, 1992; Giangreco, Dennis, Cloninger, Edelman, & Schattman, l993; Giangreco & Putnam, 1991; Lipsky & Gartner, 1989; Porter & Richler, 1991; Schaffner & Buswell, 1991; Stainback & Stainback, 1992; Stainback & Stainback, 1990; Thousand & Villa, 1990; Vandercook, York, & Johnson, 1991; Villa, Thousand, Stainback, & Stainback, 1992).

The remainder of this chapter is divided into five sections. The first section presents contextual information regarding the challenges associated with educating a diverse group of students in general education environments and activities. The second describes characteristics of effective problem solvers as well as the complete Osborn-Parnes Creative Problem-Solving (CPS) process. The third section delineates three variations of the CPS process that utilize the creative powers of children and adults to generate options for the inclusion of classmates with diverse needs. The fourth section offers suggestions for evaluating the impact of CPS strategies on the educational experiences of students, and the final section discusses implications of using CPS in education.

THE CHALLENGE OF EDUCATING
DIVERSE GROUPS IN HETEROGENEOUS
GENERAL EDUCATION ENVIRONMENTS AND ACTIVITIES

> We can, whenever and wherever we choose, successfully teach all children whose schooling is of interest to us. We already know more than we need in order to do this. Whether we do it must finally depend on how we feel about the fact that we haven't done it so far. (Edmonds, 1979, p. 29)

Edmonds's (1979) comment reflects a vision of American education that remains unfulfilled and acknowledges the challenges faced by schools in realizing this vision. Table 2 contrasts major distinctions between "traditional" approaches of dealing with student diversity and more contemporary, inclusion-oriented approaches. These distinctions are presented in order to set a context—to highlight the assumptions and approaches that enable educators to more effectively meet the challenge of educating diverse groups of students in heterogeneous general education environments and activities.

It should be noted that even if educators embrace the inclusion-oriented educational tenets presented in Table 2, they still should and do have legitimate questions about *how* educational alternatives work and what the impact of these practices will be. Their questions include:

How can I, as a teacher, accommodate such a wide array of student needs without sacrificing quality?

Is it not a lot of pressure on one person—the teacher—to generate all the accommodations that need to be made?

How will the inclusion of students with diverse needs affect the social and academic outcomes of the other students?

Table 2. Approaches to educating students with diverse characteristics

Traditional approaches	Inclusion-oriented alternatives
1. The teacher is the instructional leader.	1. Collaborative teams share leadership.
2. Students learn from teachers and teachers solve the problems.	2. Students and teachers learn from each other and solve problems together.
3. Students are purposely grouped by similar ability.	3. Students are purposely grouped by differing abilities.
4. Instruction is geared toward middle achieving students.	4. Instruction is geared to match students at all levels of achievement.
5. Grade-level placement is considered synonymous with curricular content.	5. Grade-level placement and individual curricular content are independent of each other.
6. Instruction is often passive, competitive, didactic, and/or teacher-directed.	6. Instruction is active, creative, and collaborative among members of the classroom community.
7. People who provide instructional supports are located, or come *primarily* from, sources external to the classroom.	7. People who provide instructional supports are located, or come *primarily* from, sources internal to the classroom.
8. Some students do not "fit" in general education classes.	8. All students "fit" in general education classes.
9. Students who do not "fit in" are excluded from general classes and/or activities.	9. All students are included in general class activities.
10. The classroom teacher and general education team assume ownership for the education of general education students, and special education staff assume ownership for the education of students with special needs.	10. The classroom teacher and general education team (including special educators, related service staff, and families) assume ownership for educating all students attending the school.
11. Students are evaluated by common standards.	11. Students are evaluated by individually appropriate standards.
12. Students' success is achieved by meeting common standards.	12. The system of education is considered successful when it strives to meet each student's needs.

How will the inclusion of students with diverse needs affect my capacity to provide quality education to all of my students?

Our experiences with inclusive education in Vermont and other North American schools (see Villa et al., 1992) have yielded sufficient evidence to convince us that the answers to these questions are positive, although much remains to be done. Specifically, our conclusions include:

Diverse student *needs can be accommodated* within general class activities while maintaining high quality for all students.

The responsibility for developing accommodations can and should be *shared* among many members of the classroom community that include not only the adults of the school, but students.

Well-planned inclusion can have *positive* social and academic outcomes for students with and without disabilities.

Teachers who choose to meet the challenge of educating diverse groups of students *improve* their teaching for the entire class (Giangreco, 1992; Giangreco, Dennis, et al., 1993; Giangreco, Edelman, Cloninger, & Dennis, 1993; Helmstetter, Peck, & Giangreco, 1992; Peck, Donaldson, & Pezzoli, 1990; Stainback & Stainback, 1992).

OSBORN-PARNES CREATIVE PROBLEM-SOLVING AS A METHOD FOR INCLUDING STUDENTS WITH DIVERSE NEEDS IN THE CLASSROOM

The Osborn-Parnes Creative Problem-Solving (CPS) process (Parnes, 1981, 1985, 1988, 1992) is one method for empowering teams of teachers and students to work together to meet the challenges of educating a heterogeneous school population. CPS is a generic strategy designed for addressing a variety of challenges and opportunities. The process was articulated first by Alex Osborn (1953), the person who coined the term *brainstorming*. CPS was further developed by Osborn's protegé and colleague, Sidney Parnes, who promoted the use of CPS in many fields—advertising, product development, business, and education. Clearly, creativity is recognized as a valuable process and outcome in education and a necessary skill for professionals faced with restructuring schools to meet the changing needs of modern society. Within education, CPS historically was associated with the education of children labeled "gifted." Only since the late 1980s has CPS been applied to inclusion-oriented education issues. As a consequence, people just now are recognizing that approaches to teaching students at "opposite ends" of the academic achievement continuum hold benefits for the multitude of children in between. What follows are some basic tenets of the Osborn-Parnes CPS process represented as characteristics of effective problem-solvers.

Characteristics of Problem Solvers

To be optimally successful in using the CPS process, participants must exhibit certain behaviors and dispositions identified as characteristic of effective problem-solvers. Six of these characteristics are described here.

Problem Solvers Believe Everyone Is Creative and Has the Capacity to Solve Problems   Everyone has heard statements such as, "I'm not creative," or "I could never come up with those kinds of ideas." Many people limit the many useful ideas they can generate by minimizing their personal creative potential. The fact is that people use their creative problem-solving abilities constantly in daily life without even noticing it. Creative abilities are being used every time a person rearranges the furniture, makes a substitution in a recipe, improvises by using an object in place of an absent tool, adapts a game to play with a child, or plans a schedule.

In education, as in many other fields, people have been encouraged to believe that certain experts hold the key to special knowledge or creative solutions. As a result, there is a tendency to become unnecessarily dependent on outside consultants to solve problems while becoming increasingly less confident in one's own abilities as deference is given to others. In contrast, we believe any group of people has the ability to solve the many challenges of inclusion-oriented schooling through the use of CPS. By working together, teams of people can identify solutions and take actions no individual could accomplish alone. The practice of using creative problem-solving strategies within teams can enhance individual team members' personal growth and creative capacity in a broader range of situations.

The steps of CPS take advantage of the abilities people already have and encourage people to emphasize and deliberately use their existing abilities to solve problems. Learning the basics of CPS is easy. People already know how to do most or all of what is needed, and they have been doing it naturally all their lives. The new learning comes in practicing the use of these existing skills in new and deliberate ways.

Problem Solvers Are Optimistic CPS, or any other problem-solving method, is based on optimism. Problem-solvers enter the process with the knowledge that every challenge they face *can* be solved, usually in more than one way.

Problem Solvers Alternate Between Divergent and Convergent Thinking A central concept embedded in the Osborn-Parnes CPS process is that of actively alternating between divergent and convergent thinking. This means that at each stage of the CPS process, there is a time to consider the challenge in broad, divergent ways, to open up to many possibilities. Then, within the same stage, the problem-solver is encouraged to think convergently—to narrow the focus and make a choice from among the many possibilities, allowing the process to continue.

Problem Solvers Actively Defer and Engage Their Judgment People frequently inhibit their creative abilities by prematurely engaging their judgment; in essence, they are generating ideas and attempting to evaluate them at the same time. Firestien (1989) likens this to driving a car with your feet on the brake and the gas pedal at the same time. Firestien's analogy points out that such an approach is unlikely to get anyone very far. Effective problem solvers refrain from this practice and identify times to actively defer judgment and times to engage judgment purposefully. These times correspond with divergent and convergent thinking. In a divergent phase, judgment is actively deferred. In a convergent phase, judgment is purposefully engaged.

Problem Solvers Encourage "Free-Wheeling" and Fun Having fun and being playful with ideas is crucial to effective problem-solving. We might think of humor and playfulness as the oil that keeps the creativity engine lubricated and running smooth. Creative insights as well as humor can be facilitated by bringing together things that seem incongruent. The *Far Side* cartoons of Gary Larson are prime examples of incongruency that are both creative and humorous.

Sometimes it may be difficult for people to be playful when the challenges they are facing are serious; yet, playfulness is essential. During training workshops, we have observed teachers practicing the use of CPS on noneducational examples and doing an excellent job of being playful and having fun with their ideas. However, when the same teachers were asked to apply CPS skills to educational challenges, many reverted to old "school meeting behaviors" that were anything but fun and that seriously interfered with their capacity to creatively problem solve. It is easy for people to fall back into familiar patterns and traditional group interactions. Therefore, when using CPS, it is critical to be mindful of this hazard and guard against it with collective playfulness. If people do not enjoy using CPS strategies, they will be less likely to use them in the future.

Problem Solvers Take Action　Problem-solvers extend the power of their optimism by acting upon their ideas. Ideas that are generated do not have to be earth-shattering or world-changing. Some people do not use the ideas they generate because they judge the ideas as "not good enough." Yet, as Alex Osborn observed, "A fair idea put to use is better than a good idea kept on the polishing wheel" (cited in Parnes, 1988, p. 37). As people start to use CPS and get into new habits that accentuate their creative problem-solving abilities, they find themselves generating more and better ideas. The key is to act, not to wait for the perfect solution before taking action. Better ideas always may be implemented later, when discovered.

STAGES OF THE OSBORN-PARNES CREATIVE PROBLEM-SOLVING PROCESS

The information regarding the six stages of the Osborn-Parnes Creative Problem-Solving process presented in Table 3 and described on the following pages is based on descriptions of the process outlined by Osborn (1953) and Parnes (1981, 1985, 1988, 1992) and insights gained from the authors' use of the process (Giangreco, 1993).

Developing creativity capabilities is a lifelong undertaking (Parnes, 1985, 1988) that should be thought of more as the development of a *creative attitude* than the learning and application of specific steps and procedures. Thus, the Osborn-Parnes CPS process should be used as a springboard for inventing or personalizing CPS models and techniques. Some of the variations developed by these authors to help with the challenges of school and community inclusion are highlighted later in this section. Cycling and recycling through the CPS process and its variations internalizes the creative attitude and makes creative problem solving a part of one's daily routine rather than an isolated tool used only in certain contexts (e.g., school vs. home or family) or with certain problems (e.g., student vs. systems change issues in educational reform).

Stage 1: Visionizing or Objective-Finding　Have you driven down the same road many times and later realized that there was something on that road you had not noticed before? The first stage of CPS helps us become increasingly aware of challenges and opportunities around us by *sharpening our powers of observation*. It prepares us to use all of our senses and perceptions to explore new possibilities and search for opportunities. Rules or dispositions that help a problem solver at this stage are:

Think of objective-finding as a starting point or a general challenge.
Be divergent by considering a variety of potential problems to solve. Remember to *defer judgment* and have fun.
Expand the possibilities and free yourself from real or perceived boundaries by imagining, wishing, dreaming, and fantasizing.
Be convergent by focusing in on one challenge you really want to solve.

Table 3. Stages of the Osborn-Parnes Creative Problem-Solving process

Stage 1: Visionizing or Objective-Finding At this initial stage, the problem solvers heighten their awareness through imagining potential challenges. First, they are divergent, considering a variety of possible challenges. Then, they converge by selecting one to begin solving.

Stage 2: Fact-Finding Problem solvers gather as much information as possible about the selected challenge by using all of their perceptions and senses. By asking "who, what, where, when, why, and how" questions, problem solvers are divergent in considering multiple perspectives regarding the challenge. They finish this stage by identifying facts they believe to be most relevant to the challenge.

Stage 3: Problem-Finding The purpose of this stage is to clarify the challenge or problem by redefining it in new and different ways; by rephrasing the challenge as a question, "In what ways might I/we . . .?"; and by asking the question "Why?" or "What do I/we really want to accomplish?" This process is repeated until the problem solvers restate the problem in a way that makes the most sense and is most appealing to them.

Stage 4: Idea-Finding At this stage, the objective is to defer judgment while generating as many ideas as possible to potentially solve the challenge. Playfulness and wild ideas are encouraged. To come up with ideas beyond the obvious, problem solvers attempt to make new connections between ideas through analogies, manipulation of ideas (e.g., magnifying, minifying, reversing, eliminating), and hitchhiking (i.e., making new associations by building on someone else's idea).

Stage 5: Solution-Finding At this stage of the process, a variety of criteria are considered and ultimately selected for evaluating the merit of ideas. Problem solvers use the criteria to assist in selecting the best solution.

Stage 6: Acceptance-Finding The problem solvers refine the solutions to make them more workable. The objective is to turn ideas into action through the development and implementation of an action plan. Regular evaluation of the solution helps problem solvers discover new challenges and ways of addressing them as the action plan is carried out.

Based on Osborn (1953) and Parnes (1981, 1985, 1988, 1992).

Remember that challenges come in all different sizes. Pick one that is small enough to be solved in the time available. By starting with manageable challenges, teams (and individuals) are more likely to experience success, develop a creative attitude, and practice and improve creativity skills.

Stage 2: Fact-Finding The purpose of fact-finding is to identify and list as many facts about the challenge as team members can think of. There is an important relationship between facts and potential solutions. From obvious facts come obvious ideas; from less obvious facts come less obvious and possibly more inventive solutions. To start fact-finding, set a relatively short time limit, such as 5–8 minutes. Fact-finding is a quick-paced, rapid-fire listing of what people believe to be true about the challenge situation. The facts should be presented briefly *without* explanation, judgment, or discussion. In other words, use the approach of Joe Friday (the character from the famed television series, *Dragnet*) and solicit "just the facts, ma'am; just the facts." Always record and save the list of facts for use later during the CPS process (e.g., during idea-finding). Tips for increasing the likelihood that all of the relevant facts emerge are:

Use all of your senses and perceptions to describe what you know about the challenge. Remember facts can be feelings, so they may be listed also.

Ask "who, what, where, when, why, and how" questions about what is and is not true of the challenge situation.

Be divergent and defer judgment to generate a large quantity and variety of facts. If someone states an opinion with which you do not agree, do not dispute it; rather, accept the fact as that person's opinion (e.g., Fact: "Larry believes that students act out because they simply are bored during class.").

Stretch beyond the obvious facts.

Ask, "What does the challenge or facts about the challenge remind you of?"

Be convergent by selecting a subset of relevant facts to assist problem-finding in the next stage.

Record and save the list of facts. These will be used again later in the process (especially during idea-finding).

Stage 3: Problem-Finding   Sometimes the initial selection of a challenge was right on target; at other times the initial selection was just a starting point. The purpose of problem-finding is to clarify the challenge or problem by considering different ways of viewing it. When rephrasing the challenge at this stage, it is helpful to state the challenge in positive words by using the starter phrase, "In what ways might we . . . ?" and repeating the question until the team feels comfortable that it has teased out the real issues.

Next, be convergent and select one of the new challenge statements that the team agrees it most wants to solve. Consensus may be prompted by asking team members a question such as, "Which of these challenges do we most desperately want to accomplish or solve?" Problem-finding is an important stage of CPS because, as John Dewey observed, "A problem well defined is half solved" (cited in Parnes, 1988, p. 72).

Stage 4: Idea-Finding   Ideas are *potential* solutions to the challenge statement selected at Stage 3. Where do these ideas come from? Ideas may emerge through the deliberate use of approaches such as the awareness plans described in Chapter 14, this volume. Central to idea-finding is the awareness plan of *brainstorming* (Osborn, 1953). Brainstorming is a divergent idea-generating process in which judgment (even praise) is deferred in order to help problem solvers stretch beyond the obvious. Quantity is the key, as it is likely that the first ideas generated will be the "same old" ideas. It is important to keep the flow of ideas coming as quickly as possible and to limit sessions to 5–10 minutes. Good brainstorming sessions do not look anything like a typical group meeting; in brainstorming sessions, there is little quiet time and people speak in single words or short phrases rather than sentences. Other important techniques to jar ideas loose are *forced relationships* (Parnes, 1988, p. 158), *synectics*, and *incubation*. These techniques are briefly described below.

Forced Relationships   Forced relationships are achieved when two objects, ideas, or concepts that appear to have little or no relationship to each other are combined or rearranged in some way to generate a new idea to solve a problem. These new connections between apparently unlike entities are made by looking for similarities, analogies, metaphors, or other comparisons between characteristics of the two objects or ideas.

Synectics   Gordon and Poze (1979) explain that learning occurs when we *make the strange familiar*. Creativity and invention, however, are facilitated when we *make the familiar strange*. Among the ways of making the familiar strange is to search for new ways of seeing the challenge and facts by *identifying new relationships* through paradox, analogies, metaphors, associations, and connections. (For more information, readers may refer to Gordon [1987] and Gordon and Poze [1979].)

Incubation   Incubation involves moving away from the challenge for a time to engage in different activities and returning to the challenge later.

As mentioned earlier, ideas also may emanate from facts. Thus, it is important to use facts from Stage 2 in conjunction with *idea-joggers*, by combining or manipulating facts or their dimensions. Idea-joggers include questions such as: What would the situation look like if something (e.g., a fact about the situation) were: 1) minified/ made smaller, 2) magnified/made bigger, 3) rearranged, 4) eliminated, 5) reversed, or 6) turned upside down or inside out?

Idea-joggers may involve *manipulating* dimensions of a fact; for example, if part of a problem situation is *visual* (e.g., In what ways might the school building or classroom be improved in appearance?). Applying idea-joggers to visual dimensions such as color, shade, brightness, design, or contrast can generate ideas. Although facts can lead directly to ideas, theoretically the more idea-joggers applied and combined, the more ideas that are likely to be generated.

Some ideas that are generated may be wild and unusable. These ideas have tremendous potential value, however, as other ideas may be spurred by them in a *hitchhiking* effect. For example, a class of first graders was presented with the forced relationship of a magazine photo of a tropical beach scene and the challenge, "In what ways might we help our new classmate, Amy, feel welcome?" One student enthusiastically blurted out, "Let's take her to Bermuda!" The next student said, "I could play with her in the sandbox during recess." This student apparently hitchhiked on the previous idea by identifying similarities between the beach in Bermuda and facts she knew about the schoolyard (e.g., both have sand used for play) (Giangreco, 1993). Idea-finding concludes by focusing in on promising ideas.

Stage 5: Solution-Finding Solution-finding involves evaluating and selecting from the ideas generated in Stage 4. It begins divergently, with an individual or group considering a wide variety of potential *criteria* that might be used to evaluate the ideas. For example, ideas about potential accommodations for an individual student might be judged by the following criteria framed in question form:

1. Is the accommodation feasible?
2. Is the accommodation time efficient for the teacher?
3. Does the student like the idea?
4. Will the accommodation likely enhance the image of the student among peers?
5. Will the accommodation promote independence and responsibility rather than dependence and helplessness?

Next, the individual or team needs to converge upon a subset of criteria and use them to evaluate the ideas. Selecting solutions can be facilitated by cross-referencing ideas and criteria arranged in a matrix. Ideas are listed along the side and criteria are listed across the top. The matrix offers space to rate each idea based on each criterion. Rating may be as simple as a plus versus minus scoring system or as complex as a scale that weighs criteria differently. Remember, whatever the scoring method used, is it *not* intended to be a formula that removes decision-making power. Rather, the criteria and rating method are intended to provide a rational framework for considering the merits of each idea. Fundamentally, solution-finding is a convergent stage of CPS in which judgment is engaged to select or combine ideas for which a plan of action is then devised and implemented.

Stage 6: Acceptance-Finding In acceptance-finding, the problem-solving task is to first think divergently by asking and answering "who, what, where, when, why, and how" questions in order to explore a variety of ways to make the selected solution(s) more workable and effective. The team then acts convergently developing a step-by-step plan of action. The entire process ends with the problem solvers taking action and regularly evaluating the effectiveness of the selected solution(s). New challenges that arise during implementation may be viewed as *opportunities—*

opportunities to cycle through the CPS process again, to invent yet more new solutions, to continue to develop a creative attitude and disposition, and to hone creativity skills.

VARIATIONS OF THE CPS PROCESS
THAT TAP STUDENTS' NATURAL CREATIVITY

This section describes three variations of the CPS process that have been field-tested in some Vermont classrooms. The variations are dedicated specifically to developing ways of enhancing meaningful participation for class members when the group includes students with a wide range of abilities and characteristics. The variations focus on the challenge of including an individual student. Although this approach was successful as a starting point, users of the variations are encouraged to consider the challenge as the meaningful inclusion of *all* class members in the classroom community.

The variations described in this section tap the innate creative abilities of students. Although it may be preferable to teach children a complete problem-solving process (e.g., Eberle & Stanish, 1985), less complete variations have proven to be effective for "on-the-fly" classroom use. CPS variations work so well because people are by their nature creative; the variations simply "fill in the blank" for steps missing from the creative processes each of us develops on our own. It should be emphasized that CPS and its variations are generic tools for students to use to address—individually or in groups—a range of academic, social, or personal challenges other than those described in this chapter.

Heterogeneous Grouping and Inclusion-Oriented
Education: A Prime Opportunity to Engage Creative Processes

Before detailing each of the three CPS variations, these authors would like to return to an examination of the context in which the variations are useful. We all know educators who look at students who have widely differing educational needs and use that observation to justify ability-grouping within a classroom or the exclusion of some students from typical classes rather than determine in what ways students' uniqueness can be appreciated and supported. For problem solvers with an inclusive educational orientation, placement in the classroom of students with widely differing educational needs is a naturally occurring incongruity. As such, heterogeneous, inclusive classrooms offer a prime opportunity for many creative ideas and solutions to be developed and tried. Inclusive education and creative problem solving, therefore, are positively interdependent characteristics of effective schooling.

CPS and its variations work best if a *creative attitude, atmosphere, and culture* exist within the classroom and school community. An additional issue, therefore, in using CPS with and for children in schools, is how to promote a culture of creativity so that students eventually identify and engage creative problem-solving strategies, even when they are not asked to. Strategies classroom teachers and administrators have used to establish more creative school cultures include the following.

Establish and use a collaborative team approach in which members of the classroom and school community work together toward common goals (Giangreco, Dennis, & Edelman, 1991; Thousand & Villa, 1992).

Be sure adults model collaborative, open, creative, and problem-solving behaviors (e.g., deferring judgment) for students.

Involve students in making important instructional decisions.

Give students ongoing opportunities to solve important problems in an atmosphere where their ideas are welcomed and acted upon.

Create opportunities for students to see that there can be more than one "right answer" to any problem or question.

Create ongoing opportunities for learning to be active and fun.

As adults, be ready, willing, and able to learn from your students as well as from each other.

Issues in Peer-Supported Problem-Solving

Because the problem-solving strategies described here engage children in problem solving for a peer, concerns arise as to whether having classmates focus on a particular student unnecessarily draws negative attention to the student or otherwise infringes upon the privacy and rights of the individual. Such concerns should always be considered seriously. Peer-supported problem-solving can be a powerful and effective strategy if precautions designed to protect student rights and dignity are observed. Specifically, educators should be sure to:

Obtain *parental consent* and permission.

Obtain *student consent*. Discuss in private the possibility of peer-supported problem-solving with the student who will be the focus of discussion and seek feedback and approval before proceeding. For students with communication challenges, explore various observational strategies and augmentative approaches to determine their interest in involving peers in planning processes.

Respect student *privacy and confidentiality* needs. For some students, the type of personal information that may be revealed and used in problem-solving with classmates may be very nonthreatening; for other students, the same information may be considered extremely sensitive and private.

Use CPS variations respectfully with *other* class members, whether or not they have a disability. This establishes the process as a *general* classroom tool for addressing daily challenges and building class community.

CPS Variation #1: "One-Minute Idea-Finding" or "Ask the Kids"

The simplest and quickest variation used in inclusive classrooms is to have the teacher ask the students for their ideas, using the steps presented in Table 4. It is remarkable how many excellent ideas students will generate when they simply are presented with information, a challenge, and a request for their ideas.

To illustrate the "Ask the Kids" variation, consider the experience of a class of third graders who are preparing a mural as a culminating activity of their social studies unit on cities (Giangreco, 1993).

> The teacher divided the class into four heterogeneous groups of five students each. One group included Betty, a girl with intensive educational needs. The teacher assigned each group a part of the city to paint or draw (e.g., downtown business area, residential neighborhoods, waterfront, industrial sites). Using cooperative group skills (Johnson, Johnson, & Holubec, 1986) the class had practiced throughout the year, each group was asked to reach consensus about what would be included in their part and decide who would be responsible for each part. Each group also had to coordinate with every other group so when finished the four pieces could be joined to make a single large mural of a city to be displayed in the hallway. The teacher told the students they should be prepared to explain what they did within and between groups and why.
>
> The teacher then asked the class, "How can we make sure that Betty has ways to par-

Table 4.   Steps in the "One-Minute Idea-Finding" or "Ask the Kids" strategy

Step 1.   *The teacher presents introductory lesson content or activity directions to the class.* This provides the students with some information about the challenge (i.e., fact-finding). They already know other general information about themselves and the classroom.

Step 2.   *The teacher presents a selected challenge to the class.* For example, a teacher might say, "We are going to be conducting a science experiment in small groups. In what ways can we make sure Molly (a student with educational challenges) is included in the activity?" This step combines objective-finding (CPS Stage 1) and problem-finding (Stage 3). An alternative phrasing that might be more inclusive and respectful would be to ask, "We are going to be conducting a science experiment in small groups. In what ways can we make sure that everyone in each group is included in the activity?"

Step 3.   *The teacher asks the students to offer their suggestions for 1 minute in an atmosphere of deferred judgment.* This is the idea-finding stage of the CPS process. The ideas may be recorded on the chalkboard or elsewhere.

Step 4.   *The class selects from the ideas generated the ones they wish to use.* This is the solution-finding stage of CPS.

Step 5.   *The students participate in the class activity and use their ideas.* This last step represents the acceptance-finding stage of CPS.

ticipate in this activity?" Mark said, "She's up there in her wheelchair and we're here on the floor with this big paper: we could get her out of her chair and bring her down here with us." Karen suggested, "It's good for Betty to have her arms moved and I know blue is her favorite color; I could help her hold and move the paint brush to paint the sky and water." Janet thought, "Betty could help carry our group's list of ideas to the other group so we can see how our parts will fit together." "Hey! That makes me think, maybe we could have Betty run the tape recorder so we can tape our list rather than writing it!" said Joe. (p. 122)

The key is to *ask* students for *their* ideas. So often we don't. This CPS variation is quick, easy, and effective, but limited for two reasons. First, students may come up short on ideas or, after using this strategy repeatedly, give "standard" answers rather than developing new, creative alternatives. Second, although student ideas may lead to meaningful inclusion of the classmate with disabilities, their suggestions may or may not address the individualized learning needs of the student. This represents a common problem in inclusion-oriented classrooms. A student may be welcomed and included, but individual learning objectives may not be adequately or deliberately addressed through participation in class activities.

Despite its limitations, this simple variation is consistent with the notion of developing natural supports internal to a classroom and simultaneously facilitating inclusion and a culture of creativity.

CPS Variation #2: "One-Minute Idea-Finding with a Fact-Finding Back-Up"

The "One-Minute Idea-Finding with Fact-Finding Back-Up" variation addresses the problem of students getting stuck for ideas or giving standard solutions. The variation takes advantage of the relationship between facts and ideas. As previously noted, ideas can come directly from facts or "idea-joggers" used to consider facts from new perspectives.

The steps of this variation parallel those of the first "One-Minute Idea-Finding" variation (see Table 4). The back-up procedure occurs at Step 3, as outlined in Table 5. Using the previous example about Betty participating in the social studies/mural activity, Giangreco (1993) offered the following example of how a teacher might assist students to break through to new ideas. The teacher could say, "Okay, what do we know about this activity?" As the students use their powers of observation to fact-

Table 5.   Fact-finding back-up procedure for Step 3 of "One-Minute Idea-Finding"

Step 3:	The teacher asks the students to offer their suggestions for 1 minute in an atmosphere of deferred judgment (idea-finding). The ideas may be recorded on the chalkboard or elsewhere.

Fact-Finding Back-Up Procedures

3a.	If students do not answer, offer a very limited number of ideas or offer standard ideas—the teacher stops and has the students list facts about the activity and class.
3b.	The teacher encourages the students to search for ideas that may be spurred by looking at the facts.
3c.	If an insufficient number of ideas is generated by looking at direct relationships between the facts and ideas, idea-joggers can be applied to the facts to generate additional ideas.

find, ideas might be spurred. The teacher could continue to facilitate idea-finding by asking probing, idea-jogging questions, such as "What would happen if we took that fact and reversed it, cut it in half, or made it bigger?" Perhaps the teacher then would present an object as a *forced relationship* to stimulate the students to look for similarities, connections, analogies, or metaphors between the object and the challenge that might help solve the problem.

Using these procedures, Andrea realized, "We need to get paper and paints from the supply room (fact-finding); Betty could go to the supply room with us and help carry back the stuff we need and give it to the other kids" (idea-finding). Marc added, "We'll be painting with a lot of different colors (fact-finding). Hey, maybe Betty could use her switch to turn on a fan. Then the paint would dry faster and we could do more painting."

This variation is quick and addresses the issue of what to do if students get stuck for ideas. However, it does not address the problem of inclusion-oriented classrooms mentioned previously; that is, a student being welcomed and included, but individual learning objectives not being adequately or deliberately addressed.

CPS Variation #3: "Get Some Help from SAM—a Good Friend"

The third variation was once called the "Short-Focused Option" (Giangreco, 1993) because the variation, being less extensive than the full CPS process, can be completed in a *short* period of time (i.e., less than 10 minutes), while *deliberately focusing on the individualized learning objectives* of a student. The deliberate attention on learning objectives distinguishes this third variation from the two previously described. Although the short-focused option, however, is not a friendly name, one colleague jokingly suggested renaming the variation "John." Another hitchhiked, saying, "Why not just a name?" Using the forced relationship technique in combination with metaphors and connections between a person's name and the short-focused option were explored. The name, SAM, came to mind because of a good friend named Sam. The short-focused option also could be considered a good friend in helping us pursue quality, inclusive education. Thus, this variation was fondly renamed SAM. SAM is not an acronym for anything, although it could be (e.g., Short Accommodation Method, Super Adaptation Method, Sane Approach Method, Subversive Accommodation Mishaps, Sequential Adaptation Map, Supersonic Activity Maker, Sure-Fire Analog Miracle, Stimulating Amplification Method).

When to Call on SAM for Assistance   SAM may be called upon prior to a lesson as a *pre-planning* activity by the teacher or a team (e.g., teacher and paraprofessional together, teacher and special educator together). When done in advance, the classroom teacher must have an idea of how the lesson or activity will be presented, as SAM can assist in adapting the original plans to address a mismatch between the planned lesson and the needs of one or more students.

Certain types of activities (e.g., large-group discussions, small-group tasks, independent work, quizzes, labs) may be a consistent part of a classroom scene. If the activities are reoccurring formats, with variations in content, facts generated by observations of these activities may be useful in generating adaptation ideas for a *series* of similar situations. This avoids continually having to reinvent the same wheel. For example, a series of options may be developed for each time a quiz is given, a lab experiment is planned, or a large-group lesson is implemented.

Examples: The Double-Edged Sword   Although examples are desirable because they can illustrate a process, they are included here with some hesitation. Any time an example is used, there always is the danger that it will become a standard response. The caution, therefore, is to remember that the examples offered here are not the *only* solutions. They may prompt piggy-backing or hitchhiking of ideas onto them, but they clearly are not the only usable ideas.

The examples embedded within the following steps are based on the student description presented below. As discussed previously, approaches that focus on the inclusionary challenges of an entire class rather than an individual student may be beneficial. In such instances, knowing the learning objectives for other students is needed to use the SAM variation effectively.

Molly is 11 years old and attends fifth grade at Mountainview Middle School. Molly lives at home with her mom, dad, and younger brother. She is known for her lovely smile and her pleasant personality and is sought after for friendship by her classmates and the children who live in her neighborhood. Molly is considered stubborn and noncompliant by some people, but those who know her best view her simply as strong-willed. Molly enjoys using headphones to listen to many kinds of music. She likes going on almost any kind of outing with family or friends, especially shopping trips with her parents. Her favorite activities include playing on playground equipment, going swimming, playing with her dog, and sledding in the winter.

Molly seems to enjoy being around other people, but does not always react as if she knows others are present. This may be due, in part, to the fact that Molly has some hearing and vision loss. Molly has some physical disabilities as well, and no formal mode of communication. Thus, it is difficult to determine her sensory abilities precisely. Although Molly has been labeled "intellectually delayed," those who know her have been unwilling to accept any label that limits expectations of her abilities. As her dad pointed out, "We just can't be sure how much she understands or what her potential is, so let's proceed as if she understands everything!"

Currently, Molly communicates primarily through facial expressions (e.g., smiling and frowning). She makes some sounds that family members understand to represent pleasure or discomfort. Her parents have pointed out that they would expect few other people to understand the meaning of these vocalizations unless their meaning had been previously explained. People communicate with Molly by speaking (to take advantage of her residual hearing), using gestures, and showing her objects and pictures (to accommodate for her visual impairments).

Molly gets from place to place by having others push her wheelchair. Molly has limited use of her arms and needs at least partial assistance with most daily activities. Her favorite foods are tacos, fruit, and pizza; she needs to have these and other foods cut into small pieces and fed to her. Molly, her teacher, the paraprofessional who supports her, classmates, and family members receive the support of an integration specialist (special educator), occupational therapist, physical therapist, speech-language pathologist, and a dual sensory impairment specialist.

Steps in Using SAM   Before getting assistance from SAM, it is important to become familiar enough with the basic principles of CPS (e.g., alternating between divergent and convergent thinking, deferring judgment, using idea-joggers) and the characteristics of problem solvers previously discussed in this chapter to apply them throughout the SAM process. The steps of SAM presented here parallel the six stages of the generic CPS process.

Step 1: Identify the Challenge and Develop a Challenge Statement   SAM starts by identifying a class, activity, or situation in which the needs of a particular student differ significantly from the range of educational needs of other students. For example, Molly, described earlier, attends a fifth grade science class in which much of the curricular content appears not to match her individual educational needs. Yet, there are many opportunities for Molly's educational needs to be met through existing class activities if the activities are adapted slightly or if new science activities are invented.

Next, a challenge statement is developed. Figure 1 offers a worksheet format[1] for getting assistance from SAM. As Figure 1 illustrates, with the SAM variation of CPS, objective-finding and problem-finding have been combined into a single challenge statement. The challenge statement, "In what ways might we address the educational needs of *(insert student name)* in *(insert name of class or activity)* class/ activity?" is applied to the student and the situation to become, for example, "In what ways might we address the educational needs of Molly in science class?"

Step 2: Identify the Facts About the Student's Educational Needs and the Class/ Activity   The left-hand column of Figure 1 is used to list facts about the student's program and educational needs. Student facts include a brief description of priority individualized education program (IEP) goals, desired learning outcomes beyond current IEP priorities, and the general supports necessary to successfully participate in the educational program. As the left-hand column of Figure 2 shows, current priority learning outcomes for Molly are:

Make choices when presented with options
Greet others
Follow instructions
React to people by displaying an observable change in behavior
Offer assistance to others
Engage in active leisure with others (e.g., plays group games)
Use adapted microswitch to activate battery-operated devices
Does a classroom job with peer(s)

This is only a *partial* listing of all of the learning outcomes generated by Molly's support team,[2] which includes her parents.

In the second column of the SAM worksheet (Figures 1 & 2), observations about

---

[1]The SAM worksheet presented in Figure 1 is meant to offer a format to facilitate systematic exploration of possibilities at each step of the SAM process. The authors acknowledge that the SAM form has limited space and likely will be insufficient for all of the ideas that will be generated. It may be easier, therefore, to simply have the form available as a reminder of the SAM process and to write ideas as lists on blank sheets of paper. SAM users also are encouraged to modify or develop their own SAM worksheet formats and share them with the authors.

[2]Information about the student may come from any of several sources. If using the COACH assessment (Giangreco, Cloninger, & Iverson, 1993), this information may come from one of three sources: 1) the Program-at-a-Glance, 2) the Scheduling Matrix, or 3) the student's schedule. A Program-at-a-Glance lists a full set of facts regarding the content of the student's educational program. A Scheduling Matrix provides a set of facts as they relate to particular classes or major class activities. Both identify priority objectives for a student, other anticipated learning outcomes, and general supports the child's team has decided are needed for student participation in classes. SAM has been pilot-tested in environments where COACH was used to generate information about the focus student. Of course, information about a student may be generated or collected in many other ways, directly (e.g., direct observation) and indirectly (e.g., record review, interviews with the student, family members, friends, school personnel).

OBJECTIVE-FINDING
AND PROBLEM-FINDING:

In what ways might we address the educational needs
of _____ in _____ ?
    (student's name)   (class/activity)

FACT-FINDING		IDEA-FINDING	
Facts about student's needs 1	Facts about class/activity 2	Direct Ideas 3	Indirect Ideas 4

(continued)

Figure 1. SAM creative problem-solving worksheet. (Based on Osborn-Parnes Creative Problem-Solving process [Parnes, 1981, 1985, 1988, 1992]).

Figure 1. (*continued*)

SOLUTION-FINDING

Potential Ideas	Criteria				
	Addresses student need	Neutral or positive for students without disabilities	Likely to support valued life outcomes	Perceived as usable by users (e.g., teacher)	Other: _____ _____ _____
1.					
2.					
3.					
4.					
5.					
6.					
7.					
8.					
9.					
10.					
11.					
12.					

ACCEPTANCE-FINDING

What needs to be done?

Who is going to do it?

When is it going to be done?

How can the ideas be improved?

Where will it be done?

OBJECTIVE-FINDING
AND PROBLEM-FINDING:

In what ways might we address the educational needs
of _____ Molly _____ in _____ Science _____ ?
(student's name)   (class/activity)

FACT-FINDING		IDEA-FINDING	
Facts about student's needs 1	Facts about class/activity (partial listing)	Direct Ideas (partial listing)	Indirect Ideas (partial listing)
1. Makes choices 2. Greets others 3. Follows instructions 4. Reacts to people 5. Offers assistance 6. Engages in active leisure 7. Uses "switch" 8. Does classroom job with peer(s)	1. Students greet each other and teacher before class bell rings. 2. Students hand in homework to box on teacher's desk. 3. Teacher tells students agenda for class. 4. Teacher turns off lights and shows short video. 5. Teacher assigns small groups to play educational games to reinforce video. 6. Teacher passes out quiz. 7. Some students who finish early feed class fish and gerbils.	Teach/practice greeting before bell rings. Work on active leisure (game skills) during educational games and instruction following. Caring for class pets with a peer may be a classroom job.	Student chooses which game to play. Student gets opportunity to react to classmates by having "homework box" on her desk. Student offers assistance to others and gets opportunities to react by handing out quizzes. Student uses switch to activate TV/VCR and listen to music when adapted quiz is completed.

Figure 2.   SAM creative problem-solving worksheets completed for Molly.

(continued)

Figure 2. (*continued*)

SOLUTION-FINDING

(partial listing)

Potential Ideas

	Criteria				
	Addresses student need	Neutral or positive for students without disabilities	Likely to support valued life outcomes	Perceived as usable by users (e.g., teacher)	Other: _____ _____ _____
①Student chooses game	+	+	+	+	
②Homework box on desk	+	+	+	+	
③Handout quizzes	+	+	+	+	
4. Switch for lights	+	+	+	—	
5. Switch for TV/VCR	+	+	+	—	
⑥Switch for tape player	+	+	+	+	
⑦Greeting before class	+	+	+	+	
⑧Cares for class pets	+	+	+	+	
⑨Plays educational games	+	+	+	+	
10. Grades quizzes with key	+	—	—	—	
11. Record and play tape of class agenda	+	+	+	—	
12.					

ACCEPTANCE-FINDING

What needs to be done?

Who is going to do it?

When is it going to be done?

How can the ideas be improved?

Where will it be done?

the class or activity may be listed. These facts should include the things the teacher and students actually do (e.g., teacher shows a videotape, class plays an educational game, students draw diagrams, groups of students build a model). To gain accurate information about a class may require one or more of a student's support team to observe in the classroom. Here, it is more crucial to identify what the teacher and students *do* than to identify the curricular content of the general education lesson. Thus, no observed event is insignificant, as any activity may prove to be useful in either prompting or being an idea for adapting a lesson. For example, what adaptations or accommodations for Molly do the facts about science class (see Figure 2) bring to mind?

Before the bell rings, the teacher and students *greet* each other and talk informally.
Students hand in homework to box on teacher's desk.
A *student turns off the lights* before a film is shown.
The *teacher* passes out the quiz.

Remember, when facing curriculum overlapping challenges, the nature of activity in a classroom is more important to developing adaptations than the actual lesson content. When classroom approaches are primarily passive and teacher-directed, opportunities for meaningful participation for curriculum overlapping are more limited. When classroom approaches are active and participatory, opportunities for meaningful participation expand. A goal of creative problem solving, therefore, is to increase teachers' use of more active and participatory instructional approaches.

Step 3: Generate Direct and Indirect Ideas   A "first level" of idea-finding involves a systematic comparison[3] of each fact about the student (see the first column in Figure 2) with each fact about the class/activity (see the second column in Figure 2) to look for direct, obvious relationships. Any *direct ideas* that arise through this comparison are recorded in the third column of Figure 2, labeled Direct Ideas. Given 8–10 facts in each of the two fact columns, the comparison process should take no more than a few minutes.

Let's compare the facts about Molly and her class listed in Figure 2. It is immediately apparent that there is a direct relationship between the second fact in column 1 (i.e., greets others) and first fact in column 2 (i.e., students greet each other and teacher before the bell rings). This class appears to offer a natural time to teach and practice greetings. Notice also that Molly's goal of participating in active leisure with peers relates directly with the teacher's planned activity for students to play educational games. The activity is a natural opportunity for Molly to follow instructions related to game playing (e.g., rolling dice, picking up cards, moving a marker). Another direct relationship exists between Molly's need for doing a classroom job and the activity of feeding and caring for the classroom fish and gerbils. Clearly, caring for the classroom animals could be a class job done with a classmate.

Systematically comparing facts about a student's needs and classroom routines may reveal that naturally occurring opportunities for meaningful inclusion already exist, without the need for significant changes in routine. The number of such opportunities, however, may be insufficient for an educational experience of adequate

---

[3]While the two fact-finding and the idea-finding steps are presented here in a linear, sequential fashion, these authors have found shifting attention back and forth between the two sets of facts to be a powerful technique for prompting ideas for adaptations. For example, once educational needs are listed, each new class/activity fact can be compared with the needs to see if an idea is immediately spurred. These ideas should be recorded as they are generated.

quality; therefore, it may be necessary to invent adaptations to existing routines or invent completely new experiences.

After identifying direct ideas, it may be necessary to look for *indirect ideas* by applying idea-joggers to facts. Following the same pattern used to find direct ideas, facts about the student and facts about the class/activity are compared, while applying an idea-jogger (e.g., Ask, "What would happen if we eliminated this fact, or made it bigger or smaller?"). At this point it is critical to defer judgment about the quality, usefulness, or feasibility of the ideas that result. For example, suppose the idea-jogger of *reversing* were applied to the facts in Figure 2. The teacher intends to assign small groups to play educational games to reinforce content presented in the videotape. By reversing who chooses the game from teacher to student, an idea is generated for Molly to work on choice making, a priority goal for her (see column 4 of Figure 2).

Suppose the idea-jogger of *rearranging* were applied to Molly's goal of reacting to the presence of other people and the fact that, in this science class, students hand in homework by placing it in a box on the teacher's desk. Rearranging the place where homework is turned in so that the homework box is on Molly's desk would create as many opportunities for interaction as there are students in the class.

Combining *rearranging* with the idea-jogger of *minifying/making smaller* and applying them to the fact that the science teacher passes out quizzes and Molly needs practice reacting to and offering assistance to others could lead to the indirect idea of having Molly and a classmate, rather than the teacher, pass out quizzes. To keep the pace of classroom activities typical, the task could be made smaller so that Molly hands out five quizzes in the same time that her partner hands out 20. While all of the ideas just described may seem small, they do match the student's identified needs.

Step 4: Evaluate Ideas and Choose Solutions   Step 4 involves solution-finding and convergent thinking. Here direct and indirect ideas are evaluated based on a set of criteria. The four criteria on the SAM worksheet (see Figures 1 and 2) are offered as starting points for evaluating ideas. Ideas are listed in abbreviated form in the left-hand column of the worksheet. Then, each idea is judged according to the selected criteria. Using the four criteria included on the worksheet, one may ask:

Does this idea address an identified student need?

Is the idea positive or at least neutral in terms of likely impact upon students without disabilities?

Is the idea likely to yield valued life outcomes (e.g., friendships and affiliations, access to meaningful places and activities, choice and control that matches a person's age, health, and safety)?

Is the idea perceived as feasible and meaningful by the user (e.g., the teacher)?

As already noted, the process of applying criteria to potential ideas is intended to assist decision making. Criteria, therefore, must match the situation and be adjusted, replaced, eliminated, or otherwise changed to match the unique characteristics of a situation. Items may be rated using whatever method is preferred and makes sense, as long as by the end of this step, preferred solutions have been selected.

Step 5: Refine Ideas to Develop and Carry Out an Action Plan   Once solutions have been selected, they must be refined. Idea-joggers continue to be helpful in accomplishing this end. For example, suppose that a direct idea was generated about playing an educational game as an accommodation for Molly. When looking carefully at the nature of the game, Molly's physical characteristics likely would prompt the question, "What if the game parts were bigger?" This type of simple adaptation might allow Molly to participate, at least partially, with game materials. The who, what, where, when, why, and how questions facilitate the development and delivery of a CPS action plan. As ideas are implemented, remember to be alert to new facts and new ways to "make the familiar strange." Also note how repeatedly cycling through the SAM and other CPS variations develops a creative attitude and competence.

EVALUATING THE IMPACT OF USING CPS ON STUDENTS' EDUCATIONAL EXPERIENCES

For any educational innovation, it is crucial to evaluate the innovation to determine if it is achieving its intended outcomes. The use of CPS is intended, at a minimum, to: 1) increase the frequency and quality of instructional involvement within heterogeneous groups, 2) meet the educational needs of the student with disabilities, 3) meet the educational needs of students without disabilities, and 4) provide support mechanisms and teaching adaptations for the teacher and other members of the classroom community. Measurement techniques, such as frequency counts, time samples, and item-by-item ratings, of specific target behaviors may require augmentation to answer certain evaluation questions. Teachers, however, may find more "user-friendly" (Meyer & Janney, 1989, p. 263) forms of measurement useful, such as the *CPS Impact Evaluation* offered in Figure 3.

A teacher may complete the *CPS Impact Evaluation* form before and after using CPS and its variations in a classroom. Direct observations of a student in the class combined with the pre-intervention use of the evaluation give a quick overview of the current situation without interfering with instruction or taking an inordinate amount of time. Once CPS strategies have been applied for a sufficient amount of time, the teacher may again use the *CPS Impact Evaluation* form as a post-intervention measure. Comparison of pre/post responses offers a relatively simple and quick assessment of the perceived impact of the use of CPS.

Clearly, this type of evaluation may not yield reliable responses across team members (e.g., teacher, parent, students, special educator, principal). When team members who have independently completed the evaluation form disagree on pre- or post-assessments, the tool serves another function—it prompts team members to dialogue, which should facilitate a collective understanding of educational programs, a shared framework for adjusting instruction, and improved teamwork.

EDUCATIONAL IMPLICATIONS OF USING THE OSBORN-PARNES CPS PROCESS

This chapter opened with the proposition that inclusive educational arrangements are desired alternatives to more exclusionary traditional approaches. The Osborn-Parnes Creative Problem-Solving process and its variations are offered as a set of procedures for empowering teams to meet the challenge of meaningfully instructing heterogeneous groups of learners.

There are many implications of mastering and using CPS and its variations, particularly in the education of students who otherwise might be excluded from the general education opportunities. Table 6 offers anticipated benefits for students with

Table 6. Implications of using CPS for students with and without disabilities

CPS engages students in the solution of real-life problems and challenges, which are an essential characteristic of effective education (Dewey, 1938).

CPS encourages students to believe they can solve problems, either independently or with the support of others in the class.

CPS offers students at all levels of academic achievement the opportunity to assist in solving relevant challenges faced by them or their classmates and establishes all students as valued contributors.

CPS offers opportunities for students to be included in general class activities in ways that meet their individualized educational needs.

CPS offers opportunities for students to participate in the design of their own instruction.

CPS offers opportunities for students to learn and practice problem-solving skills on an ongoing basis to address relevant challenges.

The collaborative, nonjudgmental, and action-oriented aspects of CPS encourage a sense of community building among classmates when the process is used to address challenges that are of concern to the group.

CPS can encourage and reinforce many desirable academic and affective skills (e.g., observation, analysis, evaluation, perspective taking, building on another's ideas, synthesizing ideas).

disabilities and their peers without disabilities; Table 7 suggests positive outcomes educators should expect when they use problem-solving methods described in this chapter.

Taking action is the first, middle, and culminating step for any problem solver, including those of us who are interested in excellence, excitement, and equity in education. We would do well, therefore, to follow the advice of Charles Kettering to "keep on going and chances are you will stumble on something, perhaps when you least expect it. I have never heard of anyone stumbling on something sitting down" (cited in Parnes, 1988, p. 89). The creative problem-solving strategies offered in this chapter should help us to keep on going, for as Irving Cheyette noted, "creativity is converting wishful thinking into willful doing" (cited in Parnes, 1988, p. 105).

Table 7. Implications for professionals working with students in heterogeneous groups

CPS encourages teachers to be open to the possibility that there is more than one "right" answer.

CPS encourages teachers to provide the kinds of active, problem-solving learning experiences that educational leaders have advised us are essential now and will be increasingly vital as we enter the 21st century.

CPS encourages teachers to be ongoing learners and especially to open themselves to learn from the children in their classes.

CPS provides a method for distributing the pressures of instructional accommodations in inclusive classrooms across a wider group of problem solvers.

CPS used by teachers can enhance their capacity to teach all children by recognizing existing options for teaching heterogeneous groups, adapting other existing options, and inventing new options.

CPS encourages teachers to design interesting, active approaches to education that account for student input and result in motivating learning experiences.

REFERENCES

Brown, L., Ford, A., Nisbet, J., Sweet, M., Donnellan, A., & Gruenewald, L. (1983). Opportunities available when severely handicapped students attend chronological age appropriate regular schools. *Journal of The Association for Persons With Severe Handicaps, 8,* 16–24.

Campbell, C., Campbell, S., Collicott, J., Perner, D., & Stone, J. (1988). Individualized instruction. *Education New Brunswick—Journal Education, 3,* 17–20.

Collicott, J. (1991). Implementing multi-level instruction: Strategies for classroom teachers. In

Evaluation of Intervention Impact on Inclusion: _____ PRE or _____ POST

Student name _____ Grade/placement _____

Lesson/activity _____

Lesson/activity time of day _____ Length of lesson/activity _____

Observation dates: from _____ to _____ Number of observations _____

Teacher(s) of the lesson/activity _____

Name of respondent _____
Describe the extent of involvement (e.g., how, what) for the student with special needs

in the lesson/activity: _____

_____

_____

Average number of minutes of participation: _____ min out of a total of _____ possible
  minutes
Average number of opportunities/turns for participation per lesson: _____
Compared to classmates, the time and opportunities for participation by this student
  typically are:

___ significantly less   ___ slightly less   ___ about the same   ___ more

Based on your observations of the lesson/activity prior to _____ (list
  intervention):

1. How involved was the student in the lesson/activity?
    Not involved   Very involved
    1   2   3   4   5   6   7   8   9   10
    Comments:

2. How much did the student benefit educationally (based on his/her individual
   educational program) from participation in the lesson/activity?
    Not at all   Very much
    1   2   3   4   5   6   7   8   9   10
    Comments:

3. Did you have a clear idea which of the student's individual goals and objectives
   could be addressed during this lesson/activity?
    Not at all clear   Very clear
    1   2   3   4   5   6   7   8   9   10
    Comments:

4. Did you have enough usable instructional ideas to include the student with special
   needs in meaningful ways during this lesson/activity?
    Insufficient number   More than sufficient number
    1   2   3   4   5   6   7   8   9   10
    Comments:

(continued)

Figure 3.   CPS Impact Evaluation. (From Giangreco, M.F. [1993]. Using creative problem solving methods to include students with severe disabilities in general education classroom activities. *Journal of Educational and Psychological Consultation, 4*, pp. 131–132; reprinted by permission of Lawrence Erlbaum Associates.)

Figure 3.   *(continued)*

5. Did you use an identifiable method to develop ways of including the student with special educational needs in this lesson/activity?

No identifiable method   Clearly identifiable method

| 1 | 2 | 3 | 4 | 5 | 6 | 7 | 8 | 9 | 10 |

Comments:

6. What impact did the methods used to include the student with special needs (not the presence of the student) in this lesson/activity have on the educational growth (academic/social) of other students?

Negative impact   Positive impact

| 1 | 2 | 3 | 4 | 5 | 6 | 7 | 8 | 9 | 10 |

Comments:

7. How confident are you that the methods used to include the student with special needs in this lesson/activity can be generalized to other lessons in the same content area and/or other content areas to more fully include this student?

Not confident   Very confident

| 1 | 2 | 3 | 4 | 5 | 6 | 7 | 8 | 9 | 10 |

Comments:

8. To what extent did the methods used to include the student with special needs lead to improved valued life outcomes (VLO) for the student (e.g., affected relationships with others; expanded access to settings and activities; improved health/safety; offered choice or control)?

Did not improve VLO at all   Improved VLO significantly

| 1 | 2 | 3 | 4 | 5 | 6 | 7 | 8 | 9 | 10 |

Comments:

9. Overall, how satisfied are you with the current extent and quality of involvement of this student in the lesson/activity?

Not satisfied   Very satisfied

| 1 | 2 | 3 | 4 | 5 | 6 | 7 | 8 | 9 | 10 |

Comments:

G. Porter & D. Richler (Eds.), *Changing Canadian schools: Perspectives on disability and inclusion* (pp. 191–218). Ottawa, Ontario, Canada: The Roeher Institute.

Dewey, J. (1938). *Experience and education.* New York: Collier Books, Macmillan.

Eberle, B., & Stanish, B. (1985). *CPS for kids: A resource book for teaching creative problem-solving to children.* East Aurora, NY: D.O.K. Publishing.

Edmonds, R. (1979). Some schools work and more can. *Social Policy, 9*(5), 25–29.

Firestien, R. (1989). *Why didn't I think of that? A personal and professional guide to better ideas and decision making.* East Aurora, NY: D.O.K. Publishing.

Forest, M. (1987). *More education integration: A collection of readings on the integration of children with mental handicaps into regular school systems.* Ottawa, Ontario, Canada: The Roeher Institute.

Giangreco, M.F. (1992). Curriculum in inclusion-oriented schools: Trends, issues, challenges, and potential solutions. In S. Stainback & W. Stainback (Eds.), *Curriculum considerations in inclu-sive classrooms: Facilitating learning for all students* (pp. 239–263). Baltimore: Paul H. Brookes Publishing Co.

Giangreco, M.F. (1993). Using creative problem solving methods to include students with severe disabilities in general education classroom activities. *Journal of Educational and Psychological Consultation, 4,* 113–135.

Giangreco, M.F., Cloninger, C.J., & Iverson, V.S. (1993). *Choosing options and accommodations for children (COACH): A guide to planning inclusive education.* Baltimore: Paul H. Brookes Publishing Co.

Giangreco, M., Dennis, R., Cloninger, C., Edelman, S., & Schattman, R. (1993). "I've counted Jon": Transformational experiences of teachers educating students with disabilities. *Exceptional Children, 59,* 359–372.

Giangreco, M., Dennis, R., & Edelman, S. (1991). Common professional practices that interfere with the integrated delivery of related services. *Remedial and Special Education, 12*(2), 16–24.

Giangreco, M., Edelman, S., Cloninger, C., & Dennis, R. (1993). My child has a classmate with severe disabilities: What parents of nondisabled children think about full inclusion. *Developmental Disabilities Bulletin, 21*(1), 77–91.

Giangreco, M.F., & Meyer, L.H. (1988). Expanding service delivery options in regular schools and classrooms for students with severe disabilities. In J.L. Graden, J.E. Zins, & M.J. Curtis (Eds.), *Alternative educational delivery systems: Enhancing instructional options for all students* (pp. 241–267). Washington, DC: National Association of School Psychologists.

Giangreco, M.F., & Putnam, J.W. (1991). Supporting the education of students with severe disabilities in regular education environments. In L.H. Meyer, C.A. Peck, & L. Brown (Eds.), *Critical issues in the lives of people with severe disabilities* (pp. 245–270). Baltimore: Paul H. Brookes Publishing Co.

Gordon, W.J.J. (1987). *The new art of the possible: The basic course in synectics.* Cambridge, MA: Porpoise.

Gordon, W.J.J., & Poze, T. (1979). *The metaphorical way of learning and knowing.* Cambridge, MA: SES Associates.

Helmstetter, E., Peck, C., & Giangreco, M. (1992). *Benefits of integration: A statewide survey of nondisabled high school students.* Pullman, WA: Washington State University. Manuscript submitted for publication review.

Johnson, D.W., Johnson, R.T., & Holubec, E.J. (1986). *Circles of learning: Cooperation in the classroom* (rev.). Edina, MN: Interaction Book Company.

Lipsky, D.K., & Gartner, A. (Eds.). (1989). *Beyond separate education: Quality education for all.* Baltimore: Paul H. Brookes Publishing Co.

Meyer, L.H., & Janney, R. (1989). User-friendly measures of meaningful outcomes: Evaluating behavioral interventions. *Journal of The Association for Persons with Severe Handicaps, 14,* 263–270.

Osborn, A. (1953). *Applied imagination: Principles and procedures of creative thinking.* New York: Charles Scribner's Sons.

Parnes, S.J. (1981). *The magic of your mind.* Buffalo, NY: The Creative Education Foundation Inc., in association with Bearly Limited.

Parnes, S.J. (1985). *A facilitating style of leadership.* Buffalo, NY: Bearly Limited in association with The Creative Education Foundation, Inc.

Parnes, S.J. (1988). *Visionizing: State-of-the-art processes for encouraging innovative excellence.* East Aurora, NY: D.O.K. Publishing.

Parnes, S.J. (1992). *Source book for creative problem-solving: A fifty year digest of proven innovation processes.* Buffalo, NY: Creative Education Foundation Press.

Peck, C., Donaldson, J., & Pezzoli, M. (1990). Some benefits nonhandicapped adolescents perceive for themselves from their social relationships with peers who have severe handicaps. *Journal of The Association for Persons with Severe Handicaps, 15,* 241–249.

Porter, G., & Richler, D. (1991). *Changing Canadian schools: Perspectives on disability and inclusion.* North York, Ontario, Canada: The Roeher Institute.

Schaffner, C.B., & Buswell, B.E. (1991). *Opening doors: Strategies for including all students in regular education.* Colorado Springs, CO: PEAK Parent Center, Inc.

Schnorr, R. (1990). "Peter? He comes and he goes . . . ": First-graders' perspectives on a part-time mainstream student. *Journal of The Association for Persons with Severe Handicaps, 15,* 231–240.

Stainback, S., & Stainback, W. (Eds.). (1992). *Curriculum considerations in inclusive classrooms: Facilitating learning for all students.* Baltimore: Paul H. Brookes Publishing Co.

Stainback, W., & Stainback, S. (Eds.). (1990). *Support networks for inclusive schooling: Interdependent integrated education.* Baltimore: Paul H. Brookes Publishing Co.

Thousand, J., & Villa, R. (1990). Strategies for educating learners with severe disabilities within their local home schools and communities. *Focus on Exceptional Children, 23*(3), 1–24.

Thousand, J.S., & Villa, R.A. (1992). Collaborative teams: A powerful tool in school restructuring. In R.A. Villa, J.S. Thousand, W. Stainback & S. Stainback (Eds.), *Restructuring for caring and effective education: An administrative guide to creating heterogeneous schools* (pp. 73–108). Baltimore: Paul H. Brookes Publishing Co.

Vandercook, T., York, J., & Johnson, S. (1991). *Inclusive education for learners with severe disabilities: Print and media resources.* Minneapolis, MN: University of Minnesota, Institute on Community Integration.

Villa, R.A., Thousand, J.S., Stainback, W., & Stainback, S. (Eds.). (1992). *Restructuring for caring and effective education: An administrative guide to creating heterogeneous schools.* Baltimore: Paul H. Brookes Publishing Co.

Building Connections

Mary A. Falvey,
Marsha Forest, Jack Pearpoint,
and Richard L. Rosenberg

Schools that model and reflect the values of including all their students are those that are systematically building connections between the school and the participants in the school community. Building such community connections is essential to fostering a sense of belonging to the school community (O'Brien & Mount, 1991; Strully & Strully, 1985). These community connections and friendships are critical for many reasons. To avoid loneliness; to develop social, communicative, and even cognitive skills; to feel like a valued member of the community; and to develop the support needed to co-exist in a community are just a few of the reasons for building community connections and friendships (Stainback & Stainback, 1990; Stainback, Stainback, & Wilkinson, 1992).

One of the key characteristics of building connections and friendships is that people have close proximity and frequent opportunities to interact with each other (Asher, Odem, & Gottman, 1977; Hartup, 1975; Howes, 1983; Lewis & Rosenblaum, 1975). Research has demonstrated that in order for children and adults to form the necessary bonds for friendships, they must have frequent access to one another. This access is facilitated when students are regularly in close proximity to one another. So it follows that students who attend the same school as the other students who live in their neighborhood are more likely to form bonds that are strong enough to result in friendship (Grenot-Scheyer, Coots, & Falvey, 1989).

Traditionally, special educators have been training and teaching students to be independent. Recently, emphasis has been placed on interdependence (Condeluci, 1991; O'Brien & Mount, 1991). Interdependence is the ability to connect with individuals within one's own community and develop a network of supports to assist in accomplishing life goals.

There are too many unhappy, unloving, untrusting, and just mediocre schools. These schools do not teach nor do they emulate such principles as love, passion, openness, and the love of learning. Academic subjects are important only if they are used to teach these principles, as illustrated powerfully in Figure 1.

Teachers burn out in schools and classrooms that are teaching basic core academic skills out of the context of teaching values. Schools must be places where students are taught such skills as creating a just community and society and how to care for and help one another.

For 5 years, a group of teenagers fought a school district in a Western state who refused to allow one of their peers, Louise, to enter or attend the same high school as the rest of them. The school district claimed that because of her diabetes and other severe cognitive and physical disability labels, she had to attend a special education segregated class in a different high school.

When the school district forced Louise to attend a different high school, her friends were outraged. They had learned about the United States Constitution in their eighth grade civics class and felt that by denying Louise access to her neighborhood high school, her rights and their rights were being violated. They launched a campaign seeking support from advocates and their community. Their plight and their struggle were frequently written about in the newspaper; they appeared on local television news programs; and they presented to local governmental and advocacy groups, including the local city council and the board of education. In addition, they wrote and performed a "rap" song entitled "Friends," which tells their story—what they wanted and why. In April 1993, the students struggle was over—the school district reversed its decision and granted Louise the opportunity to attend the same school and classes as her peers and friends. What is so compelling about this true story is that the students, Louise and her circle of friends, formed their relationship and subsequent friendships based upon their opportunity to go to school and classes together while in junior high school. There were no adults who told the students to care about Louise because she was "special," or to treat her differently because she had diabetes and/or severe disability labels. Going to school and classes together gave these students the opportunity to know each other and become friends; they just wanted that opportunity back.

What this true story dramatizes is the need that children naturally feel to develop friendships. This natural phenomenon would continue if policy makers and ed-

---

Dear Teacher,

I am a survivor of a concentration camp. My eyes saw what no man should witness.

Gas chambers built by learned engineers.
Children poisoned by educated physicians.
Infants killed by trained nurses.
Women & babies shot & burned by high school & college graduates.

So I am suspicious of education.
My request is that teachers help students become human.
Your efforts must never produce learned monsters, skilled psychopaths, educated Eichmanns.

Reading, writing, arithmetic are important only if they serve to make our children more human.

Figure 1.   Letter to teachers. (From Ginott, H. [1972]. *Teacher and child*. New York: Collier Books; reprinted by permission of the author's estate.)

ucators just gave all students a chance. Unfortunately, frequent opportunities and close proximity are not always enough for children and adolescents to feel connected and build a network of friends. Several tools have been used successfully to facilitate such connections and eventual friendships. These tools are designed to tap into the creative energy of students and educators. Circle of Friends, Making Action Plans (MAPs), and Planning Alternatives Tomorrows with Hope (PATH) are three tools that are person-centered and assume the theory that everyone is valued. They are based on hope for the future and begin with the assumptions that all people belong, all can learn, everyone is better off together, and diversity is one of our most critical strengths. These tools are described in detail in the remainder of this chapter.

CIRCLE OF FRIENDS

A circle of friends is something that many of us take for granted unless we do not have one. A circle of friends provides us with a support network of family and friends. A circle of friends is available when one needs someone to listen, to give loving advice, and to provide support when it is needed (Perske, 1989). In the absence of a naturally formed circle of friends, educators can facilitate a circle process, which can be used to enlist the involvement and commitment of future involvement of peers around an individual student. For a student who is not well connected or does not have an extensive network of friends, a circle of friends process can be useful.

A circle of friends involves gathering together a group of students for the purpose of discovering their own circle of friends and then reflecting on each other's circles (Sherwood, 1990). Figure 2 provides a list of the steps involved in conducting a circle of friends process.

A high school teacher's experience using a circle of friends is described to illustrate the process. This teacher decided to avoid burning out and wanted to inject life back into her students, herself, and the school. She knew she could not change everything, but for at least a few of her students who had been labeled "at risk" and severely disabled and who were on the verge of dropping out of school, she could try to instill some hope and help them build connections and relationships with other students.

The teacher gathered about 50 students together and told them she wanted to have a frank discussion about friends and how to build more solid relationships in the school. She did not single out any individual, but talked in general for half an hour about her own vision and beliefs in relationships and friendship as the core of a good school. She played music softly in the background and drew colorful images as she spoke. She then drew four concentric circles on the chalkboard. She gave each student a sheet of paper that also had four concentric circles and requested that they put their name in the center of the inner circle. She modeled this by putting her name in the center of her circle. Then she directed them to write, on the first and smallest circle, the names of all the people closest to their heart. She gave an example from her own life by putting her husband, her mother, her two children, and, for fun, her computer as she is an avid computer fan in her first circle. She also added the spirit of a friend of hers who had died 2 years prior.

Then she explained that the second circle is for people who are friends, but who are not as close as those identified in the first circle. Again, she modeled this by using examples from her own life; she has six friends who she calls all the time and two others whom she sees once a year but whom she speaks to frequently. She also in-

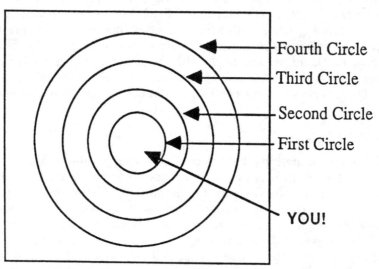

Figure 2.   Steps involved in conducting a Circle of Friends process.

cluded some family members, a few teachers she works with, and her cat. She then asked the students to fill in their second circle and found that the classroom was very quiet as the students were taking, activity seriously.

The teacher explained that the third circle was for individuals or groups of people whom they really liked, but to whom they were not very close. She modeled by identifying some of the teachers at the high school, members of the church choir where she sings, some of her tennis partners, and some members of her exercise class. She also listed individuals she sees occasionally, but who come and go, and three relatives she likes, but seldom sees.

After the students completed their third circle, she explained that the fourth circle was for people who are paid to be in their lives, such as teachers and doctors. She identified her doctor, chiropractor, and housekeeper as those people who are paid to be in her life. The students followed by identifying those people in their lives who are paid to be there. The circles were then complete.

The teacher told the students that she could tell a lot about people by looking at their completed circles. She asked for a student to volunteer his or her completed circles. She held up the completed circles of the student who volunteered and read the names of the people in each circle. Figure 3 shows the completed set of circles of this student, who has a high quality of life experiences and opportunities. She stated that she had a full life, but not perfect. Then she showed the students the completed set of circles of Jane, a student with disabilities and an "at-risk" label and asked them to describe how they would feel if those were their circles. Figure 4 shows Jane's completed set of circles. The most frequent response was that "the only people who are involved in this student's life are her family and those people who are paid to be there." In addition, the students also responded with the following descriptors:

Lonely
Depressed
Unwanted
Rejected
Isolated
Confused
Upset
Horrible
Humorless
Distraught
Frustrated
Suicidal

The teacher then asked the students to identify what they would do if this were representative of their life. Their responses were:

Commit suicide
Die
Try to make friends
Move to a deserted island
Do something really drastic
Kick
Drugs
Have a baby
Stay in bed
Drink
Kill someone
Get a tutor

A passionate discussion poured out of the students. They began talking about all the pressures they feel from their families, the school, their teachers, and society in general. They identified that they felt "pressure," as they put it, "to look good, to do well, and to achieve a lot." They felt the general attitude of teachers was that if they could not make it to a university, they were a total failure. The teacher listened and contributed to the discussion and then explained that she started the discussion to see how many students would be interested in helping her figure out how to fill in the circles of those students who were isolated and without friends.

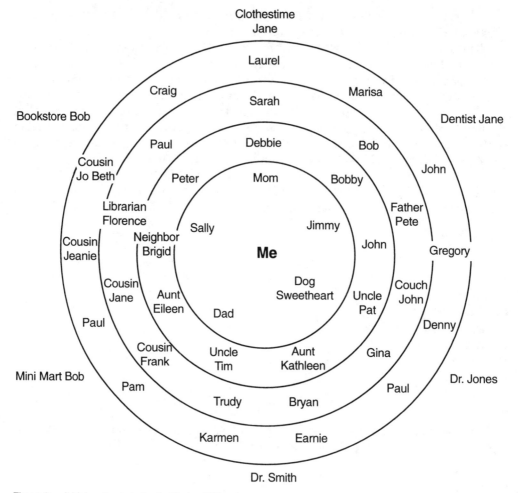

Figure 3.   A high school student's Circle of Friends.

She explained that her strategy would be to fill in circles from the outside circle to the inner circle. For example, if Jane is lonely, they would start by getting Jane involved in groups and organizations to gradually find people who are interested in more personal commitments. She explained that she was not asking, "Who wants to be Jane's friend?", which is a question searching for failure. Rather, she would ask, "Who knows Jane and is willing to brainstorm with me ideas for getting Jane more involved? For example, if Jane likes films, maybe we can identify someone who would invite her to the film club."

The teacher asked the students if there was anyone who wanted to carry on this discussion and help to figure out ways to build community and circles in their school. To her surprise, all but three students signed up and said they wanted to meet again and often.

Circle of Friends is not a trick or a gimmick; it is a powerful tool. Like a chisel, it can be used to pry open one's heart, soul, and thoughts, or create a work of art. A work of art does not happen overnight, and neither does building circles or communities. Circles and community building is a commitment. It is as important as math, physics, or history. It is part of a curriculum of caring. It is holistic, powerful, and not

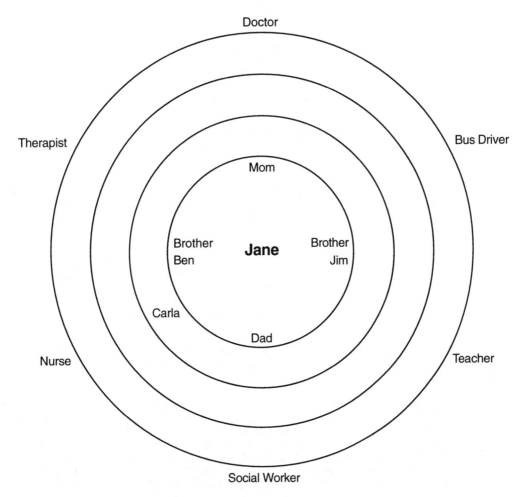

Figure 4. Circle of Friends for Jane, a student with disabilities and an at-risk label.

a thing you do once, then walk away. It is an ongoing strategy for growth, change, and development.

A young man named Tracy learned to read and write at the age of 33, after years of believing he was "learning disabled" and "retarded." As an adult, he spent time at a high school that was implementing circles and including all students in general education. He wondered what would have happened if someone would have gently and slowly helped him to build circles of friends and understand the difference between a drug pusher and a friend, or a "gang" and a group of friends. After hearing about and observing "circles" in action, he wrote the powerful poem presented in Figure 5, which describes how circles are helping teachers and students not to pass each other without stopping, listening, and really seeing.

MAKING ACTION PLANS (MAPs)

MAPs are tools designed to help individuals, organizations, and families determine how to move into the future effectively and creatively. MAPs is a tool that can be used by "artists"—people dedicated to making others' lives better, richer, and stronger in

Don't Pass Me By
by Tracy LeQuyere

I'm a man at thirty-three
Who just learned to read,
I was here all the time
But people passed me by.

One day a woman said I will show you a lie.
I know you can read with
a little time.
But people just passed me by.

So I gave me a little time,
And I gave her a little time.
See this writing,
I will have more time.

Don't pass me by.

Figure 5.   Poem reflecting the need to be connected. (From LeQuyere, T. [1991]. *Don't pass me by*. Toronto, Ontario, Canada: Inclusion Press; reprinted by permission.)

the spiritual sense of life (Forest & Lusthaus, 1989, 1990; Forest & Pearpoint, 1992; Vandercook, York, & Forest, 1989).

The MAPs process facilitates the collection of information about the persons and/or family in question. In his book entitled *Reflections on Inclusive Education*, Patrick Mackan (1991) writes:

> There is a temptation for teachers and other professionals to judge people in terms of their BEHAVIOR and outward appearance. It is all too seldom that we see through the apparent and visible which makes the person who has been wounded by rejection and segregation. We fail to realize that much behavior and acting out is not inherent but learned as a response to not being truly loved and accepted as a person. Masks are worn only as long as they are needed. Only genuine acceptance and a sense of belonging will lure the rejected supposedly inferior person out from behind the mask. (p. 65)

MAPs is a tool held in the hand of a creative facilitator who can truly listen and hear the dream and the cry of pain of people or groups who have been rejected either overtly or covertly. The tool focuses on the positive, the gifts, and the strengths. The facilitator must first and foremost have a deep belief in the capacity of all human beings. The team facilitator must see the glass half full, not half empty. In this process we focus on the possibility of inclusive and heterogeneous communities that are based on the simple and yet profound premise that each person belongs, each person can learn, and that in living we can discover the truth and dignity of each person.

There are eight key questions to MAPs, as shown in Figure 6 (Forest & Pearpoint, 1992). The questions must all be asked, but the order may be flexible based on the flow of the group dynamics and contributions. The following story is about a high school student named Donna who decided to have a MAPs process developed about her life and her future possibilities. Donna and her parents made up a "guest list" of the people they wanted to invite to the MAPs session. Donna wrote a short note inviting each of these people to her house on the day they had planned (see Figure 7).

Other MAPs gatherings have been held in classrooms, school cafeterias, corporate board rooms, small offices, and so forth. The key for an individual or group is to voluntarily choose to explore the process and to choose others they want to invite. It is

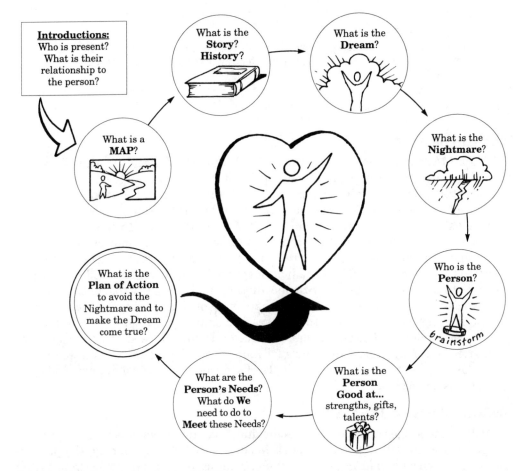

Figure 6.   Eight key questions involved in MAPs.

not a case conference or an individualized education program (IEP) where the person is the guest and the professionals are in control. With MAPs, the key people are the "person" himself or herself and those people he or she invites. The person will define his or her own problems, dreams, nightmares, and so forth with a little help from his or her friends.

Donna's parents also wrote a note that is shown in Figure 8 and sent it to the people whom Donna had decided to invite to her MAPs process. Fifteen people were invited and 16 people came. The church minister heard about the gathering and invited himself. Donna, of course, agreed. It is interesting to note that people are truly honored to be asked to attend a serious session about a person's life. In this case, two people traveled significant distances to participate. They cared. People really do care and want to be involved.

It is often better to have a facilitator (or two) who is immersed in the process and who does not know the assembled cast of characters. The facilitators can then bring out the information without a preconceived scenario. People are invited to be involved in a process that is time limited; that is, in Donna's case, she invited people for the morning, followed by an optional lunch.

Dear Maya and David,

I want to invite you to my meeting to help me think about my future. It's going to be on Saturday November 14 at 10 A.M. at my house. We are going to have lunch when it is done. I hope you can come.

Donna

Figure 7. Donna's letter of invitation to her MAPs participants.

Where to Begin

During a MAPs gathering, everyone is seated comfortably facing a wall. They are each given large sheets of paper. A leading facilitator acts as the "host." This person welcomes the group, explains the process, guides the questions, and keeps the session paced and on track. A second facilitator can be the "graphic guide." He or she records, listens, and creates a colorful record of the proceedings. In addition, the session should be audio recorded for those who understand information better with sound than with visuals. The public record is an essential part of the MAPs process. A personal, comfortable, and informal atmosphere is essential. The facilitator urges everyone to trust and be honest with one another, and not to use too much jargon or acronyms that may be a mystery to the others present. The leading facilitator begins by asking everyone to introduce themselves and share their relationship to the key person. For example, "Hi, I'm Wayne. I've known Donna since she was born.", "I've been friends of Mark and Christina's for more than 20 years.", "Donna was in my choir class during junior high school.", "Hi, I am Donna's boyfriend, Sam, and I am going to marry her."

Question #1: What Is a MAP?

A MAP includes the purpose, the specific questions to be asked, and a general description of what will happen at the gathering. At a MAPs gathering, the participants are asked what a MAP means to them. Some of the answers from Donna's team were:

Helps you get from one place an another
A guide
A way to go from here to there

The leading facilitator then said, "That's exactly what we are here for, we want to help Donna get from where she is today to where she's going. We want this day to be a guide of how to go from here to there"—a perfect start.

Question #2: What Is a Person's History or Story?

The family tells the participants their story—the history of the family member's disability and how the family relates to one another. A time limit is set; what is important are the essentials as the family or school sees it. Donna's story is similar to that of other children with disability labels—it started with fear, disappointment, and rejection. Then, through tremendous effort on the part of her family, they changed the initial expectations and realities in the community and in the family to some amount of acceptance in a regular school, regular classes, and church. This story has difficult twists and turns and very emotional parts with some intense medical stories—Donna has Down syndorme, visual impairment, and diabetes. The graphics facilitator drew the story and then summarized. At the end of each question, the

Dear Friends,

As you know Donna is just starting a process call MAPs. The purpose of this tool is to help her and us make that awesome transition from being a kid to being an adult who is a full-fledged member of the community.

The first meeting will be November 14 and Donna chose you as guests of honor. We all put a list together of everybody Donna knows, including her peers and some adults. She went through the list and circled the names of those she wanted around her, helping her to start to think about her future. You are the names she circled. This means you are the people she trusts the most and with whom she feels most comfortable. You are the ones with whom she is willing to put herself in a vulnerable position to discuss her real wants and concerns. You are her circle of support, the people she can really talk to (and you all know how tough that can be). Many of you are part of our circle of support, too, but this is Donna's list— 100%.

So please join us on Saturday, November 14 at our home. We'll start at 10 A.M. and we will have lunch (yes, taco salad!). Marsha Forest and Jack Pearpoint will be the facilitators. I think this will be an interesting morning.

Love,
Mark and Christina

Figure 8.   Donna's parents' letter of invitation to the MAPs participants.

facilitator checked that the emerging picture represented what was really said and if there was anything to add. This check constantly reaffirms the ownership of the MAP to the participants. The facilitators are pulling out information, drawing a map so that they can start on a process to reach the dream.

Question #3: What Are Your Dreams?

The question is important to answer because it helps the person and the participants know where to go in developing the eventual plan of action. Donna was abundantly clear: "My dream is to marry Sam and to be a star! I want babies. I want to live here and have friends like Greg. I also want to perform on stage with Paul Simon." The facilitator asked Donna to expand on her dream and she asked everyone else to simply listen and not add anything. She said: "This is your dream Donna—go for it. What do you really want to see in your future? Tell the graphic facilitator to draw exactly what you want." Donna was crystal clear about this dream. Figure 9 is the graphic display of Donna's dream.

The dream question is the heart and soul of the MAPs process. The facilitator must ask the person to describe his or her real dream and be nonjudgmental. Facilitators must be sure their body language does not negatively affect the process. One facilitator stymied this process for a boy named Jason, who was described by his school teacher as a major behavior problem, behavior disordered, and bad. Jason hardly spoke until his first MAPs. He declared in the dream question that he wanted to be a doctor. The facilitator, who knew him, literally stopped the process and said: "That's ridiculous! You can't even do your homework." The MAPs process ended immediately. At the next MAP, with a new facilitator, Jason again spoke about his dream. This time it was drawn and listened to with a full and accepting heart by the facilitator. As the MAP unfolded, Jason himself modified his dream. We have learned that in the seed of all dreams is the essence of a person's real desire and what might eventually be feasible. Jason really did not want to be a doctor; however, he wanted respect and he wanted to work around hospitals where his dad had worked. He liked the people at the hospital and he had been helped by a wonderful doctor friend.

Figure 9. Donna's dream.

Judith Snow, one of Canada's leading experts on the rights of people who have been excluded, relayed in her dream that she wanted to be a truck driver. Judith uses a wheelchair and has no mobility except in her right thumb. "A truck driver!" many exclaimed. But Judith has taught many of us that to be a truck driver means motion, movement, freedom, travel, adventure, and seeing the world from high up. She is living the essence of her dream today, even though there is not a truck in her life—

yet. We need to see people's dreams not as concrete or etched in stone, but as beautiful, fluid messages and images of what is possible. Many at Donna's MAP were terrified of Donna being married and having children. They noted, after all she is a person with Down syndrome. She cannot care for children, she should not . . . " People were asked to listen respectully and *not* make judgments.

Question #4: What Are Your Nightmares?

As a facilitator, the scariest question is the nightmare. We do not want people to become upset or sad, but the nightmare and the dream are equal in importance. It is the nightmare that we want to avoid, yet most of our "programs" and "projects" fuel the nightmare instead of the dream. For example, many parents of children with disabilities answer the nightmare question with this response: "I fear my son or daughter will end up in an institution." The traditional special education service delivery model that segregates students with disabilities from their nondisabled neighbors and peers essentially is preparing those students for a segregated adult lifestyle such as that found in institutions. We have never heard a nightmare that had to do with getting bad grades or getting a less-than-perfect job. It is always about more fundamental issues, such as loneliness, poverty, and death. The dream empowers families, people, and organizations to dream again. The nightmare allows people the dignity to let their monsters and demons out of the closet in an atmosphere where they are heard, recorded, and respected. The entire aim of the MAPs process is to actualize the dream and avoid the nightmare. Can there be a guarantee? Absolutely not! Does the process at least allow the chance of survival? Absolutely! The process promises nothing; however, it gives hope. The opposite of hope is despair and there is far too much of that, especially in schools.

Question #5: Who Is the Person?

This is a brainstorming step. Everyone is asked to throw words into the air and the facilitator records them as a portrait of the person. Not just good words or bad words, but words that come to the minds of the participants about the person's identity. This time the person is asked to listen. In Donna's situation, a large outline of a person was drawn and the facilitator gave each participant two Post-it note sheets to write their thoughts on. The graphic facilitator grouped words in themes. The person, Donna, is asked to identify her own words to describe herself and then to choose three favorites words from all the descriptions. Donna chose: "In love, loving, and risk taker."

To demonstrate the power of the words identified in this question, the facilitator may ask: What other words have people who are not present used to describe the person in the past? In Jason's case, for example, the words others used were troublemaker, bad, behavior disordered, and manic-depressive. None of those were mentioned at the MAP. Instead there were words such as: energetic, active, stubborn, tense, intense, terrific, and so forth.

Thomas Armstrong (1987, p. 128) illustrated how one person's negative perception of a person could actually be a positive characteristic with his suggestions of how to "turn lead into gold" (see Table 1).

Question #6: What Are the Person's Strengths, Gifts, and Talents?

Here, the concept of "giftedness" is stressed, not as an academic ability, but as a part of a well-rounded person. The graphic facilitator can draw a gift box with gifts coming out of it to portray this image. As the participants list descriptions that identify the

Table 1. Turning lead into gold

A child who is judged to be	Can also be considered
Learning disabled	Learning different
Hyperactive	A kinesthetic learner
Dyslexic	A spatial learner
Aggressive	Assertive
Plodding	Thorough
Lazy	Relaxed
Immature	Late blooming
Phobic	Cautious
Scattered	Divergent
Daydreaming	Imaginative
Irritable	Sensitive
Perseverative	Persistent

Reprinted by permission of The Putnam Publishing Group from IN THEIR OWN WAY by Thomas Armstrong. Copyright © 1987 by Thomas Armstrong.

person's gifts, strengths, and talents, they are written down and stated very positively. Some of Donna's gifts identified by the participants were her smile, personality, family, spirit, and lovingness.

Question #7: What Does the Person Need?

To answer this question, the participants must think about what it will take—people and resources—to make the dream come true. There was complete agreement that Donna needed friends her own age to be more included with other typical high school students at church and at school. It was also agreed that her parents needed some time alone to get their own lives in order. This information can help to focus the opportunities that need to be created for the person and to recognize the formal and informal supports that are needed.

Question #8: What Is the Plan of Action?

To avoid the nightmares and to facilitate the dreams, the participants are asked, in a very specific way, to identify the plans. These plans should include who will do what and when will they do it. Donna's plan involved several important components:

Increase the circle of friends at the high school.
Increase the circle of friends at church.
Teach friends and others to deal with Donna's insulin reading and monitoring.
Maintain the regular high school class participation.
Investigate possible self-advocacy support groups.
Investigate stage performing possibilities at school, church, and in the community.
Investigate the possibility of working as an assistant in the child-care program located on the high school campus.
Identify opportunities for Donna to present at local, state, and national conferences advocating for individuals, which is related to her dream to perform on stage.

This MAPs process took about 90 minutes and no one was tired or bored. The process has been completed with students whom no one believed could sit still for 5 minutes; yet, they do. It is understood through MAPs that all people are vitally interested in their own lives. For very young children, invite them to be present for as long as they wish and have people available for child care when they decide to leave.

PLANNING ALTERNATIVE TOMORROWS WITH HOPE (PATH)

PATH evolved from the MAPs process. It offers an opportunity to extend the MAPs steps and to put into place a plan of action. PATH may be a self-sustaining planning process. Figure 10 shows an outline of the PATH and Figure 11 illustrates a sample PATH graphically represented. PATH, as with the Circle of Friends and MAPs, is another strategy to address long- and short-range planning. This is another eight-step process—it is an exercise in thinking backward. Once again, this process is best undertaken with a lead facilitator and a graphic facilitator.

Schools that are involved in long-range planning for students, the student body, the school, and the community have experienced new roles and functions. In this new role, students, teachers, parents, community members, and friends are invited to participate. The teacher's task is to identify the strengths of each student and to nurture those strengths as catalysts to explore the full range of every student's capacities. By inviting the full participation of the others in "figuring it out," no teacher is given the impossible charge of "knowing it all" or being responsible to teach everyone. Everyone becomes a member of the team with the problems and challenges becoming shared goals. The spectrum of talents and energy available can be quite impressive.

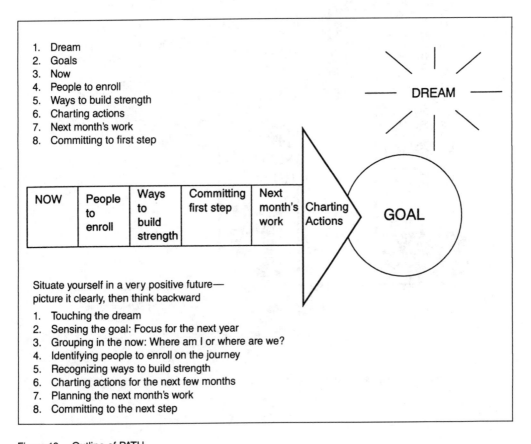

Figure 10. Outline of PATH.

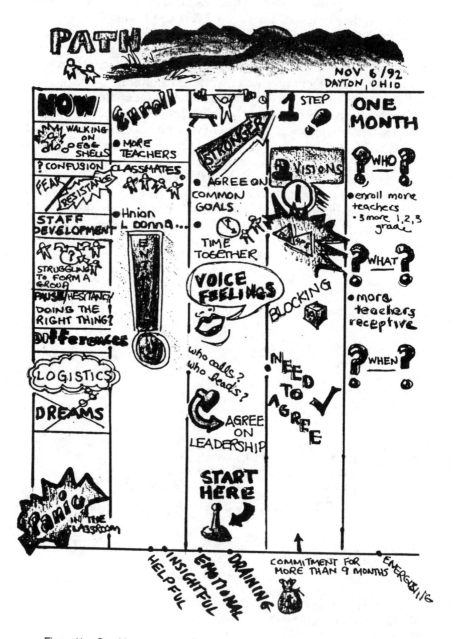

Figure 11.   Graphic representation of a PATH.

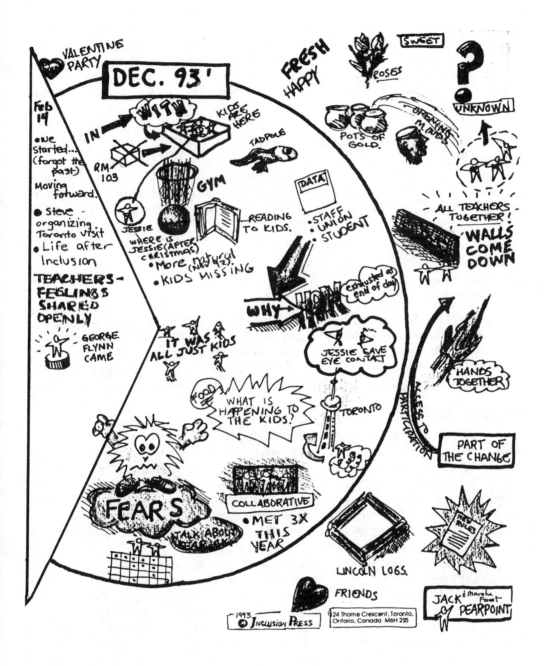

To provide an example of the PATH process, Barry, a seventh grader who uses a wheelchair and has a communicator, is described. Barry lives at home with several brothers, sisters, aunts and uncles, and his mother. He has shared with his teacher that he is not happy at home. His means of communication is using a head pointer and a typewriter, some verbal communication, and head nodding. At this time, Barry chose not to have his mother or sisters at the meeting. The meeting included Barry, his teacher, the teaching assistant, three of his friends from school, the student teacher, and his service coordinator/counselor. His brothers could not attend and were to be kept informed. These are all people whom he trusts and with whom he feels comfortable discussing personal issues.

Step 1: The North Star—The Dream

The North Star is the far-reaching dream for an individual. This may or may not be reachable; however, the North Star dream is used as a catalyst for creating a valued and desired future. Time is spent focusing on the individual identifying his or her dreams and ultimately his or her North Star. Some of the questions that can assist a person identify his or her North Star may be:

What ideals do you most want to realize?
What values do you want to guide you?
What gives direction to your life?
What drives you?

Barry's North Star was to be able to live in a home with just a few people, to have support so that he could eat when he wanted to, to go to the bathroom when he wanted-to, to have a bath when he wanted one, and to leave the house when he wanted to. The facilitator finished this step by summarizing the dream and soliciting from Barry his perspective on the accuracy of the information that have been depicted graphically.

Step 2: The Goal

The second step is to choose a future time just beyond the scope of a time that can be easily predicted, for example, 6 months, 1 year, 2 years, and pretend to go there for a few minutes. It is very important to assist the group in this visualization/planning activity. The facilitator may suggest that everyone get in a time capsule. The future is in that time capsule and everyone shares what is happening. The facilitator coaches everyone to discuss positive events that are occurring (remember they really have not occurred). The facilitator may say, "It was Barry's birthday a couple of months ago and he received a Game Boy as a gift."

Ask the person and the group to share what is happening. This is the development of the *goals* for the person. The facilitator will try to have the individual describe the smells, tastes, touches, and overall feelings in the past. For example, part of Barry's goal in the past was to go to high school and have more friends. Barry stated that in the future he goes on a number of field trips. In the past he had not been able to go because his mother did not send the permission slip. In the future, he has a new light weight electric wheelchair and a new communicator that is easier to use and can be understood by others. His friends noted that their parents bring Barry to birthday parties with them on weekends. He went to the Computer Access Center and they completed a consultation and recommended the school look into Macintosh computers with adaptations for Barry. The most important goal is that Barry is able to talk with his mother and really communicate with her.

Step 3: Now

The third step is to bring everyone back to reality. The facilitator asks the participant: "What is it like now? Don't use good words or bad words, just give a description of what life looks like now."

Barry and the group generated descriptions such as lonely, stressful, scared of his mother, hard, tiring, scary, fun and safe at school, exciting, and lots of friends. The PATH process now is a visual representation of the differences between *now* on the left, with the positive possible future (goal), and the North Star dream on the right. The facilitator helps the participants to see that this difference is often necessary and good for moving forward. The facilitator now takes more control by simply declaring that for the purposes of the PATH, the objective will be to get from *now* to the *goal* in the time span articulated. The facilitator finishes this step by summarizing the individual's sense of the now and getting confirmation that the summary is accurate.

Step 4: Who Do We Enroll?

To accomplish this step, the facilitator points out that there are some preconditions. First, no one can do PATH alone, thus "Who do you need to enroll to achieve your goal?" Again, this supports the notion that we are striving for everyone to be interdependent, not independent, working as teams and depending on each other.

It is entirely acceptable that people may answer the question with funders, government, agencies, or a whole range of generic groups that need to be enrolled. However, the facilitator needs to look for specific persons or contact persons. Participants should be encouraged to enroll themselves to assist.

Barry said that he was going to enroll his teacher and the teaching assistant to begin really communicating with his mother. Barry asked his friends to help him get to parties; if needed, he would take his old flexible wheelchair.

This process of enrolling others means more than just getting permission to participate; it means one is sharing and making a commitment in the person's life. This step also recognizes those people with whom the individual wants to build a shared commitment. When the facilitator is confident the list is complete, he or she reminds everyone this is a process and one can add, change, and delete here as well as any other place along the PATH, as long as the significant participant agrees. At this time, the facilitator also reviews the PATH and adds any names or resources needed. Then the facilitator has the group share some feeling words associated with the list of people enrolled and what they are enrolled to do.

Step 5: Getting Stronger

The fifth step is about getting stronger. The facilitator coaches the group through the reality that in order to enroll people and to move from now to the future, an enormous amount of work is required. This will be added to everyone's already busy life. So the real question is: "What do we need to do as a group, team, and/or family to be strong enough to reach the goal and keep this team moving forward. Similarly, what does each person have to do to be strong enough to be able to make his or her contribution at the personal level." Barry's list contained:

Have teachers and teaching assistants with whom to share and communicate
Communicate effectively with my mother
Be able to get out to purchase personal items
Have time to cry if and when needed

Have support to overcome the fear of rejection from my mother
Get involved in social groups
Learn from adults with disabilities about what they are able to do and how

Step 6: Three Months

In the process of events, the next two steps are very similar. Again, the facilitator gives directions and takes the group into the near future, such as 3 months from today. Everyone should think positively and assume that things have been going really well, that is, the direction of progress is correct and people are feeling some momentum. The easiest way to see this near future is to pick a clear element in the goal and think of what has happened already. If there is time, the facilitator can explore several of the elements to see what steps were (are to be) implemented within the 3 months.

The facilitator must be extremely time conscious at this point, and it is good to indicate to the participants that it is unlikely that every detail of the PATH will be completed at this time. However, once the process is understood, people can fill in their details later.

Step 7: One Month

The seventh step is a repeat of the sixth, except that the time is even closer to the present—1 month. What is important at this step is to push everyone for very precise specific steps:

Who will do what?
When will they do it?
Where?

Some members of the group may find this difficult as they realize that this exercise is getting out of the dreaming process and moving very close to reality. This step is also used to identify specifics for the more immediate future and can be used to measure people's true commitment.

Step 8: The First Step(s)

The *final* step is the *first step*. What is the first step? The facilitator should insist that this be some action that can be taken almost immediately (i.e., by tomorrow or next week). It does not need to be a gigantic step, but if the process is going to begin, it is essential that it begin *now*. If someone has to make a telephone call, a target should be set (e.g., by noon tomorrow). If someone has to contact the funding agency, another target time should be set.

At this point, as well as through the process, it is essential that the goal of interdependence be at the forefront. All the participants must form a new habit of asking for support and not assuming everything should be done. Many times the first step does not flow; that is okay. It is up to the group and the facilitator to see if there is a block. In many situations, something or someone is standing in the way of progress. The PATH is a means to identify those blocks and then take the steps to deal with the blocks. A block could have to do with funding or medical, social or emotional needs. The energy and commitment of the team, at this time, must come together to strategize any and all blocks that are identified.

Closure is important in any process. The facilitator asks the group to simply give a word or a phrase about what they felt and about the process. Barry offered: excited and scared. Others offered: trusting, energized, go for it. The excitement and reality of this process is in the implementation and the follow-up.

Each facilitator or co-facilitator has his or her own unique style and character. The goal is that the meeting and the process remain focused on the individual and that the individual and his or her significant others have a say in the development of the process. It is up to the team to allow that dream and the North Star to become a reality.

CONSIDERATIONS AND CAUTIONS

There are several cautions and considerations to be aware of when using any of the three strategies: Circle of Friends, MAPs, and/or PATH. These include:

- The facilitator always needs to remember the process is for, by, and with the individual. The facilitator needs to continually return to the individual and be sure what is being written is accurate, relevant, meaningful, and true.
- Various communication means may be necessary to ensure the focus person is involved, understands the process, and is a true participant. One may utilize facilitated communication, pictures, or someone else speaking and the individual verifying with a head nod or eye wink. The process has been successful with individuals who are highly verbal as well as individuals who do not communicate using standard means.
- Trust and confidentiality are two issues that must be addressed and reinforced. The process places the focus person in a very vulnerable position and the facilitator must reassure the person and remind the participants that this meeting is very personal and confidential.
- It is very important that the facilitator and the participants discuss when the process will be implemented and when results may be observed. The focus person may become very excited by the process and then become extremely frustrated when the dream or North Star does not come true within a week. Timing is sensitive and an issue that must be addressed during the process.
- The facilitator should be sure that a support process is in place for all participants to deal with the excitement and any other emotions that may have been brought out as a result of the process.
- Remember this is not a trick, gimmick, or quick fix. The three strategies are all long-range planning processes. The process will bring people together to have a common vision for a person, family, or organization. It will take time, commitment, and knowledge to follow through what has been generated by the Circle of Friends, MAPs, and/or PATH (Forest & Pearpoint, 1992).
- Recognizing that the three processes outlined are very personal, it may be a good strategy to provide the questions to the person ahead of time to allow them time to review them and feel comfortable with the process.
- The process does not replace the individualized education program (IEP). It can be a means to generate a very functional IEP because the process and write-up may be a strong complement to it. The process is very similar to transition planning for the school to adult transition process. The outcome can be presented as an individualized transition plan (ITP).
- The process should not be controlled by experts and is not simply an academic task. The process is to be a means to develop personal centered planning that leads to people working together for the common goals and dreams of an individual.

SUMMARY

The value of friends and colleagues cannot be emphasized enough. To embrace all children, schools and educators developing services in schools need to change their views. It is also important for schools to reflect in their educational service delivery model the principle that all children belong and all children want to belong. This chapter provides three ways to change how schools look and how services are developed: Circle of Friends, MAPs, and PATH.

REFERENCES

Armstrong, T. (1987). *In their own way.* Los Angeles, CA: Tarcher.

Asher, S.R., Odem, S.L., & Gottman, J.M. (1977). Children's friendships in school settings. In L.G. Katz (Ed.), *Current topics in early childhood education* (Vol. 1. pp. 33–61). Norwood, NJ: Ablex.

Condeluci, A. (1991). *Interdependence—The route to community.* Orlando, FL: Paul M. Deutsch Press, Inc.

Forest, M., & Lusthaus, E. (1989). Promoting educational equality for all students: Circles and MAPs. In S. Stainback, W. Stainback, & M. Forest (Eds.), *Educating all students in the mainstream of regular education* (pp. 43–58). Baltimore: Paul H. Brookes Publishing Co.

Forest, M.,& Lusthaus, E. (1990). Everyone belongs with the MAPs action planning system. *Teaching Exceptional Children, 22*(2), 32–35.

Forest, M., & Pearpoint, J. (1992). Everyone belongs: Building the vision with MAPs—The McGill Action Planning System. In D. Wetherow (Ed.), *The whole community catalogue: Welcoming people with disabilities into the heart of community life* (pp. 95–99). Manchester, CT: Communitas, Inc.

Ginott, H. (1972). *Teacher and child.* New York: Macmillan.

Grenot-Scheyer, M., Coots, J., & Falvey, M.A. (1989). Developing and fostering friendships. In M.A. Falvey, *Community-based curriculum: Instructional strategies for students with severe handicaps* (2nd ed.) (pp. 345–358). Baltimore: Paul H. Brookes Publishing Co.

Hartup, W.W. (1975). The origins of friendship. In M. Lewis & L.A. Rosenblum (Eds.), *Friendships and peer relations* (pp. 11–26). New York: John Wiley & Sons.

Howes, C. (1983). Patterns of friendship. *Child Development, 54,* 1041–1053.

LeQuyere, T. (1991). *Don't pass me by.* Toronto, Ontario, Canada: Inclusion Press.

Lewis, M., & Rosenblum, L.A. (Eds.). (1975). *Friendships and peer relations.* New York: John Wiley & Sons.

Mackan, P. (1991). *Reflections on inclusive education.* Toronto, Ontario, Canada: Inclusion Press.

O'Brien, J., & Mount, B. (1991). Telling new stories: The search for capacity among people with severe handicaps. In L. H. Meyer, C.A. Peck, & L. Brown (Eds.), *Critical issues in the lives of people with severe disabilities* (pp. 89–92). Baltimore: Paul H. Brookes Publishing Co.

Perske, R. (1989). *Circles of friends.* Nashville: Abingdon Press.

Sherwood, S.K. (1990). A circle of friends in a 1st grade classroom. *Educational Leadership, 48*(3), 41.

Stainback, W., & Stainback, S. (1990). Facilitating peer supports and friendships. In W. Stainback & S. Stainback (Eds.), *Support networks for inclusive schooling: Interdependent integrated education* (pp. 51–64). Baltimore: Paul H. Brookes Publishing Co.

Stainback, W., Stainback, S., & Wilkinson, A. (1992). Encouraging peer supports and friendships. *Teaching Exceptional Children, 24*(2), 6–11.

Strully, J., & Strully, C. (1985). Friendship and our children. *Journal of The Association for Persons with Severe Handicaps, 10*(4), 224–227.

Vandercook, T., York, J., & Forest, M. (1989). The McGill Action Planning System (MAPs): A strategy for building the vision. *Journal of The Association for Persons with Severe Handicaps, 14,* 205–215.

RESPONSES FOR CHILDREN EXPERIENCING BEHAVIORAL AND EMOTIONAL CHALLENGES

Richard A. Villa, Jonathan Udis, and Jacqueline S. Thousand

> *In America they have begun to talk of troubled children as "throw-away" children. Who can be less fortunate than those who are thrown away?*
>
> *(Thom Garfat, as cited in Brendtro, Brokenleg, & Van Bockern, 1990, p. 12)*

Mariah just spent the last 3 weeks in the psychiatric ward of her local community hospital. She is 16 years old and lives with her father and 14-year-old sister. Prior to her hospitalization, Mariah had begun "experimenting" with drugs and alcohol. Her father is concerned that Mariah's substance use may have turned to "substance abuse" and may have been a catalyst for her hospitalization. There is a history of alcoholism in the family. Last year, Mariah's mother died of injuries sustained when driving a car while intoxicated. Teachers describe Mariah as a "good, solid B student"; they were shocked to learn of her hospitalization. While in the psychiatric ward, she revealed that her father has sexually abused her. Mariah was hospitalized for a nearly successful suicide attempt.

"F—you! You can't make me do it," Billy yelled at his eighth grade social studies teacher for the fourth time

The authors wish to acknowledge the thoughtful contribution of the following Vermont educators who provided feedback on the content of this chapter: Steve Brauer, Ann-Marie Carron, Carol Delos, Lu Christie, Cynthia Cole, Ruth Hamilton, Tracy Harris, Jim Merrill, Ed Sanders, Karen Topper, and Nadine Zane.

369

this week as he threw a chair toward the corner of the room and stormed out of the room. Billy lives with his parents and two sisters. He usually comes to school dressed in dirty clothes and occasionally smells of urine. Although he often comes to school late, he rarely misses a day. Billy reads at a third grade level; math is his area of strength. Billy's guidance counselor states that he has no "real friends." A review of discipline records reveals that Billy spends more than 50% of his time in the "in-school" suspension room or with the guidance counselor or the assistant principal.

Ricardo enrolled as a new student on the second day of the school year. Because his family had moved seven times in the past year, no records of his past schooling have been located. For the first 6 weeks of school, Ricardo would walk into his fourth grade classroom, put his head on his desk, and sleep. Whenever the teacher was able to get Ricardo to communicate, he would speak in a whisper and turn his eyes to the floor. Despite repeated efforts by school personnel to contact Ricardo's parents by phone, letter, and home visits, contact has yet to be made with an adult in his home. In mid-October Ricardo stopped coming to school.

WHO ARE THEY—CHILDREN WHO ARE TROUBLED OR TROUBLING?

Mariah, Billy, and Ricardo—we all know or know of these children. For a variety of administrative, fiscal, legal, educational, and theoretical reasons, many different labels (and accompanying definitions) have been developed and attached to students who appear troubled or troubling in school. Labels include emotionally disturbed, disruptive, delinquent, acting out, unmanageable, conduct disordered, socially maladjusted, anti-social, noncompliant, and serious behavior problem (Hobbs, 1982). Regardless of the origins of these labels and definitions, they all have an extraordinary impact upon the children to whom they are applied. Specifically,

> Once a particular verbal commitment has been made in describing a child or an adolescent, there follows inexorably a chain of actions bent to institutional forms. . . . Thus, it makes a big difference how one talks about a child or an adolescent and what encompassing rubrics one uses to define his [or her] status. (Hobbs, 1982, p. 23)

At the local school level, what gets labeled as a *serious* behavior problem or a *significant* emotional disturbance varies from one school to the next and from class to class. Such variability is contingent upon a community's beliefs about and successes (or failures) with students whose emotional, social, behavioral, or psychological needs go beyond what is viewed as the school's standard discipline, guidance, curriculum, or instructional responsibility or capacity. For example, members of a school community with little experience individualizing for any particular student might view and label Mariah, Billy, and Ricardo as candidates for exclusion, expulsion, or restrictive placement outside of general education. Another school, with extensive experience educating students with a broad range of needs, might view them as three of *many* students with unique needs that must be met. This phenomenon of "relativity" combined with the chain of often negative, institutionalized reactions that result when a label is attached to a child has led these authors to be very deliberate about the terms they use. Therefore, throughout this chapter, we use terms such as *children who are troubled or troubling, students who are challenged or challenging, children who demonstrate high rates of rule-violating behavior,* or *students who have acquired nonadaptive ways of relating* to represent Mariah, Billy, and Ricardo and other students who, for whatever reason, are perceived as the "most challenging" to the current school organizational structure or culture.

HOW MANY CHILDREN ARE TROUBLED OR TROUBLING?

How many of our children are troubled or troubling to their teachers, community, or family? This question is difficult to answer. But consider the following:

- Morgan and Jenson (1988) noted that the prevalence data vary widely—from 1% to 40% of school-age students—depending upon the method of counting or "guess-timation."
- The 1980 Carnegie Council on Children reported that up to one third of all American children live in conditions likely to assault their physical, emotional, and intellectual health (Gliedman & Roth, 1980).
- The 1989 Carnegie Council on Adolescent Development estimated that in America "7 million young people—one in four adolescents—are extremely vulnerable to multiple high-risk behaviors and school failure. Another 7 million may be at moderate risk, but remain a cause for serious concern" (p. 8). Furthermore, "the U.S. Department of Justice National Crime Survey indicates that teenagers are victims of crime more frequently than any other age group and that a quarter of crimes committed against them take place in or near schools" (p. 65).
- Fink and Janssen (1992) noted that in 1989 almost 2 million reports of child abuse and neglect officially were filed and that conservative estimates suggest two or three times this number of youth actually are systematically abused. Their review of the literature demonstrated that systematic abuse leads to significant dysfunction in emotional, developmental, and intellectual capacities and at-risk psychological, medical, motivational, academic, and legal conditions. The difficulties experienced by maltreated youth resemble those usually associated with youth who are labeled behaviorally or emotionally disabled.
- From the 1989–1990 to the 1990–1991 school year, special education enrollment in the United States grew by 130,000 students (2.8%), representing the largest percentage increase in 10 years. The largest increases in numbers were in the categories of specific learning disabilities (81,000), serious emotional disturbance (16,000), and speech-language impairment (16,000). Furthermore, a report to Congress noted that the number of students identified as seriously emotionally disturbed underrepresented the *actual* number for at least two reasons. First, school personnel and families resist using the label. Second, characteristics of emotional distress, such as withdrawal and depression, are easily overlooked in school environments (National Association of State Directors of Special Education, 1992).
- Kunc (1992) observed that "teen-age suicide is increasing at an exponential rate and has now become the second leading cause of adolescent death. Extreme violence, drug dependency, gangs, anorexia nervosa, and depression among students have risen to the point that these problems now are perceived almost as an expected part of high school culture (Health & Welfare Canada, 1987; Patterson, Purkey, & Parker, 1986)" (p. 37).
- The Children's Defense Fund & The Robin Hood Foundation (1992) reported that 20% of American children live below the official poverty level (21% more than in 1977), approximately 100,000 are homeless, and 2.5 million are reported as abused or neglected.
- Students identified as having a behavior or emotional disability have one of the lowest rates of promotion as well as one of the highest rates of dropout and exit prior to graduation (Leone, McLaughlin, & Meisel, 1992).

What does the above information suggest about the emotional turmoil, stress, and preoccupations our children bring with them when they walk through a school's doors? What does it suggest about how their life circumstances affect their behavior, their interactions with others, and their capacity to learn?

WHERE ARE THE CHILDREN WHO ARE TROUBLED OR TROUBLING BEING EDUCATED?

Currently, American public schools employ the self-contained separate classroom as the predominant service delivery model for children identified as "behaviorally disordered" (Leone et al., 1992). They also employ, in descending order of frequency, resource rooms, special schools, itinerant support, out-of-district placements, and homebound instruction (Morgan & Jenson, 1988). With the exception of itinerant support in regular classrooms, the common characteristics of these service options is that they immerse children in a *community and culture of disturbance and dysfunction* where students have limited access to pro-social models and where they are given the message that they *do not belong* with their peers (Kunc, 1992). Yet, as Kunc (1992) emphasized, "belonging—having a social context—is requisite for the development of self-esteem and self-confidence" (p. 30). The predicted consequences of not belonging combined with lackluster efficacy data regarding segregated special education programs (Lipsky & Gartner, 1989; Stainback, Stainback, & Forest, 1989; Wagner, 1989) have convinced these authors that educators have a professional and social responsibility to discover, invent, and share with others successful strategies for addressing the needs of troubled or troubling children in *integrated* general education and community environments. Furthermore, emerging data (Burchard & Clarke, 1990) suggest that it is considerably more cost effective to individualize services for a child with severely maladjusted behavior in the community than to place the child in a segregated residential program, and the services provided are considered to be "better."

RATIONALE AND OBJECTIVES

The purpose of this chapter is to present an alternative to a *continuum of placement* conceptualization and approach to providing support and services for children who are troubled or troubling. The alternative has been described as a "constellation of services" (Nevin, Villa, & Thousand, 1992, p. 44) approach in which supports and services are brought to the child rather than the child being *taken* to the services. The constellation is an assemblage of approaches and strategies that represents current research and writing concerning discipline, social skills, and the promotion of responsibility, and that which has been discovered when traditional strategies have failed. The constellation further reflects the assumptions and beliefs presented in Table 1. Before describing the constellation, however, these authors offer a "student bill of rights" that reminds us of the purpose of schooling.

Student Bill of Rights

The characteristics of schooling described in this section are intended to create, promote, and/or sustain a caring, responsive, and quality learning environment. Collectively, they serve as a keystone to effectively supporting and serving troubled or troubling learners and making school a desirable and motivating place for all students.

Table 1. Assumptions and beliefs underlying the constellation of resources, supports, and services

- Each child is an individual and, no matter what we do, our foremost responsibilities are to *cause no harm* to the child and to help the child meet his or her *need to belong* in a valued community (Brendtro, Brokenleg, & Van Bockern, 1990; Knitzer, Steinberg, & Bleisch, 1990; Kunc, 1992).
- All behavior is an attempt to communicate.
- Parents and families are central to solution-finding processes; the responsibility of educators is to work with and for families rather than blame them or their child for their troubles.
- Interagency collaboration promotes a unified community response that is more likely to meet the individual needs of children, their families, and the school personnel who work with and for them.
- Creative outcomes result from collaborative teaming and creative problem solving among people committed to establishing caring and effective communities of learners.

The authors conceptualize this collection of school characteristics as the "Student Bill of Rights," which is represented in Table 2. A brief explanation of these rights follows.

Effective Instruction and Personalized Accommodations Fifteen years ago, Ron Edmonds (1979) noted that the field of education had the knowledge and tools to enable any school to be effective. Specifically, he wrote, "we can, whenever and wherever we choose, successfully teach all children whose schooling is of interest to us; . . . we already know more than we need to do that" (p. 22). Edmonds's statement is even more true today, as more is learned about quality instruction and *meaningful* accommodations. When children are active participants in developmentally appropriate activities, they are less likely to present troubling behaviors. They may still be troubled, but not troubling. With the presence of effective instruction and meaningful accommodations for individual differences, it is less likely that teachers will need to resort to emotional responses and interventions that are based upon punishment, control, conformity, and obedience (e.g., humiliation, public sarcasm, detention, demerits, suspension, expulsion).

What are the characteristics of effective instruction? At a minimum, effective instruction involves high rates of active student involvement, student use of higher-level reasoning skills, and discovery and constructivist learning approaches. The literature is rich with descriptions of practices that promote effective instruction. Among the highly promoted and researched practices are: 1) outcome-based instructional models, 2) computer-assisted instruction, and 3) collaborative learning models. See Brandt (1992), Glatthorn (1987), and Thousand and Villa (1991) for discussions of these practices. Of course, the *foundations* of all effective instruction are positive teacher–student relationships and teacher reflection and decision making for the purpose of matching task demands and learner characteristics.

A Motivating School Climate Children who are troubled or troubling often *do not seem* motivated or are unable to change their interpersonal behaviors or their relationship with school or learning. Different theorists (e.g., Bandura, 1977; Brendtro et al., 1990; Glasser, 1975, 1986; Johnson & Johnson, 1991; Maslow, 1970;

Table 2. Student bill of rights

Students have the right to experience and schools have a responsibility to ensure:
- Effective instruction
- Personalized accommodations
- A motivating school climate in which basic human needs are met and students are provided supports in dealing with the societal stresses of late 20th century life

Skinner, 1974) offer different conceptualizations of motivation—how to enhance learner interest in engaging in learning versus troubling behaviors. Educators are more likely to succeed in motivating students if they take an eclectic, divergent approach to understanding and enhancing student motivation. What this requires is that all educators study as much as they can about theory and practice regarding human motivation and use that knowledge to: 1) increase students' capacity to sustain problem-solving efforts in the face of frustration, and 2) entice students to engage in the acquisition of knowledge and skills.

Adversity at home and in the community always has affected some or many of the children attending school; there always have been troubled and troubling youth. However, the number and intensity of stressors of late 20th century life (e.g., poverty, neglect, abuse, divorce, lack of adequate health care, lack of family or informal community support networks) have increased so that more and more students come to school with their ability and motivation to learn negatively affected. To create a motivating school climate for these students, educators must *acknowledge* and *attempt to address* stressors by offering a variety of supports (e.g., a breakfast program, free lunch, mental health and other human services available as on-campus school support services), including the constellation of resources, responses, and services described in the remainder of this chapter. This, of course, makes the job of educator more complex, broadening it to include the issues of safety, health, and the psychological well-being of children.

A CONSTELLATION OF RESOURCES, RESPONSES, AND SERVICES

Suppose a school community made a commitment to actualize the Student Bill of Rights presented in Table 2 and to meet the needs of all students, including those who are troubled or troubling. To fulfill this commitment, members of the school community must be able to answer "yes" to at least the following three questions:

1. Are the adults of the school equipped and empowered to deliver effective instruction, personalize accommodations for learners, and create a motivating school climate?
2. Do students of the school community know and understand their Bill of Rights?
3. Are students empowered to exercise their rights and the responsibilities that accompany these rights?

What are your responses to these three questions? In these authors' experience, in even the most committed schools, many educators and students answer "no" to at least one of these questions. The remainder of this chapter offers a constellation of resources, responses, and services for equipping and empowering educators and students to change their answers from "no" to "yes." The constellation includes strategies for: 1) promoting student responsibility, 2) supporting and empowering students, 3) involving and supporting families, 4) redefining the role of adults in the school, and 5) reconceptualizing "schooling" and the student's day. Table 3 outlines the strategies of the constellation that are detailed in the text that follows.

Teaching Students Responsibility

Educators recognize that student mastery of content areas (e.g., language arts, mathematics, science) specified in most schools' scope and sequence frameworks requires continuous and complex instruction during a period of 10–12 years. When

Table 3.   A constellation of resources and services for serving troubled or troubling learners

Strategies for promoting student responsibility
    Schoolwide discipline system
    Social skills training
    Teaching students anger management and impulse control strategies
    Setting limits to ensure safety

Strategies for involving, empowering, and supporting students
    Students as instructors
    Students as advocates
    Students as decision makers

Strategies for involving, supporting, and empowering family members
    Home–school partnerships
    The individualized education program (IEP) planning process
    Core teams for individual students
    Intensive family-based services
    Local and state-level interagency collaboration

Redefining the role of the adults
    Collaborative planning for the development of accommodations
    Teaching teams of educators, community members, and students
    Awareness training for all staff
    Mentors and advisors to students
    Adult advocates for students
    Individual assistants for students

Rethinking the traditional paradigm of schooling and the student's day
    "Jumping the tracks"
    Creative placements
    Shortened days
    Altered school weeks and years

students fail to learn new skills or concepts, we respond by re-teaching the material, providing additional or different types of supports, and making accommodations. We respond with a "teaching response" to a student's inability to learn material. Yet, for the content area known as "responsibility," the teaching of patterns of behavior and habits of mind representative of "responsible" behavior often is relegated to "add on" or "quick fix" instructional methods (e.g., seeing the guidance counselor, attending a 6-week social skills group, making an oral or a written plan, talking about it after school). Furthermore, when a student demonstrates a lack of responsibility (frequently in the form of rule-violating behavior such as tardiness, verbal aggression, rudeness, and failure to follow instructions), we (the adults of the school) often "take the behavior personally" and respond with an emotional, punishing response rather than an emotionally neutral teaching response. The teaching of responsibility is no less demanding a task than the teaching of any other curriculum area; it requires careful thought and reflection, complex instruction starting at the earliest ages and continuing throughout the school years, and patience.

    It is within the context of a caring relationship that the concept of responsibility acquires meaning. Thus, a condition for promoting the learning of responsibility is that students perceive that someone in the school community cares about them. In order to facilitate students' acquisition of responsible values, attitudes, and behaviors, educators must engage in positive, systematic approaches for developing relationships with students. Relationships may be promoted by teachers acknowledging and validating students' achievement, progress, or goal attainment. With students who are troubled or troubling, it is particularly important to demonstrate caring, concern, and support by *teaching responsibility* through: 1) the establishment of a schoolwide discipline system that promotes the learning of responsibility, 2) direct instruction of pro-social communication skills, 3) direct instruction of anger management and impulse control techniques, and 4) the setting of limits to ensure safety.

A Schoolwide Disciplinary System that Promotes Responsibility Proactive discipline systems are those that promote positive behavior and respond to troubling (rule-violating) behavior in ways that teach the relationship between a behavior and its consequence as well as alternative ways of getting needs met (Curwin & Mendler, 1988; Glasser, 1986). Such systems are based upon a solid understanding of the differences between discipline and punishment. They recognize that responsibility is learned over a period of time and only with opportunities for students to make meaningful choices and to make mistakes without retribution. While safety and orderliness are desired outcomes of a disciplinary system, obedience and compliance are not, as they fail to instill or teach ownership for one's own behavior (i.e., responsibility). Proactive disciplinary models acknowledge that the adults of the school have a responsibility to control the learning environment, but not to control the students. Instead, students are expected and supported to acquire the coping strategies to control themselves.

With responsibility-based models of discipline, responses to rule-violating behavior are congruent with the goals of the system and strive to ensure that each student is treated "fairly," but not necessarily "equally" (Curwin & Mendler, 1988, p. 68). Although classroom and schoolwide rules may be the same for everyone, responses to rule violations are individualized. They are based upon the unique characteristics of the student and the situation, *not* predetermined, arbitrarily established, and rigidly enforced "if-then" consequences (e.g., 10 absences equals a grade of "F" in the missed classes, three tardies equals a detention). Arbitrary consequences are few. Instead, creative disciplinary interventions and the establishment of consequences are guided by the questions "What will the student learn?" and "How will responsibility be promoted?"

Responsibility-based models of discipline acknowledge that conflict is a natural and ongoing part of human existence. Such models take teachers and administrators out of the traditional role of *police officer* and place them in the role of *facilitator*. Behavior is treated as contextual. Therefore, responses to either rule-following or rule-violating behavior are dependent on a variety of factors, such as the time of day, the activity during which the behavior occurred, the frequency and severity of the behavior, and the number of people demonstrating the behavior. Reminders, warnings, cues and self-monitoring techniques, positive practice, restitution, oral or written plans, behavioral contracts, redirection, prompts, direct teaching of interpersonal behaviors, "sit and watch" (being asked to briefly sit and watch classmates who model acceptable behavior), and "time out" from positive reinforcement are all potential responses to rule-violating behavior that, when delivered in a thoughtful, calm, and predictable manner, are *teaching* versus *punishment* responses to rule-violating behavior (Curwin & Mendler, 1988; Glasser, 1986; Jackson, Jackson, & Monroe, 1983). A caution here is that removal from reinforcement may be a traumatic experience, especially for youth who have been victimized by being locked up or whose pattern of response to abuse is to escape from reality through fantasy (Fink & Janssen, 1992).

Perhaps most important to the promotion of student responsibility is an acknowledgment that:

The development of student responsibility should be primarily concerned with teaching young people how to have their needs met.

The development of student responsibility is part of a school's curriculum.

The development of student responsibility is as important as any other curriculum area.

The development of student responsibility requires modeling, coaching, and ongoing thought and reflection on the part of school staff.

Social Skills Instruction   Students who are troubled or troubling often express their thoughts and feelings in ways that violate either explicit or implicit rules governing communication within the school environment (e.g., no swearing, no name calling of teachers). "Rule-violating" communication often results in the student "getting into trouble"; it also makes it more difficult for people to "hear" and understand what the student needs or is requesting. Teaching children and youth how to communicate their thoughts, feelings, and needs in ways that allow adults and peers to hear them is the goal of social skills instruction (Kahler, 1988).

The teaching of prosocial skills encompasses a wide range of instructional strategies that include behavioral, cognitive, and affective approaches (e.g., Elias & Clabby, 1992; Goldstein, 1988; Hazel, Schumaker, Sherman, & Sheldon-Wildgen, 1981; Jackson et al., 1983; Vernon, 1989). One of the greatest challenges associated with social skills instruction is student generalization of learned skills to "real life" situations, particularly stressful situations. Some strategies for promoting generalization include:

- Teaching social skills in heterogeneous "regular classrooms" versus "pull-out" situations
- Direct teaching of social skills in association with intentional cooperative group learning structures (Johnson & Johnson, 1991)
- Frequent, thoughtful teacher feedback and group processing of students' social skill performance
- Frequent recognition, within classrooms and schoolwide, of student effort and skill mastery
- Opportunities for practice of social skills in "real life" community situations
- Social skills newsletters for parents and community members
- Use of social skills in cross-age and same-age partner learning/peer tutoring structures
- Bulletin boards and assemblies that remind students of the importance of social skills to school climate

Teaching Students Anger Management and Impulse Control Strategies   Many students labeled troubled or troubling are characterized as impulsive or having difficulty managing their anger. It is not adequate or satisfactory to simply request, tell, or remind students to "stop and think" prior to acting. Instead, to promote students' control over anger and impulsiveness, schools must offer direct, quality instruction in anger management and impulse control strategies. Anger management strategies often include:

1. Teaching students to recognize and monitor the dimensions and cycle of anger— the external triggers (e.g., someone says or does something you do not like), the

internal triggers (e.g., internal dialogue about the external trigger, such as "That's not fair, I'll get her!"), and physiological signals of anger (e.g., sweaty palms, increased heartbeats).

2. Teaching students a series of anger reducing techniques, such as pleasant images, deep breathing, counting strategies, relaxation strategies, and new internal dialogue scripts.

3. Strategies for self-assessment, self-monitoring, and self-reinforcement through hassle logs and journals (Workman, 1982).

Toomey (1990) offers an explanation for students having difficulty with impulse control. She describes a student's inability to "stop and think" prior to some social or interpersonal interaction as a lack of *tentativeness*. Tentativeness is "the disposition or ability to identify all of the relevant information in order to make the best possible response" (pp. 15–16). To be tentative, a person needs to know how to do five things:

1. Differentiate between tasks that provide all of the necessary information in an explicit way and tasks that require searching for information.

2. Differentiate between closed (one right answer) and open (many possible answers) tasks.

3. Differentiate between relevant and irrelevant information.

4. Discriminate what constitutes the best response.

5. Decide at what point a search must stop and a commitment should be made to some response.

Students demonstrating poor impulse control experience difficulty in one or more of these five areas. Classroom teachers may promote tentativeness and impulse control by offering choices on how to approach tasks, teaching and encouraging self-correcting procedures, teaching the difference between open- and close-ended tasks and offering opportunities to do both, implementing long-term projects, identifying and rewarding different levels of performance, and asking students to think and teach out loud.

Behavioral, cognitive, and affective instructional strategies have been employed, often in combination, to assist students to develop impulse and anger control. For instance, Kendall and Braswell (1985) delineated an intervention based on a cognitive-behavioral framework that includes an interpersonal problem-solving approach, self-control instruction, behavioral contingencies, modeling, affective education, and role playing. Goldstein (1988) also took a cognitive-behavioral approach in *The Prepare Curriculum* and offers problem-solving training, social skills training, aggression replacement training, stress management, empathy training, moral reasoning, recruitment of supportive models, and cooperation training as elements of a comprehensive program. Of course, critical to any self-control training program are activities for promoting the generalization of acquired skills such as role-playing, coaching, and ongoing practice and reinforcement of learned self-control strategies in a broad range of contexts.

Setting Limits to Ensure Safety   It is the responsibility of the school to ensure that students are free from physical danger. It must be recognized that at times youth who are troubled or troubling present safety concerns to the school community and themselves. Therefore, part of a school's commitment to ensure safety for all must be a well-articulated and well-understood crisis management system that promotes student responsibility and choice at each stage of a crisis. Allowing students opportunities to "calm down" in a less stressful environment; allowing students the choice to leave the school grounds or to go home for a certain amount of time; in-school suspension; parent, social service, mental health, and even police removal are all possible options within a crisis response system. Although an unpleasant and a *last resort* intervention, passive physical restraint is something a number of school personnel need to know how to perform. People most likely to need to restrain a student must receive training in this last resort procedure. Finally, "out of school suspension" is an option that may need to be considered for short periods of time until a team (which includes the student) can convene to consider the "next steps." It is critical that, if a student is asked to leave the school, he or she has a safe and supervised place to go.

Involving, Supporting, and Empowering Students

The term *collaboration* usually brings to mind *adults* working together. Schools attempting to include, support, and empower students who are troubled or troubling have expanded the list of potential collaborators to include *students*. Villa and Thousand (1992) offer three reasons for empowering students by placing them in collaborative roles as instructors, decision makers, self-advocates, and advocates for others. First, given the diverse needs of an increasingly heterogeneous student population, school personnel need to take advantage of any and all available human resources; students offer a rich source of expertise, enthusiasm, and refreshing creativity at no extra cost to the school district. Second, educational reform leaders have called for more opportunities for students to develop and use higher level thinking skills through "a new collaborative role . . . in which students accept an active senior partnership role in the learning enterprise" (Benjamin, 1989, p. 9). Having students plan, teach, problem solve, and evaluate educational activities responds to these calls for active involvement. Third, reform leaders have advised schools to expand opportunities for students to develop empathy for others and practice being contributing and caring members of society (Benjamin, 1989; Falvey, Coots, & Bishop, 1990). By encouraging students to advocate for their own and fellow classmates' educational interests, schools create such opportunities.

Enfranchising students as responsible citizens of a school is the goal of collaborative student–student and student–adult arrangements. Identified in Table 4 are collaborative strategies intended to:

1. Empower students to better advocate for and support one another.
2. Increase the likelihood that any student (including one who is troubled or troubling) will experience a sense of belonging and community.
3. Motivate and support students to engage as positive members of a school community.

A caution in giving one student responsibility over another is that students who have been identified as sexual offenders should not be given responsibility or power over other children unless the interaction is supervised by an adult (Fink & Janssen, 1992).

Involve, Support, and Empower Families

The Education for All Handicapped Children Act of 1975 (Public Law 94-142) promised the design and delivery of a free and appropriate education for every child with a disability. It also provided for strong parent involvement. The architects of this document were astute in their recognition of the critical role that families play in deter-

Table 4.   Collaborative roles for students as instructors, decision makers, and advocates for themselves and others

- Students as instructors in partner learning, cooperative group learning, and adult–student teaching team arrangements
- Students as members of collaborative planning teams that determine accommodations for themselves and other classmates experiencing academic or behavioral challenges
- Students supporting a challenged classmate through a "peer buddy" system or a Circle of Friends (Forest & Lusthaus, 1989)
- Students as coaches for their teachers, offering feedback regarding the effectiveness and consistency of their instructional and discipline procedures
- Students who are troubled or troubling serving on a student council to help set school rules and consequences for students and teachers and make recommendations on how to improve the school climate (Curwin & Mendler, 1988)
- Students trained to serve as *peacemakers* in conflict situations on the playground, in the school building, and in life outside of school (Johnson & Johnson, 1991; Kreidler, 1984; Schrumpf, Crawford, & Chu Usadel, 1991a, 1991b)
- Older students teaching violence prevention information to younger students
- Students establishing a violence- or crime-prevention club in which they identify crime problems and develop strategies to reduce them (Pitcher & Poland, 1992)
- Students as members of curriculum, inservice, and other school governance committees, such as the school board or a student-operated "Jury of Peers" for dealing with student behavioral infractions

mining and evaluating the appropriateness of academic and behavioral interventions for their children. One of the most powerful interventions for meeting the needs of children who are troubled or troubling is the development of a strong, meaningful home–school partnership, one characterized by equity and parity in decision making.

For a variety of reasons, the establishment of a meaningful partnership is not always easy. Many parents may have had negative experiences themselves in school. Previous patterns of interaction with the school may have consisted primarily of frequent phone calls home to report how poorly their child was doing, academically and behaviorally. School personnel may not be available when parents are able to meet (i.e., in the evenings, on weekends). At times, parents may be overwhelmed with life's circumstances and unable to participate more meaningfully in their child's education. Finally, school personnel may, intentionally or unintentionally, communicate to parents that they are failing as parents and that their child does not belong in school. Clearly, school personnel committed to meeting the needs of children who are troubled or troubling must confront and attempt to overcome these obstacles.

The annual individualized education program (IEP) meeting required by law for children eligible for special education provides one avenue for developing a trusting home–school partnership. To be meaningful, these meetings must afford parents opportunities to express their feelings as well as share their expertise and knowledge regarding their child's unique needs and the successful strategies they have used to meet these needs. School personnel must be open to and invite parent input. Otherwise, as parents report happening far too often, educators end up talking *at* parents and presenting them with already completed documents and plans.

School-Based Supports and Services for Families   In a number of Vermont school districts, *core teams* have been assembled to support children who are troubled or troubling and their families. Ideally, a student's core team includes the parent(s), a support person for the parent, the student, a peer who provides support to the student, a classroom teacher, a special educator, an individual aide (if one is assigned to work with the student), and, perhaps, an administrator. Initially, core teams meet weekly or biweekly for 30 minutes to 1 hour to plan and problem solve with regard to the target student. Sometimes, the student and/or family members are reluctant to participate fully in the collaborative decision-making process. In some cases, it has taken a year or two for a student or parent to actively and regularly participate as a core team member because it took that long for a meaningful and trusting relationship to develop. Yet, waiting is worth the effort. For many families, the ongoing trust and communication that results from the core team's frequent face-to-face interaction has transformed their relationship with the school and the lives of their troubled children.

Schools may show respect for and support families in a number of other ways. First, personnel should avoid talking in jargon, in their respective discipline-specific expert language. Second, schools can respond to parents' requests for training related to their rights, current best practices (Fox & Williams, 1990), collaboration and conflict resolution, meaningful accommodations, appropriate academic and behavioral interventions, and transition services (Villa, 1989). This information is intended to empower parents to participate more fully in the design of their child's program as equal partners on collaborative teams. Third, it is recommended that information for parents be delivered through a team teaching arrangement of a parent and a professional, so that parents observe in the instructor role another parent with whom they can identify and who has credibility because of similar experiences. The parent–teacher teaching arrangement also models equity and parity between school personnel and families.

Finally, parents may choose to influence decisions that affect them and their child by serving the greater school community as members and leaders of school organizations such as the PTO and the school board. Parents in these roles can provide a powerful perspective as well as strong advocacy for their own and others' children as they volunteer time and energy in service to the school.

Community-Based Supports and Services for Families   Given the current organizational structure of public schools, school personnel often are not able to provide all of the supports a family may need in order to deal with the family dynamics and the behavior of a child who is troubled or troubling. Families of many children who are troubled or troubling require the services of multiple agencies (e.g., social services, mental health). In recognition of this need, federal legislation established a Child and Adolescent Service System Program (CASSP) to promote interagency coordination of services in each state (Nelson & Pearson, 1991). In Vermont, one positive outcome of CASSP has been that state leadership of mental health, human services, and education agencies has acknowledged that:

> Meeting the needs of a child or adolescent with a severe emotional disturbance and his/her family is a complex task. It begins with taking a careful look at the total child, and proceeds to networking with local service providers to design and implement an individualized treatment plan. This sounds simple, but it is not. (The Vermont Agency of Human Services and The Vermont Department of Education, 1990, pp. 3–4)

As a consequence of this understanding, in 1988, Vermont state legislators passed legislation that created one state-level and 12 local interagency teams. The goal of these teams was to facilitate access to and coordinate educational, residential, mental health, and other treatment services for children and adolescents with a severe emotional disturbance and their families. Since the formation of these teams, there has been a higher degree of service coordination statewide, an increased level of support to families and school personnel, and a significant reduction (more than 50%

from April 1991 to September 1992) in the percentage of students labeled behaviorally or emotionally disturbed who are educated in out-of-state residential facilities (G. DeCarolis, personal communication, December 3, 1992).

Family counseling often is a proactive intervention for addressing the needs of a family that, for whatever reason, is in distress. School personnel can facilitate a family's participation in counseling by serving as a "linking pin," helping the family to access appropriate, affordable counseling services.

A promising intensive community-based intervention for families of children who are troubled or troubling is known as Intensive Family-Based Services (IFBS). In Vermont, when a family participates in IFBS, it becomes possible for an IFBS worker (e.g., social worker, counselor) to be available to work with the family in the home for as many as 15 hours a week for up to 6 months. Together, the family and the IFBS worker set goals and plan how to attain those goals. The IFBS worker provides modeling and support for parents as they attempt to break old patterns with and practice new responses to their child's challenging behavior. After the 6-month intervention, parents may continue to participate in support groups and educational opportunities offered through the IFBS program.

Respite, foster care, and emergency mental health placements are other community-based supports that have proven to be effective in assisting families with a child who is troubled or troubling. School personnel can facilitate the family's access to these important resources through interagency coordination. A benefit of available respite and emergency care is that the family gets a break and has the opportunity to come together to work out problems in a less stressed state. Occasionally, short-term foster care is deemed in the best interest of the child and the family. It must be emphasized that the goals of respite or foster care are family reconciliation and, when necessary, positive change in traditional family behavior patterns.

Regrettably, in many communities, school- and community-based supports and services for families such as those described in this section are the exception rather than the rule. School personnel are encouraged to advocate for more creative and collaborative interagency responses for accessing, designing, and delivering family-centered supports for children who are troubled or troubling.

Redefining the Role of the Adult in the School

In these authors' view, we cannot expect children to support and respect others (children and adults) as equals if we are not willing to do the same. This proposition suggests a shift in the role of the adults of the school from *authority figure*—a type of policing official, responsible for ensuring that students conform to standardized rules, norms, and standards—to *support person*—an active listener and partner in the construction of meaningful educational experiences for each individual learner. Skrtic, in an interview with Thousand (1990), further proposes viewing the educator as a collaborative *inventor,* who through *adhocracies*—ad hoc collaborative teams that pool skills and knowledge to invent unique, personalized programs for each student—exercises an implicit understanding that educational programs must be "continuously invented and reinvented by teachers in actual practice with students who have unique and changing needs" (p. 32). What follows are strategies for supporting students identified as troubled or troubling that assume that the appropriate role of the educator is that of collaborative supporter and inventor.

Adults as Members of Planning and Teaching Teams   Personnel in schools that have been most successful in responding to the needs of students who are troubled or troubling consistently identify as the cornerstone to their success the establishment of individual student *core teams* that meet regularly to address the challenges experienced and presented by a student. Any adult or student interested in supporting the education of a student is a potential member of that student's core planning and support team. The strongest, most effective core teams are skilled in the use of problem-solving and decision-making processes referred to as "collaborative teaming" (Thousand & Villa, 1992, p. 73).

In some schools, long-term team teaching arrangements, described as *teaching teams,* have been established. A teaching team is "an organizational and instructional arrangement of two or more members of the school and greater community who distribute among themselves planning, instructional, and evaluation responsibilities for the same students on a regular basis for an extended period of time" (Thousand & Villa, 1990a, p. 152). As with individual student core teams, members of teaching teams engage in an ongoing exchange of knowledge and skills and the generation of creative responses to children, including those identified as troubled or troubling. In teaching teams, members release professional labels and distribute job functions across formerly separate school personnel (e.g., special vs. general educators), community volunteers, and students (Thousand & Villa, 1991).

In summary, it is important to remember that each member of the school community who comes in contact with a student with challenging behaviors needs to have an adequate understanding of the student's needs and strategies for consistently managing the student's behavior. Thus, central to a student's success in a school is ongoing communication and *awareness training* with all of the people who work in and for the school, including custodial staff, secretaries, cafeteria workers, and volunteers, regarding principles of behavior management, effective communication, active listening, and conflict resolution.

Adults as Mentors and Advocates for Students Adults, consciously and unconsciously, serve as models for children. Children who are troubled or troubling may have had limited or no access to adult models who demonstrate effective communication, anger management, and creative problem-solving skills. Thus, it is critical for teachers and other adults who work with and for children who are troubled or troubling to remain aware of their potential power as positive role models. Through their consistent actions they can teach students new patterns for communicating, managing anger, and dealing with adversity in socially acceptable ways.

Adult members of the school community can also support students who are troubled or troubling by serving as *mentors* or *teacher advisors.* Typical adult mentoring or teacher advisor programs pair each adult member of the school (e.g., teachers, custodians, administrators, secretaries) with a small group of fewer than nine students. Mentors or teacher advisors meet daily with their advisee groups and attend proactive or reactive meetings in which academic or behavioral issues of an advisee are addressed. In some schools, advisor/advisee relationships are long term, extending throughout all of the secondary school years. For children who are troubled or troubling, advisors frequently begin and end each day with a brief meeting in which the day is previewed or reviewed. In some instances, more frequent contact is scheduled throughout the day. A natural extension of the mentor/advisor role that is emerging in some Vermont schools is the adult *advocate* role. An adult advocate functions not as a school representative, but as a support person for a student. It is recommended, therefore, that a student participate in the selection of his or her advocate. The advocate accompanies and represents a student at planning, discipline, and other school-related meetings. An adult advocate may prepare a student for a meeting and discuss the results with the student following the meeting. The advocate provides a "voice" for a student in dealings with authority figures (i.e., other school personnel, parents) and helps a student plan how to successfully carry out and monitor any oral or written plan developed to affect positive changes in the student's behavior.

Individual Assistants   Valuable supports for some students who are troubled or troubling have been *individual aides* or *assistants*. Serious consideration must be given as to whether or not an individual assistant (IA) is needed to assist a student in monitoring his or her behavior. Many students view the assignment of an IA as stigmatizing. However, IAs are essential if a student's behavior is very disruptive and places themselves or others in physical danger.

Thousand and Villa (1990b) offer the following advice to educators considering assigning an IA to a student. First, be sure to spend adequate time discussing and clarifying with the school community that the purpose of support is to enable a student to gain independence and form natural relationships with peers. Second, clearly delineate the IA's job as a support to the teacher and the classroom, as well as the challenged student. Third, use the collaborative teaming processes to plan, deliver, and evaluate the student's program *and* expect IAs to join the team as equally valued, vocal members. Fourth, do not presume that all students who are troubled or troubling require full-time or part-time IA support. Instead, require and establish procedures for the documentation of need for an IA that include a description of the other types of accommodations and supports that already have been attempted. Finally, develop and regularly re-examine a plan to *fade out* direct instructional and personal support provided by the IA. Many students who are troubled or troubling have expressed dissatisfaction with being assigned an IA. Through involvement on their collaborative core teams, these students have participated in designing plans for fading and, eventually, eliminating IA support (e.g., contracting to systematically reduce IA support contingent upon appropriate behavior for a set period of time).

Rethinking School and the Student's Day

> It's no secret that America's public schools are failing. . . . The time for tinkering with the current system of education is over. After a decade of trying to make the system work better by such means as more testing, higher salaries, and tighter curriculums, we must now face up to the fact that anything short of fundamental structural change is futile. (Fiske, 1992, pp. 13–14)

Fiske's observation reflects a widespread belief that schools are failing to meet the needs of a significant number of children, among whom are children who become identified as troubled or troubling. The term, *school,* conjures up various images. As the *Oxford American Dictionary* (1980) illustrates, it may be defined as:

> 1. an institution for educating children or for giving instruction; 2. its buildings; 3. its pupils; 4. the time during which teaching is done there, *school ends at 4:30 p.m.*; 5. the process of being educated in a school, *always hated school.* [emphasis added] (p. 810)

In other words, a school consists of many components—the organizational structure, the building, time usage, the students and adults, and the processes of learning. Furthermore, a school does not operate in a vacuum, but in the context of a larger local and global community. Therefore, when thinking about how to respond to the needs of students who are troubled or troubling, all of these variables must be considered.

In rethinking schools, one of the first places to look for assistance is motivational theory. Choice and empowerment are central concepts to most contemporary motivational theories. Therefore, enhancing student choice in the learning enterprise—the what, where, when, and how of learning—is a key to restructuring schools so as to entice students to be actively engaged in learning versus disrupting the process. Choice is particularly important for troubled or troubling youth who feel that life and school have been imposed upon them, that freedom and choice have been denied, or that they are the victims of adult authority. Choice can help to break a student's cycle of apathy, resistance, or defiance. Students are more likely to make a commitment to participate in schooling when the components of schooling are, at least in part, of their own design. The following are examples of nontraditional designs of the school day that afford students more choice.

"Jumping the Tracks" In 1985, Jeannie Oakes estimated that 80% of American secondary schools and 60% of elementary schools employed some form of ability grouping or tracking. Encouraging students to *jump the tracks* and enroll in any class or course usually limited to a subset of students (e.g., jumping the college preparatory track to take a vocational child care half-day internship; jumping the "slow learner" track to participate in a "gifted program," such as the Olympics of the Mind competition) has proven to be a successful strategy for reducing the level and frequency of some students' rule-violating behavior. The increased choice and empowerment resulting from this practice has resulted in increased student interest, motivation, and engagement in learning activities, and a corresponding reduction in students' need to gain attention through means that are unacceptable to teachers.

Creative Placement Creative placement involves children being allowed to sample experiences and course offerings that traditionally have been unavailable to them because of their chronological age, grade level, or location within the building walls. It expands upon the "jumping the track" notion by opening up all of the school and community as potential learning environments and experiences. For example, a sixth grader identified as "gifted," who was not motivated by the middle school social studies curriculum, was allowed to enroll in the 12th grade government class. Another middle school student, who refused to come to school, was motivated to return by enrollment in a high school automotive course. Employment, apprenticeships, and community service also represent creative placement options that not only expand the traditional curriculum, but increase the relevance of learning to future life as a worker and community member.

Shortened Days and Altered School Weeks and Years Consider a student perceived as troubling because he routinely arrived at school at 10:00 A.M. versus the usual 7:45 A.M. start time. When questioned, he revealed that both of his parents worked the late shift and that he stayed up until 3:00 A.M. so that he could spend some time with them. This was the only time they all were at home. Rather than continue to demand that the student attend first and second period classes, which he had failed to attend for 3 years, the decision was made to shift the starting and ending time of his school day so that he began school with the third period class and ended the day with his employment program, which extended his school day until 5:00 P.M. For some students, 12 years of 185 7-hour school days does not constitute the "magic formula" for learning. Some students may be most responsive to shortened or extended school days or school years. For example, some students may need support and continued education in the summer months in order to "stay out of trouble" in the community. Students who are engaged in the determination of the time, locations, and duration of their educational careers may be more motivated and committed to the learning process and less inclined to engage in behaviors that are incompatible with learning.

In summary, we advocate replacing the current categorical, multitracked educational system with a "one-track system" (Nuzzi, 1992, p. 7) where all students' differing abilities, interests, learning styles, and psychological needs are recognized, valued, and addressed. As the Reverend Ronald Nuzzi (1992) suggests:

> If we truly wish to respond to different student interests within a one-track system, we have to rethink the notion that learning happens only within the confines of the school building. Opportunities for distance learning must be created at every level; and the neighborhood, the community, and the world must become the classroom. Would this still be a one-track system? Maybe it would be one track per student, one student per track. (p. 7)

DISCUSSION

Successfully addressing the diverse psychological and educational needs of children and youth who have been identified as troubled and troubling can be a complex, frustrating, and continual challenge. In this chapter, we present a constellation of resources, supports, and services that have been employed by school personnel committed to successfully meeting this challenge. Clearly, matching intervention strategies to the life circumstances, stresses, and context from which a child operates requires careful and thoughtful consideration; in other words, the suggested strategies should not be used in a simple, "cookbook" manner.

To illustrate the power of the resources, supports, and services recommended in this chapter, we offer strategies selected by teams supporting Mariah, Billy, and Ricardo—the students introduced at the start of this chapter.

Mariah

While Mariah was still hospitalized for her unsuccessful suicide attempt, an inter-agency team that comprised Mariah, her maternal aunt, and representatives from the school and mental health and social services agencies was formed and met to design a plan to coordinate services and supports for Mariah after her hospital release. The primary goal of the team was to reduce the likelihood of future suicide attempts. The service plan that was developed for Mariah included: 1) temporary residence for Mariah and her sister with her maternal aunt; 2) a suicide contract with Mariah; 3) individual counseling for Mariah that focused upon her drug and alcohol abuse; 4) Mariah's participation in a peer support group for survivors of sexual abuse; and 5) family counseling for Mariah, her father, and her sister. Criminal charges were brought against Mariah's father. While the charges were pending, the father voluntarily agreed to participate in an out-patient sex offender program. All contact between Mariah and her sister with their father was supervised. Upon return to school, Mariah was taught creative problem-solving strategies to identify alternatives other than self-destructive behavior to manage her thoughts and feelings. She also selected an adult mentor/advisor in the school with whom she "checked in" daily, before and after school. Mariah's support team made a commitment to continue meeting to assist Mariah in planning for her transition from school to college, independent living, and work.

Billy

Billy's social studies teacher, concerned by the increase in his swearing and chair throwing, requested that a *core team* be established to support Billy and his teachers by developing interventions for dealing with his rule-violating behaviors. The core team members included Billy, a classmate selected by him, Billy's mother, the social studies teacher, the assistant principal, and a special educator. This team met weekly on Friday afternoons from 2:30 P.M. to 3:00 P.M.

One of the team's first considerations was whether an individual assistant should be assigned to Billy's classes. It was agreed that this would be a premature, excessively intrusive, and costly response at this point in time. It was decided that the special educator would team teach with the social studies teacher 4 days a week. The role of the special educator was to implement accommodations and modifications to the curriculum and instruction to enable Billy and other students to be more successful and to be available to intervene with Billy, if necessary. The social studies teacher agreed to increase the use of partner and cooperative group learning structures in order to give students more of an opportunity to work with one another and to increase Billy's opportunity to develop friendships. In addition, because Billy expressed an interest in participating in a reciprocal tutoring program, he was trained as a tutor in mathematics and delivered instruction three times a week to a small group of students in a fifth grade classroom. He also received tutoring in reading from an eighth grade classmate during their assigned study hall.

A multidimensional approach was used to address Billy's aggressive outbursts. First, he joined an anger management and impulse control social skills group facilitated by his guidance counselor. The social studies teacher also agreed to team teach with the guidance counselor so that he would be able to incorporate social skills instruction and practice into his regular social studies curriculum. Second, Billy was given the option to remove himself from class when he felt he might engage in swearing or aggressive behavior. Third, in response to the social studies teacher's request to learn appropriate passive physical restraint procedures, the teacher was given 9 hours of training from certified personnel from a recognized training organization. The training emphasized strategies for avoiding and de-escalating aggressive behavior.

Finally, in an effort to promote responsibility and enhance self-esteem, Billy was given a school job in the cafeteria. It also was arranged for Billy to shower and change into clean clothes whenever he came to school smelling of urine.

Ricardo

After repeated visits to their home at various times during the day and night, the school social worker finally made contact with Ricardo's family. Although the social worker's Spanish vocabulary was limited, she was able to communicate with Ricardo's parents and learned that they both were migrant farm workers who worked 14–16 hours a day. She also discovered that Ricardo routinely got up in the middle of the night to welcome his parents home and spend time with them. Ricardo's parents did not know that Ricardo had stopped going to school.

A core team was established for Ricardo that included a professional from the Migrant Worker Education Center, Ricardo's classroom teacher, the school social worker, and a classmate selected by Ricardo. Supports developed for Ricardo included a flexible school schedule so that he could come to school late. When the social worker visited his home, she observed that Ricardo was very good at playing with and taking care of his younger cousins. This prompted school personnel to offer Ricardo a job in the after-school child-care program on Mondays, Wednesdays, and Fridays. The job was eagerly accepted by Ricardo and it decreased the amount of time that he was alone and unsupervised. It also provided him with a healthy after-school snack. On Tuesdays and Thursdays, Ricardo was enrolled in the YMCA after-school recreation and homework support program, where he made a number of new friends from his neighborhood. Summer program options, including volunteer community service, are being explored.

Just the Beginning

Clearly, much remains to be discovered about providing appropriate support and education for children and youth who are troubled or troubling. Nevertheless, these authors are confident that teams of educators, students, and family and community members using collaborative and creative planning processes will invent solutions to the challenges faced and presented by these youth (see Thousand, Nevin, & Leff, chap. 14, this volume; Thousand & Villa, 1992). Successful inventors are passionate. They are willing to challenge the status quo, deal with the cognitive dissonance and emotional turmoil that frequently accompany change, remain focused on their vision, and learn from their experiences (Villa & Thousand, 1992). In our experience, the school personnel most successful in dealing with youth who have been identified as troubled or troubling have this passion. Given this passion, they choose to perceive problems, barriers, and challenges as opportunities. They also maintain and display a sense of humor.

As previously stated, many North American schools are failing an ever increasing number of children. To turn this around, it is imperative to recognize that far too often the disability is not in the child who gets labeled and, often, ejected from the educational system, but rather the disability is in the structure, policies, and traditions of school and social services systems. It also is imperative to recognize that it sometimes is easier to blame the victim than to struggle to change the system.

In these authors' view, children and youth labeled as troubled or troubling offer schools a *gift*. Their behavior forces us to see the inadequacies of many of the organizational, curricular, instructional, cultural, and interaction patterns that have become tradition in North American schools. If we have the courage to confront the inadequacies of the current schooling paradigm to creatively respond to the challenges posed by Mariah, Billy, and Ricardo, the gift will be new and renewed school communities with a greater capacity to be caring, respectful, effective, and inviting for children and adults alike. The gift has been offered. Will we accept it and commit?

> Until one is committed there is hesitancy, the chance to draw back, always ineffectiveness. Concerning all acts of initiative . . . there is one elementary truth, the ignorance of which kills countless ideas and splendid plans: That the moment one definitely commits oneself, then providence moves too. (W.H. Murray as quoted in Gore, 1992, p. 16)

REFERENCES

Bandura, A. (1977). *Social learning theory.* Englewood Cliffs, NJ: Prentice Hall.

Benjamin, S. (1989). An ideascape for education: What futurists recommend. *Educational Leadership, 47*(1), 8–14.

Brandt, R. (Ed.). (1992). *Educational Leadership, 49*(7).

Brendtro, L.K., Brokenleg, M., & Van Bockern, S. (1990). *Reclaiming youth at risk: Our hope for the future.* Bloomington, IN: National Educational Service.

Burchard, J.D., & Clarke, R.T. (1990). The role of individualized care in a service delivery system for children and adolescents with severely maladjusted behavior. *The Journal of Mental Health Administration, 17*(1), 48–60.

Carnegie Council on Adolescent Development. (1989). *Turning points: Preparing American youth for the 21st century.* Washington, DC: Author.

The Children's Defense Fund & The Robin Hood Foundation. (1992). Maybe America really is going to hell in a hand basket. *Rolling Stone, 643,* 239.

Curwin, R., & Mendler, A. (1988). *Discipline with dignity.* Alexandria, VA: Association for Supervision and Curriculum Development.

Edmonds, R. (1979). Effective schools for the urban poor. *Educational Leadership, 37*(1), 15–24.

Elias, M., & Clabby, J. (1992). *Building social problem-solving skills.* San Francisco: Jossey-Bass.

Falvey, M., Coots, J., & Bishop, K. (1990). Developing a caring community to support volunteer programs. In W. Stainback & S. Stainback (Eds.), *Support networks for inclusive schooling: Interdependent integrated education* (pp. 231–240). Baltimore: Paul H. Brookes Publishing Co.

Fink, A.H., & Janssen, K.N. (1992). The management of the maltreated adolescent in school settings. *Preventing School Failure, 36*(3), 33–36.

Fiske, E.B. (1992). *Smart schools, smart kids: Why do some schools work?* New York: Touchstone.

Forest, M., & Lusthaus, E. (1989). Promoting educational equality for all students: Circles and maps. In S. Stainback, W. Stainback, & M. Forest (Eds.), *Educating all students in the mainstream of regular education* (pp. 43–57). Baltimore: Paul H. Brookes Publishing Co.

Fox, T., & Williams, W. (1990, October). *Quarterly progress report. Statewide systems change: Vermont model for statewide delivery of quality comprehensive special educaton and related services to severely handicapped children.* Burlington: University of Vermont, Center for Developmental Disabilities.

Glasser, W. (1975). *Schools without failure.* New York: Harper & Row.

Glasser, W. (1986). *Control theory in the classroom.* New York: Harper & Row.

Glatthorn, A. (1987). How do you adapt the curriculum to respond to individual differences? In A. Glatthorn (Ed.), *Curriculum renewal* (pp. 99–109). Alexandria, VA: Association for Supervision and Curriculum Development.

Gliedman, J., & Roth, W. (1980). *The unexpected minority: Handicapped children in America.* New York: Harcourt Brace Jovanovich,

Goldstein, A. (1988). *The prepare curriculum.* Champaign, IL: Research Press.

Gore, A. (1992). *Earth in the balance: Ecology and the human spirit.* Boston: Houghton Mifflin.

Hazel, J., Schumaker, J., Sherman, J., & Sheldon-Wildgen, J. (1981). *ASSET: A social skills program for adolescents.* Champaign, IL: Research Press.

Health and Welfare Canada. (1987). *Suicide in Canada: Report of the national task force on suicide in Canada* (Catalogue No. H39-107/1987E). Ottawa, Ontario, Canada: Author.

Hobbs, N. (1982). *The troubled and troubling child.* San Francisco: Jossey-Bass.

Jackson, N.E., Jackson, D.A., & Monroe, C. (1983). *Getting along with others: Teaching social effectiveness to children.* Champaign, IL: Research Press.

Johnson, D.W., & Johnson, R.T. (1991). *Teaching children to be peacemakers.* Edina, MN: Interaction Book Company.

Kahler, T. (1988). *Quality relations: Using the Process Communication model.* Little Rock, AK: Kahler Communications, Inc.

Kendall, P., & Braswell, L. (1985). *Cognitive behavioral therapy for impulsive children.* New York: Guilford Press.

Knitzer, J., Steinberg, Z., & Bleisch, B. (1990). *At the schoolhouse door: An examination of programs and policies for children with behavioral and emotional problems.* New York: Bank Street College of Education.

Kreidler, W.J. (1984). *Creative conflict resolution.* Glenview, IL: Scott, Foresman.

Kunc, N. (1992). The need to belong: Rediscovering Maslow's hierarchy of needs. In R.A. Villa, J.S. Thousand, W. Stainback, & S. Stainback (Eds.), *Restructuring for caring and effective education: An administrative guide to creating heterogeneous schools* (pp. 25–39). Baltimore: Paul H. Brookes Publishing Co.

Leone, P., McLaughlin, M., & Meisel, S. (1992). School reform and adolescents with behavioral disorders. *Focus on Exceptional Children, 25*(1), 1–24.

Lipsky, D.K., & Gartner, A. (Eds.). (1989). *Beyond separate education: Quality education for all.* Baltimore: Paul H. Brookes Publishing Co.

Maslow, A. (1970). *Motivation and personality.* New York: Harper & Row.

Morgan, D.P., & Jenson, W.R. (1988). *Teaching behaviorally disordered students: Preferred practices.* New York: Macmillan.

National Association of State Directors of Special Education. (1992). Special ed enrollment nears 5 million. *Counterpoint, 13*(1), 1, 12.

Nelson, C.N., & Pearson, C.A. (1991). *Integrating services for children and youth with emotional and behavioral disorders.* Reston, VA: The Council for Exceptional Children.

Nevin, A., Villa, R., & Thousand, J. (1992). An invitation to invent the extraordinary: A response to Morsink. *Remedial and Special Education, 13*(6), 44–46.

Nuzzi, R. (1992). Issue: The practice of "tracking" students is under heavy attack. How can schools offer only one track and still address students' different abilities and interests? *ASCD Update, 34*(9), 7.

Oakes, J. (1985). *Keeping track: How schools structure inequity.* New Haven, CT: Yale University Press.

Oxford American Dictionary. (1980). New York: Oxford University Press, Inc.

Patterson, J., Purkey, S., & Parker, J. (1986). *Productive school systems for a nonrational world.* Alexandria, VA: Association for Supervision and Curriculum Development.

Pitcher, G.D., & Poland, S. (1992). *Crisis intervention in the schools.* New York: The Guilford Press.

Public Law 94-142, Education for All Handicapped Children Act of 1975. (23 August 1977). 20 U.S.C. 1401 et seq: *Federal Register, 42*(163), 42474–42518.

Schrumpf, F., Crawford, D., & Chu Usadel, H. (1991a). *Peer mediation: Conflict resolution in schools—Program guide.* Champaign, IL: Research Press.

Schrumpf, F., Crawford, D., & Chu Usadel, H.

(1991b). *Peer mediation: Conflict resolution in schools—Student manual*. Champaign, IL: Research Press.

Sizer, T.R. (1992). *Horace's school: Redesigning the American high school*. Boston: Houghton Mifflin.

Skinner, B. (1974). *About behaviorism*. New York: Alfred A. Knopf.

Stainback, S., Stainback, W., & Forest, M. (Eds.). (1989). *Educating all students in the mainstream of regular education*. Baltimore: Paul H. Brookes Publishing Co.

Thousand, J. (1990). Organizational perspectives on teacher education and school renewal: A conversation with Tom Skrtic. *Teacher Education and Special Education, 13*(1), 30–35.

Thousand, J., & Villa, R. (1990a). Sharing expertise and responsibilities through teaching teams. In W. Stainback & S. Stainback (Eds.), *Support networks for inclusive schooling: Integrated interdependent education* (pp. 151–166). Baltimore: Paul H. Brookes Publishing Co.

Thousand, J., & Villa, R. (1990b). Strategies for educating learners with severe disabilities within their local home schools and communities. *Focus on Exceptional Children, 22*(3), 1–24.

Thousand, J., & Villa, R. (1991). Accommodating for greater student variance. In M. Ainscow (Ed.), *Effective schools for all* (pp. 161–180). London: David Fulton Publishers.

Thousand, J.S., & Villa, R.A. (1992). Collaborative teams: A powerful tool in school restructuring. In R.A. Villa, J.S. Thousand, W. Stainback, & S. Stainback (Eds.), *Restructuring for caring and effective education: An administrative guide to creating heterogeneous schools* (pp. 73–108). Baltimore: Paul H. Brookes Publishing Co.

Toomey, F. (1990). *Learning and individual differences: A cognitive-developmental model*. Unpublished manuscript, St. Michaels College, Department of Education, Winooski, VT.

The Vermont Agency of Human Services and The Vermont Department of Education. (1990, January). *The 1990 Vermont system of care plan for children and adolescents who have a severe emotional disturbance and their families*. Waterbury: Vermont Department of Mental Health.

Vernon, A. (1989). *Thinking, feeling, behaving*. Champaign, IL: Research Press.

Villa, R. (1989). Model public school inservice programs: Do they exist? *Teacher Education and Special Education, 12*, 173–176.

Villa, R.A., & Thousand, J.S. (1992). Student collaboration: An essential for curriculum delivery in the 21st century. In S. Stainback & W. Stainback (Eds.), *Curriculum considerations in inclusive classrooms: Facilitating learning for all students* (pp. 117–142). Baltimore: Paul H. Brookes Publishing Co.

Wagner, M. (1989). Youth with disabilities during transition. An overview and description of findings from the national longitudinal transition study. In J. Chadsey-Rusch (Ed.), *Transition institute at Illinois: Project director's fourth annual meeting* (pp. 24–52). Champaign: University of Illinois.

Workman, E. (1982). *Teaching behavioral self-control to students*. Austin, TX: PRO-ED.

BEYOND BENEVOLENCE

FRIENDSHIP AND
THE POLITICS OF HELP

*Emma Van der Klift
and Norman Kunc*

The move toward cooperative and inclusive education is part of a larger move out of social oppression for individuals with disabilities. It is part of a groundswell movement of social reform that holds as a central tenet the belief that all children, including those with disabilities, are capable of learning and contributing to their classrooms and communities.

Students formerly educated in separate schools or segregated classrooms are appearing in increasing numbers in neighborhood schools and regular classrooms. Across North America, we are coming to recognize that full participation in communities and schools should be the right of all individuals and that segregation on the basis of physical, mental, or cultural differences is fundamentally wrong.

This is the first generation of children with and without disabilities to grow up and be educated together. Consequently, within inclusive education we have come to entertain a cheerful optimism that the generation growing up now will be different than those of the past. We are hopeful that greater contact between children will begin to break down the barriers of misunderstanding and dispel the myths that have created society's response to disability.

At first glance, this change might seem to be taking place. Individuals with disabilities are more visible and increasingly involved in community life. If we believed that greater proximity leads to greater acceptance, it could be argued that we are successfully participating in the creation of a new social order. Unfortunately, this is only partly true. Instead, we are finding that increased visibility and "presence" alone do not necessarily ensure that those with disabilities are fully included.

True inclusion is dependent on the development of meaningful and reciprocal relationships between children. As classrooms become increasingly diverse, new strategies are being developed to ensure that the new students are more than simply present. Friendship circles, school clubs, and special buddy systems have been implemented as formalized attempts to foster interaction and develop relationships.

While increased interaction may result from such efforts, friendship often remains elusive. Children may have successful buddy systems during school hours and still be isolated and friendless after 3:00. Children without disabilities may be helpful and involved, but a reciprocal relationship upon which genuine friendship is based does not always develop. The difficult and often frustrating question is, therefore, "What are the barriers impeding the development of friendship and how can we move past them?"

FRIENDSHIP AND HELP

At the end of the 20th century, the most significant barriers preventing individuals with labels of disability from fully participating in schools and communities are still attitudinal. Specifically, our society still perceives those with disabilities as perpetual receivers of help. Descriptors such as "less fortunate" and "needy," telethons, and tear-jerker journalism all continue to perpetuate this view.

Unfortunately, there is still a distressing tendency in some schools to base interactions with students on these broader societal misperceptions, despite a sincere desire to end the isolation experienced by so many children with disabilities. Friendship clubs and buddy systems based on stereotypical beliefs risk perpetuating prejudices and myths and even exacerbating the problem.

Obviously, it is essential that students be provided with opportunities to interact. Formalized friendship and support circles may be effective ways to building relationships. However, an overemphasis on the "helper–helpee" relationship can easily skew the delicate balance of giving and receiving that is the precursor of true friendship. It is critical, therefore, to examine regularly and carefully the nature of the interaction we facilitate and the attitudes that inform it.

Consider the following scenario:

Four third grade children from a local elementary school have come to speak to a room full of adults. They have been invited, with their teacher, to talk about friendship. Actually, three of them are there to talk about their friendship with the fourth child. Children in third grade make friends all the time. We ask ourselves, "What could possibly be unusual enough about this situation to bring these children here today?"

What is unusual is soon apparent. Three of the four children in the room can speak, one of them cannot. Three of the four children in the room can walk, one of them cannot. The three walking, talking children are here to tell us about their relationship with the young man in the wheelchair.

Adults in the room begin to smile as the first classmate talks. Approving nods accompany the child's words, "He's different on the outside, but inside he's just like me."

The conversation whirls around the boy in the wheelchair as he scans the room, looks at his communication board, and sometimes watches his classmates. "We take turns being his buddy," offers one young girl. "Everyone has a turn."

As the children talk and answer questions, it is interesting to watch the interplay between the subject of the discussion and the girl to his left. She has one arm around his shoulders and in the other hand she holds a washcloth. She wipes his mouth repeatedly.

At one point, he appears to lose patience and struggles a bit. One hand jerks forward. His friend seizes his hand and holds it still. He makes a noise of clear irritation and attempts to pull his hand free. His classmate smiles fondly at him, continuing to restrain his hand, and wipes his mouth again.

Is there anything wrong here? Not much, we might say. A 9-year-old who in other times or other places might have been attending segregated classes and a group of nice third graders together are learning a few lessons about differences and similarities.

We might even agree with comments made by audience members. We heard the boy's three classmates being called "the hope for tomorrow" and "exceptional kids." All over the room, adults were beaming. After all, this relatively new phenomenon seems to hold out some hope for an end to discrimination and distance between those who have disabilities and those who do not.

However, as the presentation continued, it became increasingly apparent that while both adults and children thought they were talking about friendship, much of the discussion taking place was really about help. While there was undeniable warmth between the children, most of the comments and nonverbal interactions reflected a helper–helpee relationship, not a reciprocal friendship.

When initially attempting to foster relationships between children with disabilities and their classmates without disabilities, it is common practice to have children "help" the new student. Such help may take the form of physical care, "keeping company" during breaks, or schoolwork assistance. Help-giving contact can reduce an initial sense of strangeness or fear and can, if carefully done, lay the groundwork for friendship.

Clearly, there is nothing wrong with help; friends often help each other. However, it is essential to acknowledge that help is not and can never be the basis of friendship. We must be careful not to overemphasize the helper–helpee aspect of a relationship. Unless help is reciprocal, the inherent inequity between helper and helpee will contaminate the authenticity of a relationship.

Friendship is not the same as help. Attempts to include children with disabilities have sometimes blurred this distinction. Friendship clubs are often really assistance clubs. For example, how much time is spent on the logistics of help? "Who can take Jane to the library on Monday?" "Who can help George eat lunch on Friday?" Still more insidious, how much time is spent bringing George's classmates into a "multidisciplinary team system" to analyze the effectiveness of his current behavior management plan?

Professional caregivers are made, not born. How does it happen? Put a third grade "helper" next to a third grade "helpee." Add a sizable amount of adult approval, and there you have it.

It is not entirely thrilling that kids who take part in friendship circles during school go on to careers in human services. Don't misunderstand—lots of wonderful people choose such professions. However, an unfortunate result is that lots of children and adults with mental and physical disabilities have legions of professional caregivers, but no friends in their lives. We must guard against merely creating another generation of "professionals" and "clients," with the former group seen as perpetually competent and the latter as perpetually needy.

But what is a teacher to do? To create a helper is relatively easy; to facilitate a friendship is tough. After all, friendship cannot simply be mandated. At best, it seems to be made up of one third proximity and two thirds alchemy!

Perhaps we must begin by acknowledging what should be, but is not always obvious. That is, no one has the power to conjure up friendship at will. Maybe that is just as well. Friendship is about choice and chemistry and cannot even be readily defined, much less forced. This is precisely its magic. Realizing this, we can acknowledge without any sense of inadequacy that we are not, nor need to be, friendship sorcerers.

However, teachers and others do have some influence over the nature of proximity. Thus, to create and foster an environment in which it is possible for friendship to emerge might be a more reasonable goal. To achieve this goal, it is essential that we examine the nature of the interactions we facilitate. In particular, we must look closely at the role of help in our classrooms and look not so much at whether children should help each other, but how that help takes place.

THE POLITICS OF HELP

Let's "begin at the beginning" and examine what help means to all of us. In most societies today, helping others is viewed as a socially admirable course of action. Those of us who are in a so-called "privileged position" are asked to give to others. We know we should give to our families, our communities, and most of all, to those "less fortunate" than ourselves. Yet, why is it that most of us, while perfectly comfortable offering help, are decidedly uncomfortable receiving it?

The answer to this question is at once relatively simple and enormously complex. Consider the contrasting perceptions regarding the giving and receiving of help as presented in Table 1. As Table 1 illustrates, although our society associates a host of positive attributes to help, these attributes clearly are reserved for the "helper."

When people without disabilities are asked to imagine their lives with a disability, their reactions reveal interesting assumptions about disabilities and the meaning of "quality of life." "I'd lose my autonomy," says one man. "I'd be so helpless," says another. "I'd be vulnerable and I wouldn't be able to do things for myself!" These are typical responses. In fact, a close look at the controversial right to die issue reveals a disturbingly clear extrapolation of these sentiments; in today's society, many of us would rather die than lose our independence.

Those of us who still are able-bodied and young seldom think about these issues, having the luxury of viewing help as something that is ours to offer or withhold at will. Unless we happen to break a bone or become incapacitated with some temporary illness, we usually do not think about how it feels to be the receiver of help. However, as age and the possible prospect of infirmity approach, it is not uncommon for the always-uncertain future to be viewed with apprehension, if not dread.

Is it the need for help itself that causes us to feel this way, or is it the kind of help we expect to get? Those who have closely examined this issue believe that the problem lies primarily with the lack of self-determination commonly experienced by "helpees." It seems that often dignity must be forfeited in order to receive help. The power to decide where and when help should take place, who should help us, and whether in fact help is needed is stripped away.

People with disabilities sometimes do need help. However, if they are uncomfortable receiving it, as most of us are, they are left in a classic "no win" position of either doing without help or enduring the underlying demeaning messages. Furthermore, it is almost impossible to confront the issue directly. If the helper's motives are questioned, the inevitable response is an indignant or sorrowful "I was only trying to help." Consequently, for many people with disabilities, help is a four-letter word.

Table 1.   Contrast between offering and receiving help

Personal dimension	Why we like offering help	Why we dislike receiving help
Ability	Affirms capacity	Implies deficiency
Value	Affirms worth	Implies burden
Position	Affirms superiority	Implies inferiority
Obligation	One is owed	One is obligated
Vulnerability	Masks our vulnerability	Reminds us of our vulnerability

In inclusive and cooperative education, we are working toward a time when asking for and receiving help is not considered an admission of inferiority, when being the helper does not imply moral or social superiority. The goal is a future in which the human community learns to merge help with respect. However, in the interim, it is important to acknowledge that the broader societal perception of help does not yet match this ideal, especially as it relates to individuals with disabilities.

RESPONSES TO DIVERSITY: FROM MARGINALIZATION TO VALUING

Conformity and uniformity are highly valued in today's society. In general, we are uncomfortable with those who are different. However, rather than admit this, our discomfort is often masked by rationalization. We cover our fears by asserting that our actions toward those with disabilities are for their own good. "It's a dangerous world," we say. "Those who are different must be protected from the potential evils of the world." Then, without any apparent sense of contradiction, we go on to say, "Differences are potentially dangerous. We must protect society from those who are different."

Isolation in the name of safety is a double-lock on the door of community. It effectively prevents those relegated to the outer circle from entering and belonging, while still allowing those within to feel that lofty moral imperatives have been well served. We know that good intentions based on unacknowledged fears can result in oppression. Some of the cruelest actions committed by humanity upon its members have been the result of so-called "good intentions."

The act of forcible segregation for those seen as different is not reserved for those with disabilities alone. Throughout history, the dominant cultures have avoided, marginalized, and even aggressed against so-called minority groups. For those with disabilities, avoidance and marginalization usually occur under the auspices of "protection." The result, however, is still systematic removal from regular society. Institutionalization and segregation in special schools and work environments have been the means of enforcement.

In the past 2 decades, more attention has been paid to the injustices and inherent problems created by segregation. As a society, we are beginning to examine some of the underlying motives and are finding that our actions lack justification. But even as some of the more blatant forms of marginalization and discrimination are changed or eliminated, other hurdles are raised for those labeled different.

We have gone on to say, "You can be with us but you must first be like us." In other words, if you can reform and reduce the evidence of your disability, look and behave "normally," then you can come back into society.

Many remedial, therapy, and life-skill programs have been expressly designed to help minimize the evidence of disability and to create an impression of greater "normalcy." The intent is to improve quality of life through increased "functioning" and skill development. The carrot held up is the promise of future belonging and acceptance. The real message is, "You are not valuable as you are."

Those who work on social justice issues are stripping the mask of good intention from the faces of both marginalization and reform. The hurtful results are made more public, their legitimacy and continued existence now in question.

There is, however, another response toward those who are different. At first glance, it is more appealing, and is consequently more difficult, to recognize as oppressive. In our society, we believe that dealing well with diversity will require tolerance. In fact, we are regularly exhorted to become more tolerant toward others. Many view intolerance as morally reprehensible and wish and work for a truly tolerant society. The intent—to create more acceptance of diversity—can hardly be questioned. Tolerance has seemed, for many, a worthy goal. However, if it is the ultimate and only goal, true social justice will never be realized.

If we comply with the demands made by those with disabilities "because we have to," if our response is merely lukewarm resignation, or even benign patronage, we will not create a society in which equity and respect will be afforded to all its members. Simply being tolerated is not necessarily being valued. Being present does not automatically mean being included. Having an endless parade of well-intentioned helpers is not the same as having a group of friends who value and respect you.

In summary, to move beyond mere tolerance, another response to diversity— that of valuing—must prevail. In a valuing paradigm, diversity is viewed as normal, people are considered of equal worth, relationships are of mutual benefit, and belonging is a central societal theme. Table 2 lists the varied responses to diversity.

We live in a society that tells us there is only one "right" way to be. At times, all of us feel measured against an unfairly strict standard: white, able-bodied, young, intelligent, successful, attractive, thin, and preferably male. Normalcy is a tight bell curve, allowing little deviance without societal repercussion. Even those of us who find ourselves encompassed well within the confines of the curve feel pressure to conform to the middle, while those who fall outside its range feel that they are seen not only as deviant, but deficient.

It is puzzling that this standard of normalcy includes so few of us. We know that diversity, not uniformity, is the real societal norm. After all, the human community consists of great variety—race, gender, language, color, religion, ability, and sexual orientation. People of color make up most of the world's population. Women comprise 51% of the global population. Most of the world does not live in a state of affluence.

Table 2. Responses to diversity

Marginalization	Segregation
	Avoidance
	Aggression
Reform	Rehabilitation
	Assimilation
Tolerance	Resignation
	Benevolence
Valuing (Diversity as normal)	Equal worth
	Mutual benefit
	Belonging

There have always been people with disabilities in society. Social justice for individuals who carry labels of disability will only come about as we learn to value diversity and recognize the multiplicity of gifts within the human community. Our strength is our diversity. We need a paradigm shift of the most profound kind, and, clearly, this paradigm shift will require a change in attitude.

However, the problems inherent in the creation of attitudinal change continue to be difficult for the agents of any social movement. Attitudinal barriers stubbornly defy legislation, do not respond to architectural adaptations, and do not necessarily improve with the application of more money or better programming. They are notoriously slippery; they are the insidious products of unconscious socialization.

To further complicate things, as any good social reformer with a modicum of honesty will admit, attitudinal barriers do not exist only among "those retrogressive oppressors out there," but are just as often within ourselves. In the immortal words of Pogo, "We have met the enemy, and he is us."

Inclusive education has begun to push society beyond blatant forms of oppression such as marginalization and reform. On a daily basis we are confronted by our prior assumptions, called upon to question them, and asked to move toward a new awareness that differences do not imply deficiency and that people with disabilities are capable of significant contributions.

Genuine valuing of diversity will require further confrontation with the more subtle forms of discrimination (e.g., tolerance) and the courage to examine our own beliefs and practices as part of the process.

FROM TOLERANCE TO VALUING

How, then, do we move beyond mere tolerance to true valuing of diversity? For many of us, the struggle is often not in understanding why we should do something, but in knowing what we should do next.

Rather than seeking answers, perhaps it might be more helpful to begin by developing a new set of questions. We need questions that are broad in scope and that will challenge the paradigms both inside and outside the context of inclusive education. What kind of educational system do we want? What can schools become? What kind of society do we want to live in?

Schools will be transformed only as we move away from a narrow "that's the way we've always done it" mind set, and begin to focus on creating a classroom community that promotes belonging and acceptance for all and does not rely on competition and stratification to provide its members with a sense of worth. We know that cooperative learning strategies are one way to accomplish this goal. A further task for teachers in inclusive classrooms is to create the space in which relationships can develop by consciously thinking about and working on the nature of proximity. The following are some practical ideas to assist the process.

Do Not Make Friendship a Big Deal

Friendship between children is wonderful. However, it is not a big deal. If we commend and praise children without disabilities for their interactions with their peers with disabilities (either publicly or in other ways), we inadvertently make friendship a big deal and imply that all children are not created equal. We reinforce the idea that it is morally and socially admirable to "help the handicapped" and, therefore may remove the opportunity for equality and reciprocity.

Respect Personal Boundaries

Adults are seldom comfortable talking about childhood sexuality. But the truth is that children start noticing each other in kindergarten. People with disabilities, however, often receive messages that tell them they are asexual; these messages begin early. Boundaries of touch that would not be crossed between kids without disabilities should never be crossed with their classmates with disabilities.

An unfortunate side effect of tolerant or benevolent interaction is a tendency to treat the "different" child like a life-size doll or pet or a classroom mascot with whom the usual physical boundaries of touch may be violated. We must always ask, "Do the interactions between children in any way compromise the dignity of the individual with the disability?"

Modeling Behavior

There is a lot of discussion of how kids model behavior from each other and how a child's peers are effective arbiters of social appropriateness. While this is most certainly true, we must also remember that teachers remain the most powerful modeling agents in the classroom. If interactions between the teacher and the child with the disability are respectful, the other students will take their cues accordingly.

A child's classmates may provide useful information about the nature of puzzling behaviors. Sometimes children will see things that remain invisible to adult observers. However, the risk involved in eliciting input about behavior may be the development of an increased sense of difference and distance. People with disabilities tell us that it is easier to be ignored than to be patronized or seen as a "class project."

We can still get the information we need without compromising the equity of peer relationships by positing the issue as the school's problem, rather than the child's problem. This way, it is we who do not yet have the insight, experience, or information necessary to support the student, not the student who is in need of "fixing." It may emerge that the real issue, one well worth discussing, has more to do with how we might make schools more responsive to all of their members.

Reciprocity and Contribution

Although a majority of educators acknowledge that the rights of students with disabilities should be respected, there is an ongoing debate about whether reciprocity is really possible and what kind of contribution is realistic to expect. "What," we are often asked, "can a student with a disability really bring to a relationship?"

This question usually reveals more about our own stereotypical views about the *idea* of disability than about the limitations of a disability itself. After all, there is nothing universally "true" about any disability. Generalizations about "the disabled" will never generate the information necessary to address serious questions about the nature of reciprocity or contribution.

Dembo, Leviton, and Wright (as cited in Wright, 1983) first identified a societal tendency to generalize and make broad inferences about the nature of disability. They called this common phenomenon "disability spread." Specifically, "disability spread" is what happens when we extrapolate the characteristics we associate with the notion of disability to the particular individuals we meet. These perceptions are often based on stereotypes and what we think we know about a particular disability. They are expressed in predictable ways. For example, "All people with Down syndrome are happy," or "People with cerebral palsy usually have a mental disability." In fact, these characteristics may or may not actually be true of any one individual. Figure 1 illustrates this concept.

Many inferences and assumptions are made about disability in our society. For example, we are inclined to see people with disabilities as a collection of needs and deficiencies (McKnight, 1989). We are led to evaluate people based on what is missing rather than what is present. When our perceptions are based on stereotypical myths and misperceptions we will not see a real person with any clarity.

In fact, every individual is a complex collection of components. Each of us has a variety of interests, skills, capacities, and a unique background. We all have different physical characteristics and our own idiosyncratic personalities. In our interactions with others, we want most to be understood and seen for who we are, and we hope that we will not be judged simply at face value. However, for individuals who have visible disabilities, being judged at face value is precisely what happens most often.

When disability is seen as the largest component of a person, much of what is unique and "human" about him or her will be obscured. When needs and deficits are what we see, we only see what that person cannot do.

We will not recognize the diverse contributions of those who wear obscuring labels until we move our focus from the disability and look for the complexity and individuality we take for granted in ourselves. Only getting to know a person in all his or

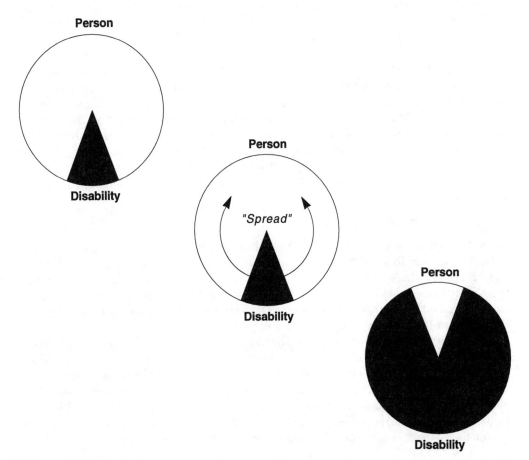

Figure 1.   Disability spread.

her multifaceted individuality can cause the "huge" disability to magically shrink and assume its real proportion—only one small facet of a person. Only then will we find ourselves able to see and receive the variety and richness of possible gifts.

Merging Respect and Help

Too much help can be a disabling force. One of the biggest challenges teachers face in inclusive classrooms is getting other kids to stop doing everything for the child with a disability. Too much help, even when enthusiastically given, is fundamentally disempowering. Help should always be "natural and situation-rooted" (Wright, 1983, p. 311) and should only be what subjects of a fascinating study on help and disability termed *necessary help* (Ladieu, Hanfmann, & Dembo cited in Wright, 1983, p. 310).

Help outside the context of choice and self-determination is disrespectful. We all want to feel necessary. However, when our desire to feel needed is at the expense of someone else's sense of competence and autonomy, we commit a lasting act of injustice. People with disabilities literally spend lifetimes struggling to be heard. We must learn to listen. Marsha Saxton (1985) wrote:

> All of those people trying so hard to help me . . . All of them hoping for me to . . . do well, all wanting to be kind and useful, all feeling how important helping me was. Yet never did anyone of them ask me what it was like for me. They never asked me what I wanted for myself. They never asked me if I wanted their help. I do not feel entirely grateful. I feel, instead, a remote anger stored beneath my coping pattern of complacent understanding. People do the best they can to help in meaningful ways, I know. I just wish all the disabled children would say to their helpers: "Before you do anything else, just listen to me." (pp. 133–134)

We must listen to both the verbal and nonverbal messages expressed by someone who may or may not want help. We must use this information to guide our actions and increase our sensitivity. It does not sound like much, but the ramifications are enormous. It is often during times when we are hell-bent on helping that we listen least well. We all know stories about people with visual impairments being forcibly "escorted" over crosswalks by well-meaning pedestrians, of people in nursing homes being fed when they are not hungry, or of what the participants in the Dembo study aptly called "unexpected attacks" of help (Ladieu, Hanfmann, & Dembo, as cited in Wright, 1983, p. 309).

Empathy and Social Justice

Most children are acutely conscious of what is fair and what is not. It is not usually difficult to appeal to a child's sense of justice. Furthermore, powerlessness and social stigma are not the sole experience of those with disabilities. Children, by virtue of their status in society, generally understand what it feels like to be without influence. They know how it feels to be silenced, to be disregarded, and to have decisions that concern them made arbitrarily and regularly by others.

We have downplayed and underutilized these experiences, thinking that "white, middle class, able-bodied children" do not experience oppression and will not understand. In fact, most children experience rejection, isolation, and a sense of powerlessness at some time. Whether these are children of color, children who must learn English as a second language, children who dress differently, children who eat different foods or have ethnically "different" last names, or children who just do not seem to fit in somehow, there is a kernel of commonality in these experiences.

Too often, in discussions of social justice between educators and children, the issues are portrayed as "theirs." We show kids what institutional life looks like, we talk about the negative effects of segregation, and we ask them to think about how it feels to be teased because of a disability. We even subject them to simulated situations or "role plays" that supposedly allow participants to feel, for example, what it is like to be blind.

Unfortunately, the unintentional result is more distance and a greater sense of fundamental "otherness." At best, this approach fosters sympathy, and at worst, a guilty relief—"thank heaven it's not me."

We must take care not to inadvertently reinforce the notion that those with disabilities are objects of pity. Equitable relationships cannot be built on a foundation of pity. Instead, we must build on the shared experiences, the shared stories between us to create a sense of empathy, and a sense of "I know what you mean." This does not disregard our different experiences. It is certainly true that having a disability and being an immigrant are not completely comparable experiences. Likewise, being left out of games on the playground and being the victim of racist behavior are not the same. However, where experiences do intersect, we have an opportunity to build connection and understanding that may extrapolate to other situations in unexpected ways. Social justice is an important aspect of education. The development of empathy and shared understanding between individuals of diverse background and ability is critical if our world is to survive the next century. We need young women and men who will work together to address the issues of inequity and injustice that still face us.

You may wonder why, in a book primarily devoted to cooperative learning within heterogeneous schools, this epilogue has focused almost exclusively on inclusive education. We believe that individuals with mental and physical disabilities may well prove to be the proverbial canaries in the experimental coal mines of education. These are the people who will teach us most about the nature of help. Through our interactions with those who have disabilities, we stand to learn valuable lessons that will lead us to greater appreciation of diversity in all its forms. The creation of a better world is dependent on our collective ability to learn these lessons well.

REFERENCES

McKnight, J. (1989). *Do no harm: A policymaker's guide to evaluating human services and their alternatives.* Evanston, IL: Center for Urban Affairs & Policy Research.

Saxton, M. (1985). The something that happened before I was born. In A.J. Brightman (Ed.), *Ordinary moments—The disabled experience* (pp. 127–140). Syracuse, NY: Human Policy Press.

Wright, B.A. (1983). *Physical disability—A psychosocial approach* (2nd ed.). New York: Harper & Row.

Awareness Plan A conceptual tool developed by Herbert Leff (1984) that refers to one's mental procedure for soliciting and processing information.

Base Groups A classroom arrangement suggested by David and Roger Johnson, in which students are assigned to the same "base group" for a semester, year, or during several years. Such long-term affiliation provides peer support both socially and academically and holds members accountable for performance. (See also *Formal Groups* and *Informal Groups*.)

Brainstorming Brainstorming is a procedure developed by Alex Osborn (1953) and is a commonly used term to describe the awareness plan of forcing yourself or a group to generate a large number of alternative ideas.

Circle of Friends The circle of friends process was developed by Marsha Forest and Jack Pearpoint and is described by Falvey, Forest, Pearpoint, and Rosenberg in Chapter 16. Teachers structure a circle of friends by gathering together a group of students for the purpose of discovering the existence or absence of their own circle of friends and then reflecting on each other's circles.

Classwide Peer Tutoring (CWPT) Classwide Peer Tutoring consists of four major components: 1) weekly competing teams, 2) highly structured teaching procedures, 3) daily earning of points for work accurately completed and public posting of the points, and 4) direct practice of functional academic skills. (See Chapter 9.)

Classwide Student Tutoring Teams (CSTT) Classwide Student Tutoring Teams is an adaptation of CWPT and the Teams-Games-Tournaments (TGT) program developed by Robert Slavin and colleagues. CSTT actively engages students in content-related discussions and review of a series of 10–30 questions developed by the teacher for weekly study guides. (See Chapter 9.)

Collaborative Approach James Britton and Douglas Barnes developed the collaborative approach in the United Kingdom primarily in literature and language arts. It focuses on the creation of personal meaning and internally persuasive understandings through dialogue and discussion. Five phases of instruction include engagement, exploration, transformation, presentation, and reflection.

Complex Instruction   Complex instruction is a cooperative learning approach developed by Elizabeth Cohen and associates for investigations in math and science. Multiple-ability tasks are designed to: 1) incorporate all levels of performance (cognitive, psychomotor, visual, skills, and so forth); and 2) emphasize unique talents or knowledge that each member of the group brings to the investigation.

Components of Effective Partner Learning Programs   As discussed by LaPlant and Zane (chap. 11), components of effective partner learning programs include identification of participants, recruitment, training, supervision, evaluation, and reinforcement (or maintenance).

Cooperative Education Team   As developed by Jacqueline Thousand and Richard Villa, a cooperative education team is an instructional arrangement of two or more people in the school and greater community who share cooperative learning planning, instructional, and evaluation responsibilities for the same students on a regular basis for an extended period of time. Members of an effective cooperative education team practice the same critical elements that are structured for cooperative learning groups (positive interdependence, promotive face-to-face interaction, individual accountability, practice of small-group interpersonal skills, and periodic assessment and reflection of group effectiveness).

Cooperative Learning Groups   Students work together in groups ranging in size from two to six members. They work cooperatively to achieve a common goal. Interdependence and social interaction skills are fostered by assigning roles and responsibilities to each group member. The completion of the academic task is dependent upon the participation of all group members.

Curricular Adaptations   Curricular adaptations are modifications that teachers make in their curricular content to accommodate the specific learning needs of students with disabilities. Changes can be made in lesson format, teaching style or delivery of instruction, time required to complete a task, amount of assignment to be completed, objectives (goals), evaluation criteria, environmental and social conditions, learning materials, and level of support or assistance.

Formal Groups   A classroom arrangement suggested by David and Roger Johnson and colleagues in which the teacher assigns groups of students for a number of days or across several weeks to work together on completing specific learning tasks or projects.

Group Investigation   A six-stage model of cooperative learning developed by Yael and Shlomo Sharan and colleagues at Jerusalem University in which a complex topic is divided into multiple subtopics studied by different research groups. Critical components of the group investigation model include investigation, interaction, interpretation, and intrinsic motivation.

Inclusive Education   As suggested by Giangreco, Cloninger, Dennis, and Edelman (chap. 15), inclusive education involves heterogeneous grouping, a sense of belonging, shared activities with individualized outcomes, use of settings frequented by persons without disabilites, and an educational experience that balances academic/functional and social/personal aspects of schooling.

Independent or Individual Seat Work   The student works alone on assigned homework or material that has been presented in class or previously explained. Independent work can also be accomplished in the library on student-selected areas of interest. An outcome of many cooperative group learning assignments is students who independently seek additional information about a subject to enrich the group's product.

Individual Accountability   Individual accountability in cooperative group learning exists when the performance of each student is assessed, the results are provided to the individual and the group, and the student is held responsible by teammates for contributing his or her fair share to the group's success. Individuals who need more assistance, support, encouragement, and other accommodations to complete the assignment are acknowledged.

Informal Groups   A classroom arrangement suggested by David and Roger Johnson in which students are assigned temporarily to a group on a short-term basis (i.e., one discussion or class period) to help each other focus on class material, organize information, formulate questions, and ensure that they are understanding the information.

Instructional Strategies   Instructional strategies are actions and behaviors that are practiced by teachers to enable students to learn.

Large-Group (Whole-Class) Instruction   The entire class learns the same content from the teacher—primary source of information. Students are usually expected to assimilate the information and work at approximately the same rate.

Learning Together   A conceptual approach to cooperative group learning developed by David and Roger Johnson at the University of Minnesota that emphasizes five basic elements: positive interdependence, face-to-face interaction, direct teaching of interpersonal and small-group interaction skills (often through assigning specific roles such as facilitator, encourager, paraphraser, etc.), reflective evaluation of the skills and the achievement of the academic task, and individual accountability. (See Chapter 3.)

Making Action Plans (MAPs)   Developed by Forest and Pearpoint and described by Falvey, Forest, Pearpoint, and Rosenberg in Chapter 16, MAPs are tools designed to help individuals, organizations, and families determine how to move into the future effectively and creatively so as to make people's lives better, richer, and stronger in the spiritual sense of life.

Multilevel Teaching   Multilevel teaching involves students working on similar instructional objectives or with the same material but at different academic levels.

Multimodality Teaching   Multimodality teaching involves assigning students academic tasks that involve multiple forms of active involvement (reading, writing, performing through acting, listening, dancing, singing, drawing).

Numbered Heads Together (NHT)   First described by Stanley Kagan and subsequently researched by Larry Maheady and colleagues, Numbered Heads Together is an alternative teacher questioning strategy designed to engage all students during teacher-led instruction. Students are assigned to four-member heterogeneous learning teams who sit together and number themselves from one to four. When the teacher directs a question to the entire class, pupils are instructed to "put their heads together," decide on their best answer, and make sure that everyone on their team can discuss it. The teacher randomly selects from the students with the number 1 (or 2, 3, or 4) to answer the question and then asks for elaborations (e.g., "Can number 1 [or 2, 3, or 4] expand on that answer?"). (See Chapter 9.)

One-to-One Teacher/Student Instruction   The student receives direct instruction, supervision, or guidance from an adult. Instruction may be provided by the classroom teacher, specialist, related service personnel (e.g., speech therapist), classroom volunteer, and so forth.

Osborn-Parnes Creative Problem-Solving (CPS)   A problem-solving process that was first articulated by Alex Osborn (1953) and further refined by his protégé Sidney Parnes, who promoted its use in many fields of business and in education. The process facilitates creative thinking and action by systematically alternating between divergent ways of thinking (e.g., brainstorming) and convergent ways of thinking (e.g., applying specific criteria to judge whether ideas are feasible and usable).

Partial Participation   The principle of partial participation acknowledges that many students, particularly those with severe disabilities, might never learn the skills to perform an activity with complete independence. Partial participation involves designing instruction so that students with severe disabilities have at least some degree of active involvement in a task or activity.

Partner Learning (Peer Tutoring or Cross-Age Tutoring)   With partner learning, a student is coached on a particular topic or assignment by a classmate or older student. Students may take turns as tutor or tutee for different academic subjects. (See also *Components of Effective Partner Learning Programs*.)

Peer Buddy   A peer buddy is a student of the same age who agrees to cultivate a friendship with another student for the purpose of acclimating him or her to the school, assisting him or her to or from classes, and introducing him or her to other friends.

Peer-Influenced Interventions   Teachers structure learning academic and social skills to capitalize on the natural social interactions and consequences that peers provide one another.

Peer Interventions   Peer interventions include a range of strategies that involve teachers and peers working together to help a particular student by implementing a strategy (intervention) to increase or decrease specified behaviors. Peer intervention strategies have the dual purpose of teaching academic skills and managing certain social skills and behaviors of a specific student.

Peer-Mediated Interventions   Peers systematically implement behavior-change programs and are trained and monitored by a teacher (or guidance counselor) to serve in peer mediation roles. (See Chapter 12.)

Peer Mediation   Peer mediation refers to conflict resolution programs that teach students to be peer mediators (peacemakers or conflict managers) who can proactively and positively assist students in handling their conflicts. (See Chapter 12.)

Piagetian Theory   Piagetian theory is a theory of cognitive development developed by Jean Piaget and his colleagues through observation of children's interactions with the environment. He documents that children's cognition consists of progressive organization and adaptation through a sequence of phases or periods (sensorimotor, preoperational, concrete operational, formal operational), each characterized by distinct patterns of behavior and thinking (schemata). Conceptual conflict occurs when children interact with other children who have developed different ideas or methods to solve problems. During cooperative group learning, children participate in conceptual conflict resolution processes that result in greater learning.

Planning Alternative Tomorrows With Hope (PATH)   Developed by Forest and Pearpoint and described in Chapter 16 by Falvey, Forest, Pearpoint, and Rosenberg, PATH evolved from the MAPs process. It is an eight-step process that extends the results of the MAPs process to create a plan of action.

Positive Goal Interdependence   When students perceive they can achieve their learning goals if and only if all the members of their group also attain their learning goals, the group is united around a common goal.

Positive Interdependence The technical term for that dual responsibility between a member of a cooperative learning group and his or her teammates, positive interdependence involves learning the assigned material and ensuring that all members of the group learn the assigned material. Teachers can structure positive interdependence so that students believe "they sink or swim together" and care about how much each other learns through goal, reward, resource, and role interdependence.

Positive Resource Interdependence Each group member has only a portion of the resources, information, or materials needed to complete a task, and the members' resources must be combined for the group to achieve its goals.

Positive Reward (Celebration) Interdependence Each group member receives the same reward when the group achieves its goal. Celebrations of group efforts and success enhance the quality of cooperation.

Positive Role Interdependence Each member is assigned complementary and interconnected roles that specify responsibilities that the group needs in order to complete the joint task. Role assignments can include reader, recorder, checker of understanding, encourager of participation, elaborator of knowledge, and so forth.

Processing Group Interactions Effective group work is influenced by whether or not groups reflect on (i.e., process) how well they are functioning. Processing group interactions occurs when group members describe what actions were helpful and unhelpful and when group members subsequently agree on what actions to continue or change. The purpose of group processing is to clarify and improve the effectiveness of each member's contributions to the collaborative effort to achieve the group's goals.

Promotive (Face-to-Face) Interaction Defined as group members encouraging and facilitating each other's efforts to achieve, complete tasks, and produce in order to reach the group's goals, promotive interaction is fostered by positive interdependence. It is characterized by group members providing each other with efficient and effective assistance, exchanging needed resources such as information and materials, processing information more effectively, and providing feedback to improve subsequent performance.

Reciprocal Friendship As discussed by Van der Klift and Kunc in the Epilogue, unless help is reciprocal, the inherent inequity between "helper" and "helpee" will contaminate the authenticity of a friendship relationship.

Reciprocal Teaching Derived from a cognitive science perspective that analyzes expert and novice thinking processes, reciprocal teaching is a method in which the teacher and students take turns as teacher. When the pupil takes a turn as the teacher, the pupil is carefully coached in the skills of comprehending, questioning, and extending the concepts being learned. It is hypothesized that the pupil's learning is enhanced by being exposed to the strategies used by the "expert" learner (i.e., the teacher or a peer tutor).

Responsibility Curriculum As discussed by Villa, Udis, and Thousand in Chapter 17, educators are charged with designing a curriculum that explicitly teaches students how to be responsible through: 1) the establishment of a schoolwide discipline system that promotes the learning of responsibility, 2) direct instruction of pro-social communication skills, 3) direct instruction of anger management and impulse control techniques, and 4) the setting of limits to ensure safety.

Role Reversal An awareness plan suggested by Thousand, Nevin, and Leff (chap. 14), role reversal invites members of a cooperative education team to deliberately take the perspective of another. For example, the teacher might take the student's perspective, the special educator might take the classroom teacher's perspective, the teaching assistant might take the role of parent, and the parent might take the role of the classroom teacher. Team members switch roles several times to explore alternative actions for accommodating instruction, materials, and classroom arrangements.

Small-Group Learning   Students work together to complete a project or socialize and share ideas while completing individual work. This arrangement differs from cooperative group learning because students are not assigned roles and they do not work together to complete a common task.

Social Learning Theory   A theoretical perspective from which teamwork (a key aspect of cooperative group learning) is derived.

Structural Approach   As categorized by Stanley Kagan, the structural approach is an array of simple group structures such as think-pair-share, roundtable, Numbered Heads Together, three-step interview, jigsaw, and pairs check that can be implemented immediately in any classroom for any academic subject.

Structured Team Meeting Process   As developed by Jacqueline Thousand and Richard Villa, cooperative education teams create positive interdependence through a structured team meeting process. During team meetings, team members rotate from one meeting to the next using different leadership roles that promote either the completion of the agenda or the maintenance of relationships among members. Agenda items are solicited from each team member and time limits are decided mutually, outcomes and agreements are recorded publicly, and time is allocated to process members' use of collaborative skills and their progress toward completion of agenda items.

Student Team Learning   A series of cooperative learning strategies developed by Robert Slavin and associates at The Johns Hopkins University, including Student Teams Achievement Divisions (STAD), Teams-Games-Tournaments (TGT), Cooperative Integrated Reading and Composition (CIRC), and Team Accelerated Instruction (TAI) for math. (See Chapter 2.) Student team learning strategies combine individual accountability and either group rewards or group goals.

Teacher-Directed Small-Group Instruction   The teacher instructs a small group of students (five to eight members). The instruction focuses on a particular topic, subject, or content area.

Vygotskian Theory   Russian psychologist L. S. Vygotsky defined "the zone of proximal development" as the distance between the actual developmental level (as measured by individual problem-solving performance) and the level of potential development (measured through problem solving under adult guidance or through interactions with more capable peers). In cooperative group learning, children participate in community collaboration in which the zone of proximal development is evidenced.

REFERENCES

Leff, H. (1984). *Playful perception: Choosing how to experience your world.* Burlington, VT: Waterfront Books.

Osborn, A. (1953). *Applied imagination: Principles and procedures of creative thinking.* New York: Charles Scribner's Sons.

INDEX